ベルセルク

BERSERK 12

BY
KENTARO MIURA
三浦建太郎

TRANSLATION
DUANE JOHNSON
LETTERING AND RETOUCH
DAN NAKROSIS

DARK HORSE MANGA
DMP Digital Manga Publishing

PUBLISHERS
MIKE RICHARDSON, DARK HORSE MANGA
HIKARU SASAHARA, DIGITAL MANGA PUBLISHING

EDITORS
CHRIS WARNER, DARK HORSE MANGA
FRED LUI, DIGITAL MANGA PUBLISHING

COLLECTION DESIGNER
DAVID NESTELLE

ART DIRECTOR
LIA RIBACCHI

English-language version produced by
DARK HORSE MANGA and DIGITAL MANGA PUBLISHING.

BERSERK vol. 12 by KENTARO MIURA

Dark Horse Manga
A division of Dark Horse Comics, Inc.
10956 S.E. Main Street
Milwaukie OR 97222

DarkHorse.com

Digital Manga Publishing
1487 West 178th Street, Suite 300
Gardena CA 90248

DMPBooks.com

To find a comics shop in your area, call the Comic Shop Locator Service toll-free at 1-888-266-4226

First edition: July 2006
ISBN: 978-1-59307-484-5

10 9 8 7
Printed in the United States of America

BERSERK

ベルセルク⑫

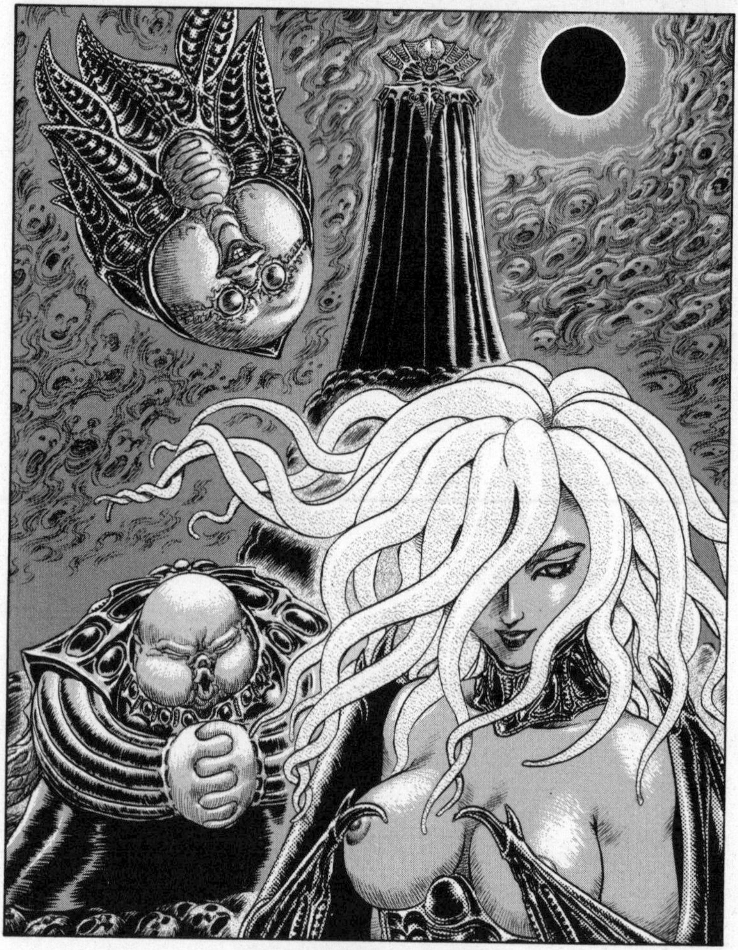

三浦建太郎

ベルセルク 12

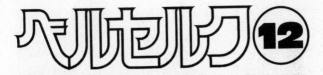

CONTENTS

ベルセルク

風の鎮魂歌（レクイエム）

REQUIEM OF THE WIND

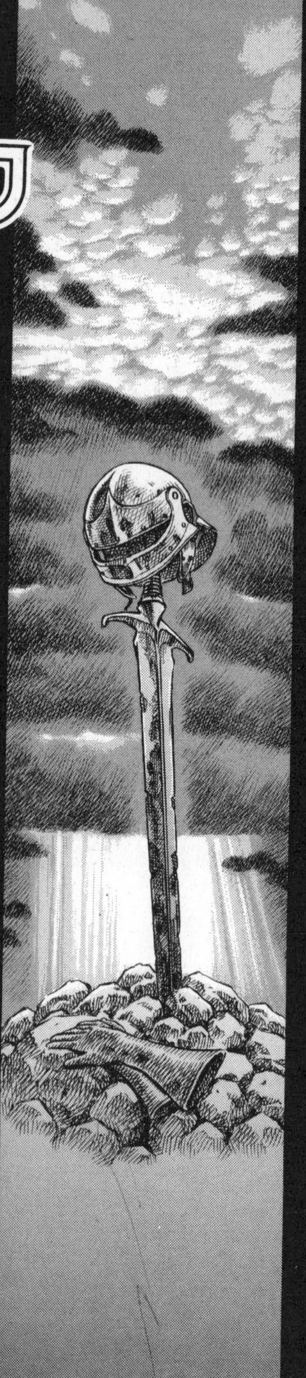

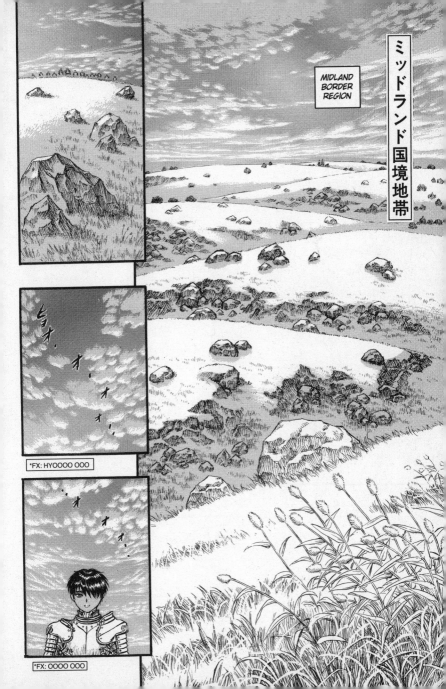

MIDLAND
BORDER
REGION

ミッドランド国境地帯

*FX: HYOOOO OOO

*FX: OOOO OOO

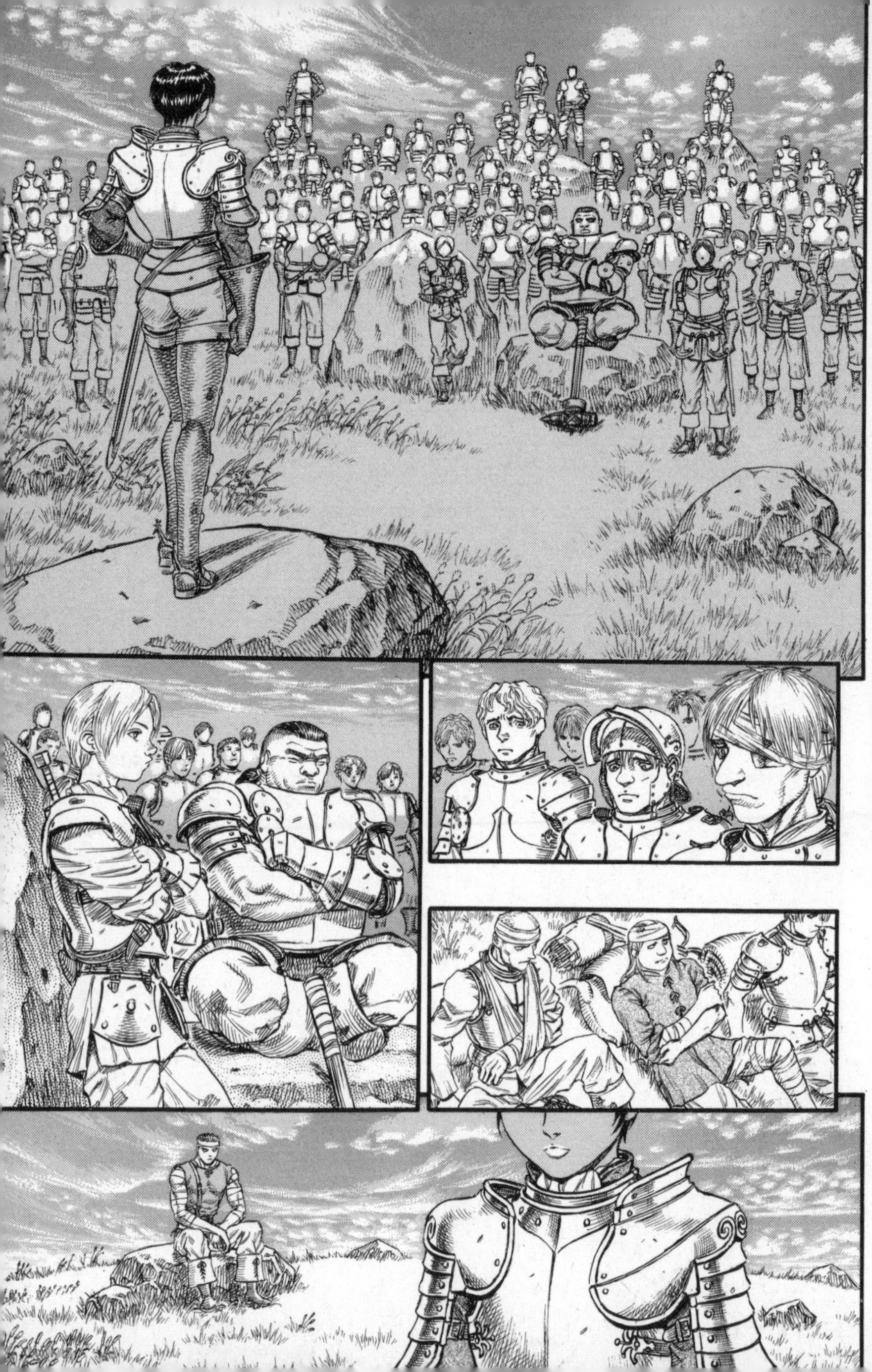

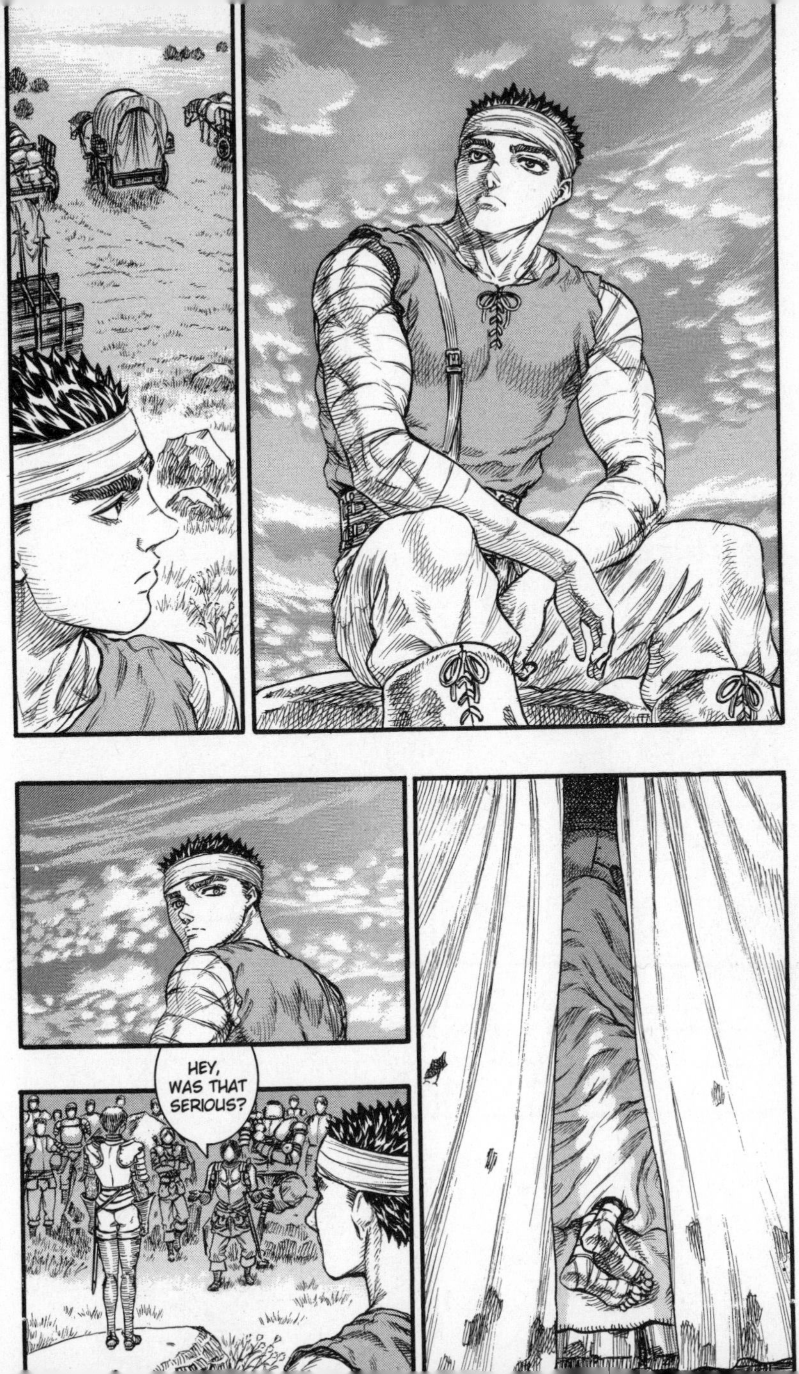
HEY, WAS THAT SERIOUS?

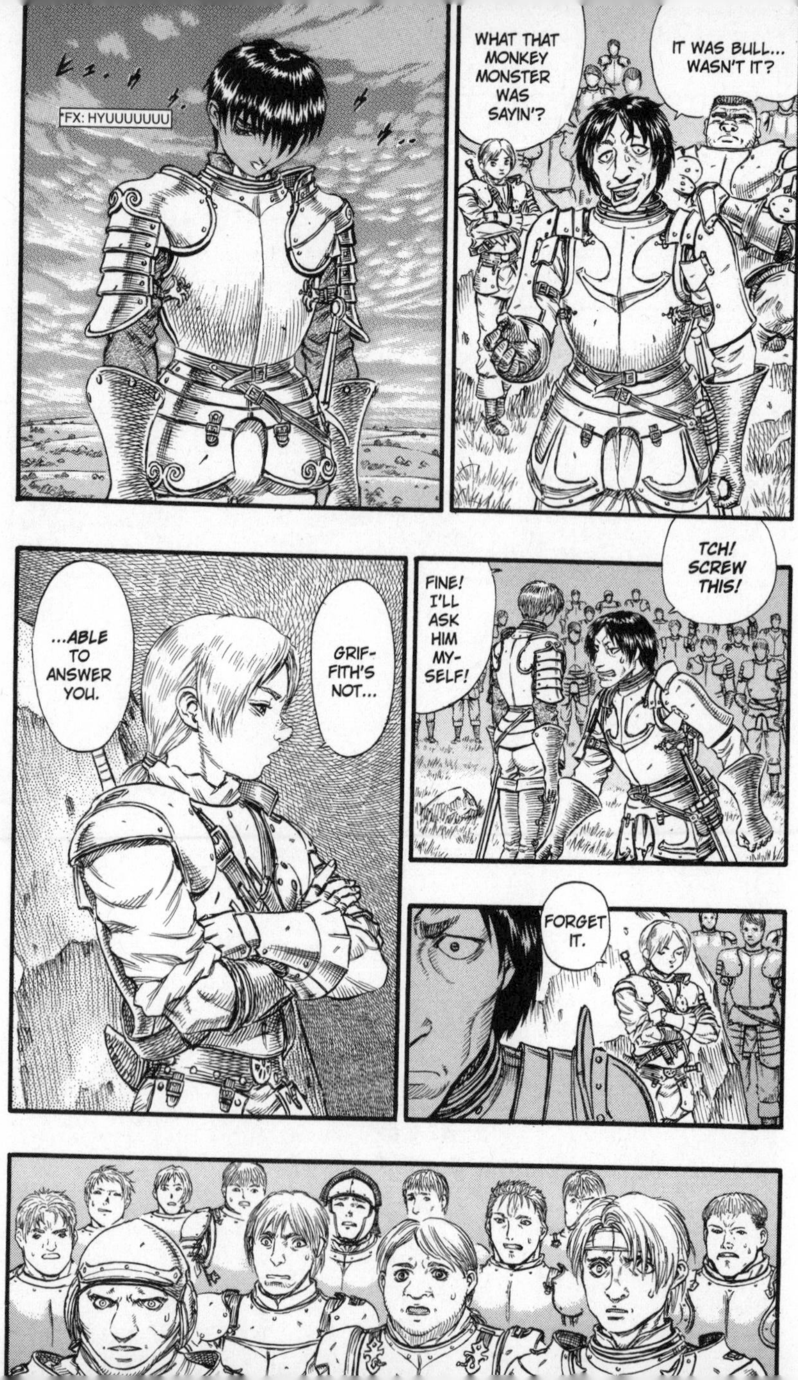
IT WAS BULL... WASN'T IT?
WHAT THAT MONKEY MONSTER WAS SAYIN'?
*FX: HYUUUUUUU
TCH! SCREW THIS!
FINE! I'LL ASK HIM MY-SELF!
FORGET IT.
GRIF-FITH'S NOT...
...ABLE TO ANSWER YOU.

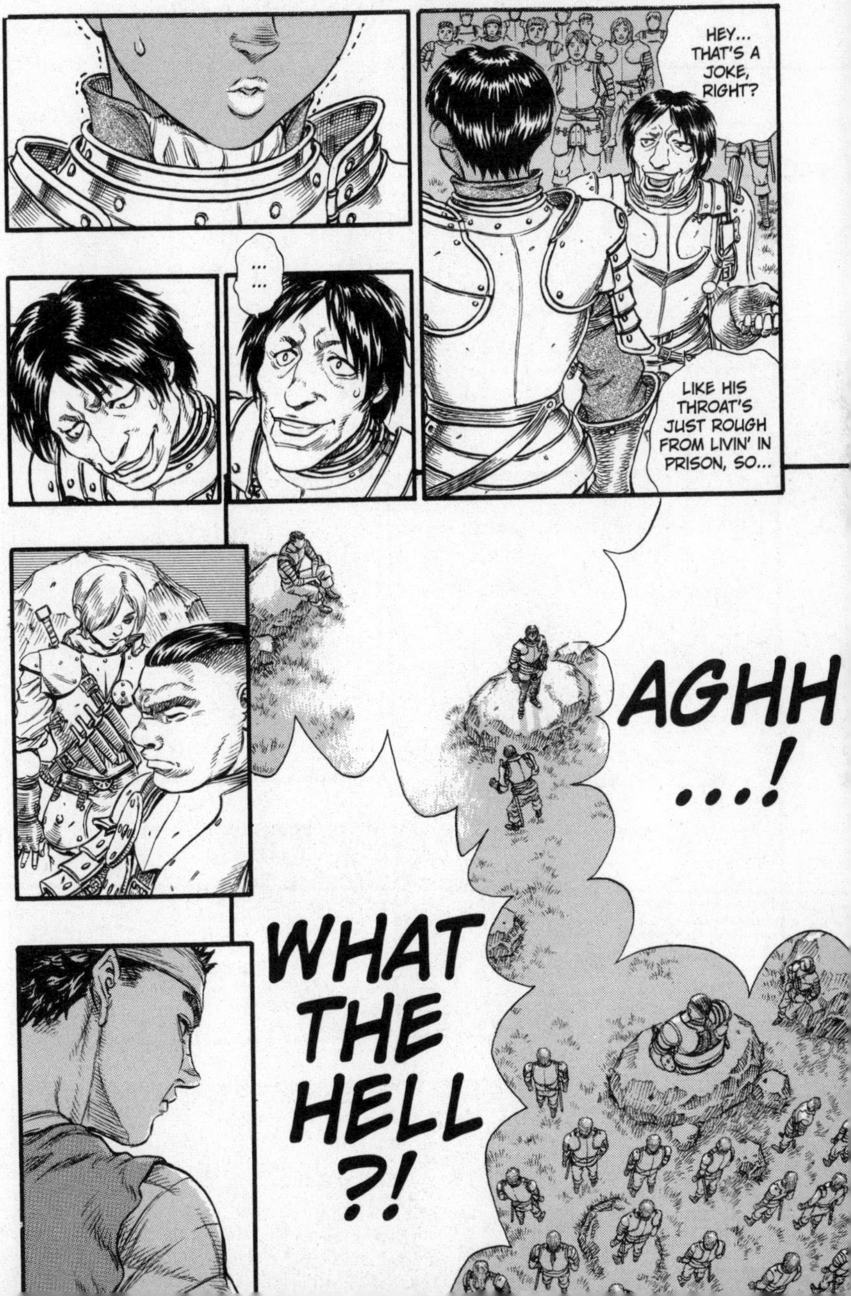
HEY... THAT'S A JOKE, RIGHT?
LIKE HIS THROAT'S JUST ROUGH FROM LIVIN' IN PRISON, SO...
... ...
AGHH ...!
WHAT THE HELL ?!

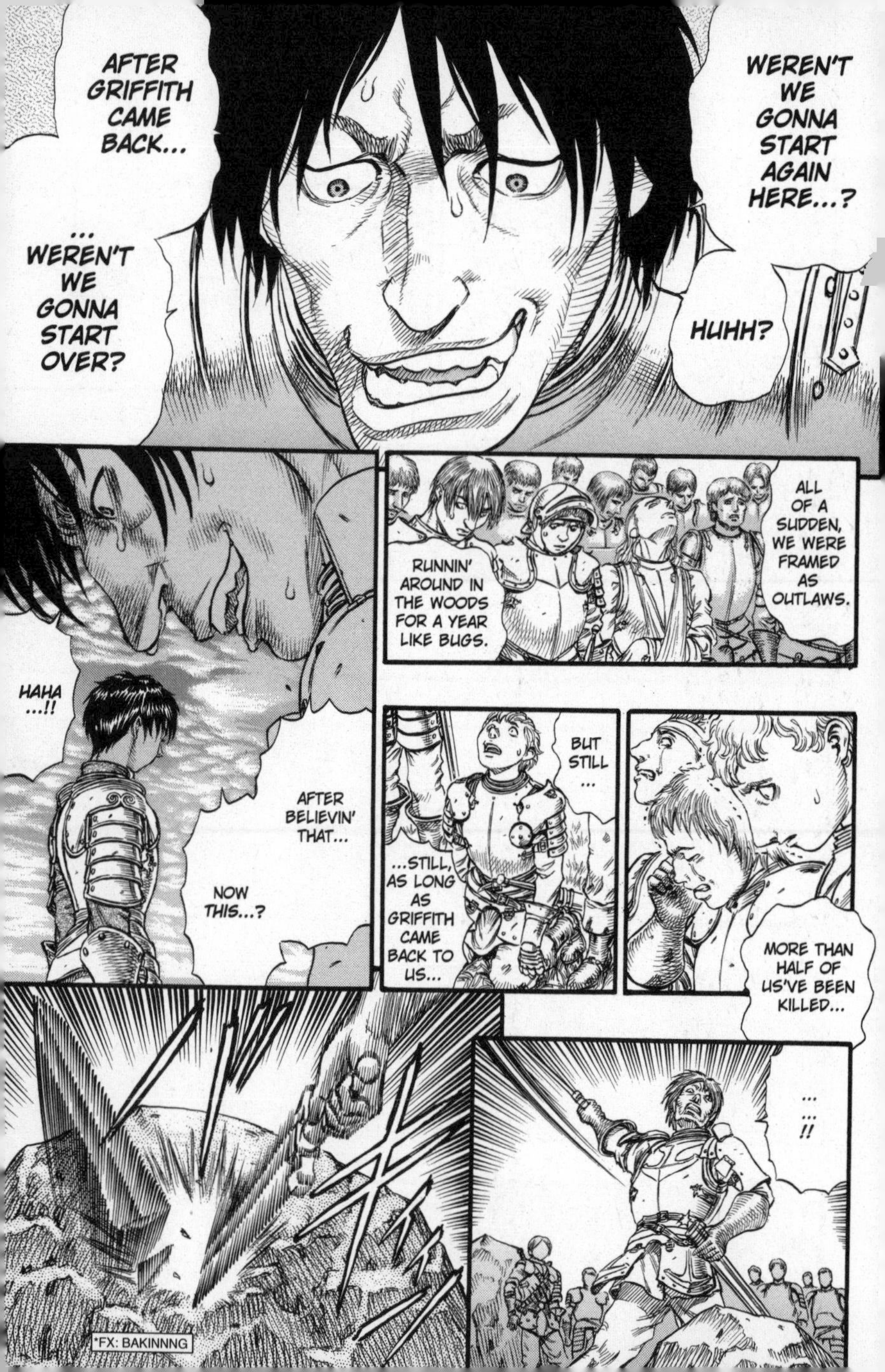
WEREN'T WE GONNA START AGAIN HERE...?
AFTER GRIFFITH CAME BACK...
HUHH?
...WEREN'T WE GONNA START OVER?
ALL OF A SUDDEN, WE WERE FRAMED AS OUTLAWS.
RUNNIN' AROUND IN THE WOODS FOR A YEAR LIKE BUGS.
MORE THAN HALF OF US'VE BEEN KILLED...
BUT STILL ...
...STILL, AS LONG AS GRIFFITH CAME BACK TO US...
HAHA ...!!
AFTER BELIEVIN' THAT...
NOW THIS...?
... ... !!
*FX: BAKINNNG

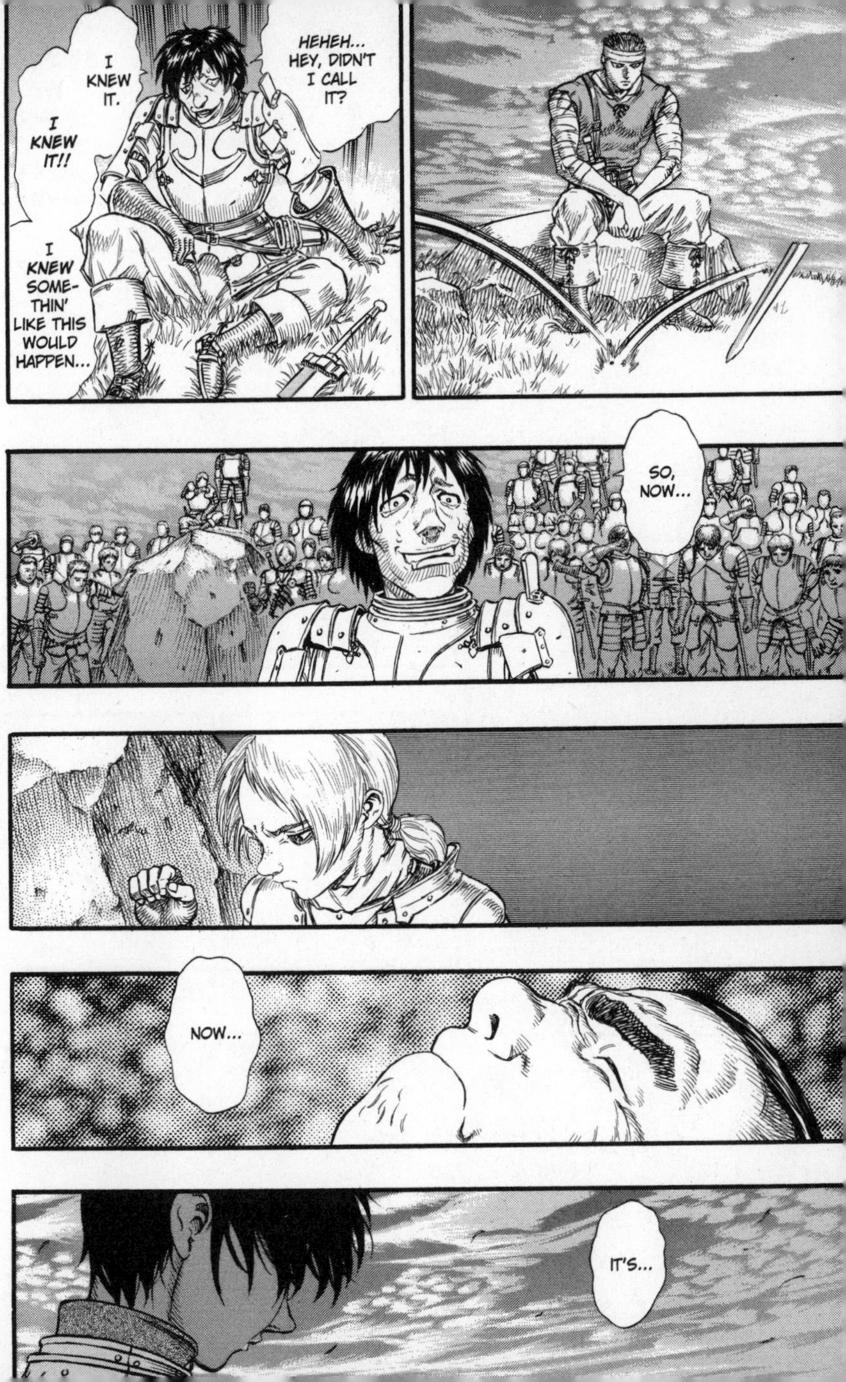
HEHEH... HEY, DIDN'T I CALL IT?
I KNEW IT.
I KNEW IT!!
I KNEW SOME-THIN' LIKE THIS WOULD HAPPEN...
SO, NOW...
NOW...
IT'S...

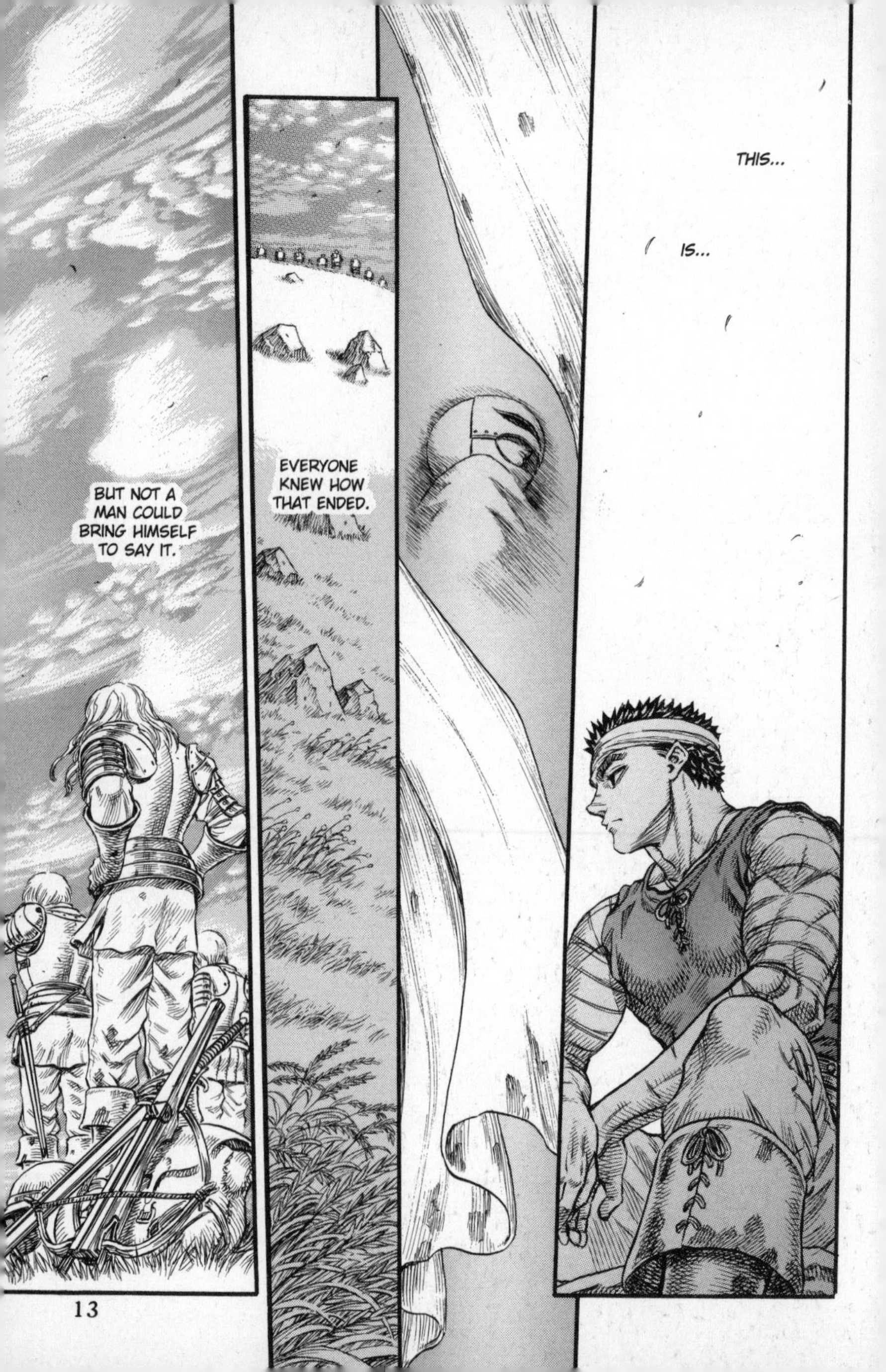
THIS...
IS...
EVERYONE KNEW HOW THAT ENDED.
BUT NOT A MAN COULD BRING HIMSELF TO SAY IT.

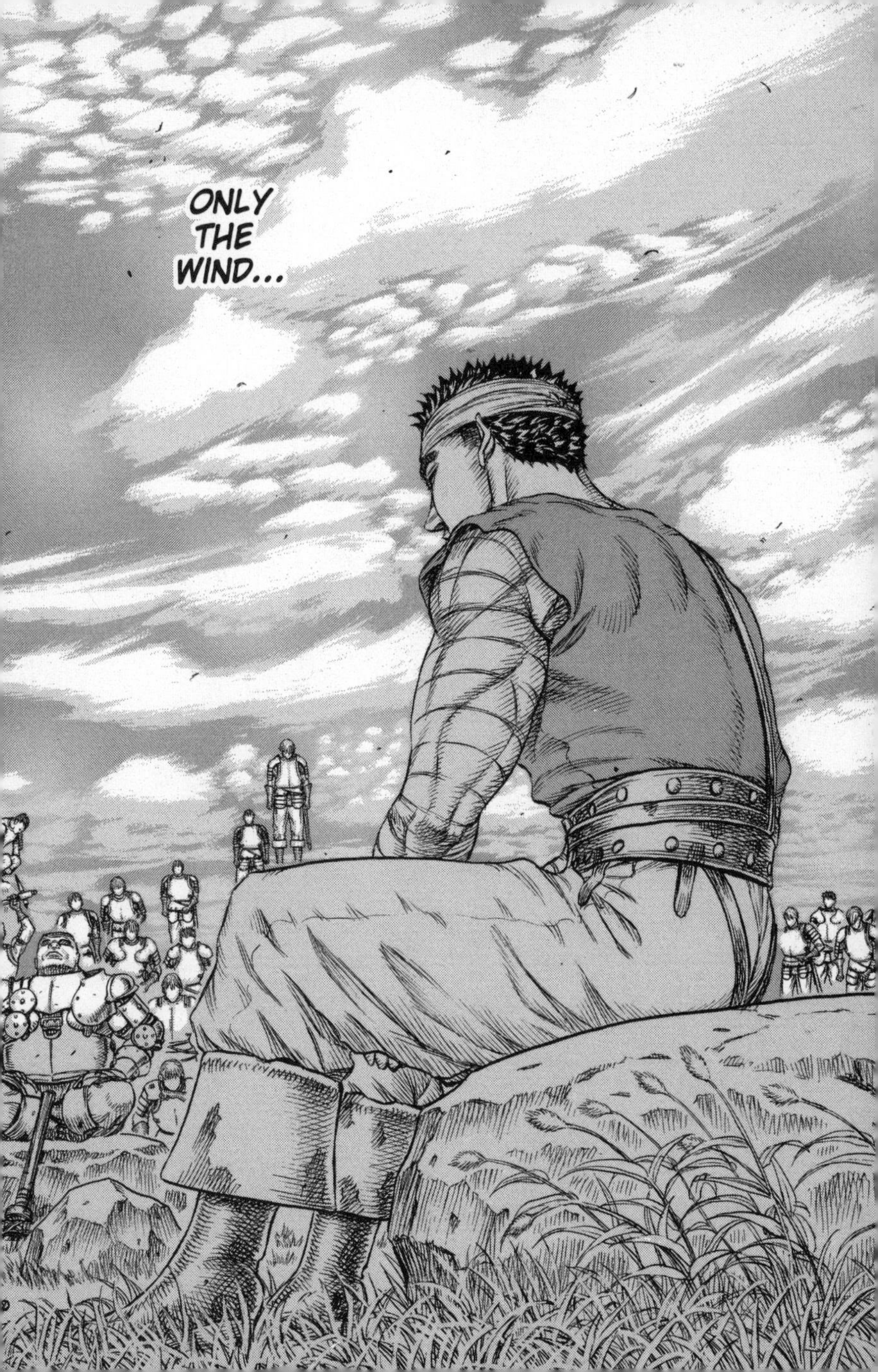
ONLY THE WIND...

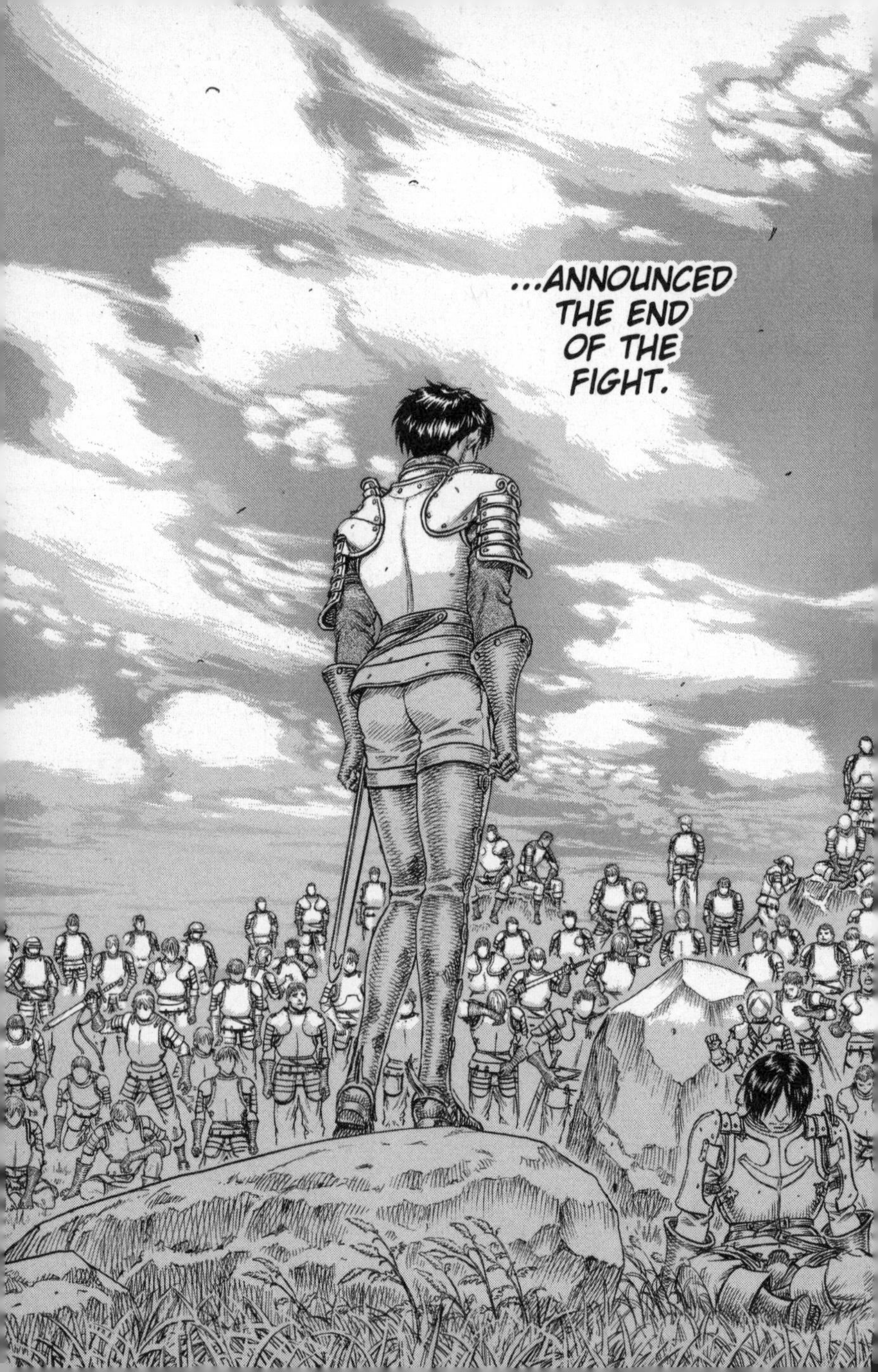
...ANNOUNCED THE END OF THE FIGHT.

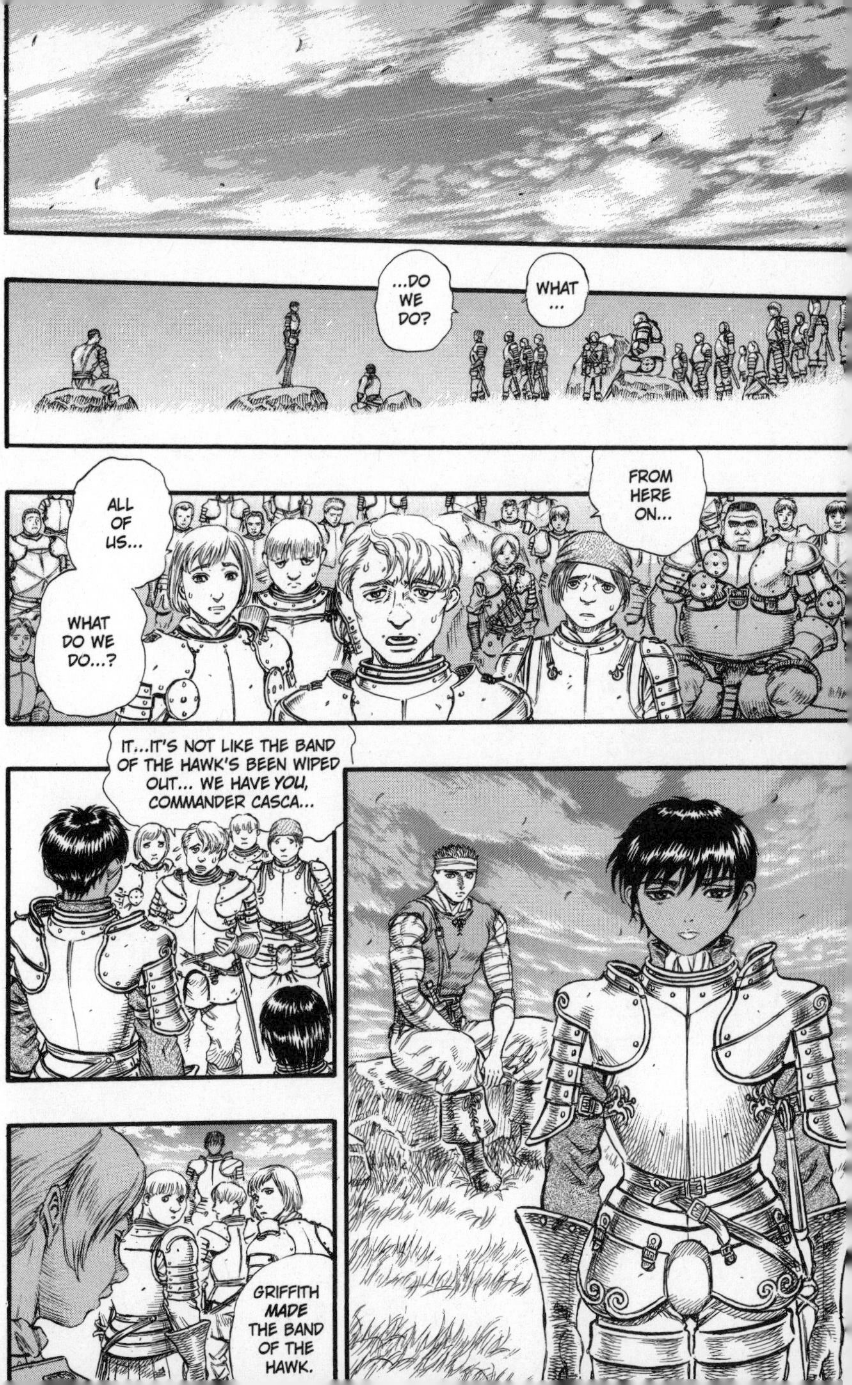
WHAT...
...DO WE DO?
FROM HERE ON...
ALL OF US...
WHAT DO WE DO...?
IT...IT'S NOT LIKE THE BAND OF THE HAWK'S BEEN WIPED OUT... WE HAVE *YOU*, COMMANDER CASCA...
GRIFFITH *MADE* THE BAND OF THE HAWK.

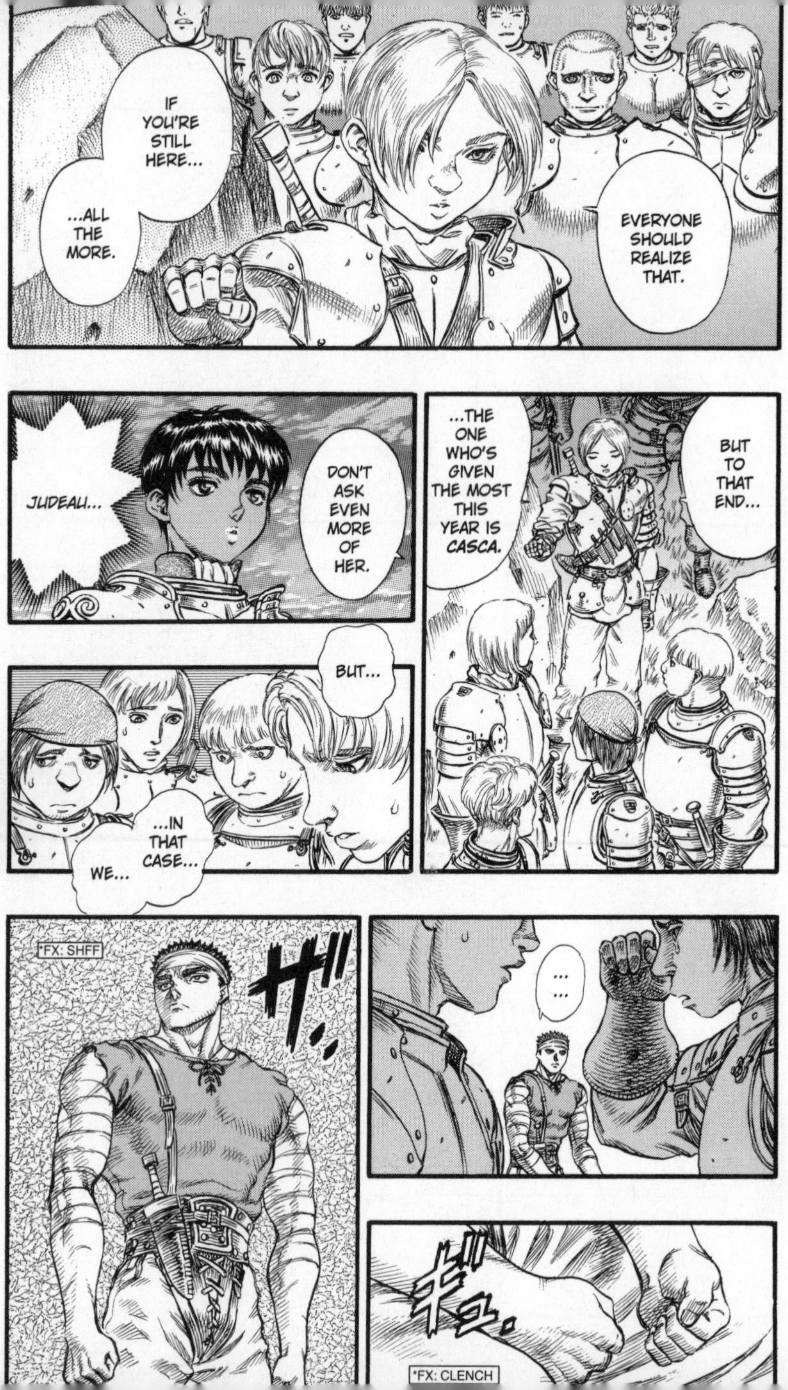
EVERYONE SHOULD REALIZE THAT.
IF YOU'RE STILL HERE...
...ALL THE MORE.
BUT TO THAT END...
...THE ONE WHO'S GIVEN THE MOST THIS YEAR IS CASCA.
DON'T ASK EVEN MORE OF HER.
JUDEAU...
BUT...
...IN THAT CASE...
WE...
......
*FX: CLENCH
*FX: SHFF

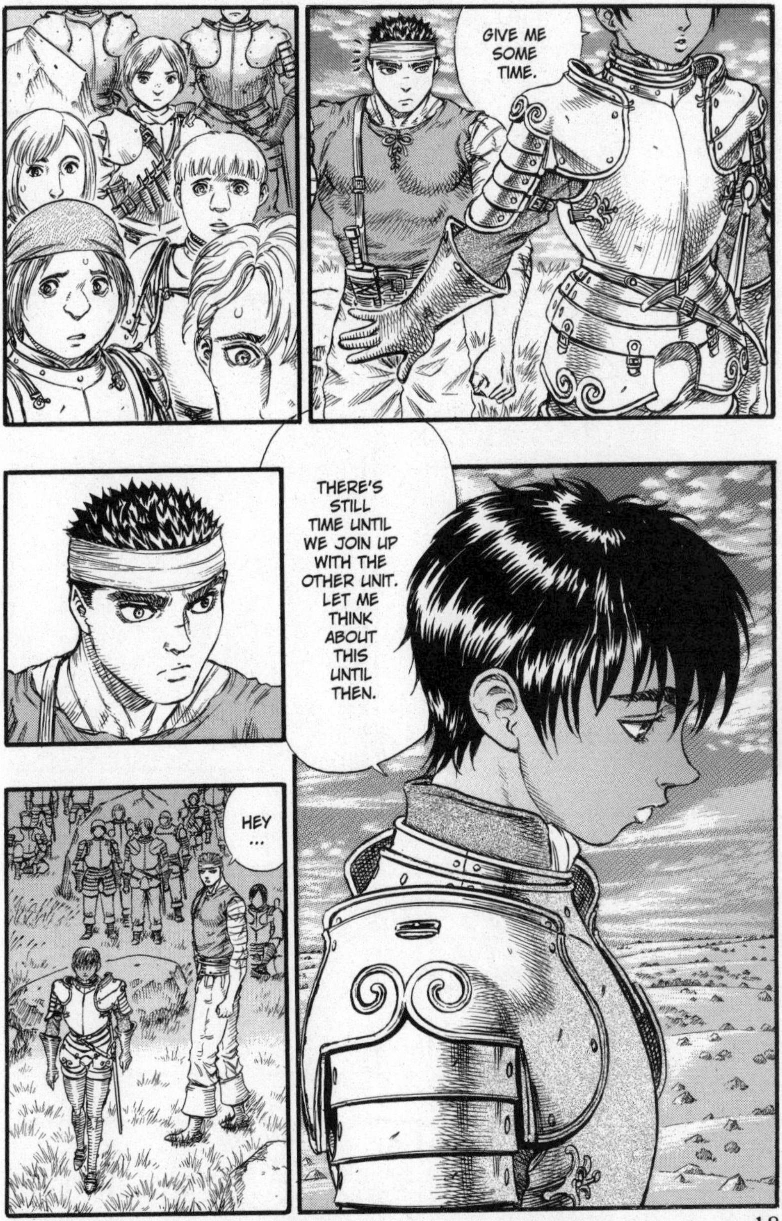
GIVE ME SOME TIME.
THERE'S STILL TIME UNTIL WE JOIN UP WITH THE OTHER UNIT. LET ME THINK ABOUT THIS UNTIL THEN.
HEY ...

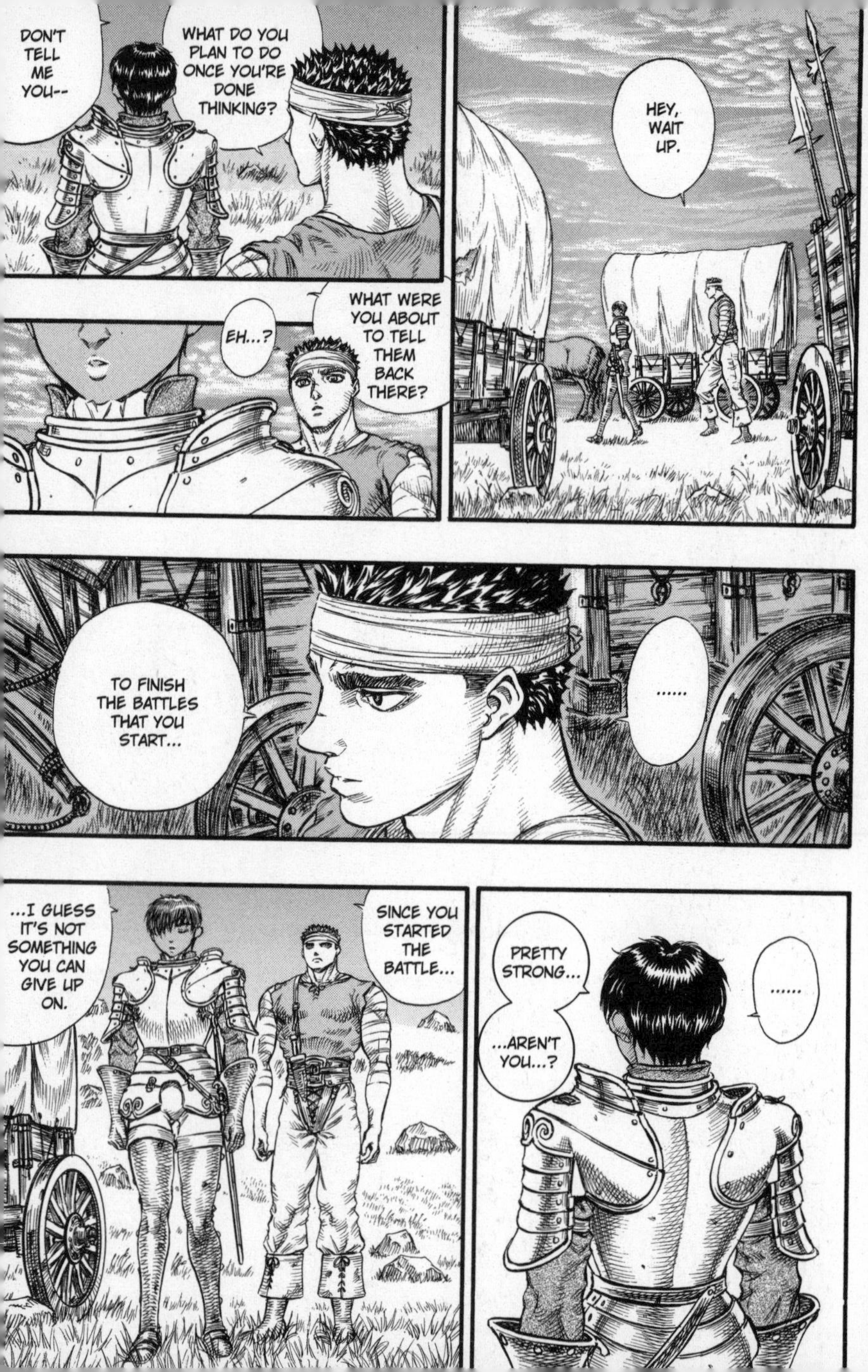
HEY, WAIT UP.
WHAT DO YOU PLAN TO DO ONCE YOU'RE DONE THINKING?
DON'T TELL ME YOU--
WHAT WERE YOU ABOUT TO TELL THEM BACK THERE?
EH...?
......
TO FINISH THE BATTLES THAT YOU START...
......
PRETTY STRONG...
...AREN'T YOU...?
SINCE YOU STARTED THE BATTLE...
...I GUESS IT'S NOT SOMETHING YOU CAN GIVE UP ON.

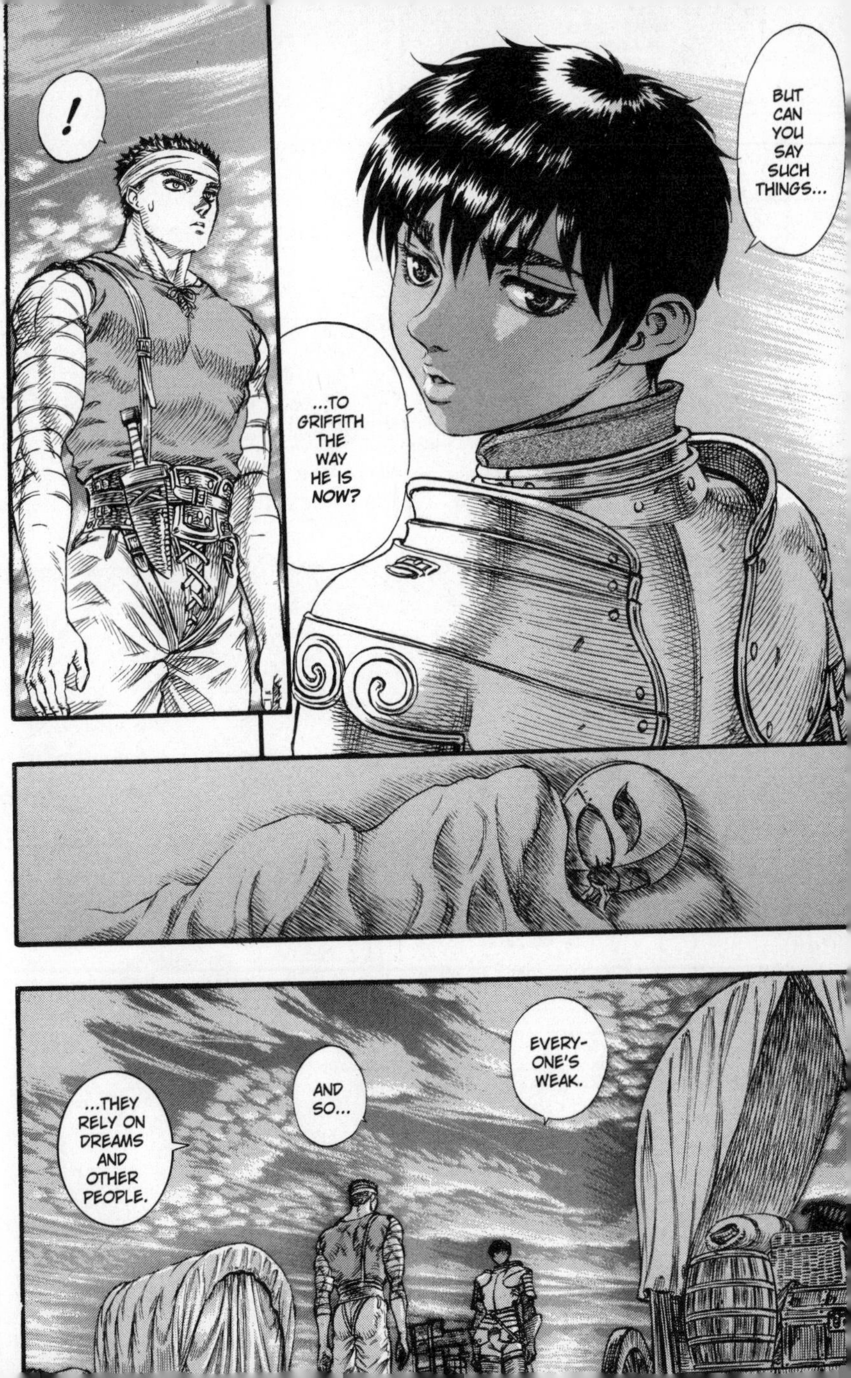
BUT CAN YOU SAY SUCH THINGS...
...TO GRIFFITH THE WAY HE IS NOW?
!
EVERY-ONE'S WEAK.
AND SO...
...THEY RELY ON DREAMS AND OTHER PEOPLE.

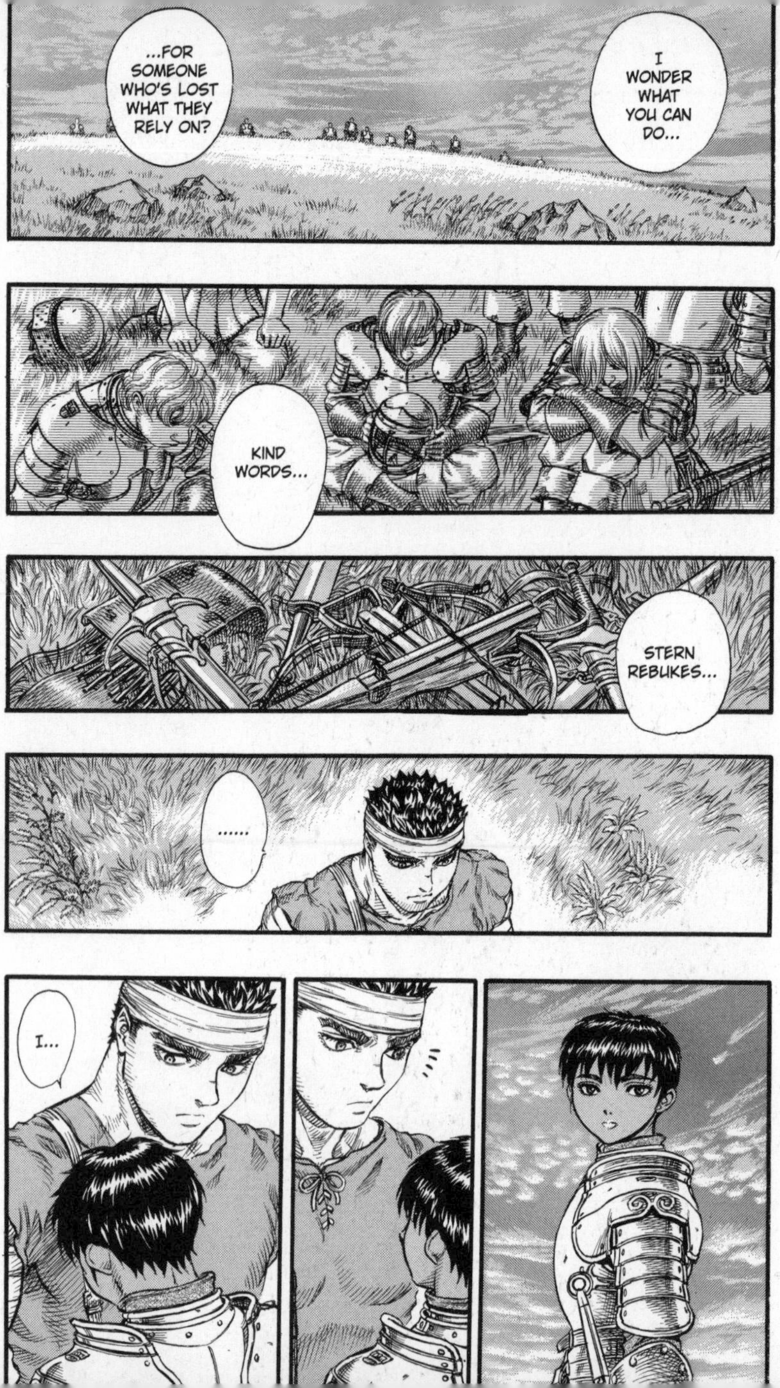
I WONDER WHAT YOU CAN DO...
...FOR SOMEONE WHO'S LOST WHAT THEY RELY ON?
KIND WORDS...
STERN REBUKES...
......
I...

...WANTED...

...SOMEONE
TO BE
NEAR ME.

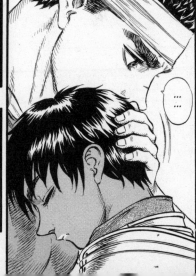

...
...

......

...ON GRIF-FITH.

I'M GOING TO CHECK...

LET'S CHANGE THOSE BANDAGES.

GRIF-FITH...

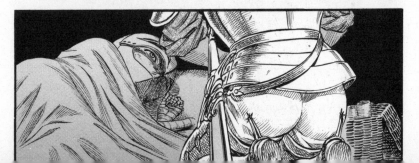

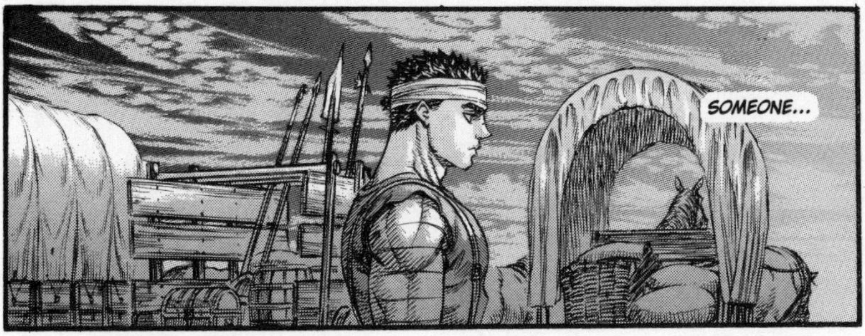
SOMEONE...

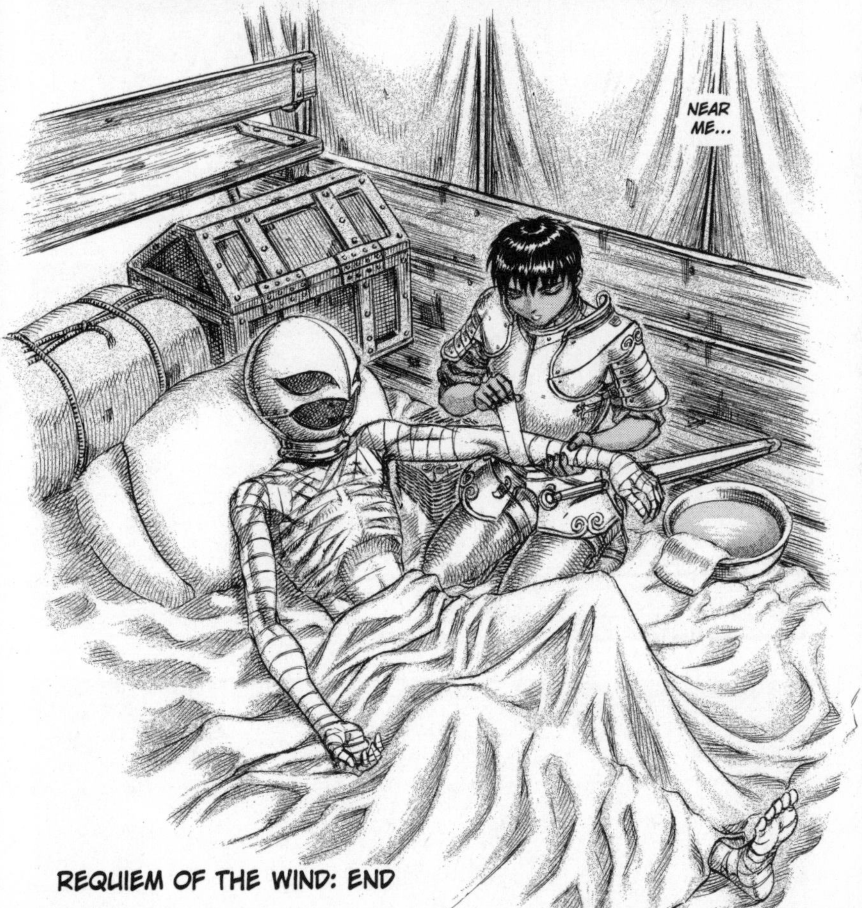
NEAR ME...
REQUIEM OF THE WIND: END

ベルセルク

THE WARRIORS OF TWILIGHT

黄昏(たそがれ)の戦士達

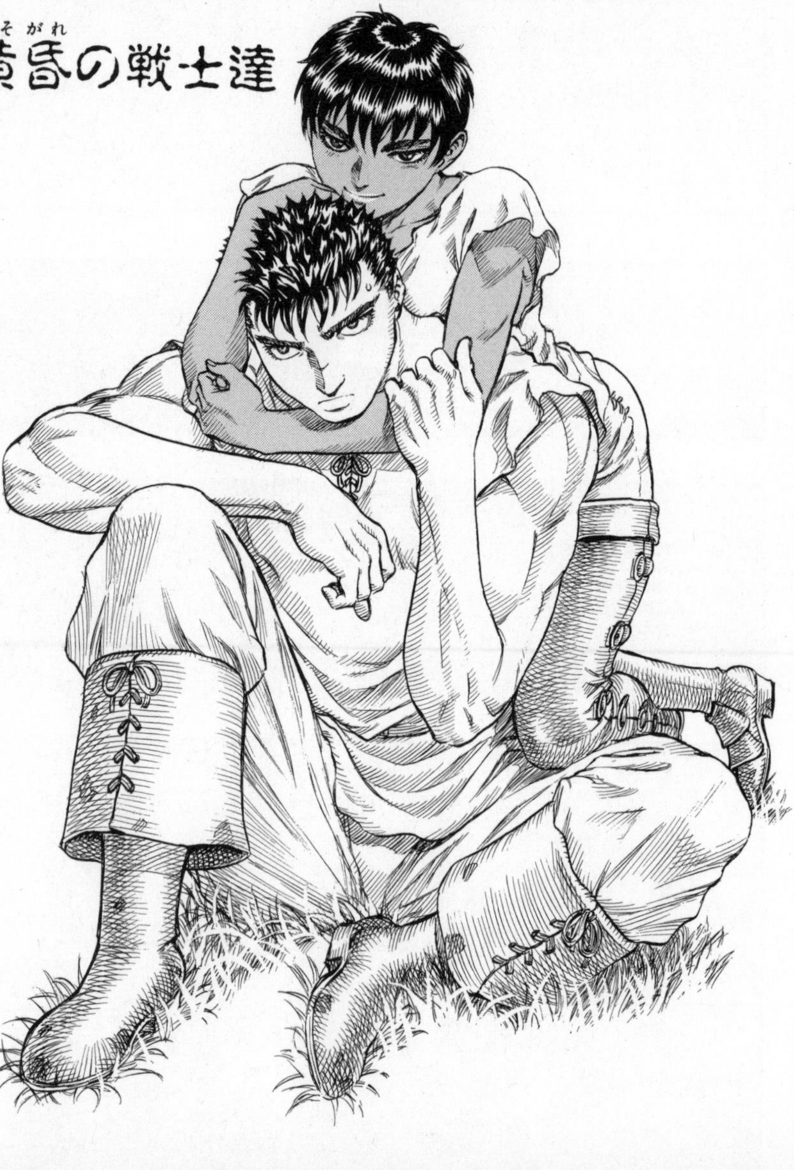

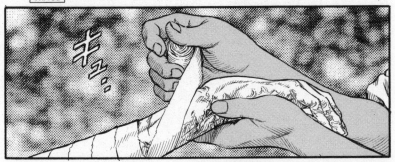

I DIDN'T KNOW HIS HANDS WERE THIS SMALL.

...TO GRASP EVERYTHING WITH THESE HANDS...

HE TRIED...

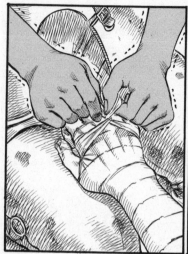

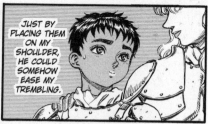

JUST BY PLACING THEM ON MY SHOULDER, HE COULD SOMEHOW EASE MY TREMBLING.
TIME AFTER TIME...
...THEY WOULD ERASE MY ANXIETY.
WHOOPS...
HUH?

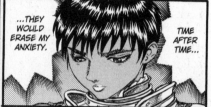

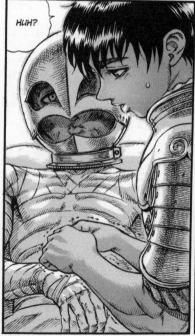

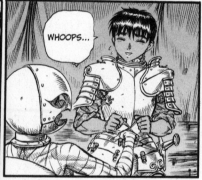

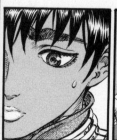

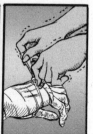

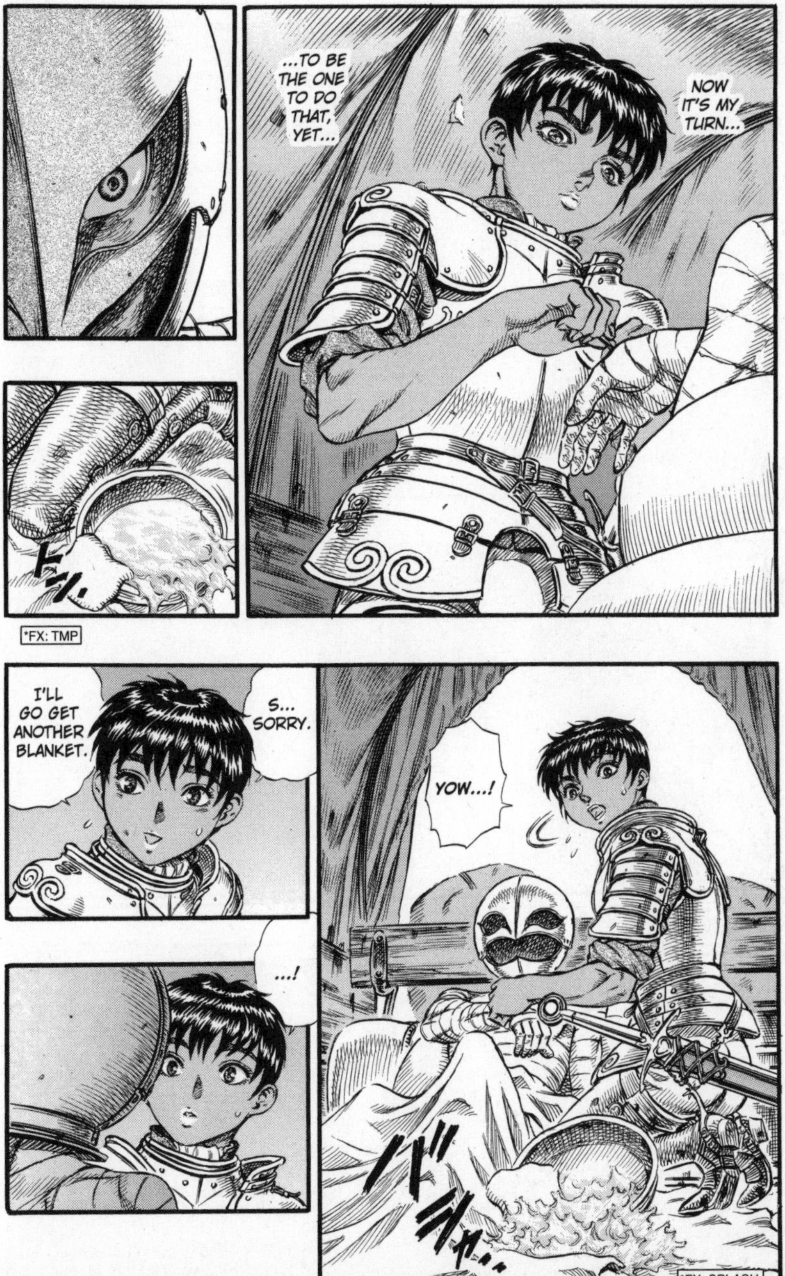
NOW IT'S MY TURN...
...TO BE THE ONE TO DO THAT, YET...
*FX: TMP
YOW...!
*FX: SPLASH
S... SORRY.
I'LL GO GET ANOTHER BLANKET.
...!

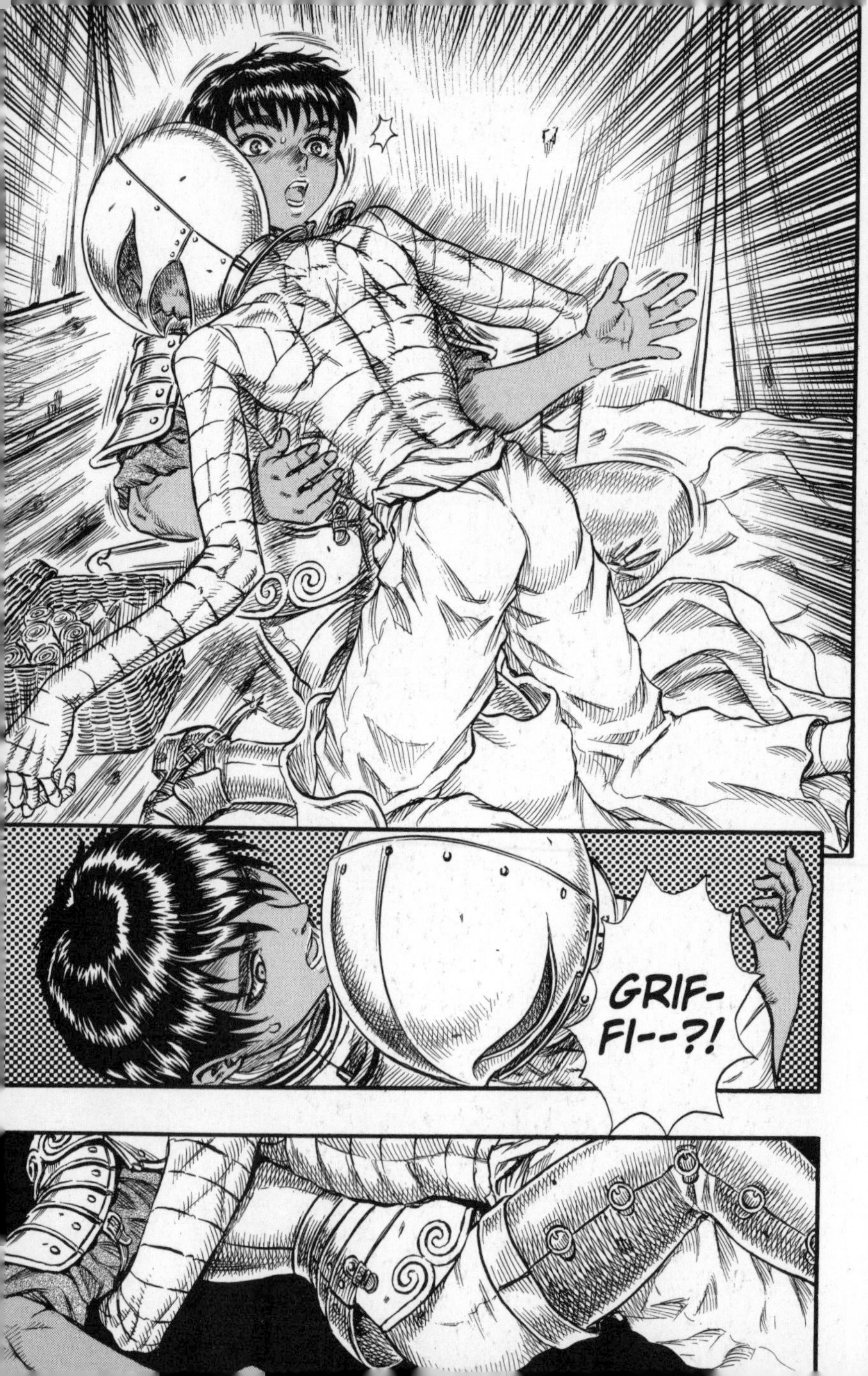
GRIF-
FI--?!

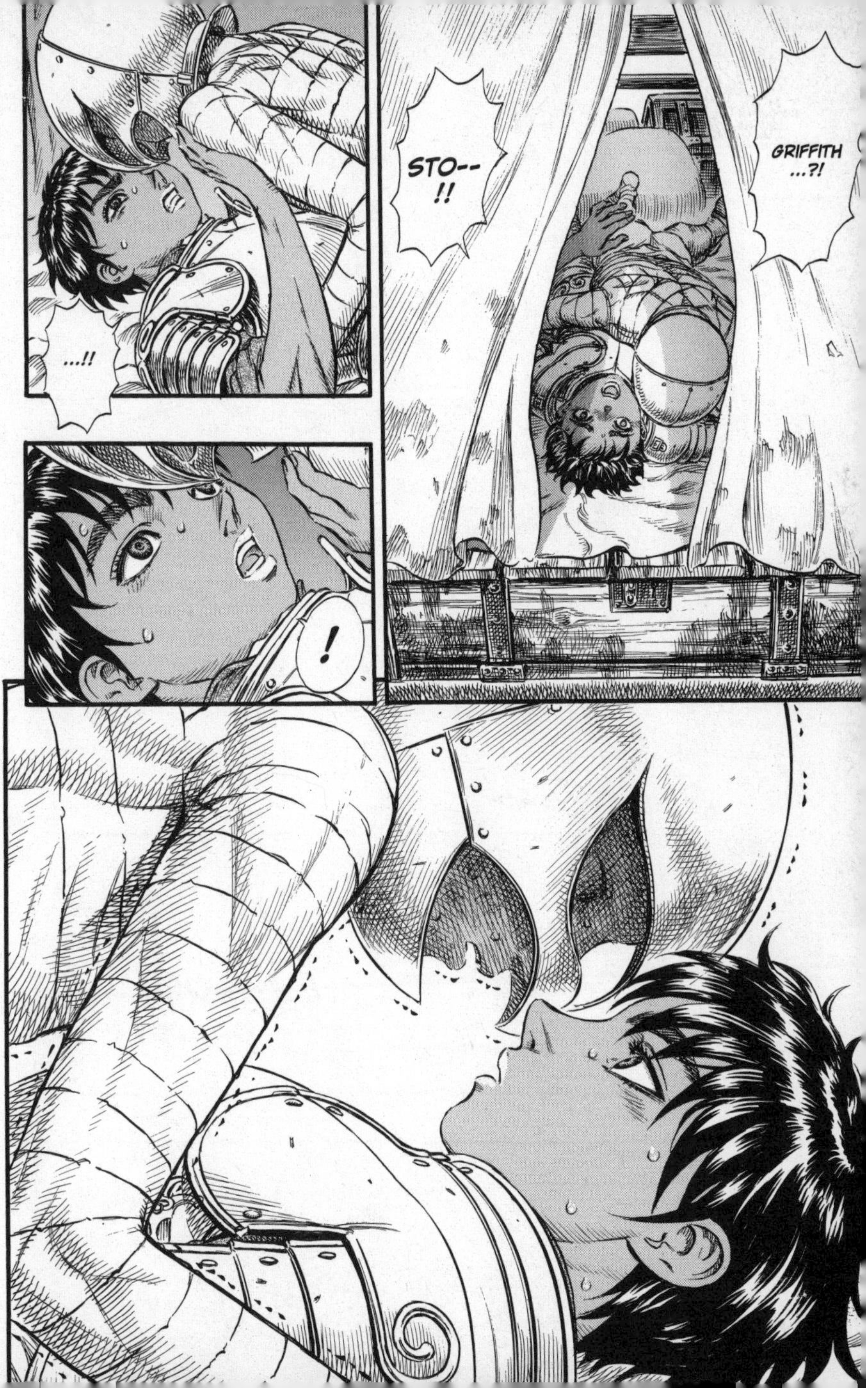
GRIFFITH ...?!
STO-- !!
...!!
!

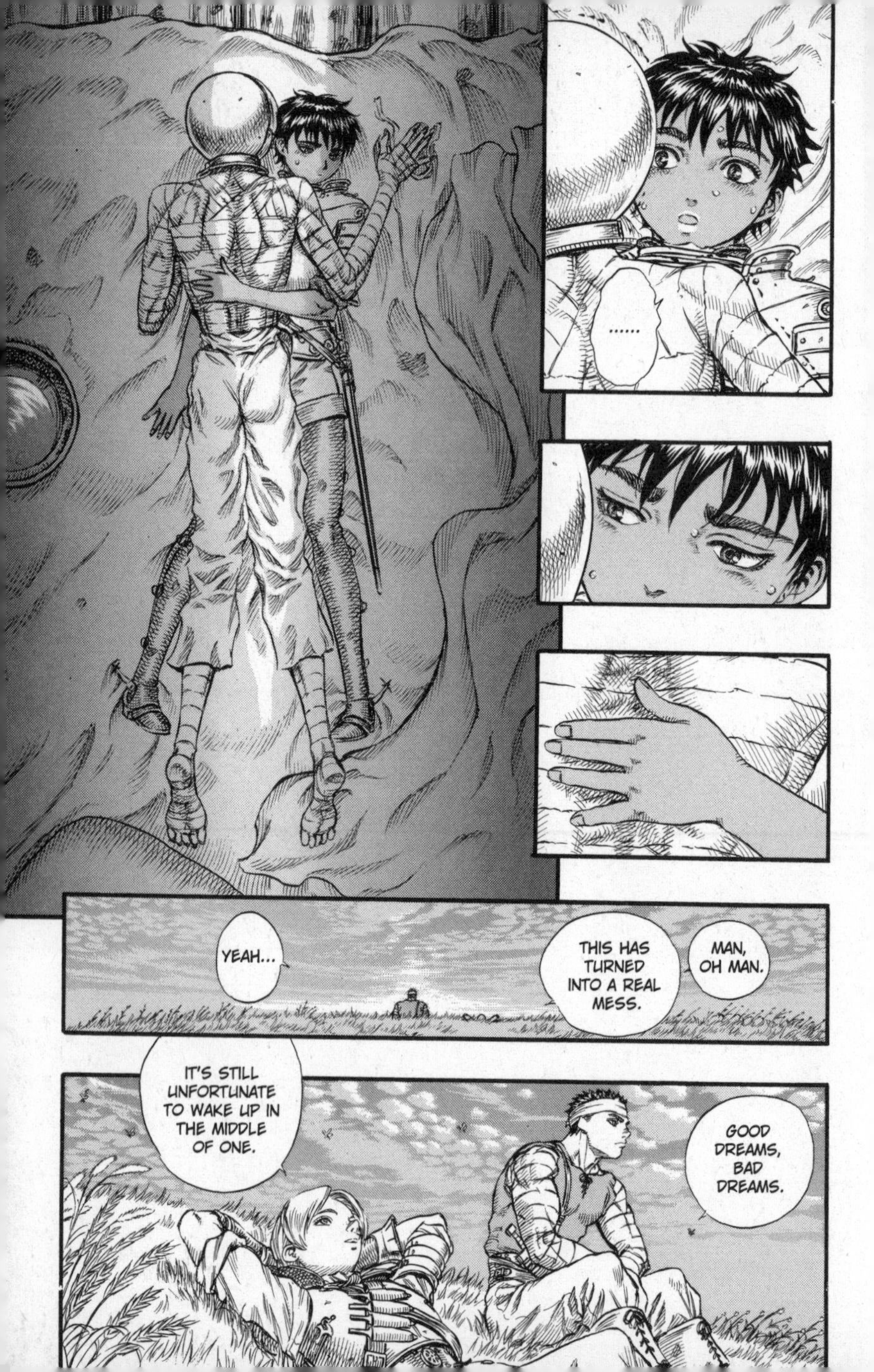
......
MAN, OH MAN.
THIS HAS TURNED INTO A REAL MESS.
YEAH...
GOOD DREAMS, BAD DREAMS.
IT'S STILL UNFORTUNATE TO WAKE UP IN THE MIDDLE OF ONE.

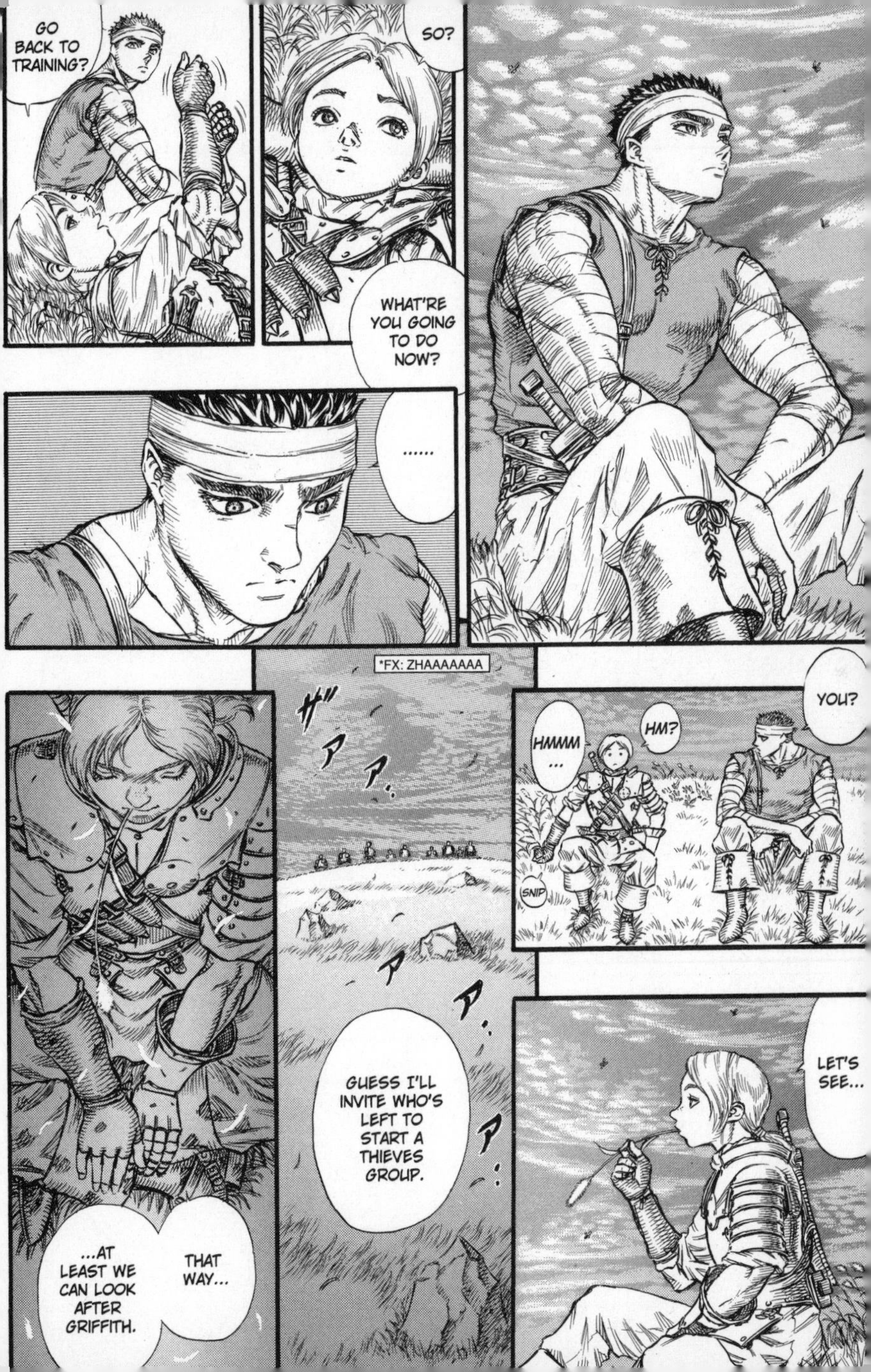
WHAT'RE YOU GOING TO DO NOW?
SO?
GO BACK TO TRAINING?
......
YOU?
HM?
HMMM ...
SNIP
LET'S SEE...
*FX: ZHAAAAAAA
GUESS I'LL INVITE WHO'S LEFT TO START A THIEVES GROUP.
THAT WAY...
...AT LEAST WE CAN LOOK AFTER GRIFFITH.

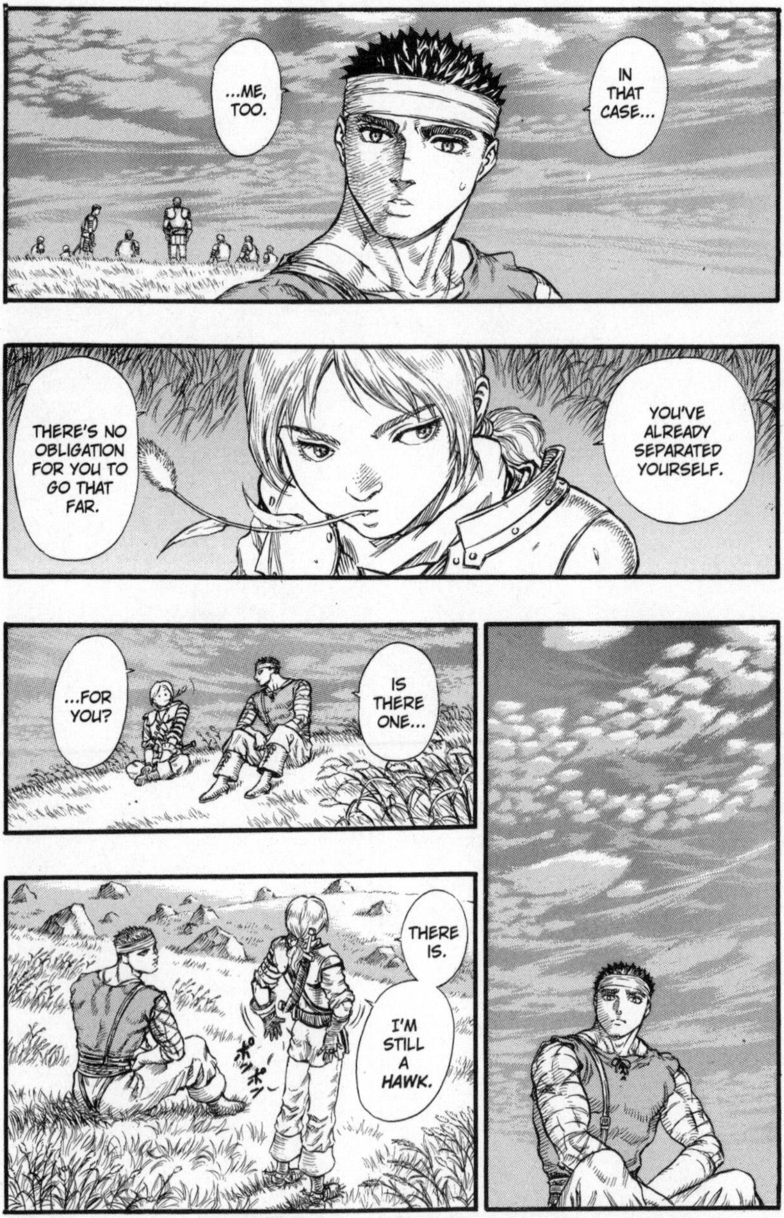
IN THAT CASE...
...ME, TOO.
YOU'VE ALREADY SEPARATED YOURSELF.
THERE'S NO OBLIGATION FOR YOU TO GO THAT FAR.
IS THERE ONE...
...FOR YOU?
THERE IS.
I'M STILL A HAWK.

*FX: PAT PAT

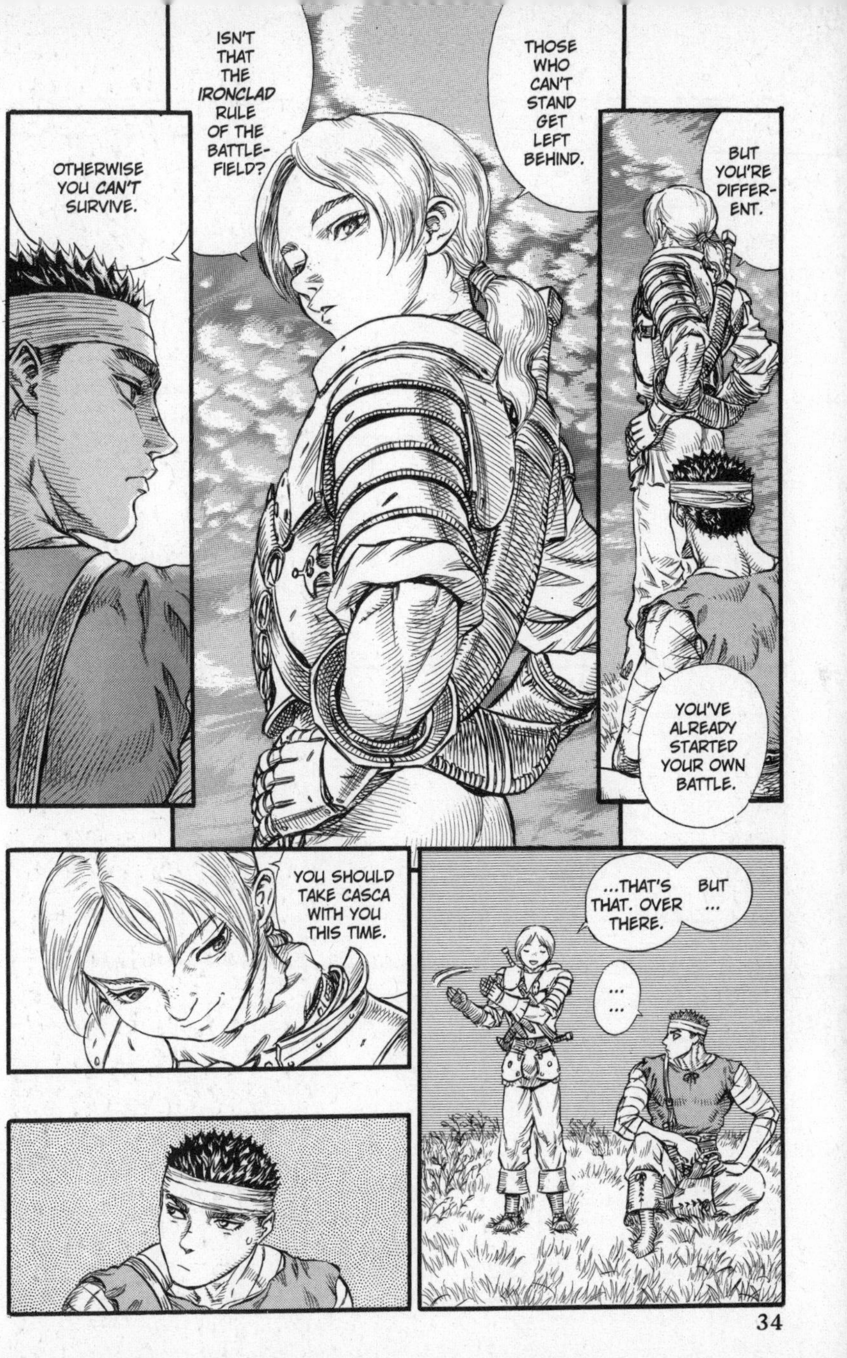
THOSE WHO CAN'T STAND GET LEFT BEHIND.
ISN'T THAT THE IRONCLAD RULE OF THE BATTLE-FIELD?
OTHERWISE YOU CAN'T SURVIVE.
BUT YOU'RE DIFFER-ENT.
YOU'VE ALREADY STARTED YOUR OWN BATTLE.
YOU SHOULD TAKE CASCA WITH YOU THIS TIME.
BUT ...
...THAT'S THAT. OVER THERE.
... ...

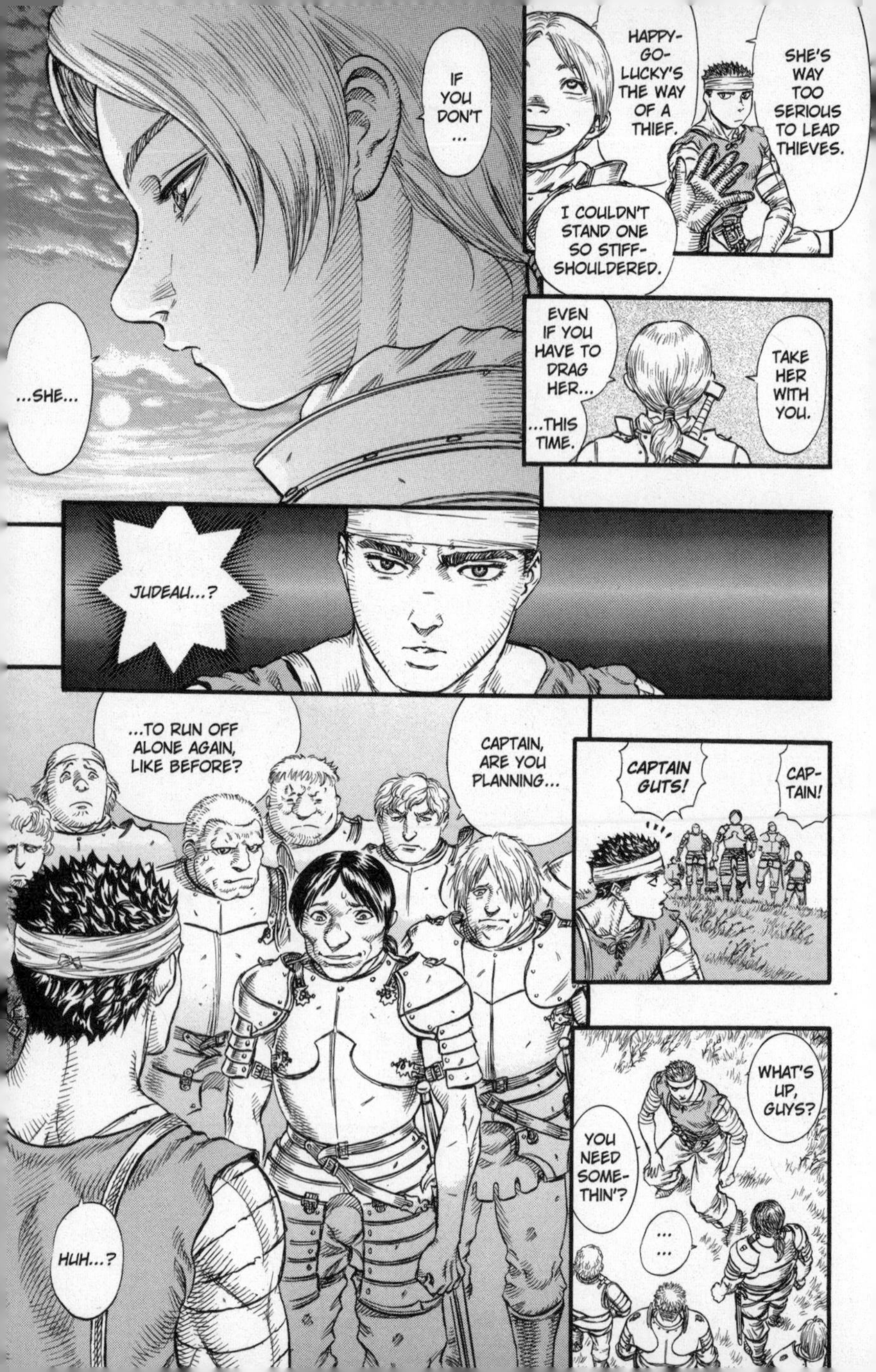
SHE'S WAY TOO SERIOUS TO LEAD THIEVES.
HAPPY-GO-LUCKY'S THE WAY OF A THIEF.
I COULDN'T STAND ONE SO STIFF-SHOULDERED.
TAKE HER WITH YOU.
EVEN IF YOU HAVE TO DRAG HER...
...THIS TIME.
IF YOU DON'T ...
...SHE...
JUDEAU...?
CAP-TAIN!
CAPTAIN GUTS!
WHAT'S UP, GUYS?
YOU NEED SOME-THIN'?
... ...
CAPTAIN, ARE YOU PLANNING...
...TO RUN OFF ALONE AGAIN, LIKE BEFORE?
HUH...?

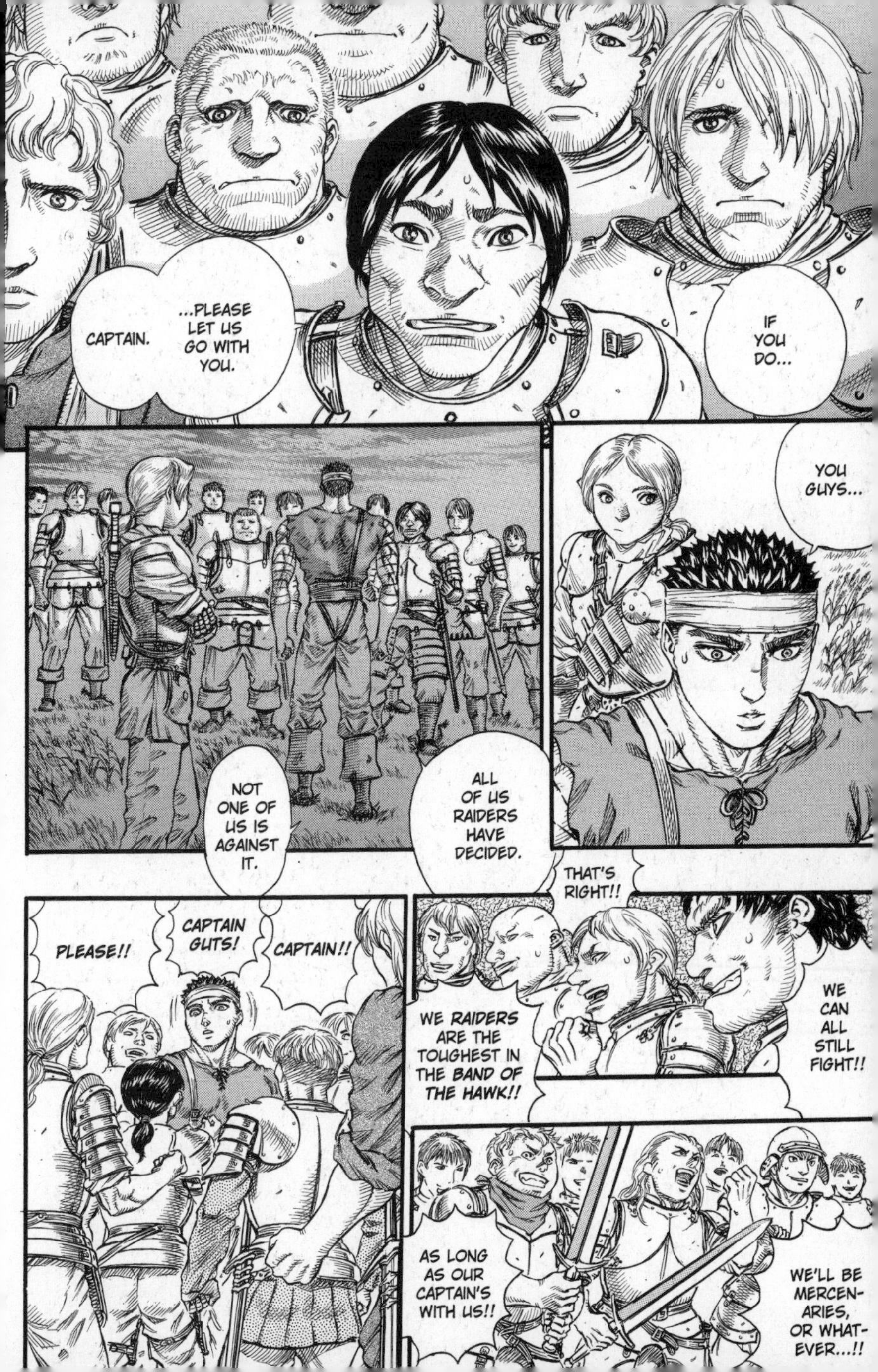
IF YOU DO...
...PLEASE LET US GO WITH YOU.
CAPTAIN.
YOU GUYS...
ALL OF US RAIDERS HAVE DECIDED.
NOT ONE OF US IS AGAINST IT.
THAT'S RIGHT!!
WE CAN ALL STILL FIGHT!!
WE RAIDERS ARE THE TOUGHEST IN THE BAND OF THE HAWK!!
WE'LL BE MERCENARIES, OR WHATEVER...!!
AS LONG AS OUR CAPTAIN'S WITH US!!
CAPTAIN!!
CAPTAIN GUTS!
PLEASE!!

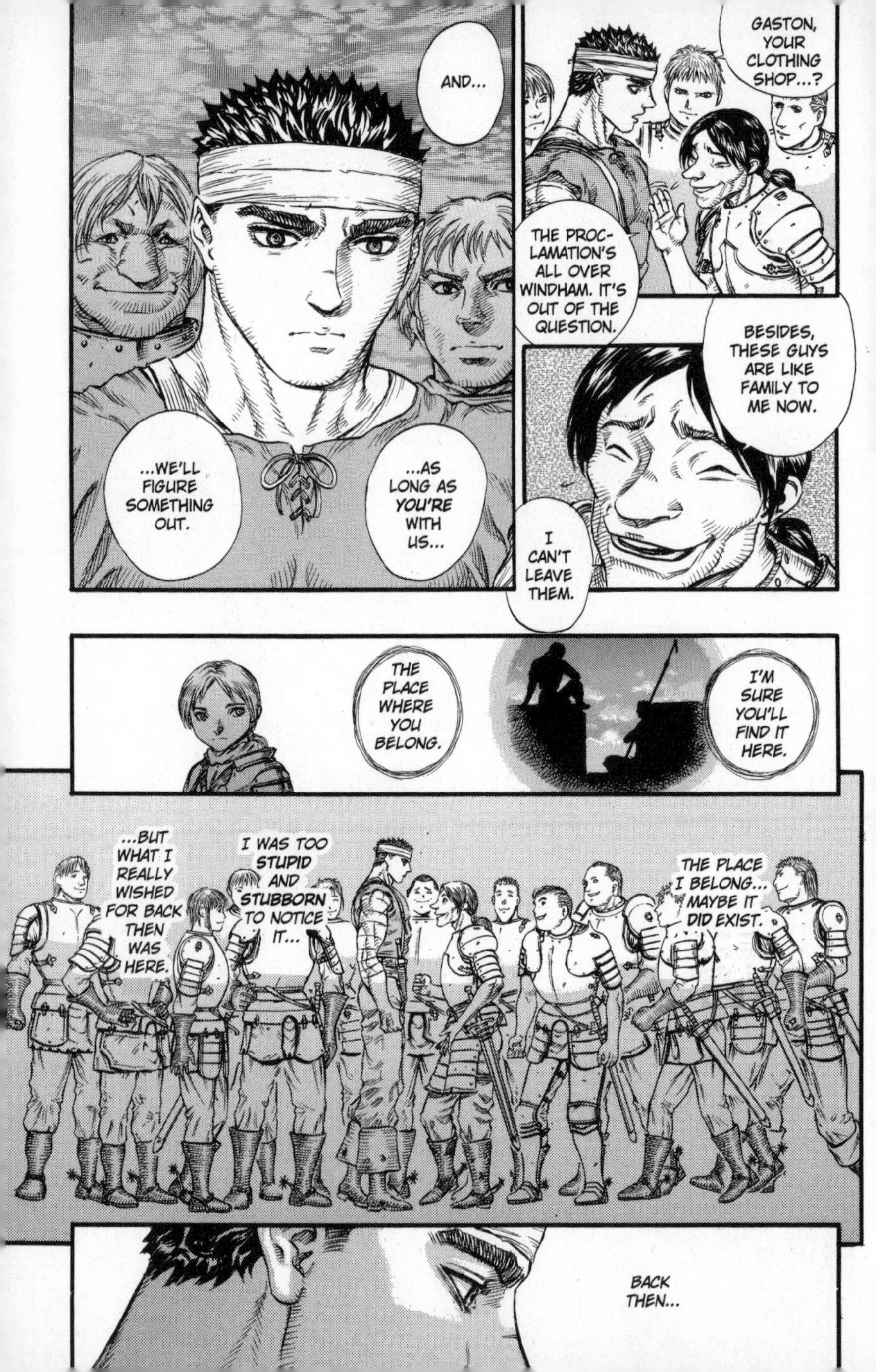
GASTON, YOUR CLOTHING SHOP...?
THE PROC-LAMATION'S ALL OVER WINDHAM. IT'S OUT OF THE QUESTION.
BESIDES, THESE GUYS ARE LIKE FAMILY TO ME NOW.
I CAN'T LEAVE THEM.
AND...
...AS LONG AS YOU'RE WITH US...
...WE'LL FIGURE SOMETHING OUT.
I'M SURE YOU'LL FIND IT HERE.
THE PLACE WHERE YOU BELONG.
THE PLACE I BELONG... MAYBE IT DID EXIST.
I WAS TOO STUPID AND STUBBORN TO NOTICE IT...
...BUT WHAT I REALLY WISHED FOR BACK THEN WAS HERE.
BACK THEN...

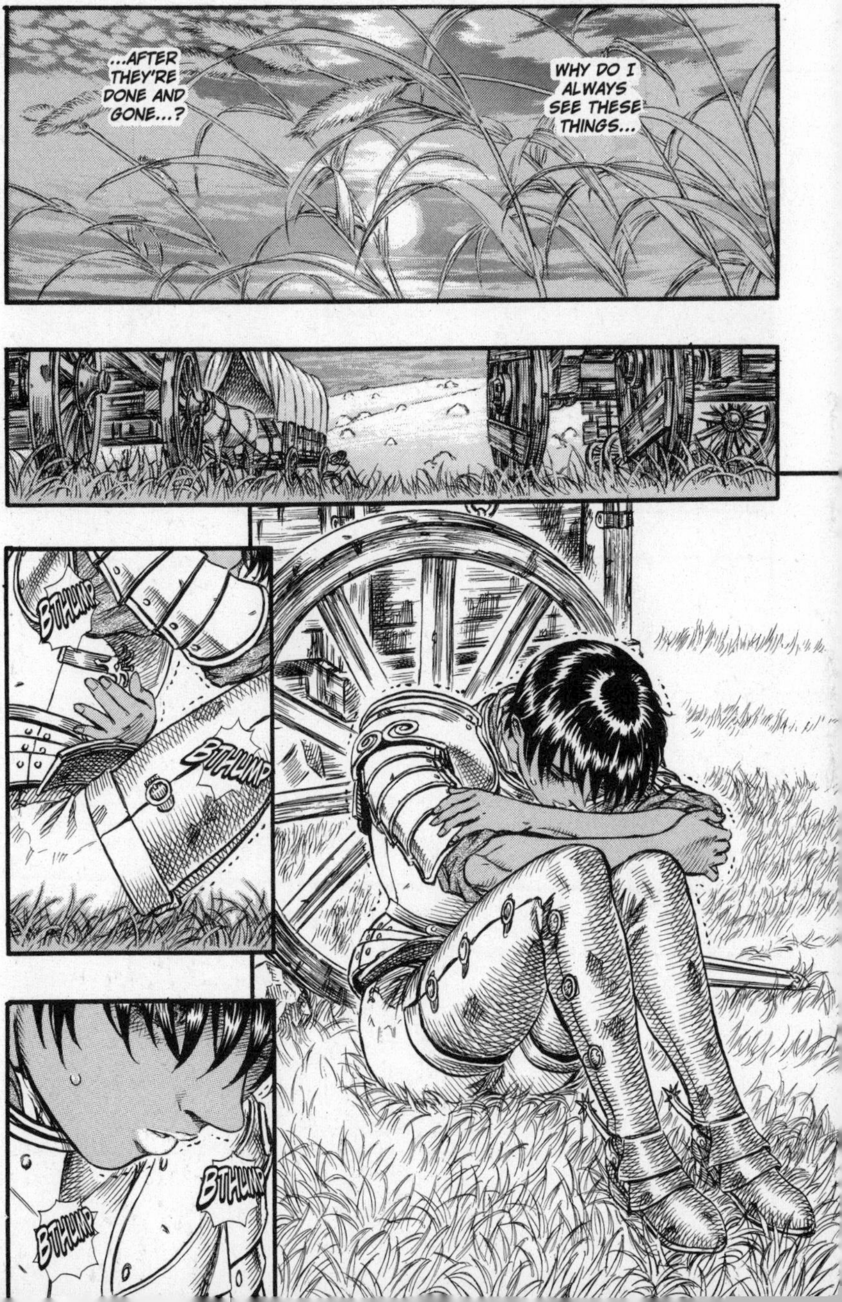
WHY DO I ALWAYS SEE THESE THINGS...
...AFTER THEY'RE DONE AND GONE...?
BTHUMP
BTHUMP
BTHUMP
BTHUMP

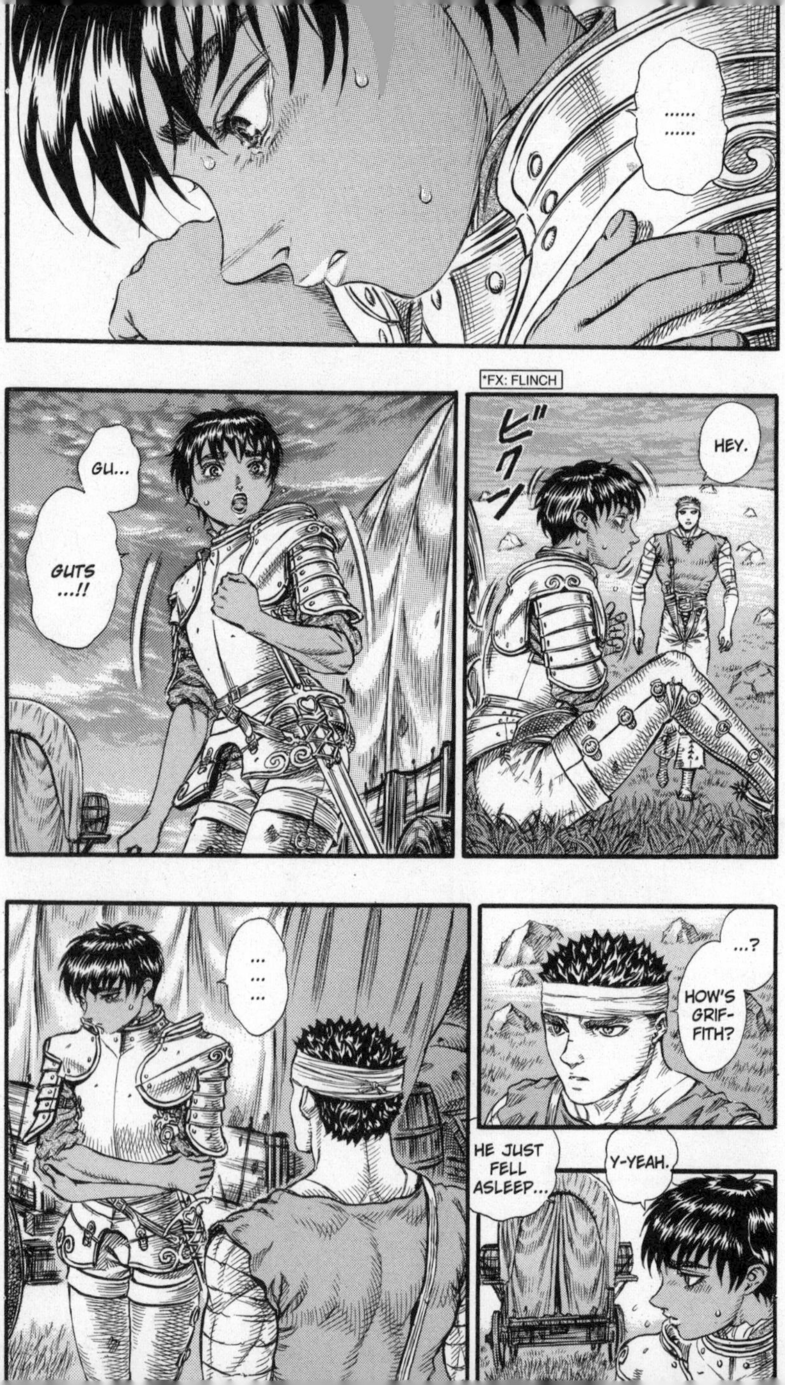
......
......
*FX: FLINCH
ビクン
HEY.
GU...
GUTS ...!!
...?
HOW'S GRIF-FITH?
Y-YEAH.
HE JUST FELL ASLEEP...
...
...
...

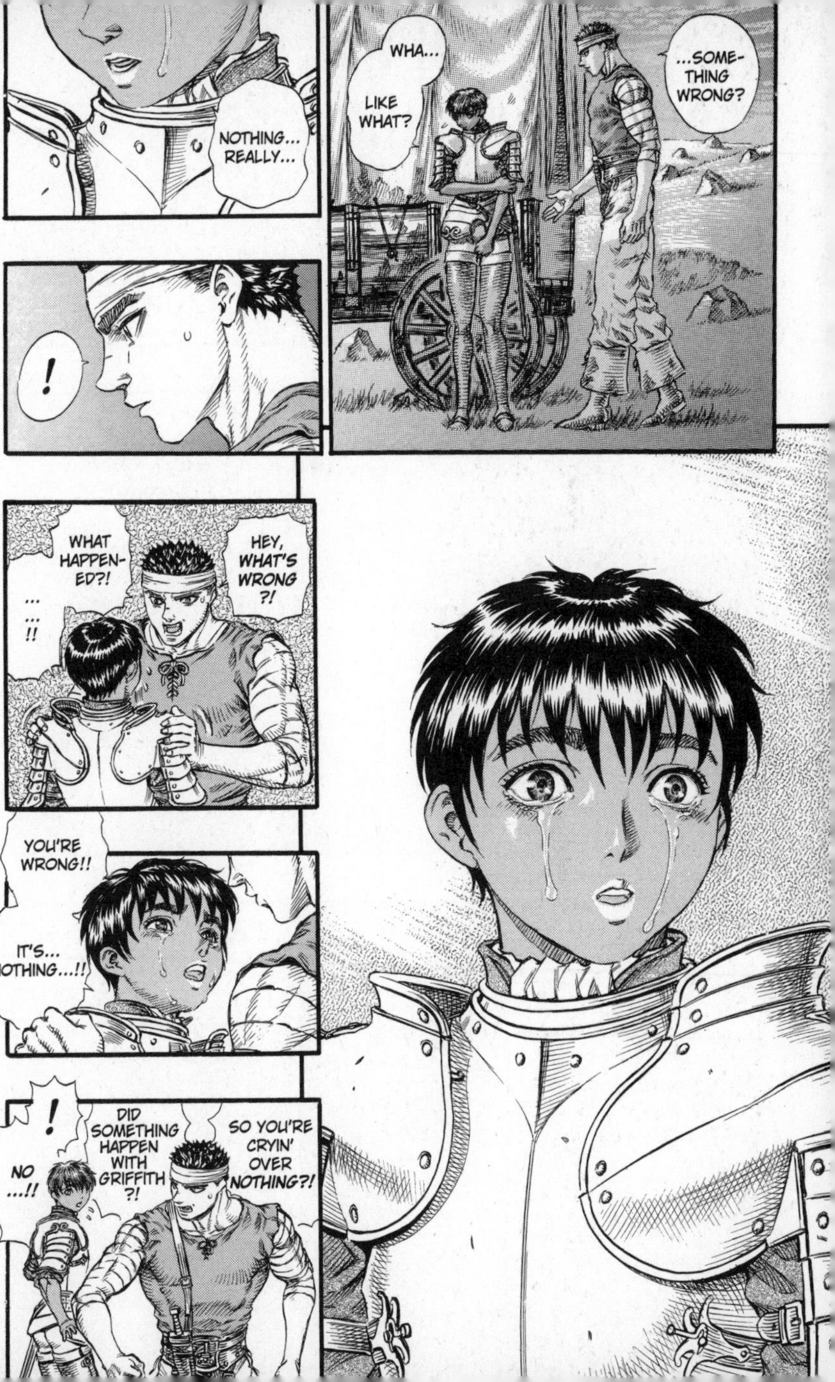

...SOMETHING WRONG?
WHA... LIKE WHAT?
NOTHING... REALLY...
!
HEY, WHAT'S WRONG?!
WHAT HAPPENED?!
... ... !!
YOU'RE WRONG!!
IT'S... NOTHING...!!
SO YOU'RE CRYIN' OVER NOTHING?!
DID SOMETHING HAPPEN WITH GRIFFITH?!
!
NO...!!

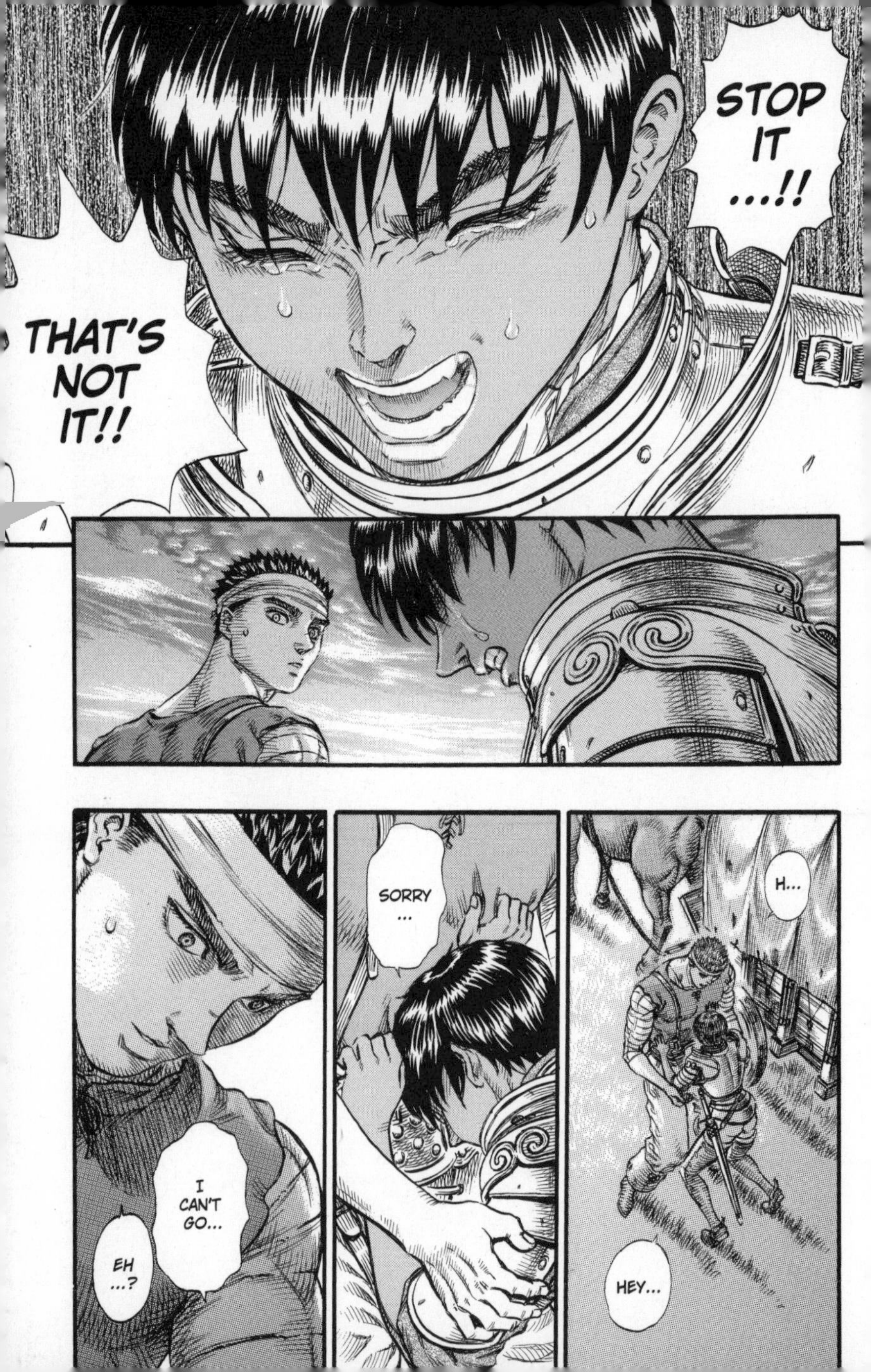
STOP IT ...!!
THAT'S NOT IT!!
H...
HEY...
SORRY ...
I CAN'T GO...
EH ...?

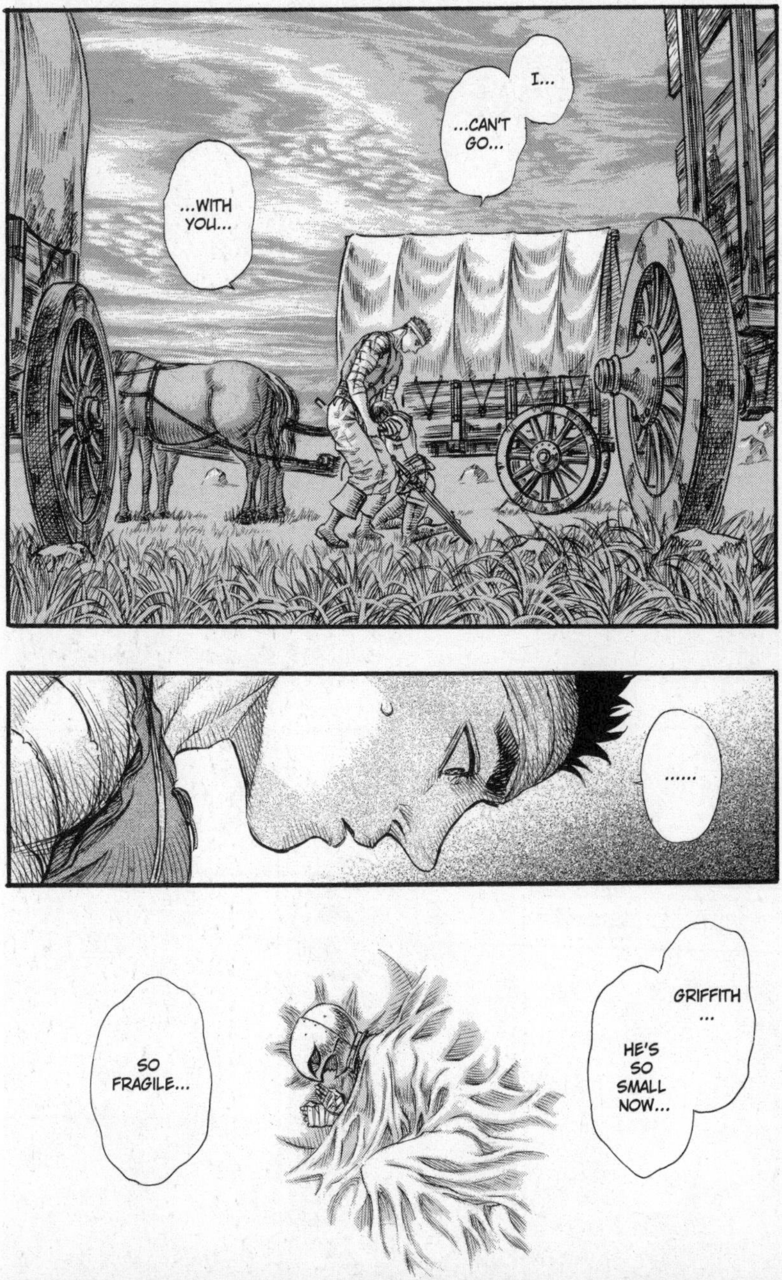
I...
...CAN'T GO...
...WITH YOU...
......
GRIFFITH ... HE'S SO SMALL NOW...
SO FRAGILE...

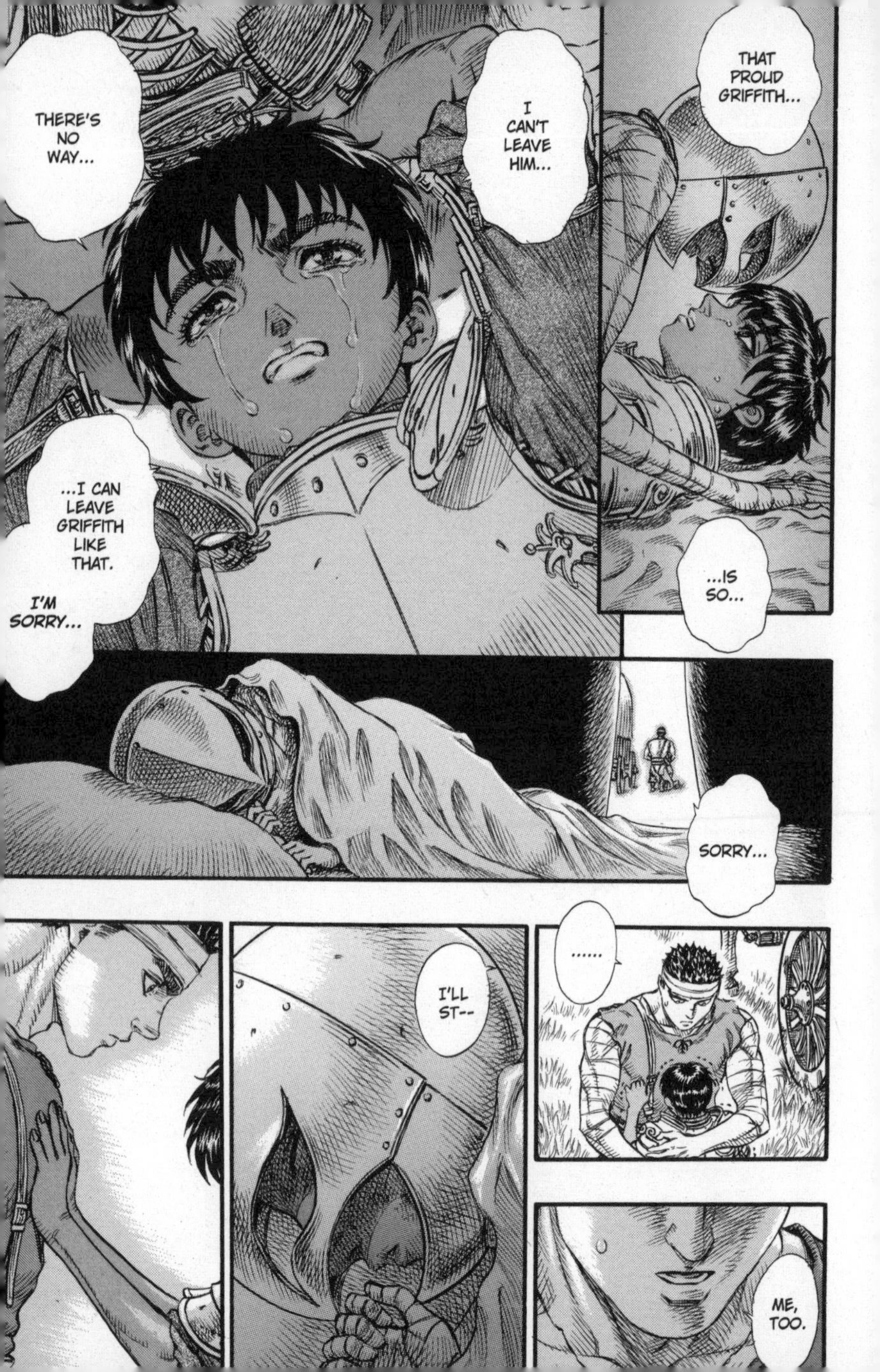
THAT PROUD GRIFFITH...
...IS SO...
I CAN'T LEAVE HIM...
THERE'S NO WAY...
...I CAN LEAVE GRIFFITH LIKE THAT.
I'M SORRY...
SORRY...
......
ME, TOO.
I'LL ST--

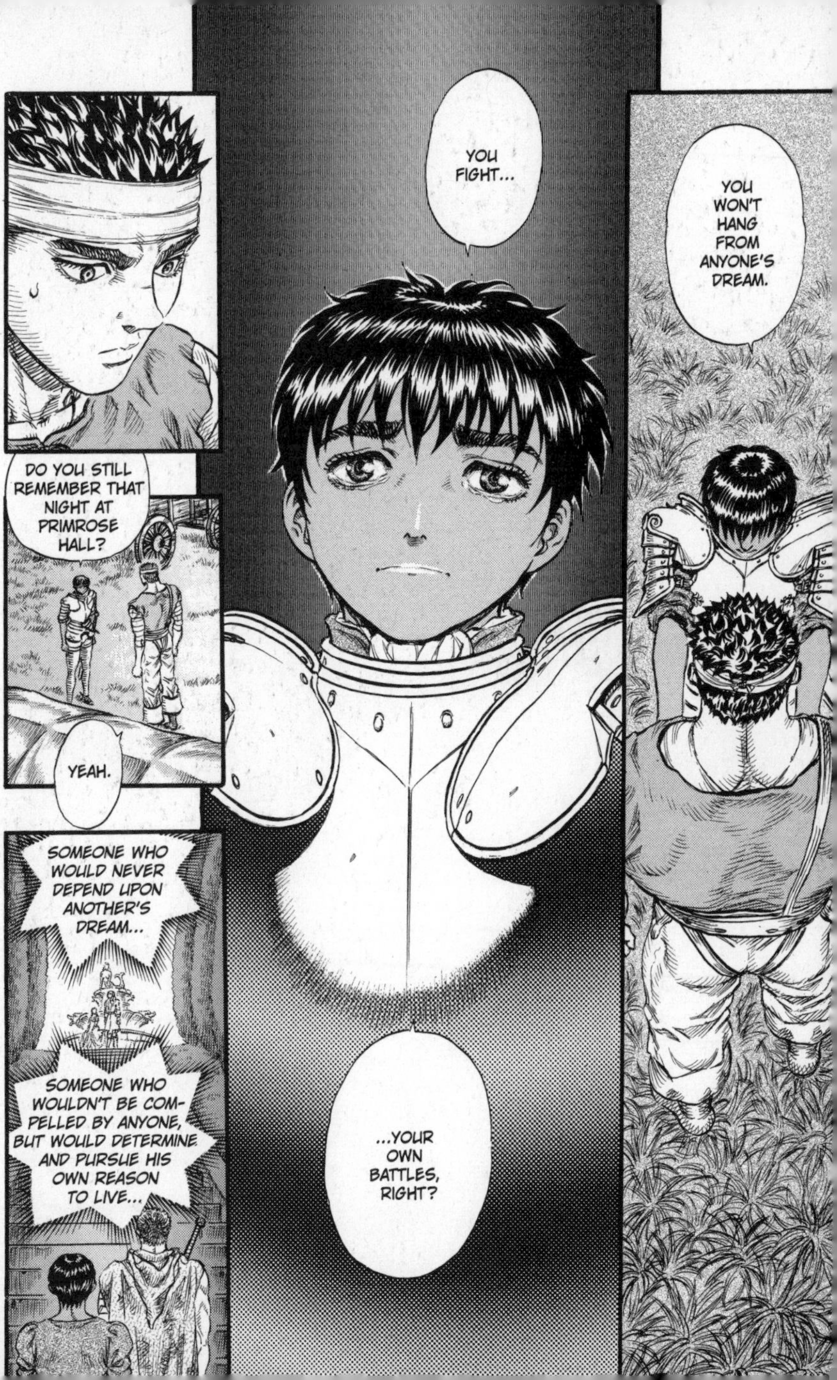
YOU WON'T HANG FROM ANYONE'S DREAM.
YOU FIGHT...
...YOUR OWN BATTLES, RIGHT?
DO YOU STILL REMEMBER THAT NIGHT AT PRIMROSE HALL?
YEAH.
SOMEONE WHO WOULD NEVER DEPEND UPON ANOTHER'S DREAM...
SOMEONE WHO WOULDN'T BE COM-PELLED BY ANYONE, BUT WOULD DETERMINE AND PURSUE HIS OWN REASON TO LIVE...

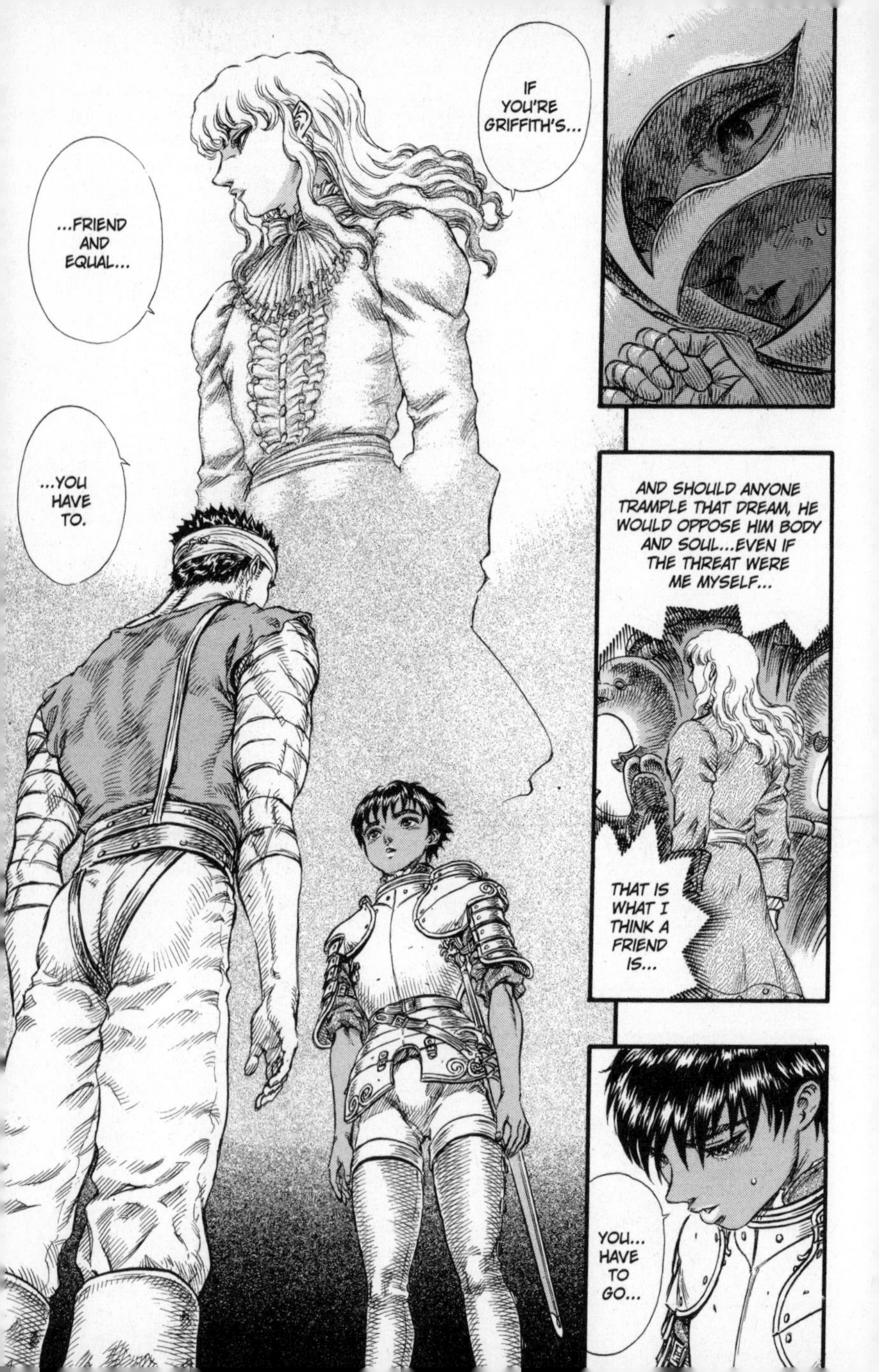
AND SHOULD ANYONE TRAMPLE THAT DREAM, HE WOULD OPPOSE HIM BODY AND SOUL...EVEN IF THE THREAT WERE ME MYSELF...
THAT IS WHAT I THINK A FRIEND IS...
YOU... HAVE TO GO...
IF YOU'RE GRIFFITH'S...
...FRIEND AND EQUAL...
...YOU HAVE TO.

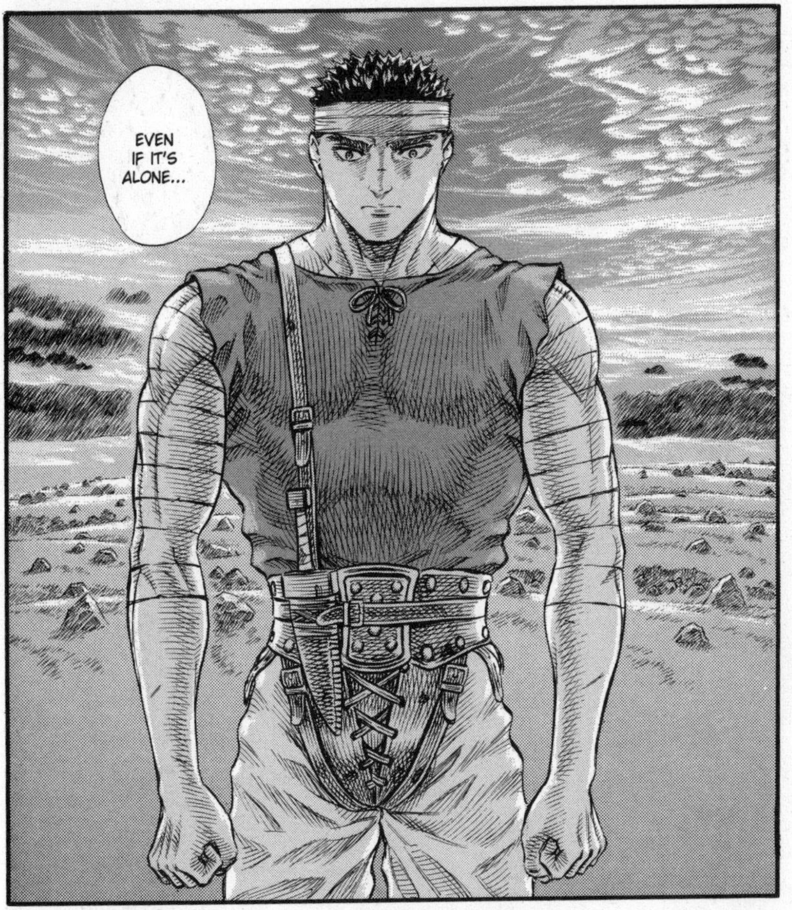
EVEN IF IT'S ALONE...
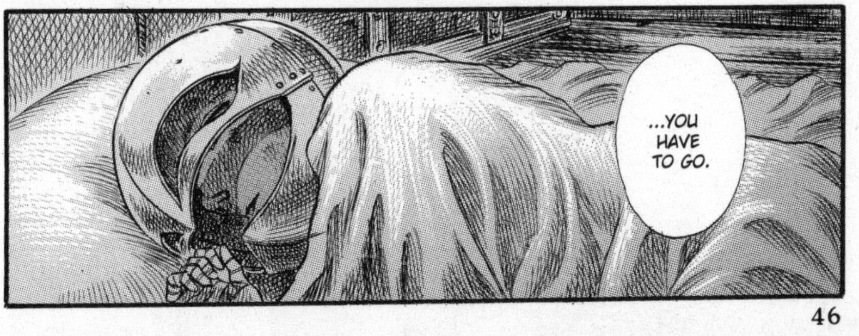
...YOU HAVE TO GO.

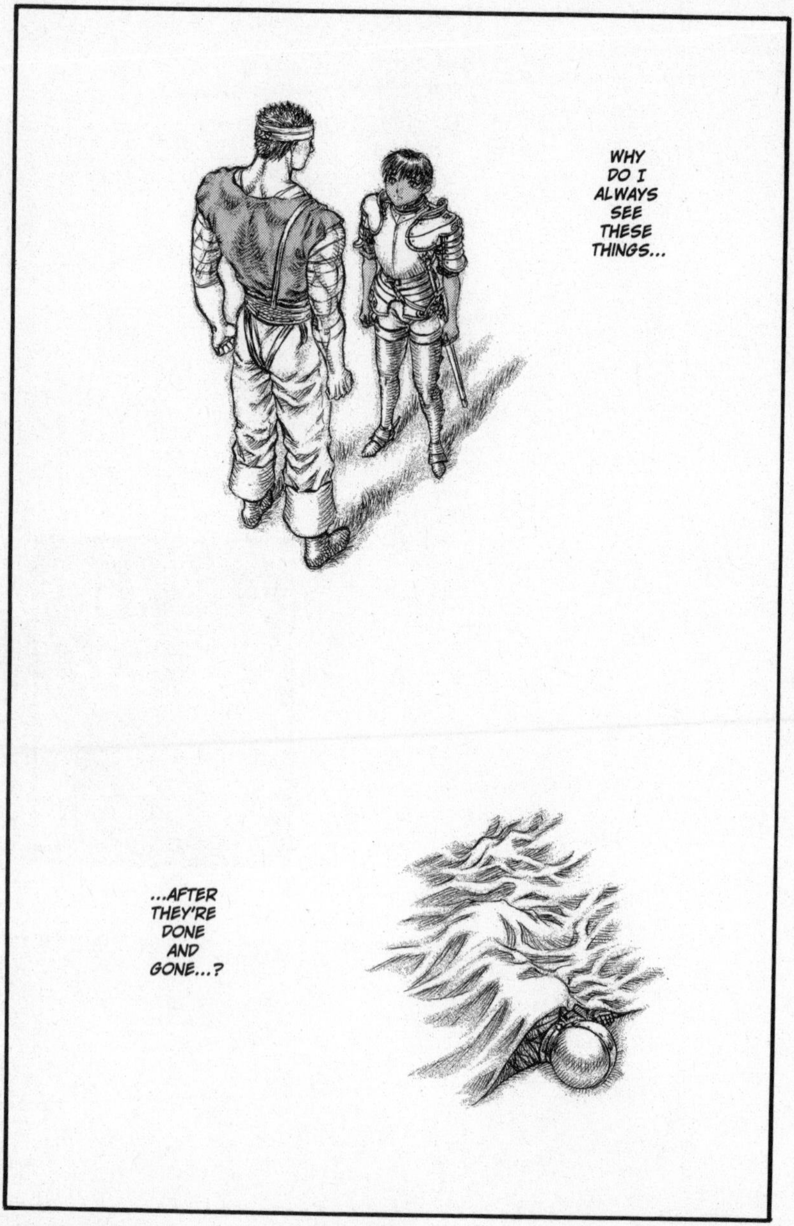
WHY DO I ALWAYS SEE THESE THINGS...
...AFTER THEY'RE DONE AND GONE...?

THE WARRIORS OF TWILIGHT: END

...YOU HAVE TO GO.

EVEN IF IT'S ALONE...

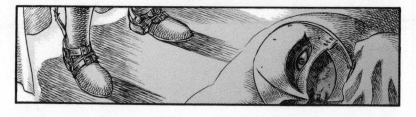

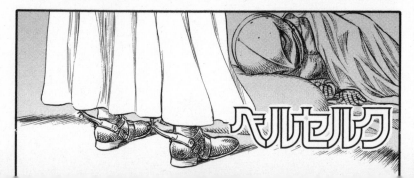

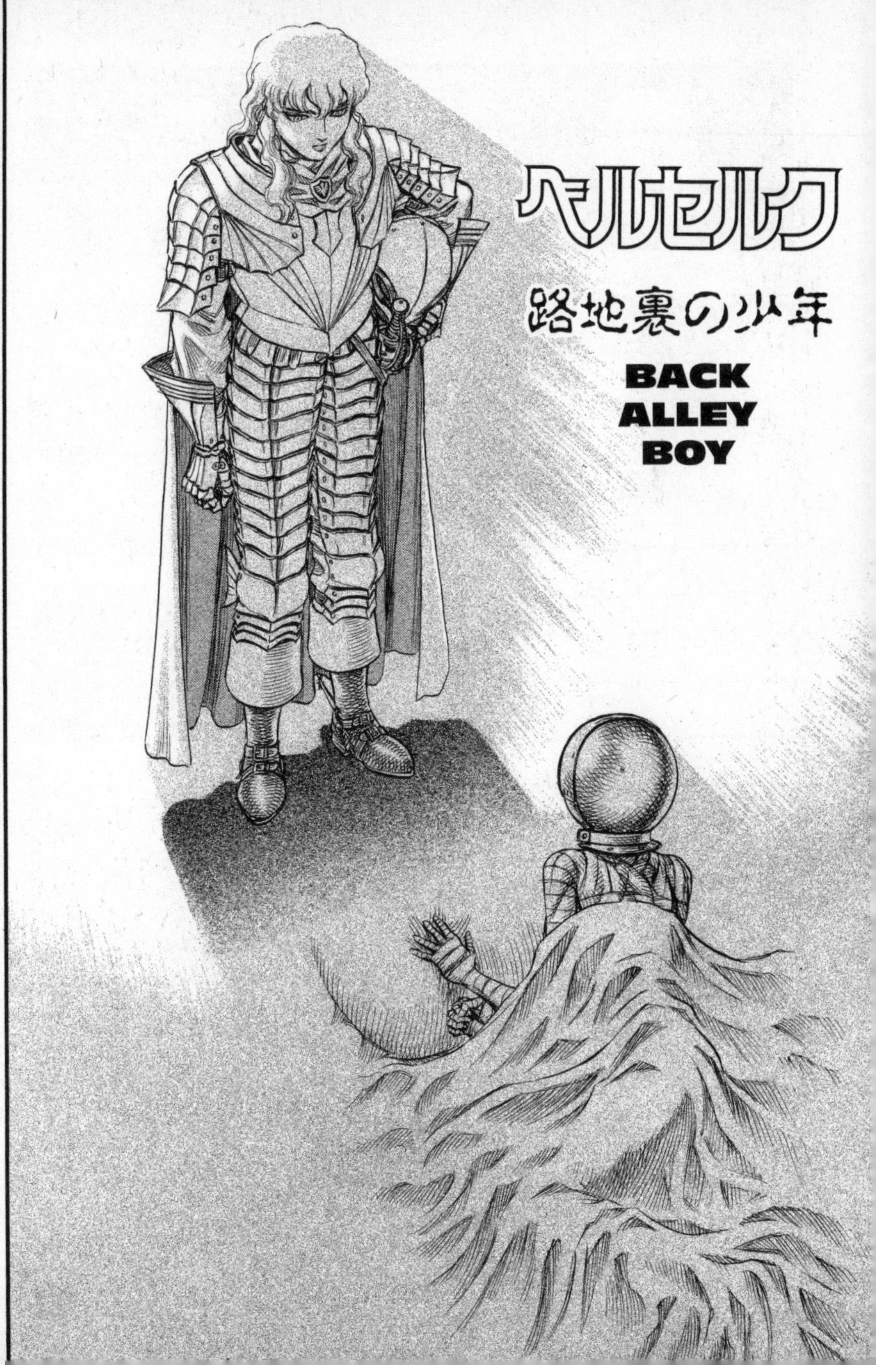
ベルセルク
路地裏の少年
BACK ALLEY BOY

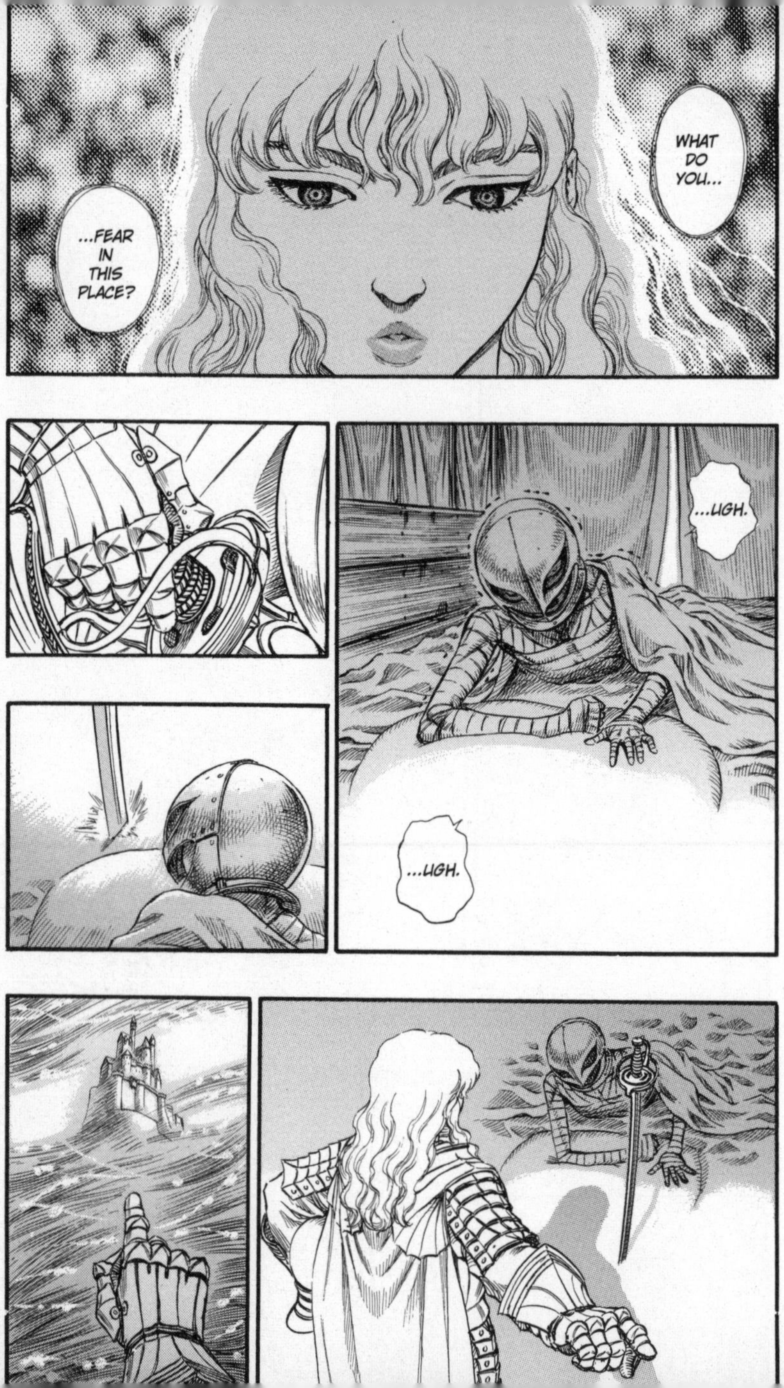
WHAT DO YOU...
...FEAR IN THIS PLACE?
...UGH.
...UGH.

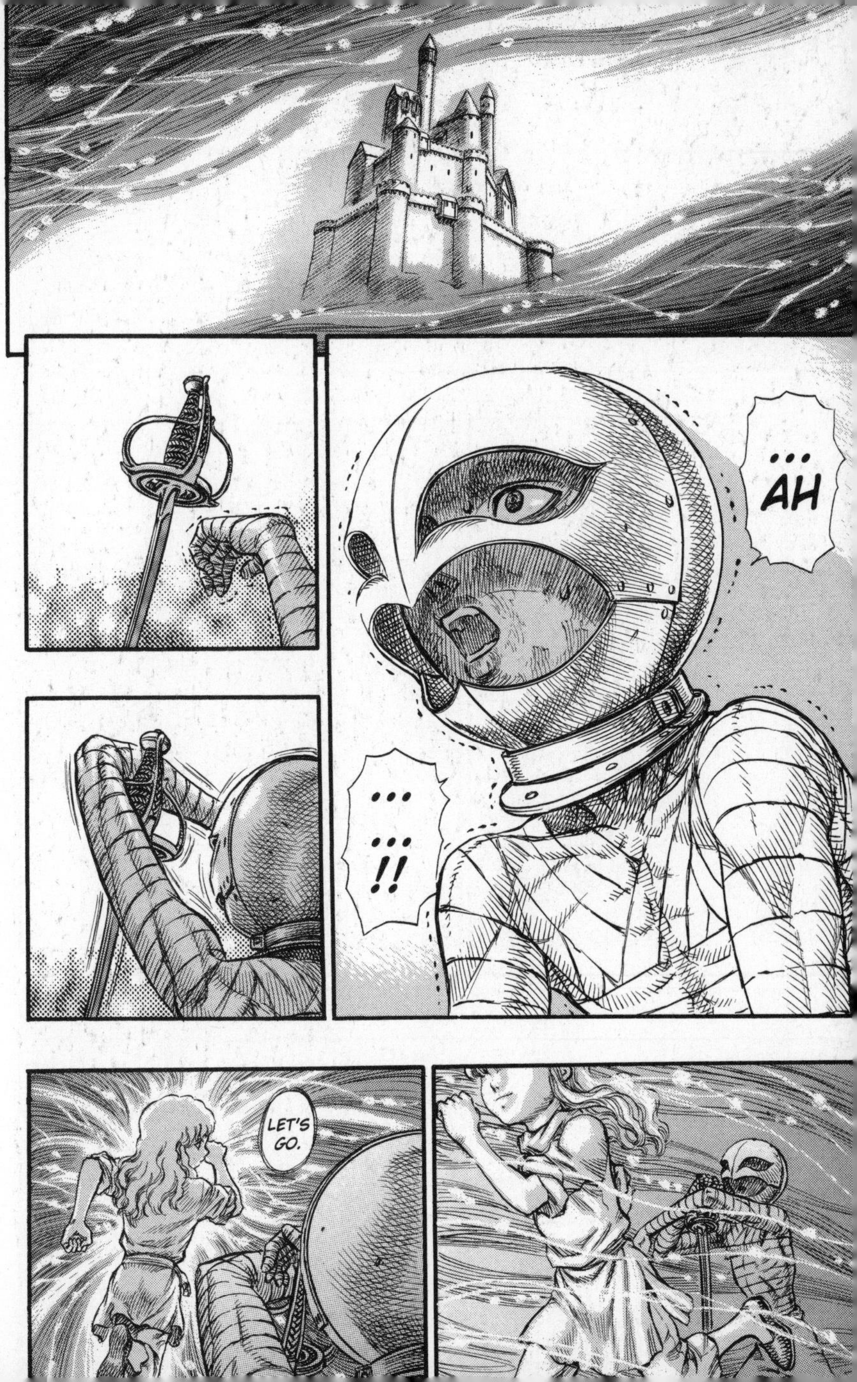
...AH
......!!
LET'S GO.

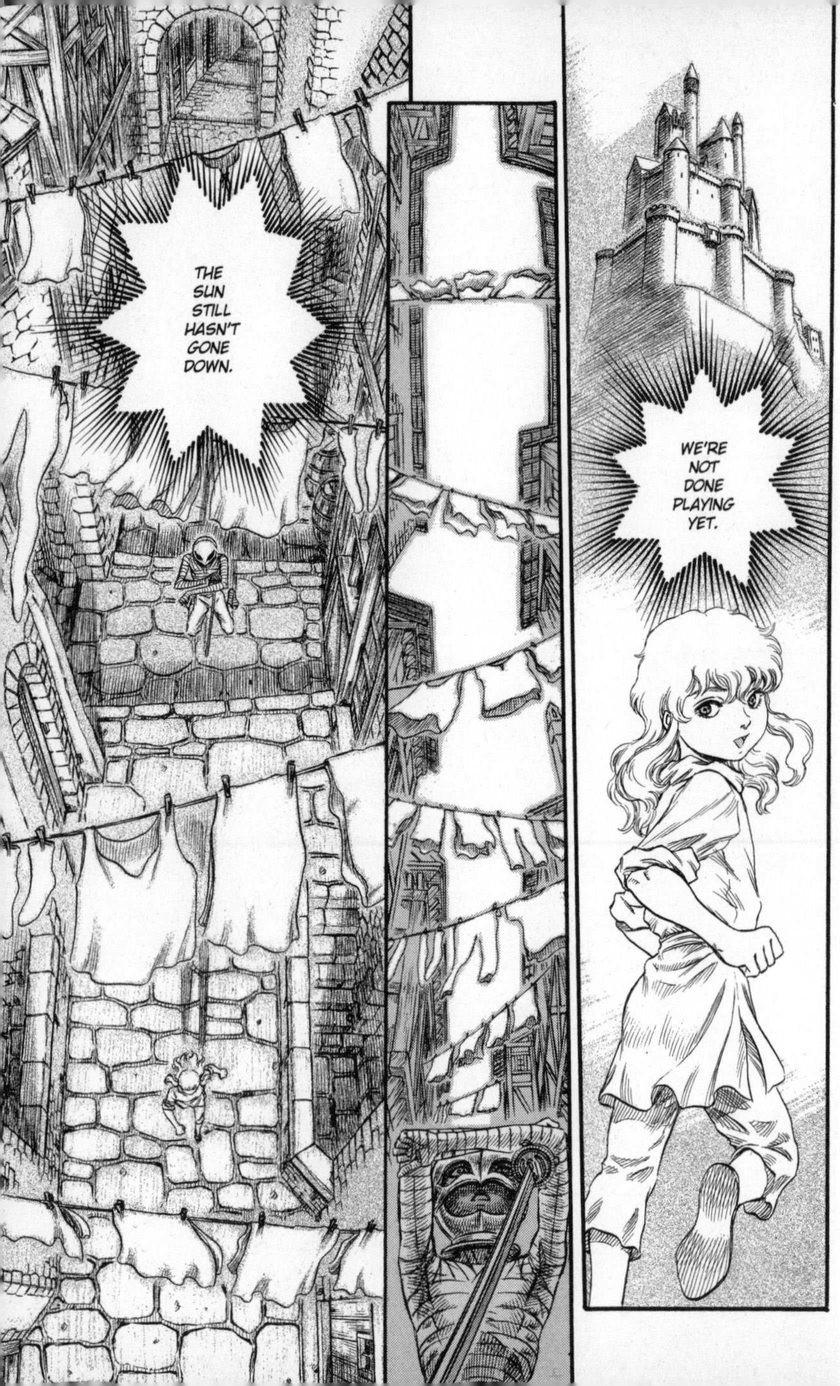
WE'RE NOT DONE PLAYING YET.
THE SUN STILL HASN'T GONE DOWN.

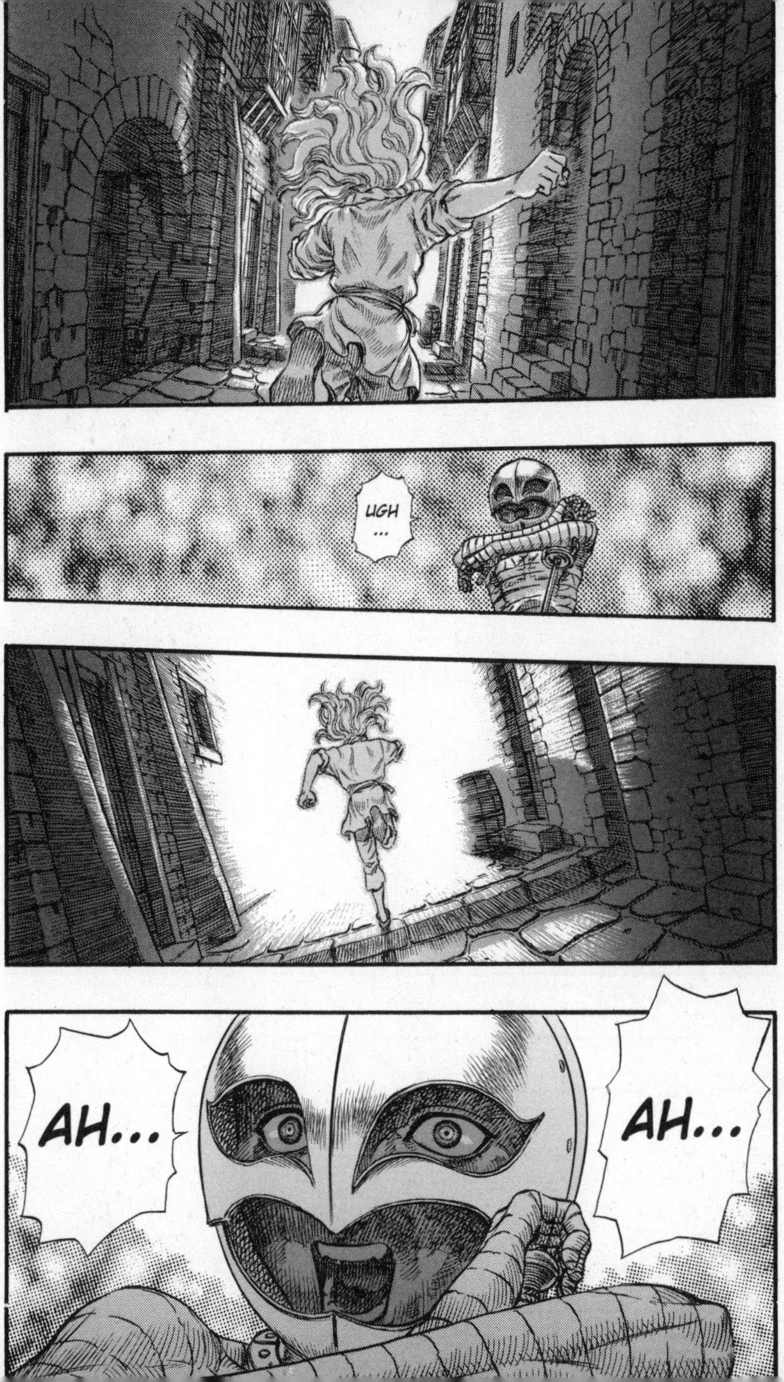
UGH ...
AH...
AH...

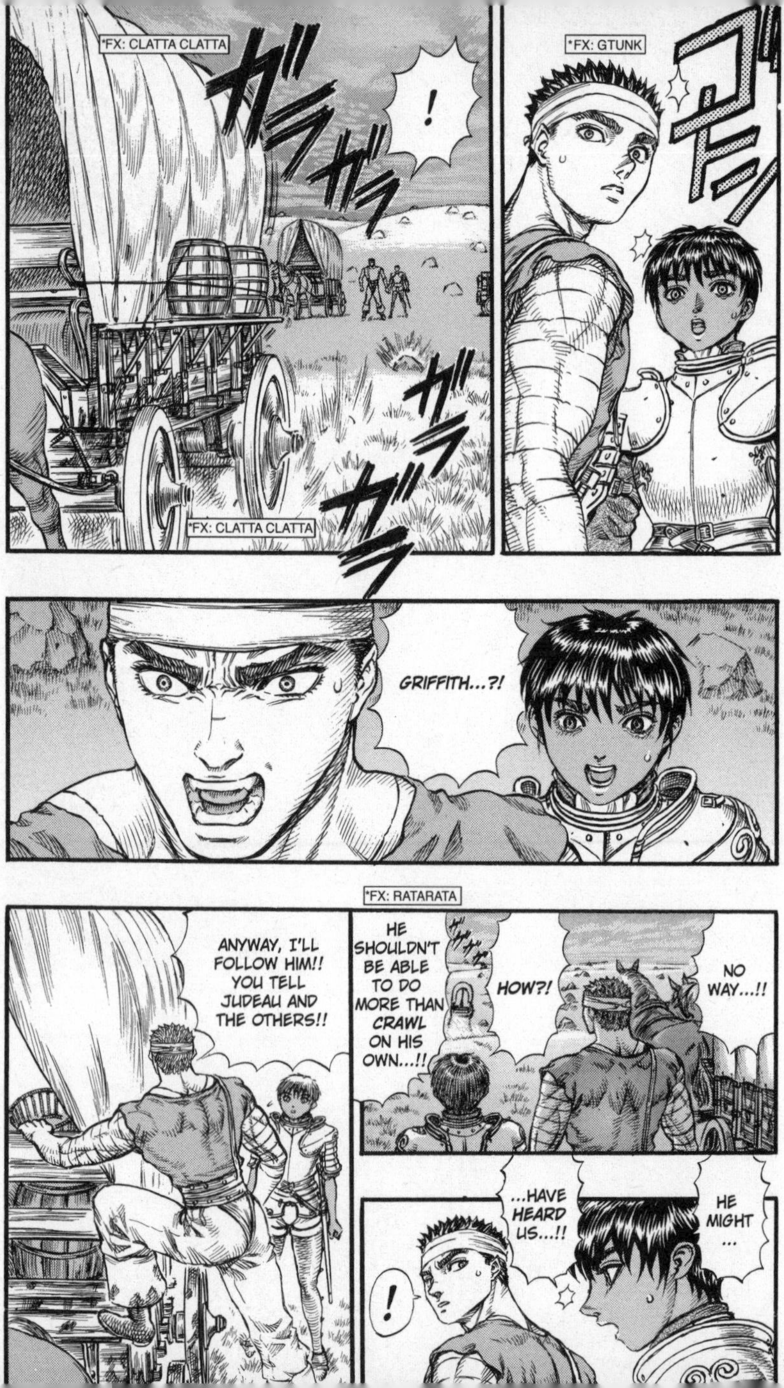
*FX: GTUNK
*FX: CLATTA CLATTA
!
*FX: CLATTA CLATTA
GRIFFITH...?!
*FX: RATARATA
NO WAY...!!
HOW?!
HE SHOULDN'T BE ABLE TO DO MORE THAN CRAWL ON HIS OWN...!!
HE MIGHT ...
...HAVE HEARD US...!!
!
ANYWAY, I'LL FOLLOW HIM!! YOU TELL JUDEAU AND THE OTHERS!!

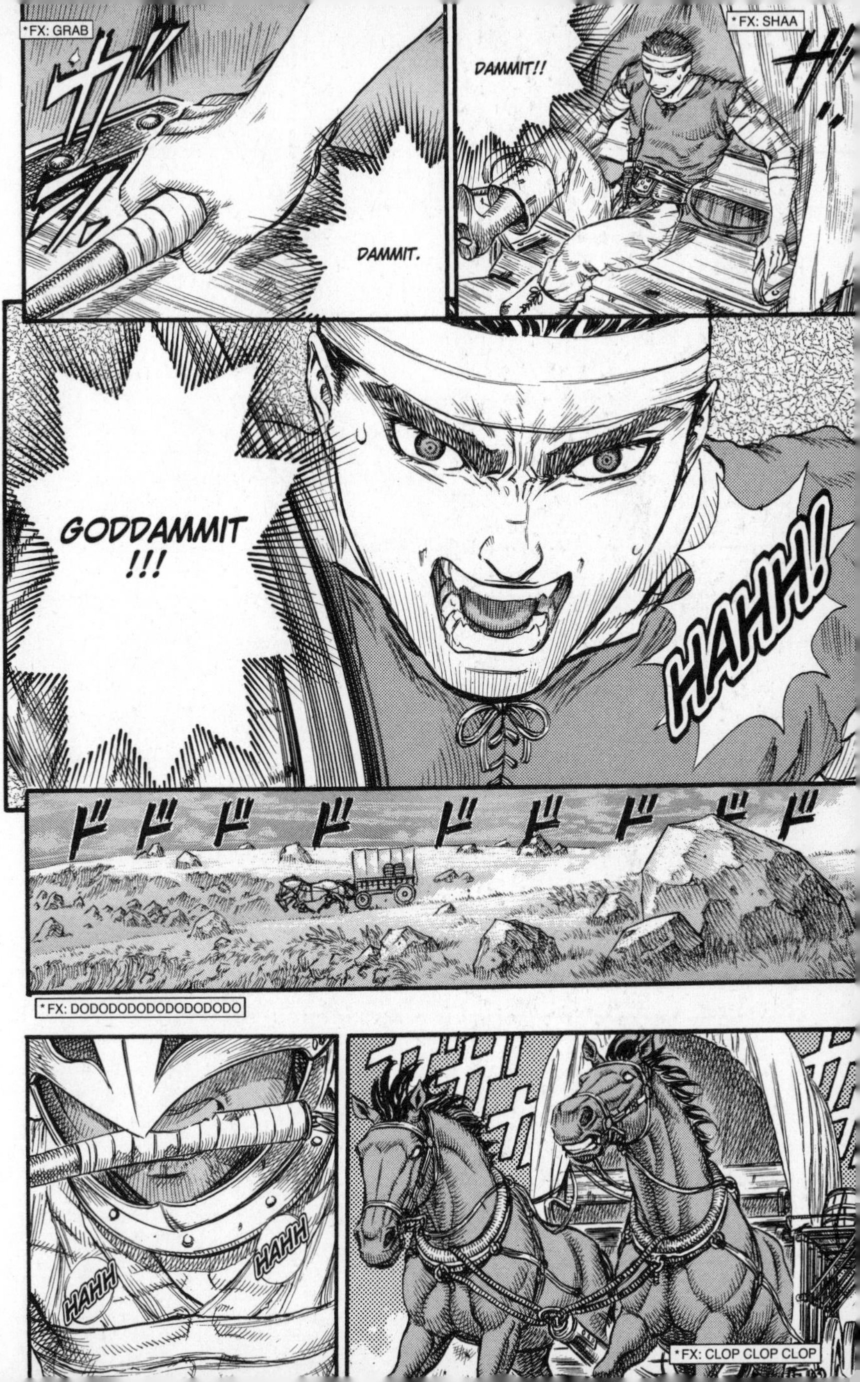
*FX: SHAA
DAMMIT!!
*FX: GRAB
DAMMIT.
GODDAMMIT !!!
HAHH!
*FX: DODODODODODODODODO
*FX: CLOP CLOP CLOP
HAHH
HAHH

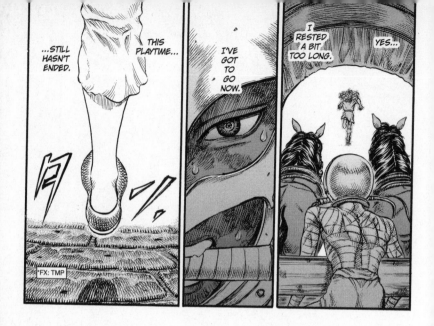

YES...
I RESTED A BIT TOO LONG.
I'VE GOT TO GO NOW.
THIS PLAYTIME...
...STILL HASN'T ENDED.
*FX: TMP
THAT BACK ALLEY COBBLESTONE PATH...
...STILL GOES ON.

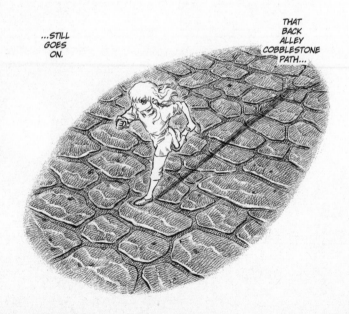

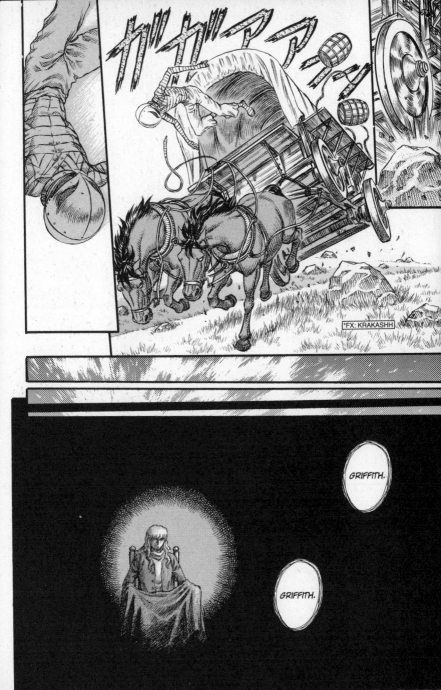

*FX: KRAKASHH

GRIFFITH.

GRIFFITH.

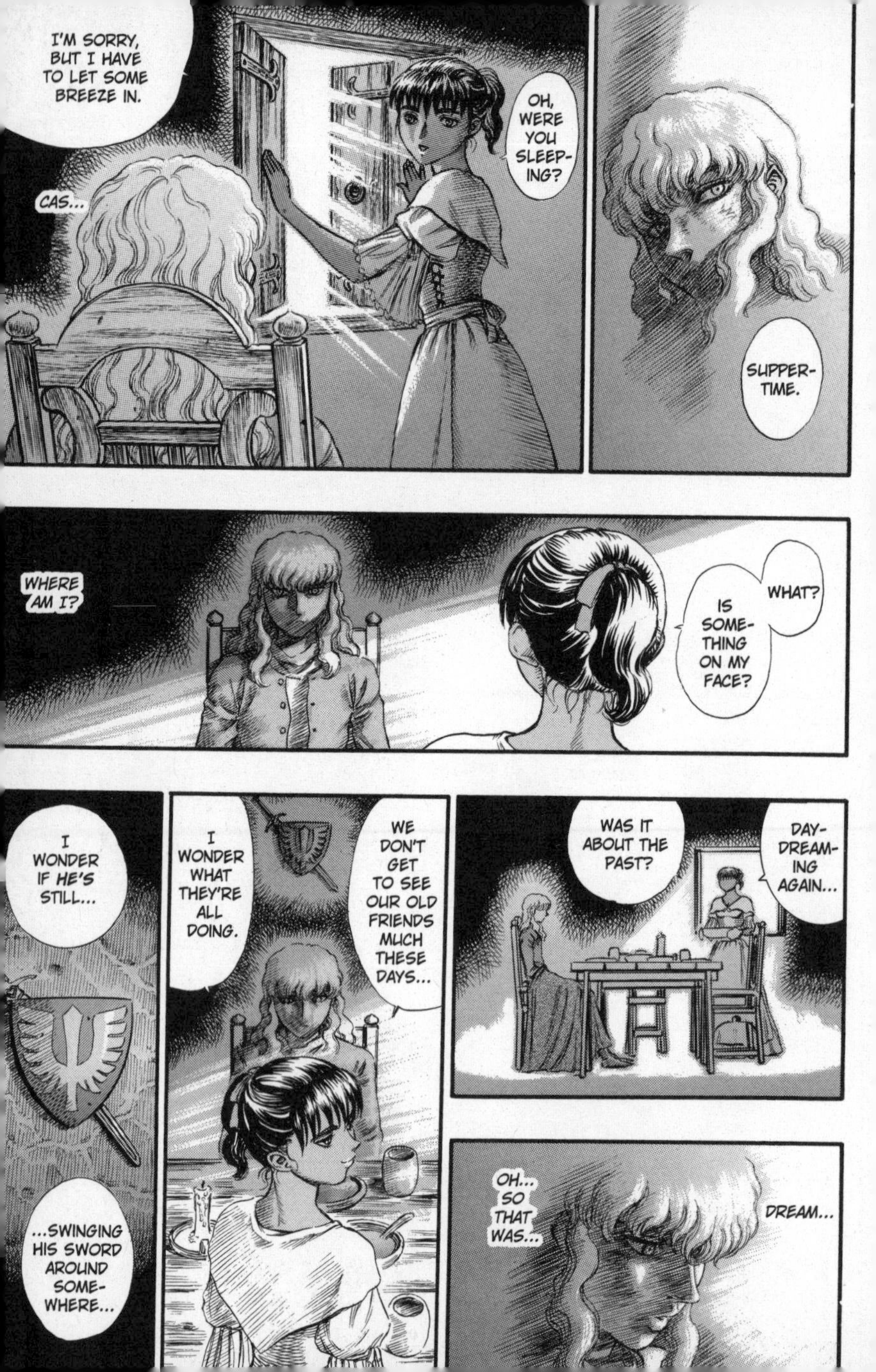
SUPPER-TIME.
OH, WERE YOU SLEEPING?
I'M SORRY, BUT I HAVE TO LET SOME BREEZE IN.
CAS...
WHAT?
IS SOMETHING ON MY FACE?
WHERE AM I?
DAY-DREAMING AGAIN...
WAS IT ABOUT THE PAST?
DREAM...
OH... SO THAT WAS...
WE DON'T GET TO SEE OUR OLD FRIENDS MUCH THESE DAYS...
I WONDER WHAT THEY'RE ALL DOING.
I WONDER IF HE'S STILL...
...SWINGING HIS SWORD AROUND SOMEWHERE...

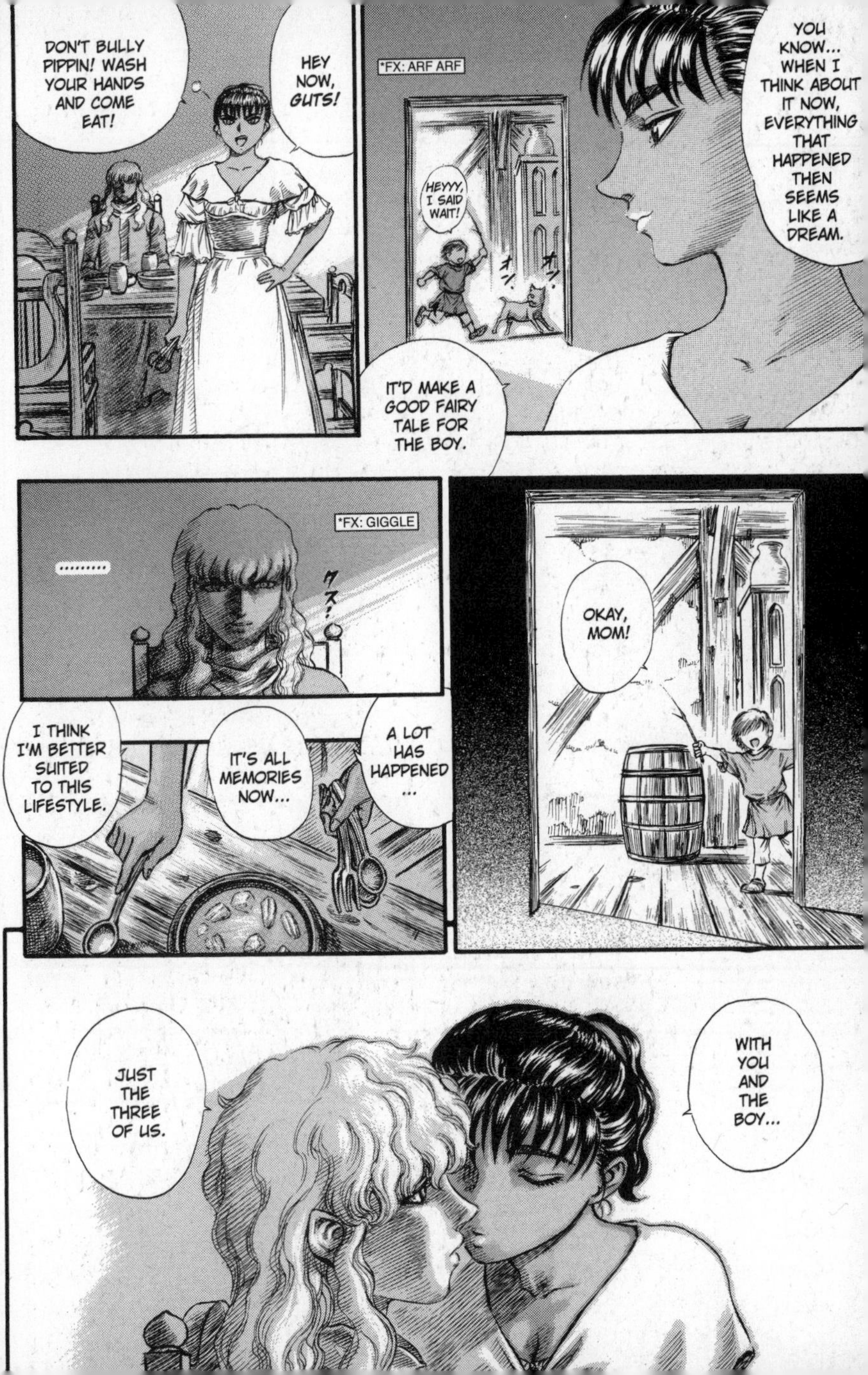
YOU KNOW... WHEN I THINK ABOUT IT NOW, EVERYTHING THAT HAPPENED THEN SEEMS LIKE A DREAM.
*FX: ARF ARF
HEYYY, I SAID WAIT!
IT'D MAKE A GOOD FAIRY TALE FOR THE BOY.
HEY NOW, GUTS!
DON'T BULLY PIPPIN! WASH YOUR HANDS AND COME EAT!
OKAY, MOM!
*FX: GIGGLE
....
A LOT HAS HAPPENED ...
IT'S ALL MEMORIES NOW...
I THINK I'M BETTER SUITED TO THIS LIFESTYLE.
WITH YOU AND THE BOY...
JUST THE THREE OF US.

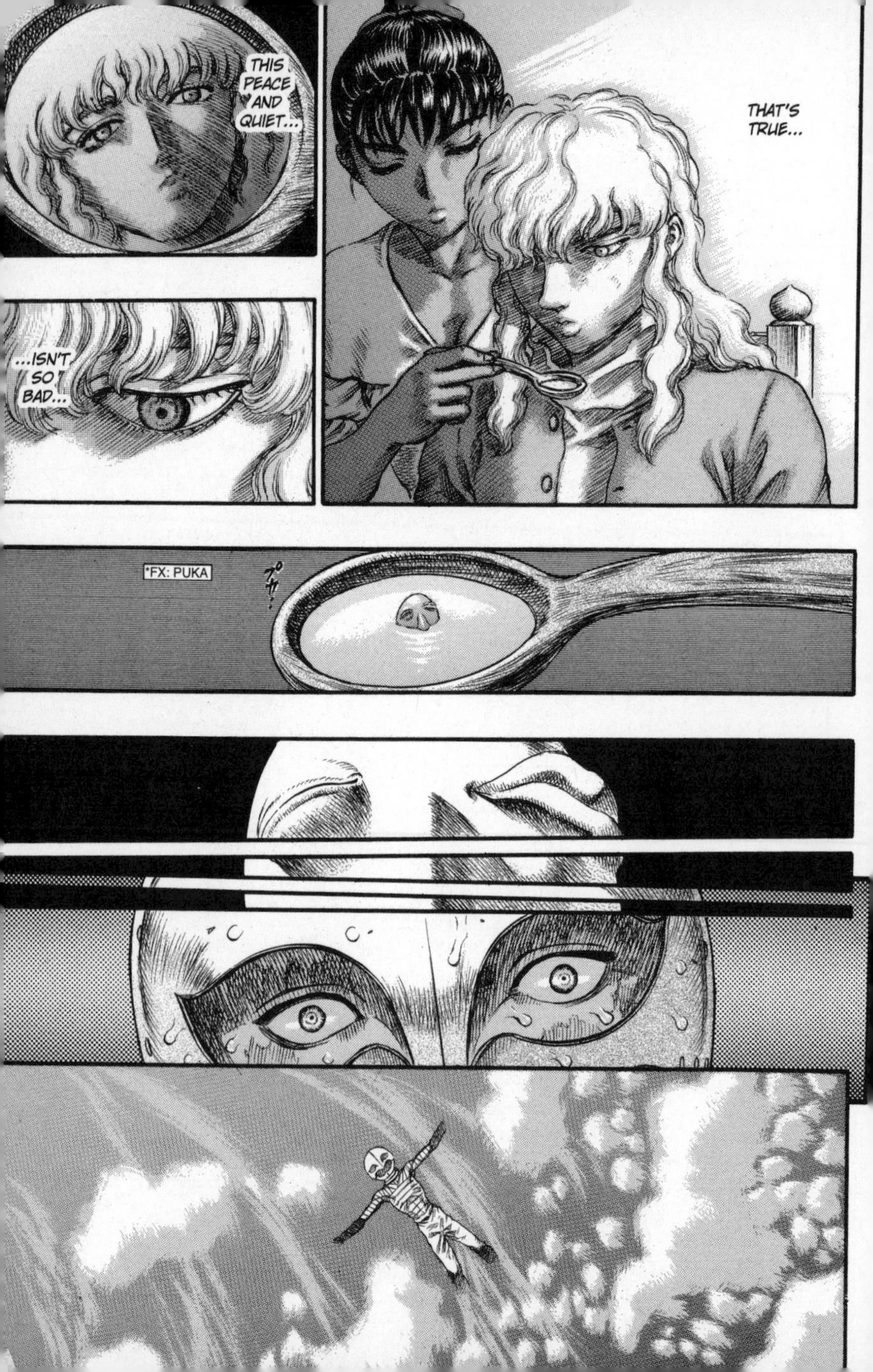
THAT'S TRUE...
THIS PEACE AND QUIET...
...ISN'T SO BAD...
*FX: PUKA

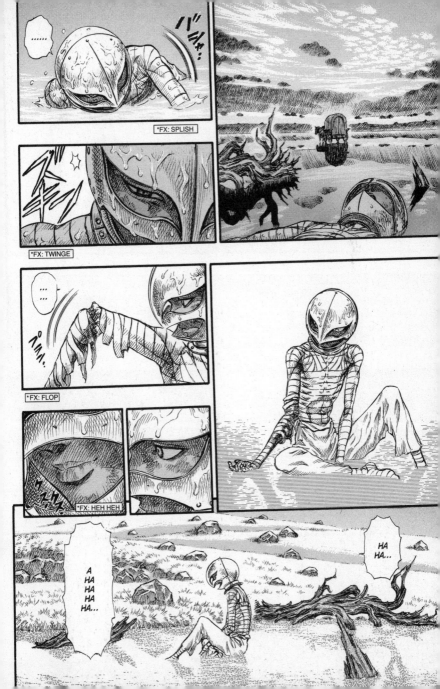

*FX: SPLISH

*FX: TWINGE

*FX: FLOP

*FX: HEH HEH

A
HA
HA
HA
HA...

HA
HA...

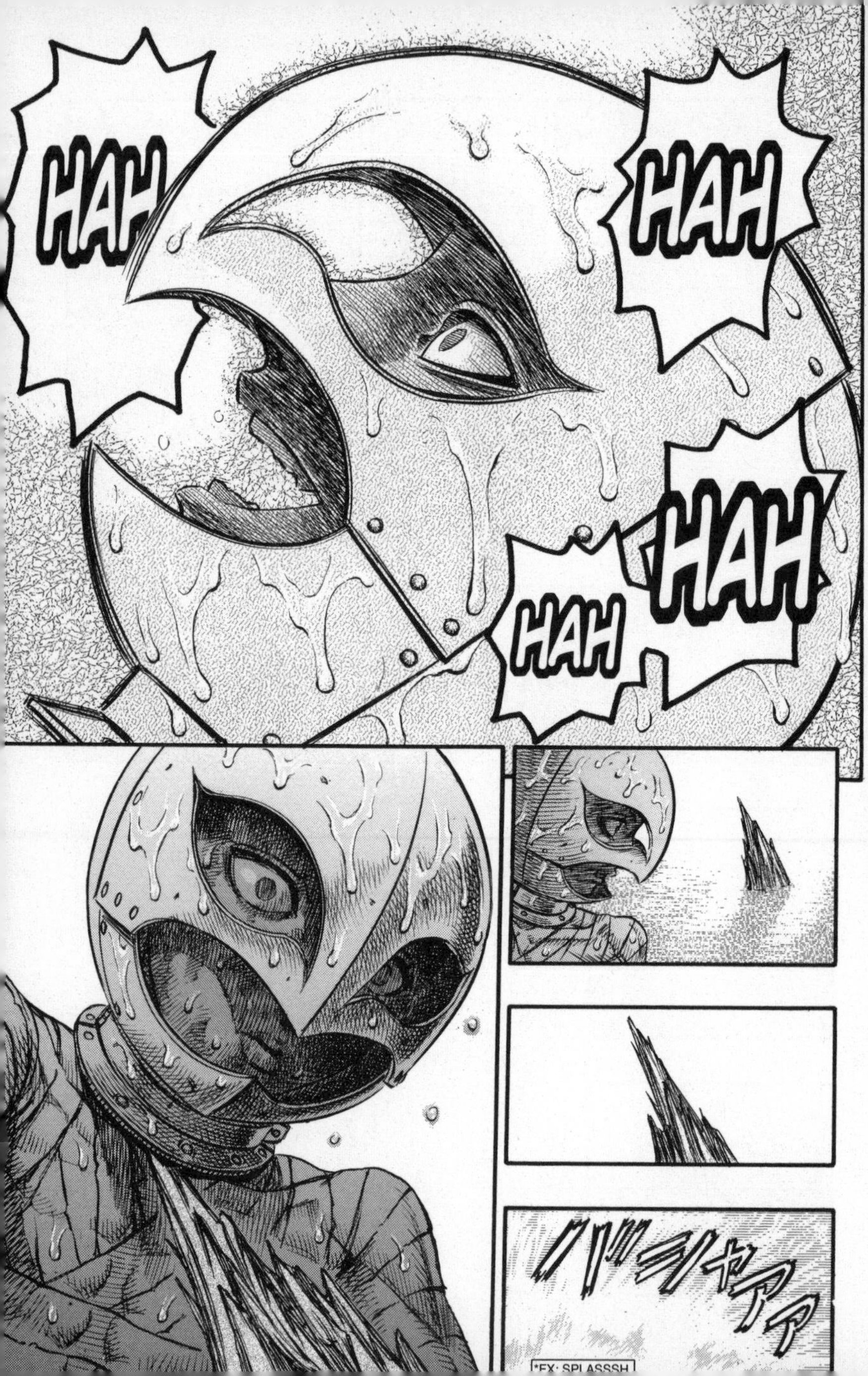
HAH
HAH
HAH
HAH
バシャアア
*FX: SPLASSSH

ズグ…
*FX: ZHNK

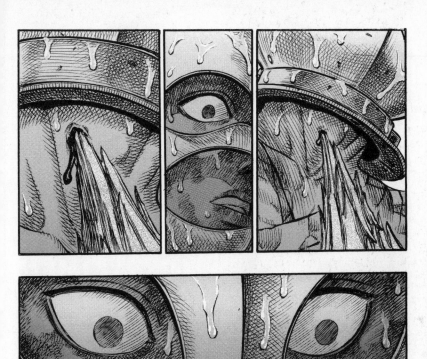

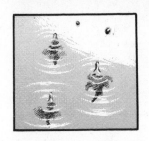

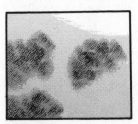

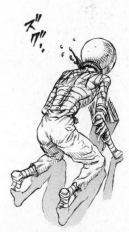

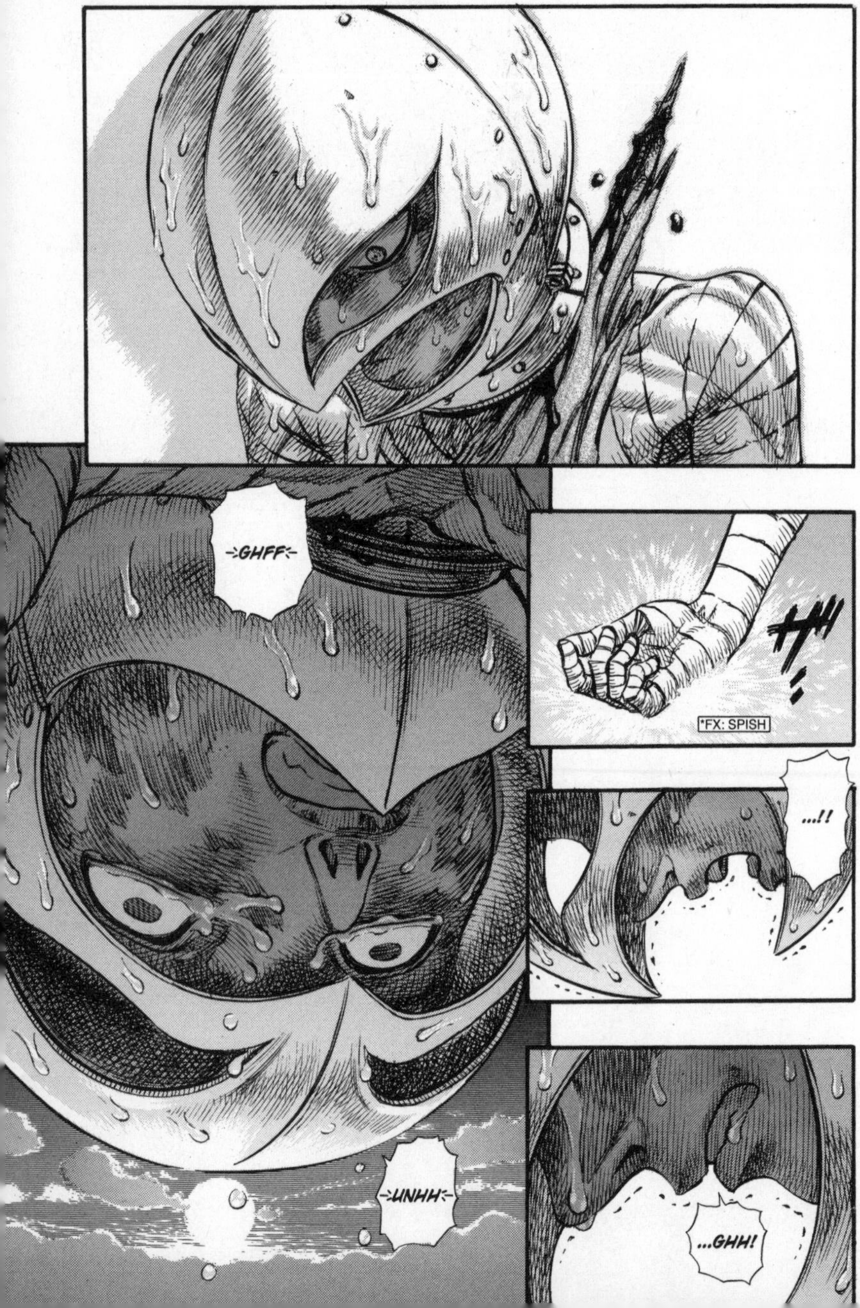
*FX: SPISH
...!!
...GHH!
GHFF
UNHH

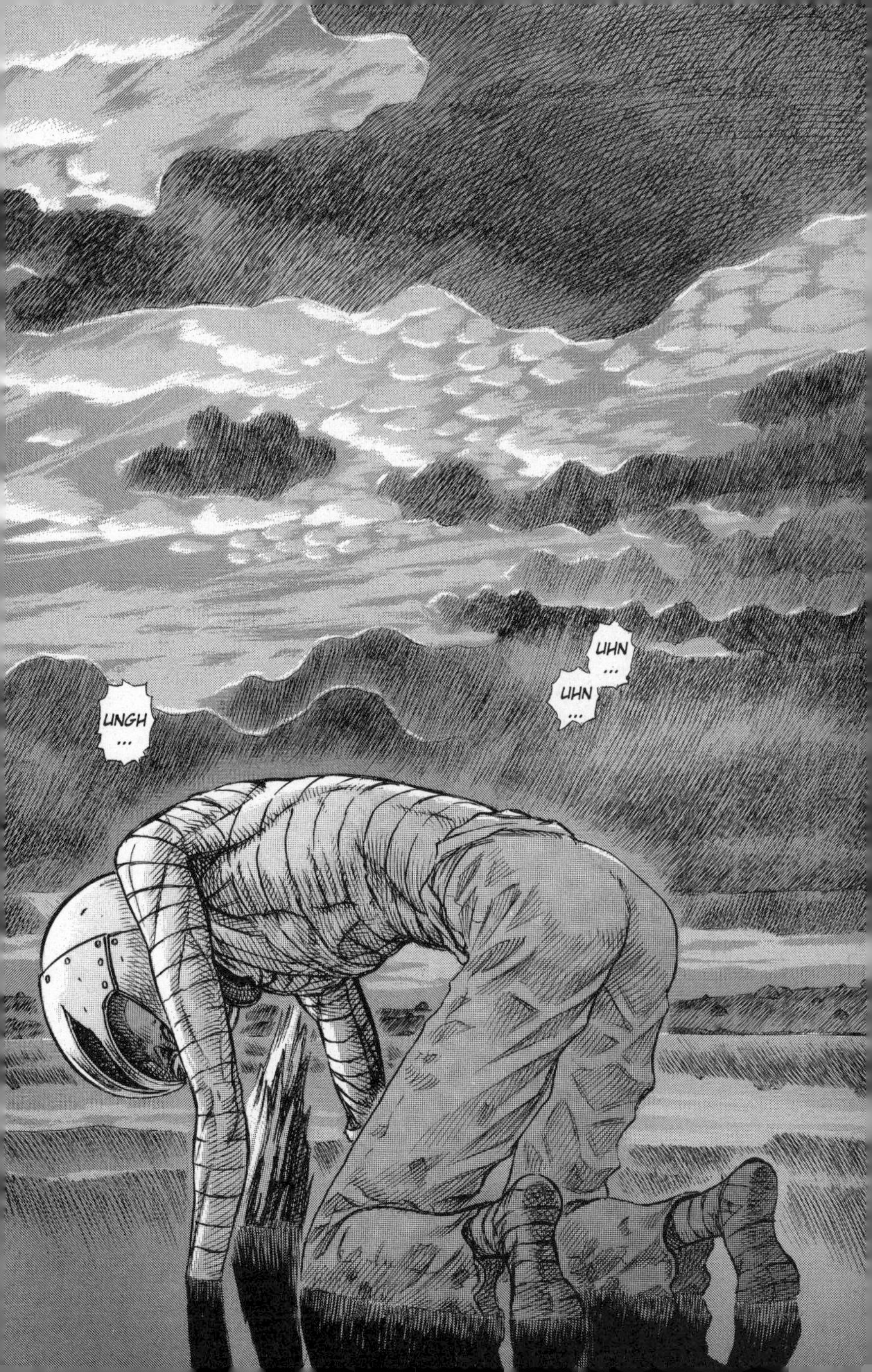
UHN ...
UHN ...
UNGH ...

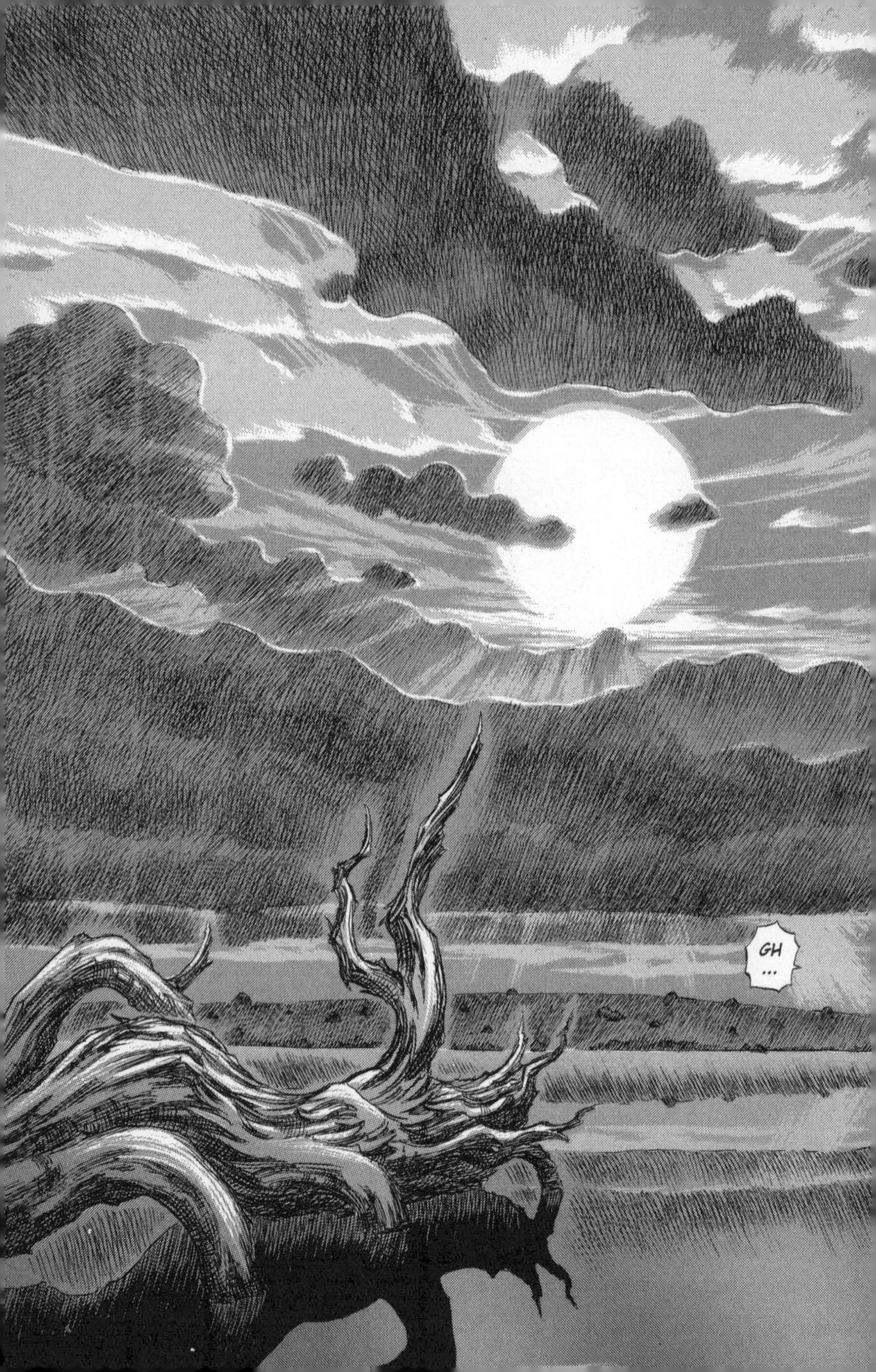
GH ...

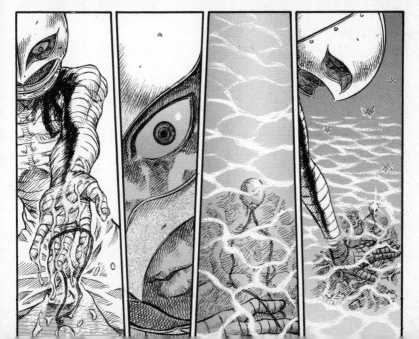

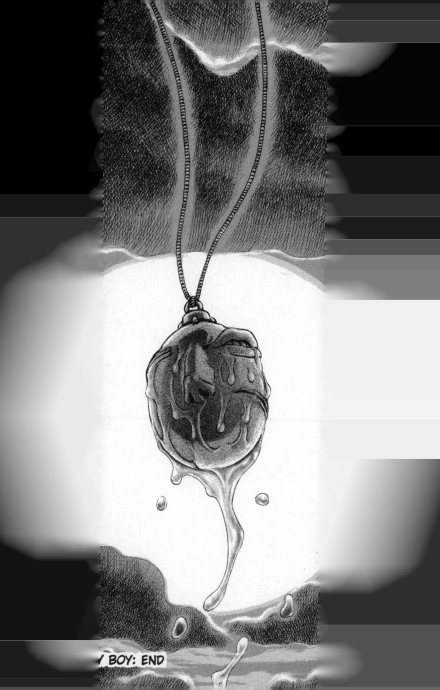

BOY: END

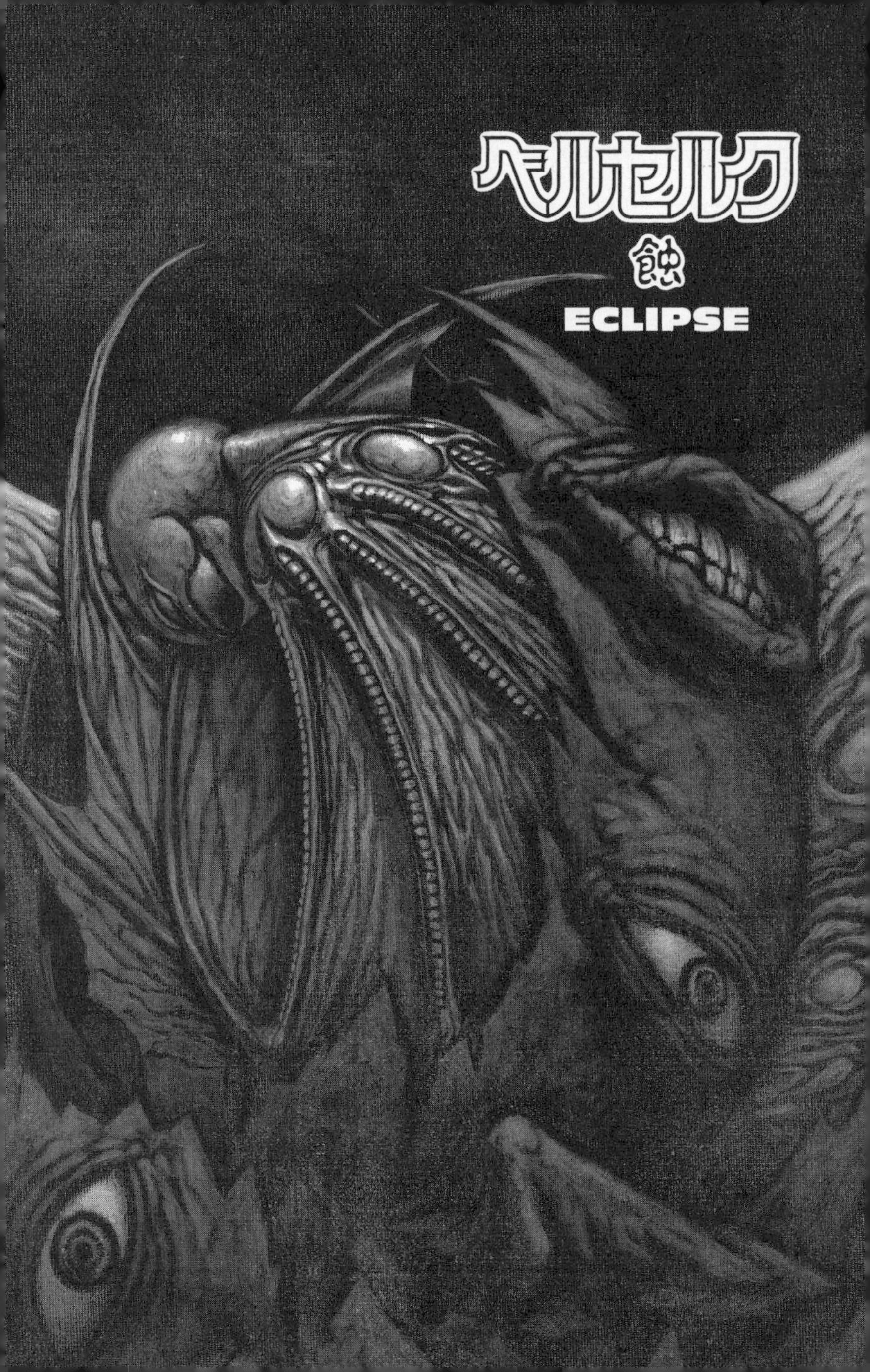
ベルセルク
蝕
ECLIPSE

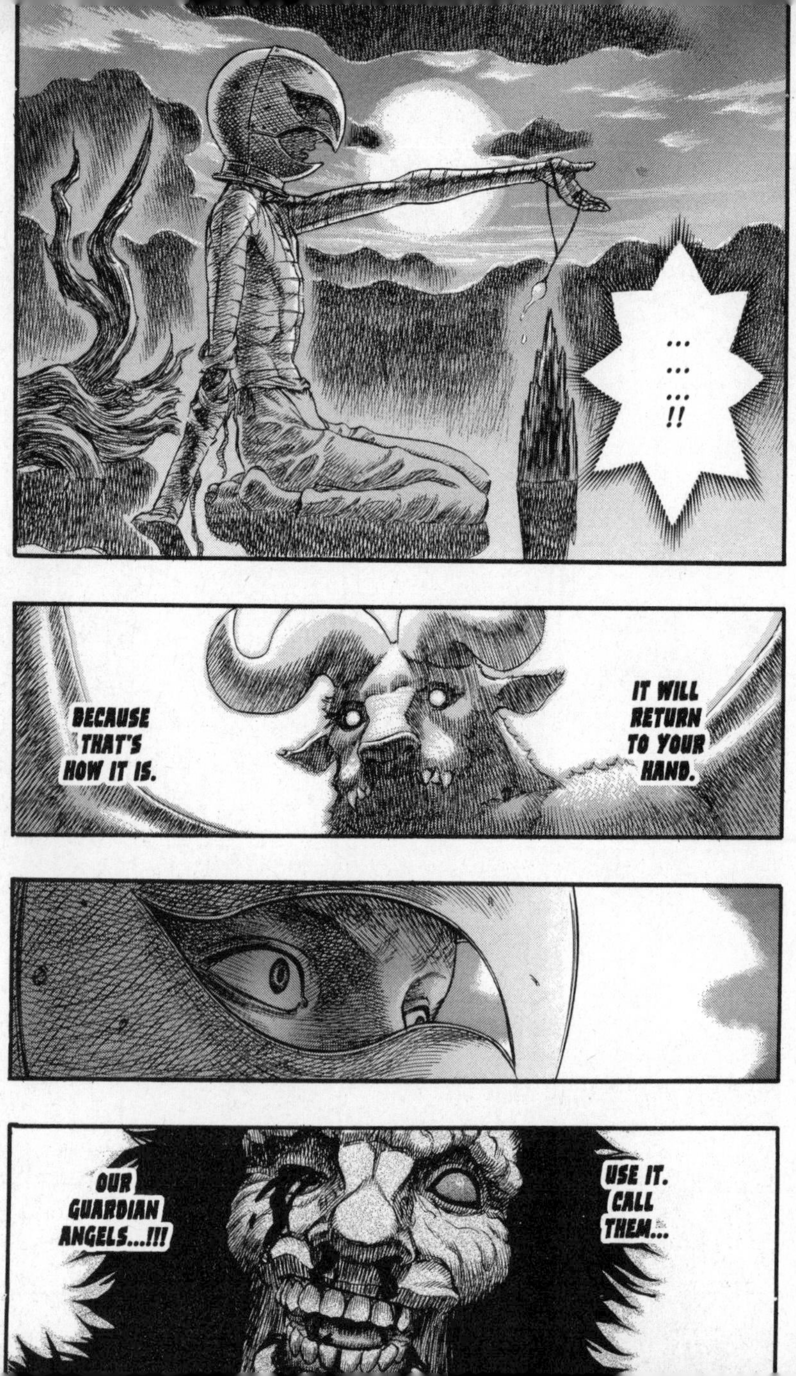

… … … !!
IT WILL RETURN TO YOUR HAND.
BECAUSE THAT'S HOW IT IS.
USE IT. CALL THEM…
OUR GUARDIAN ANGELS…!!!

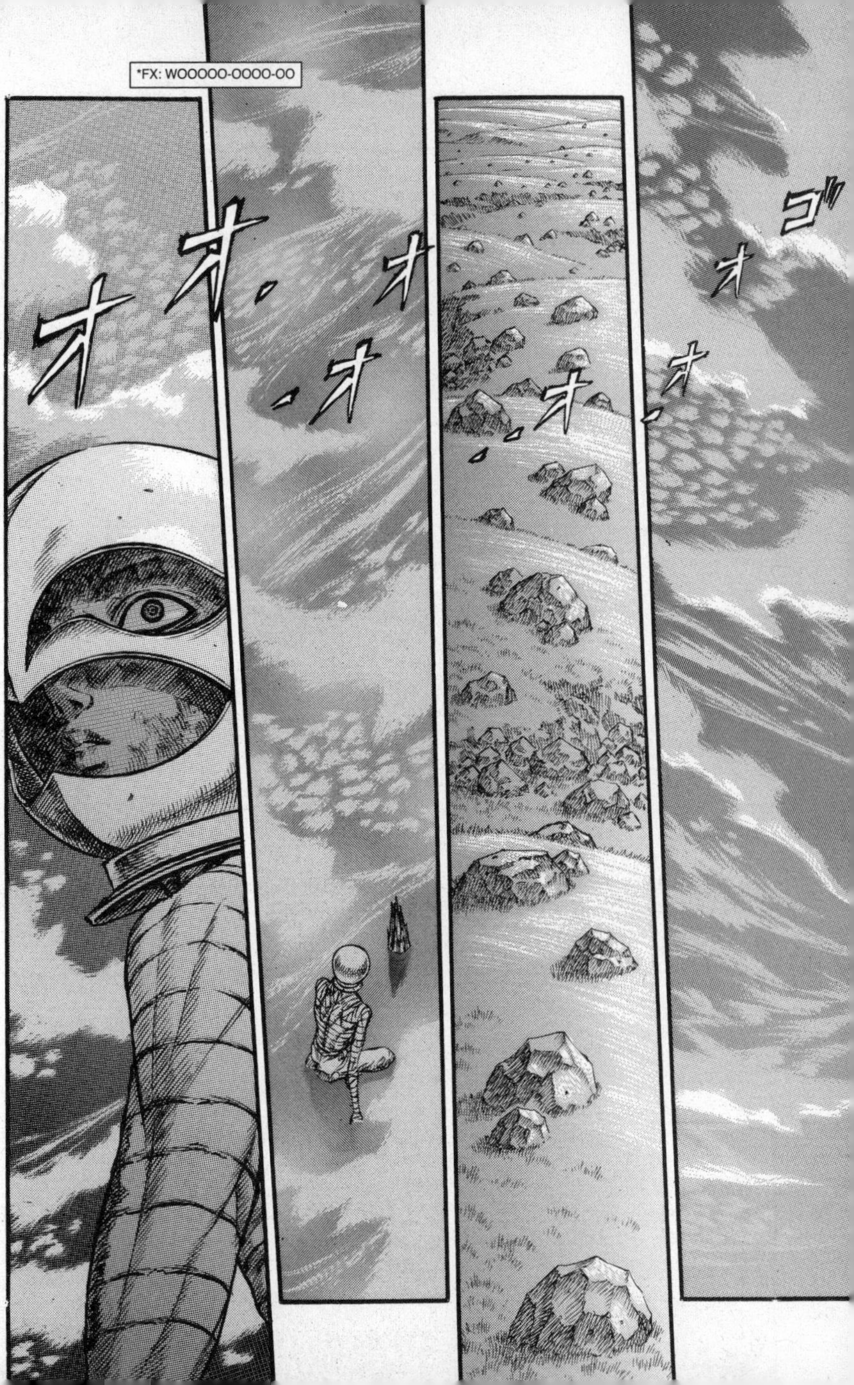
ゴオオオオオオオオ
*FX: WOOOOO-OOOO-OO

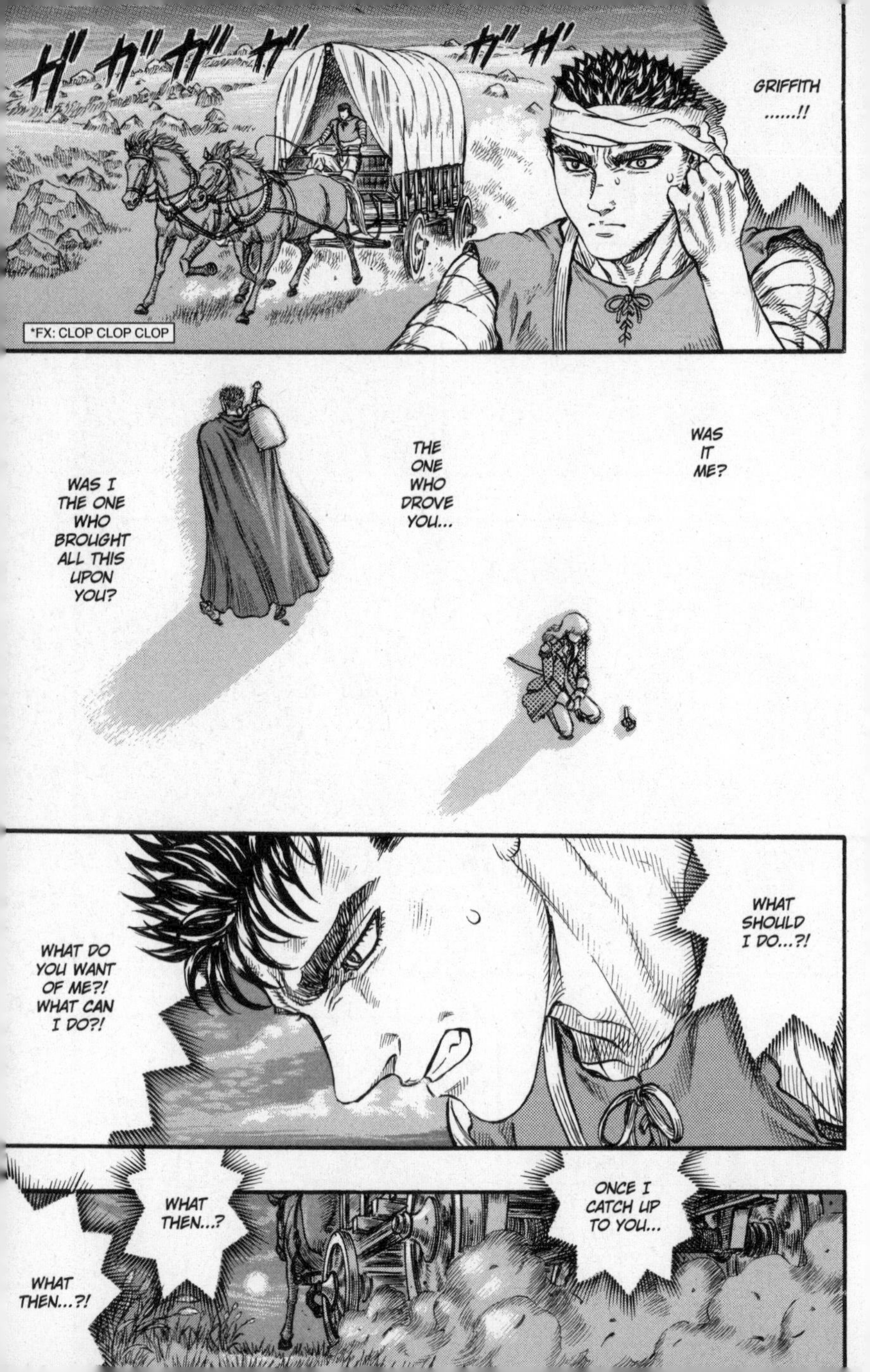
GRIFFITH ......!!
*FX: CLOP CLOP CLOP
WAS IT ME?
THE ONE WHO DROVE YOU...
WAS I THE ONE WHO BROUGHT ALL THIS UPON YOU?
WHAT SHOULD I DO...?!
WHAT DO YOU WANT OF ME?! WHAT CAN I DO?!
ONCE I CATCH UP TO YOU...
WHAT THEN...?
WHAT THEN...?!

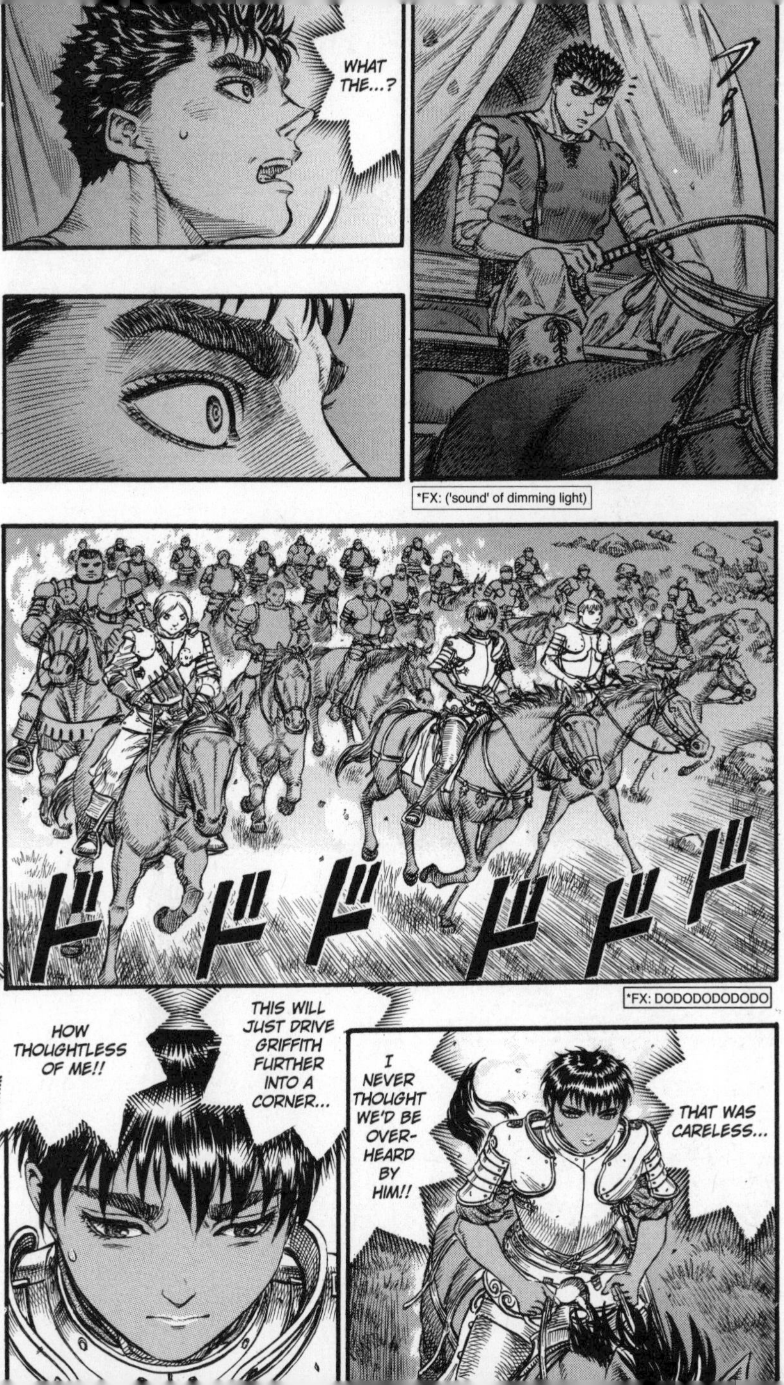
*FX: ('sound' of dimming light)
WHAT THE...?
ドドドドドド
*FX: DODODODODODO
THAT WAS CARELESS...
I NEVER THOUGHT WE'D BE OVER-HEARD BY HIM!!
THIS WILL JUST DRIVE GRIFFITH FURTHER INTO A CORNER...
HOW THOUGHTLESS OF ME!!

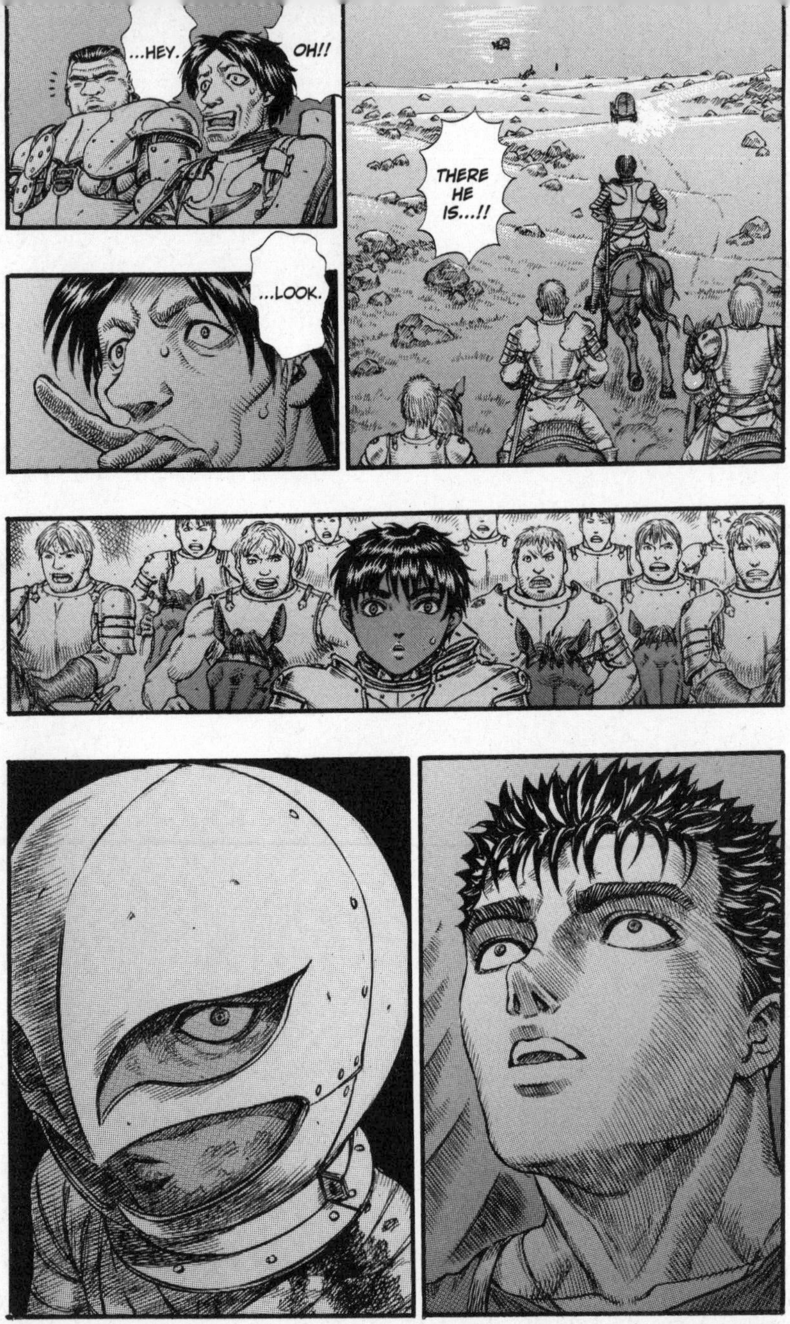
THERE HE IS...!!
OH!!
...HEY.
...LOOK.

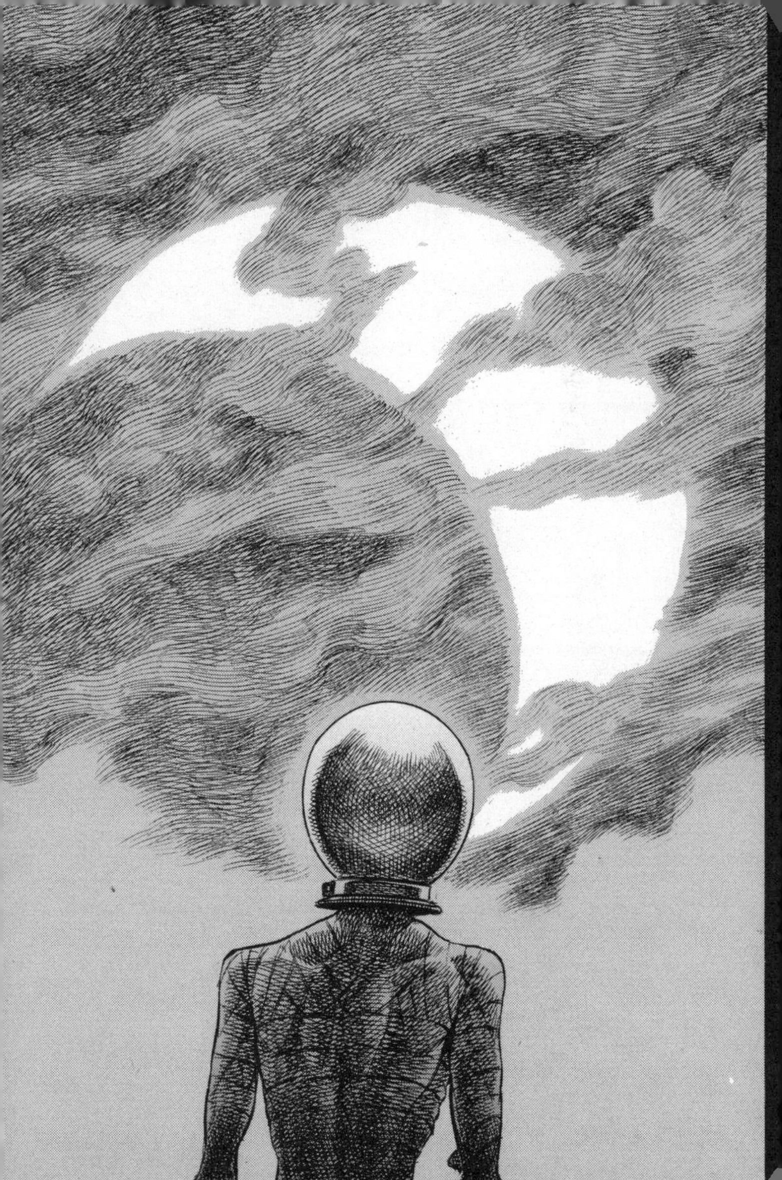

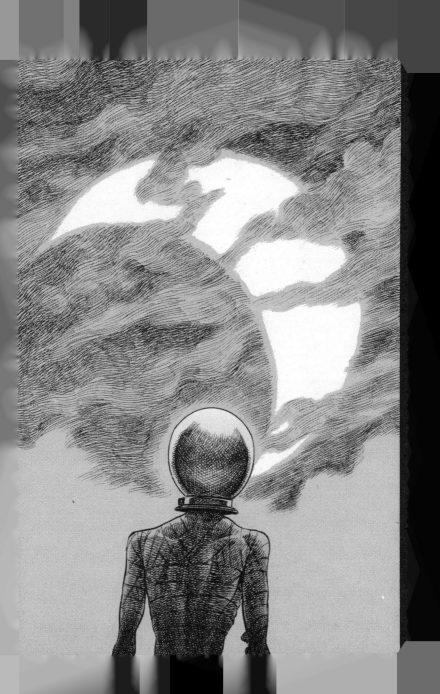

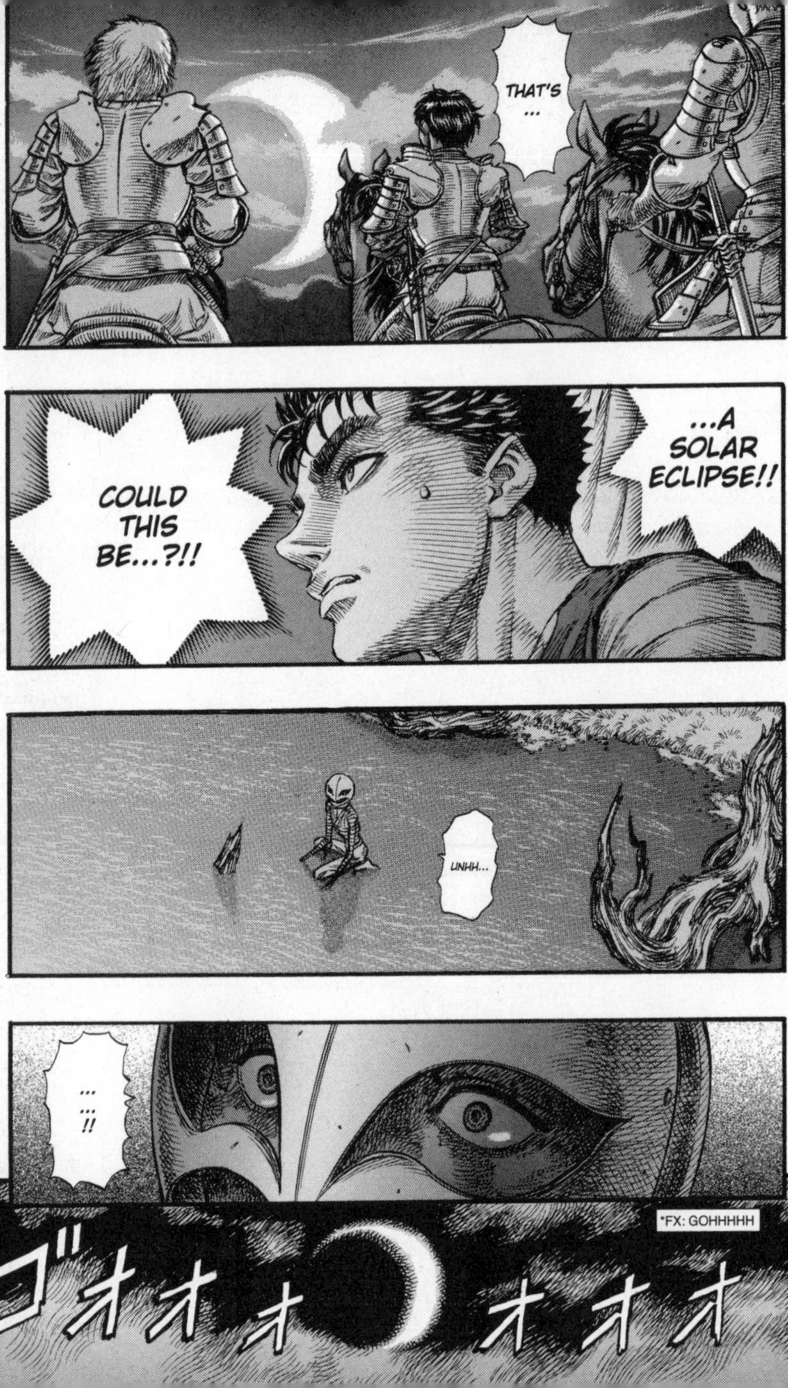
THAT'S ...
...A SOLAR ECLIPSE!!
COULD THIS BE...?!!
UNHH...
... ... !!
*FX: GOHHHHH
ゴオオオ オオオ

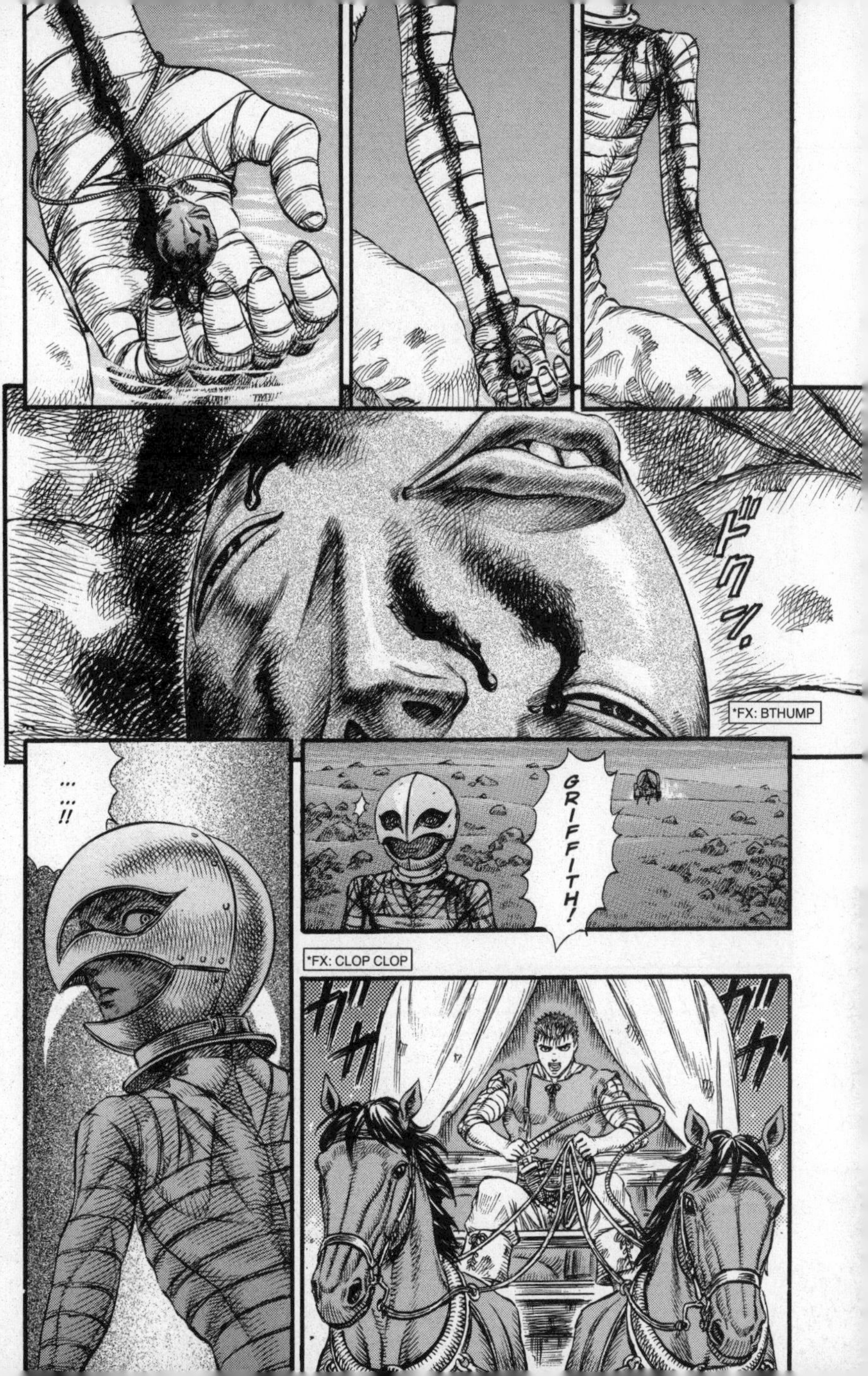
ドクッ
*FX: BTHUMP
GRIFFITH!
*FX: CLOP CLOP
......!!

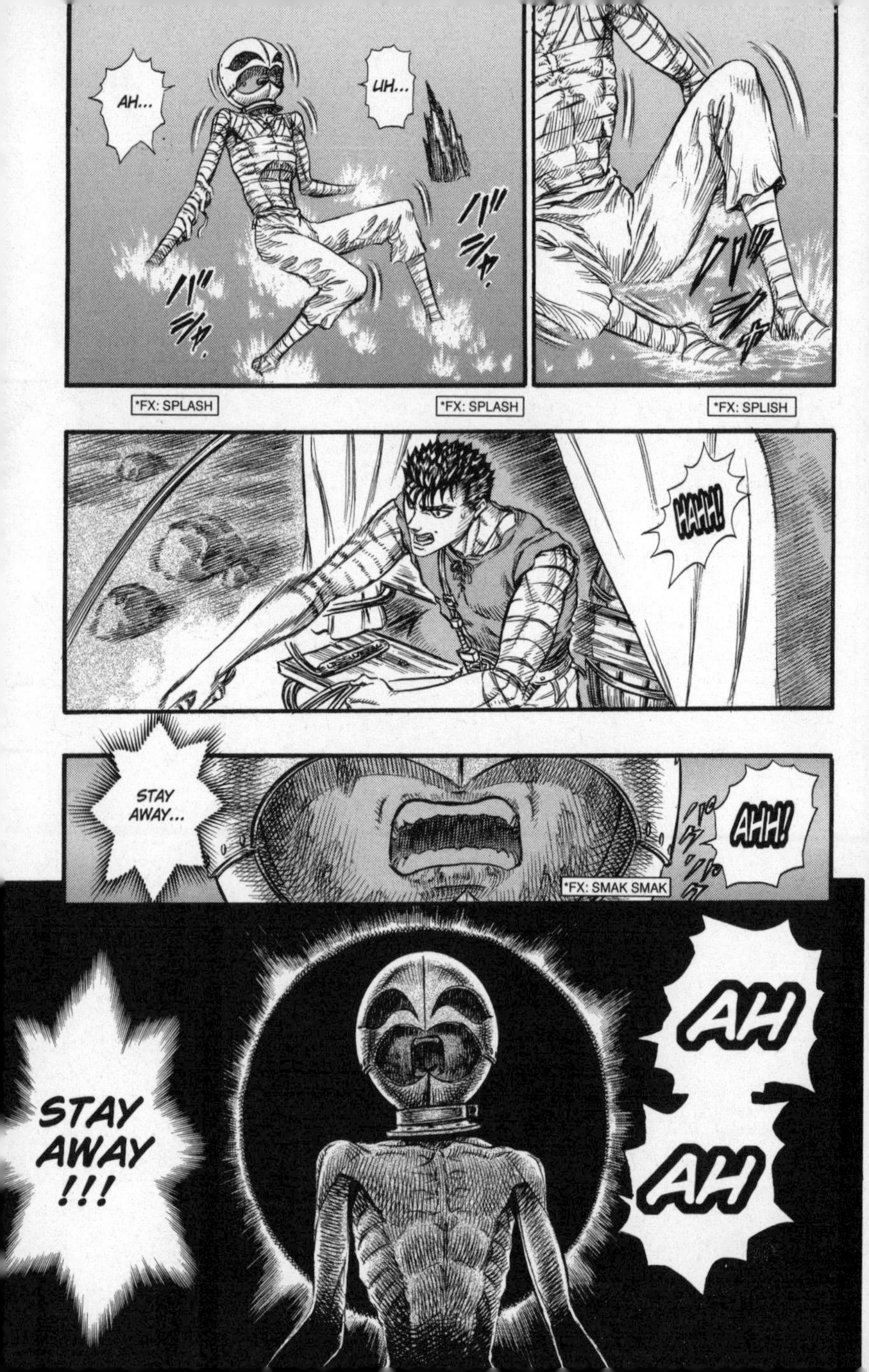
*FX: SPLISH
UH...
*FX: SPLASH
AH...
*FX: SPLASH
HAHH!
AHH!
*FX: SMAK SMAK
STAY AWAY...
AH
AH
STAY AWAY !!!

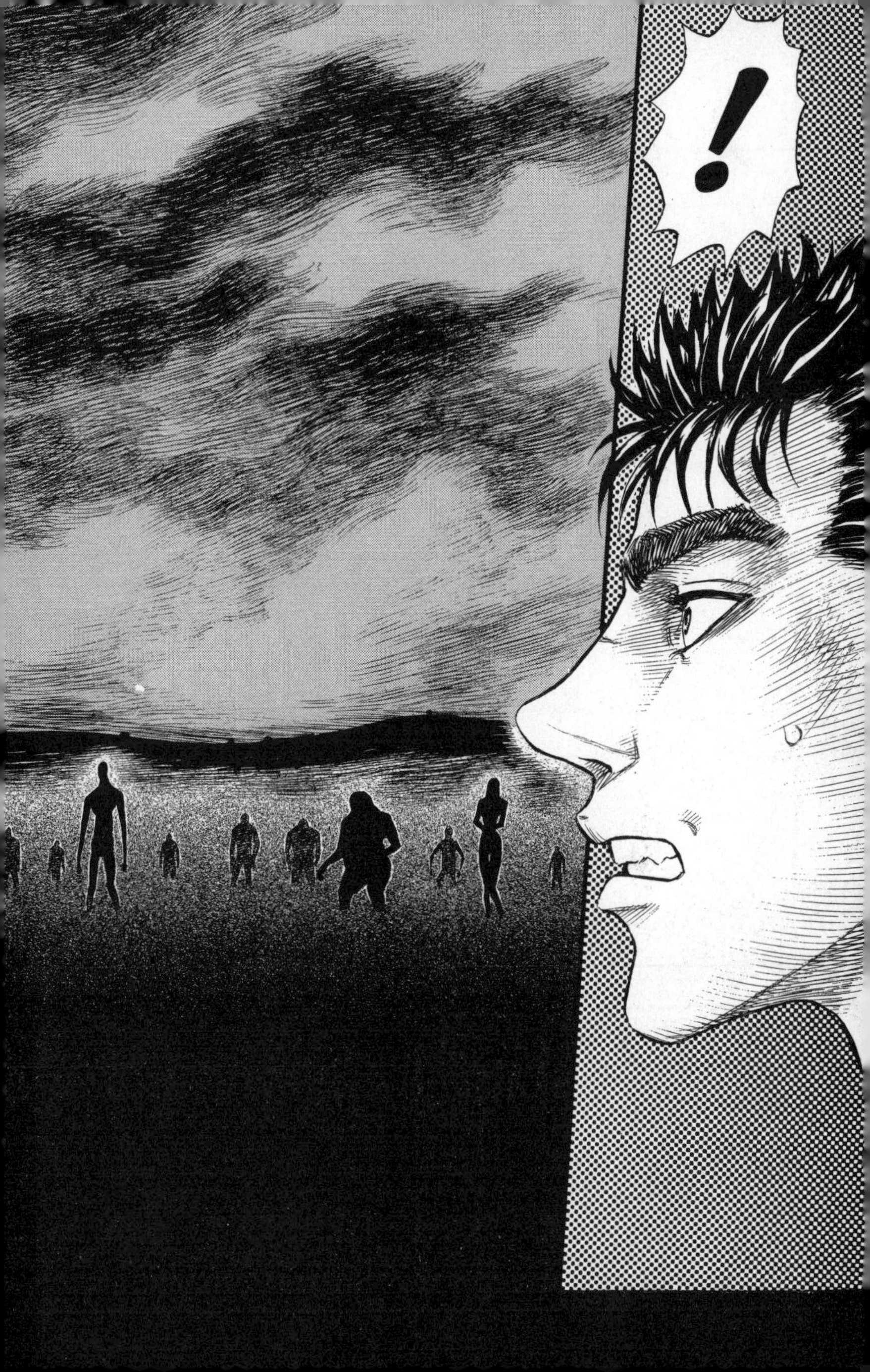
!

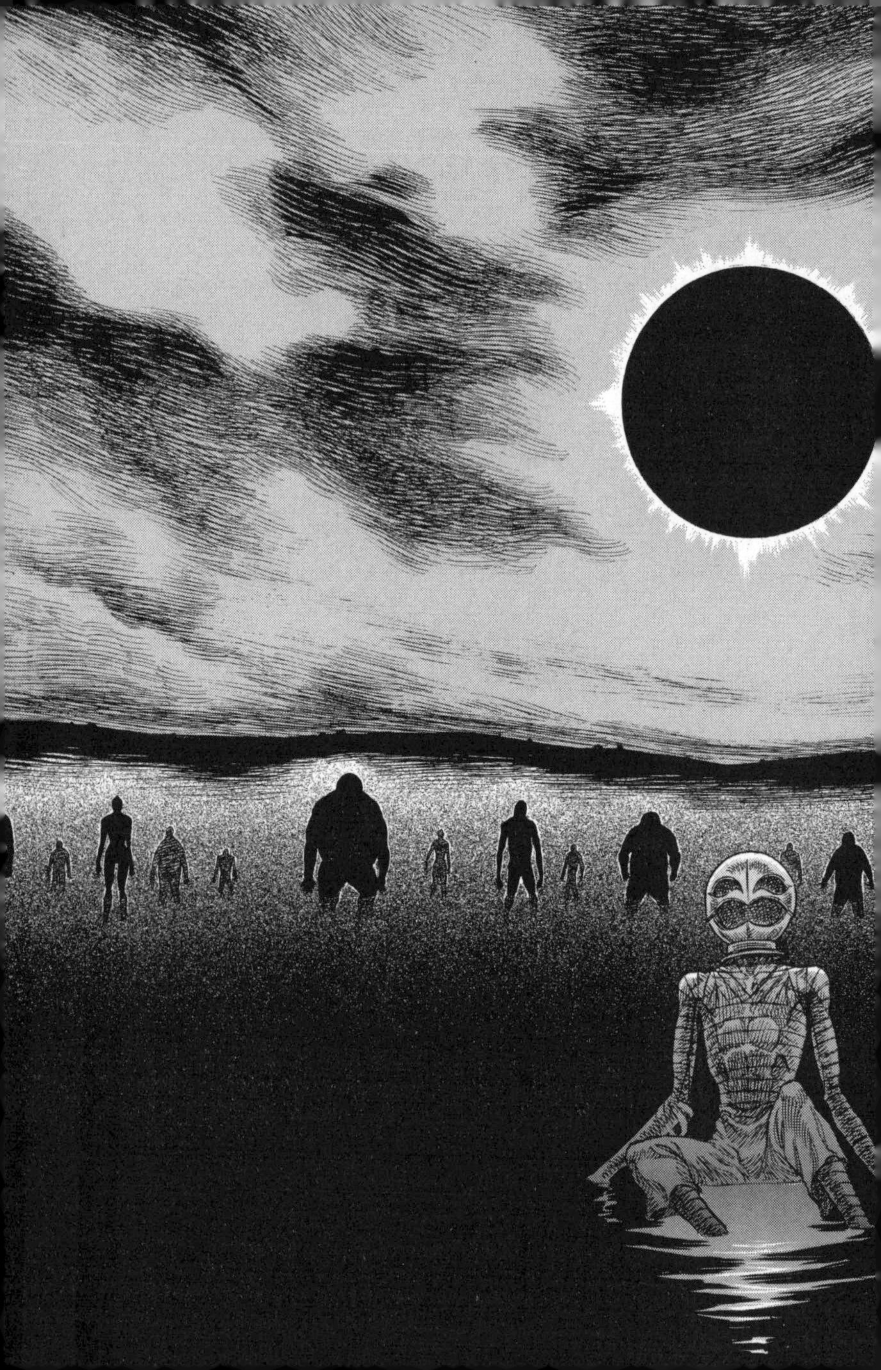

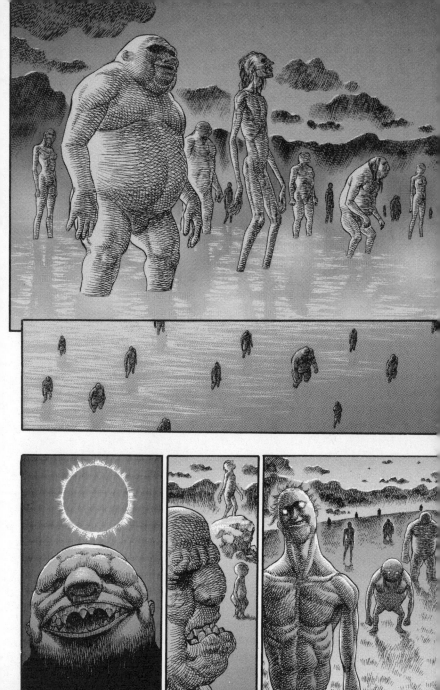

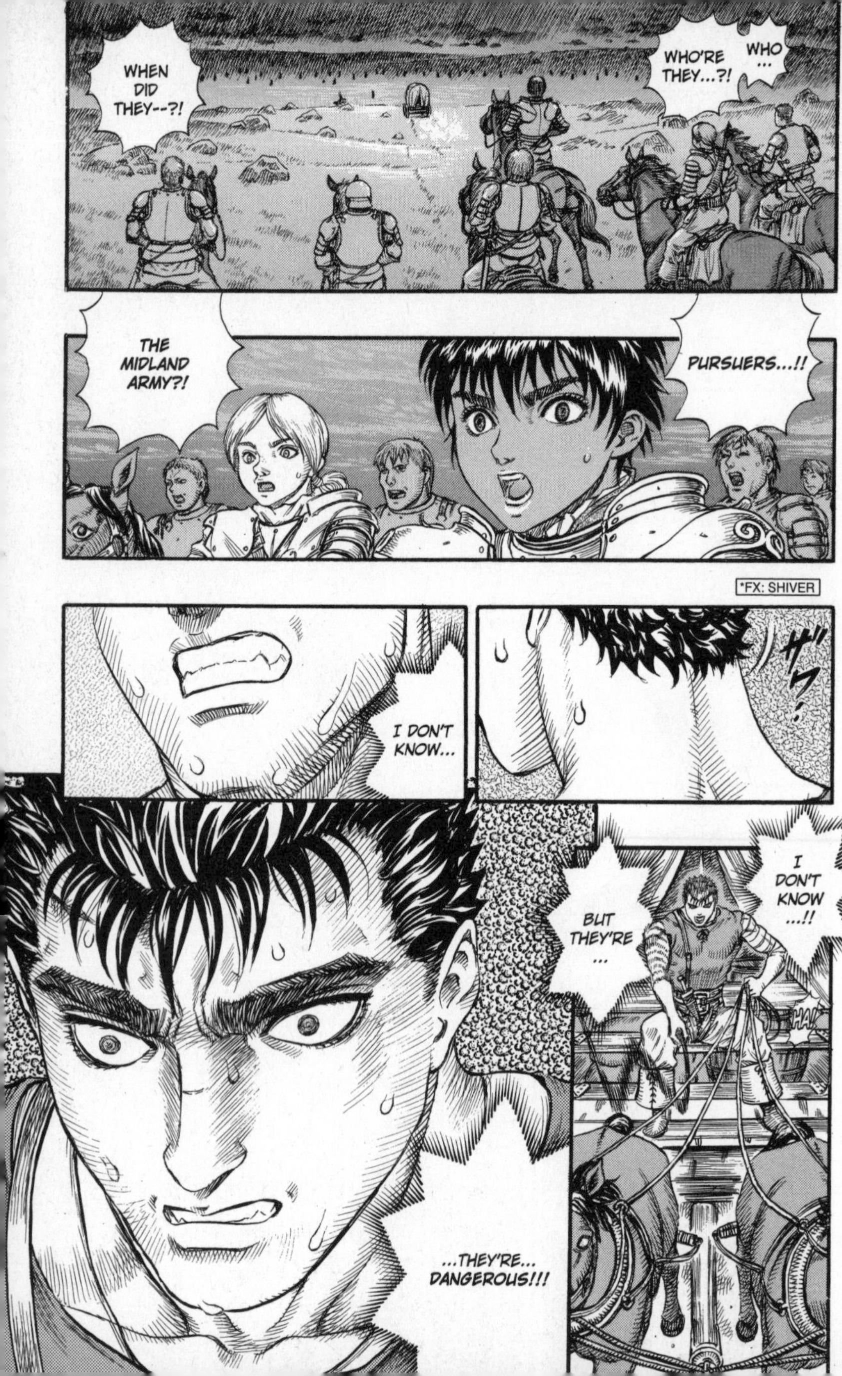
WHO ...
WHO'RE THEY...?!
WHEN DID THEY--?!
PURSUERS...!!
THE MIDLAND ARMY?!
*FX: SHIVER
I DON'T KNOW...
I DON'T KNOW ...!!
BUT THEY'RE ...
HA!
...THEY'RE... DANGEROUS!!!

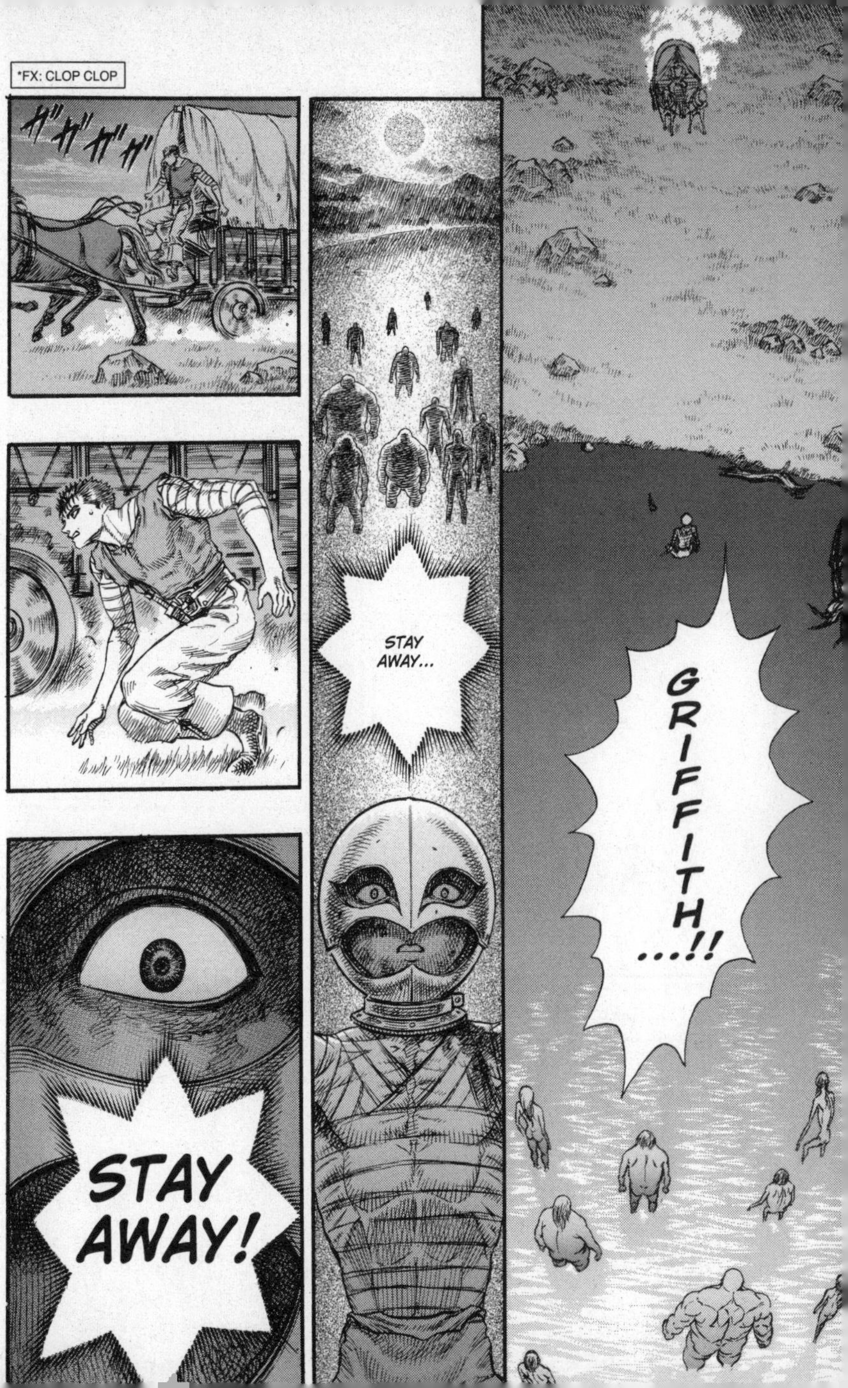
GRIFFITH...!!
STAY AWAY...
*FX: CLOP CLOP
STAY AWAY!

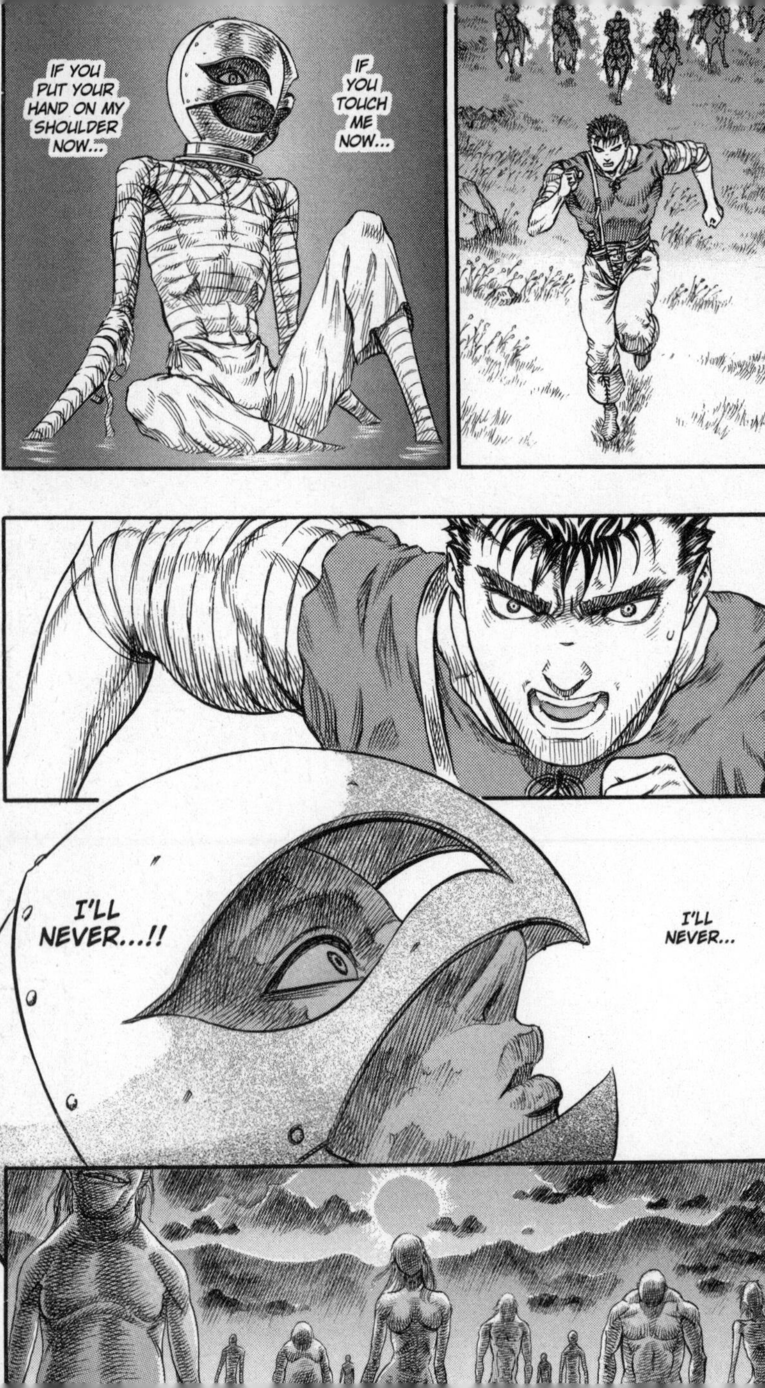
IF YOU TOUCH ME NOW...
IF YOU PUT YOUR HAND ON MY SHOULDER NOW...
I'LL NEVER...
I'LL NEVER...!!

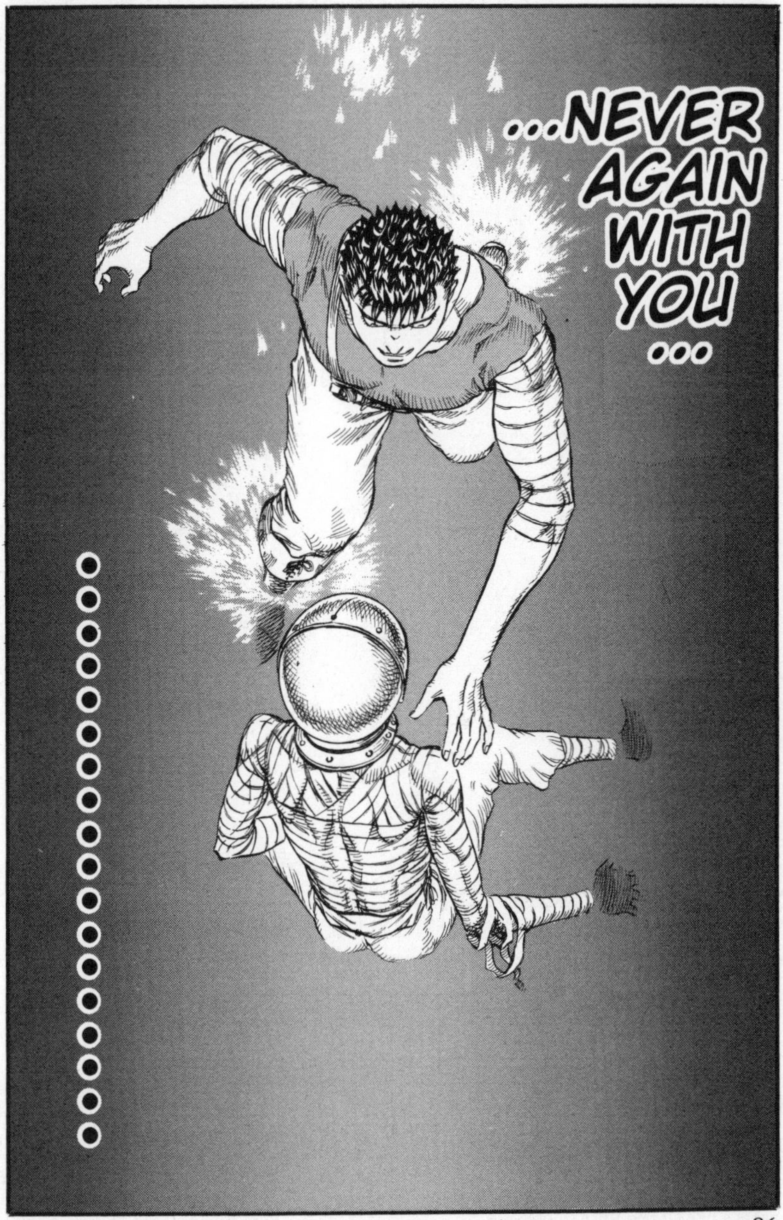
...NEVER AGAIN WITH YOU ...

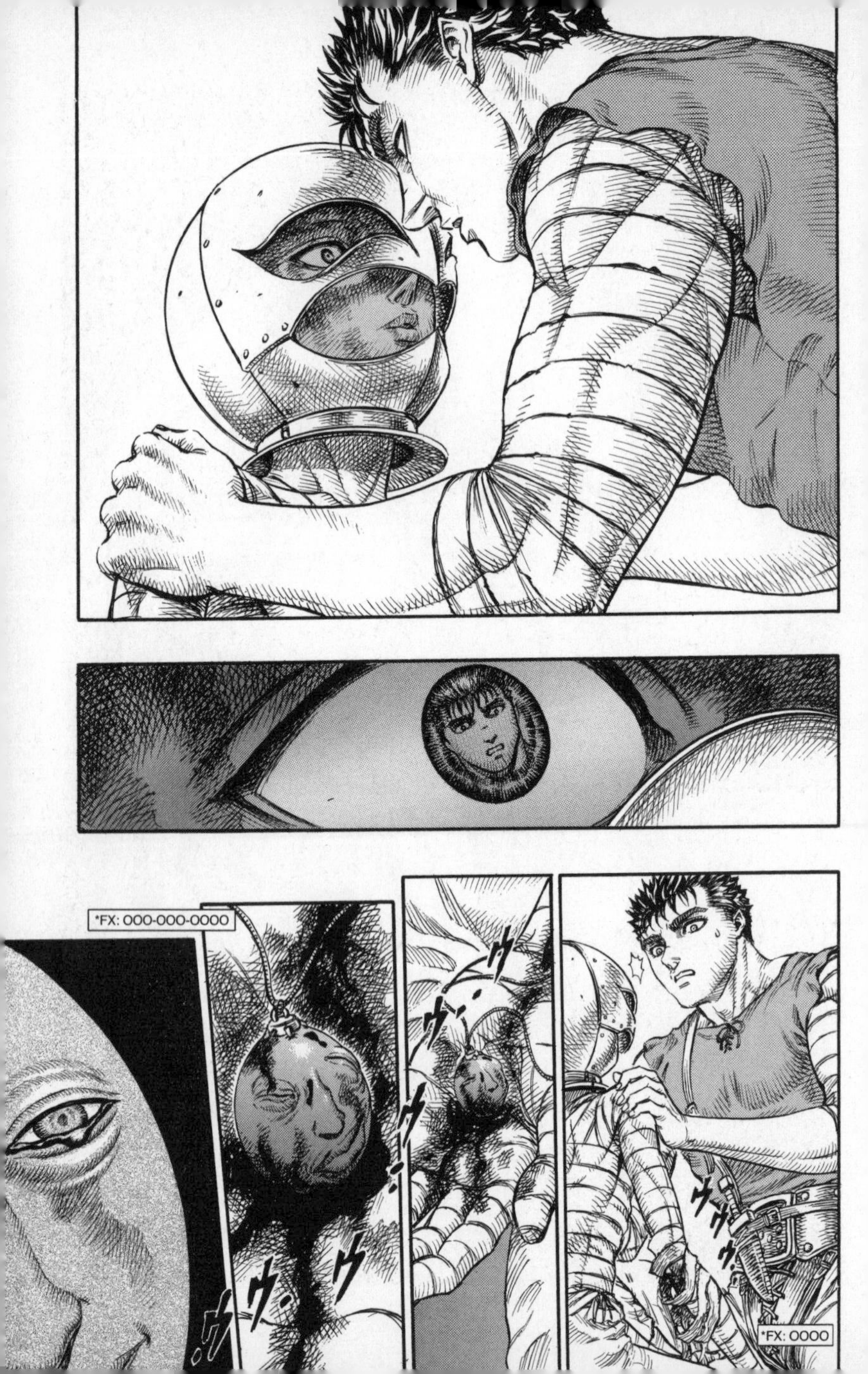
*FX: OOOO
*FX: OOO-OOO-OOOO

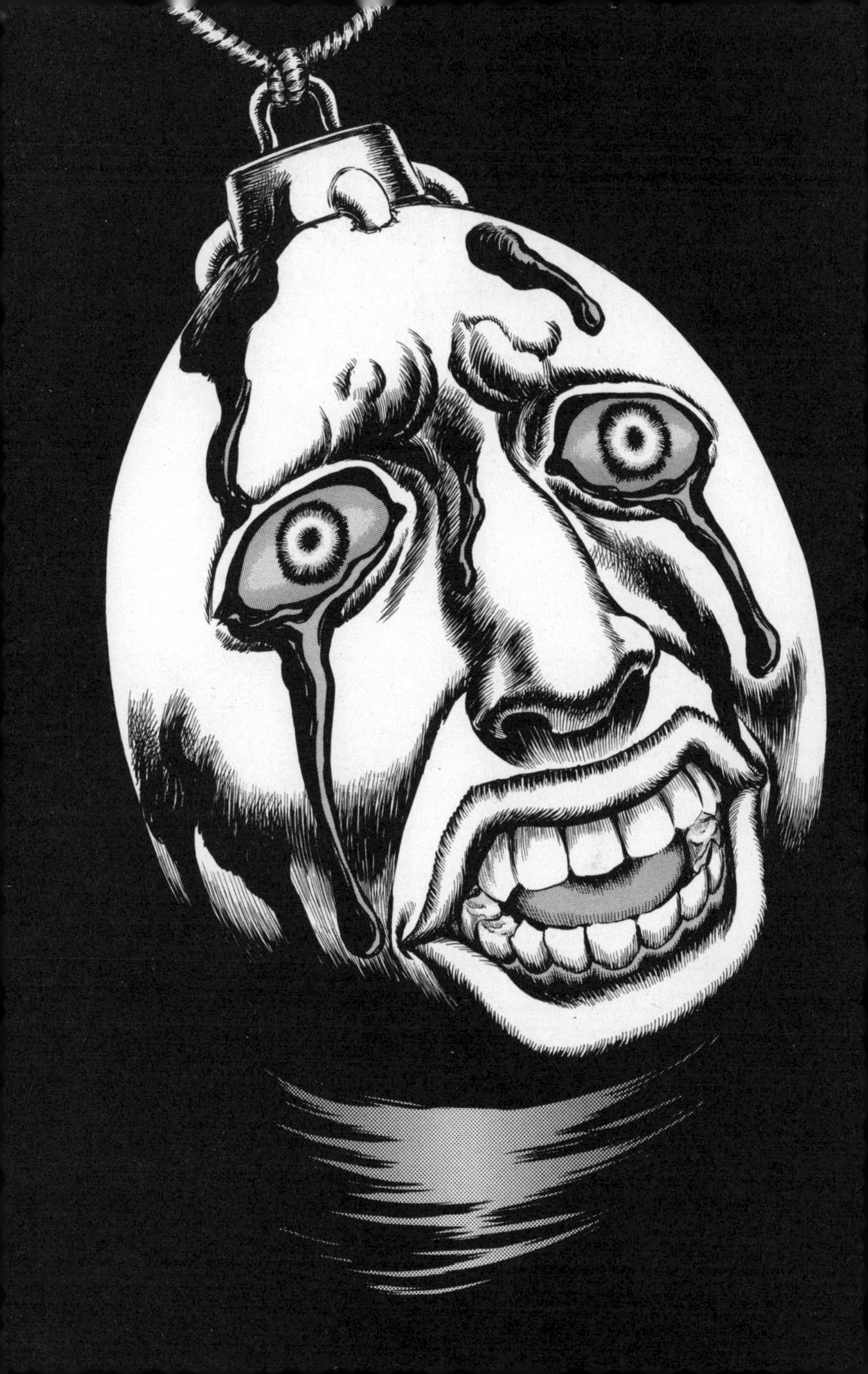

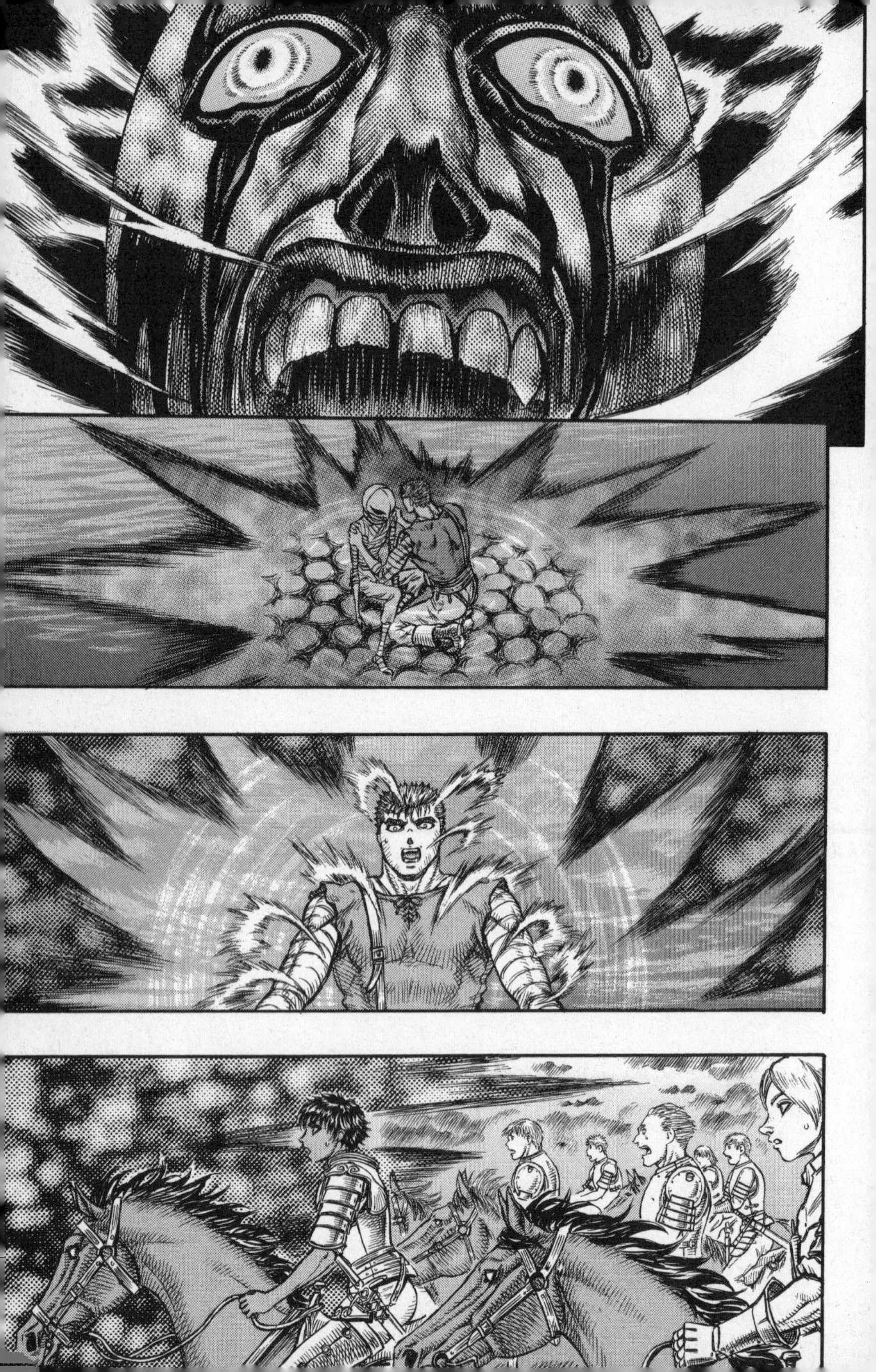

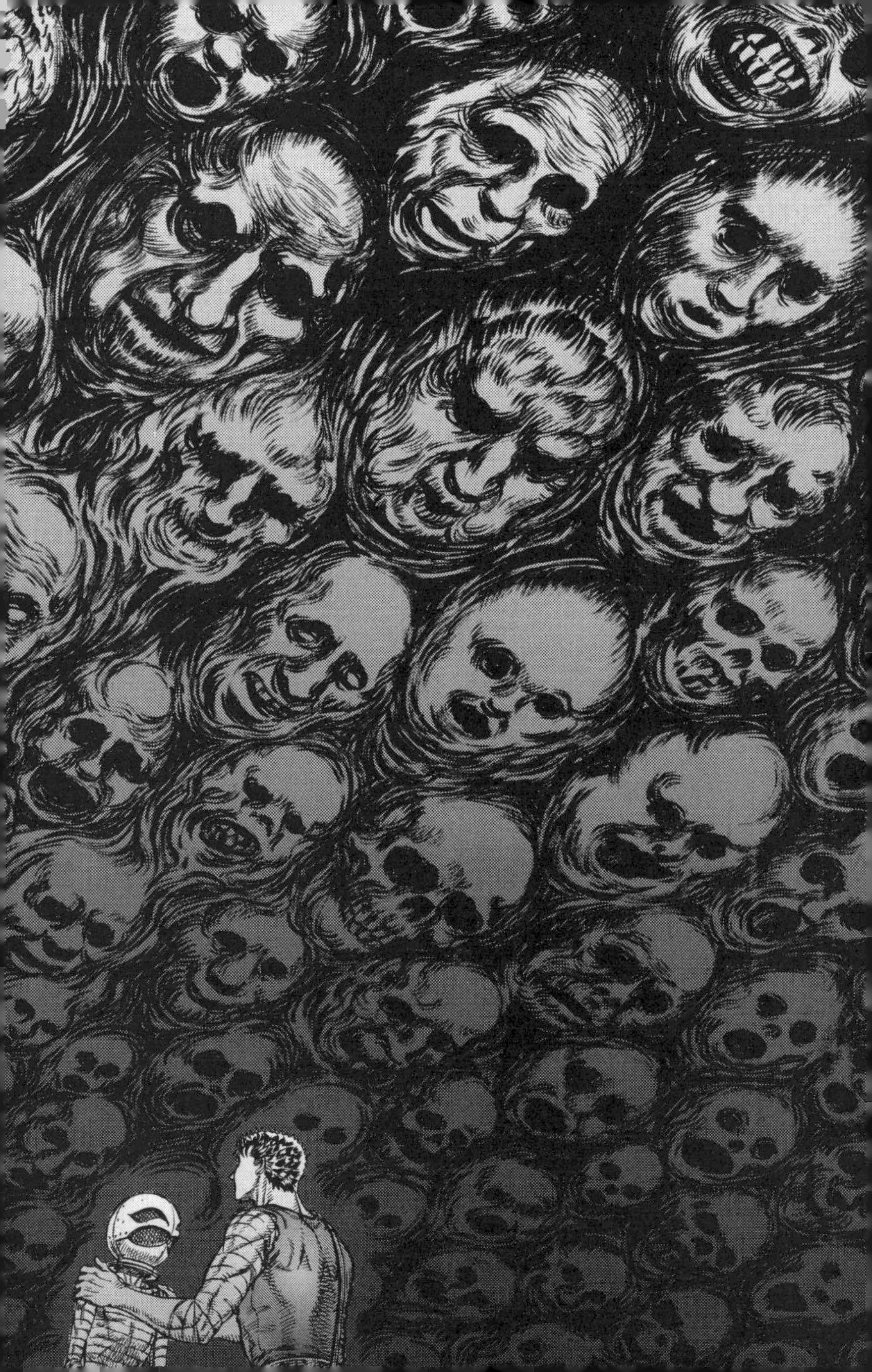

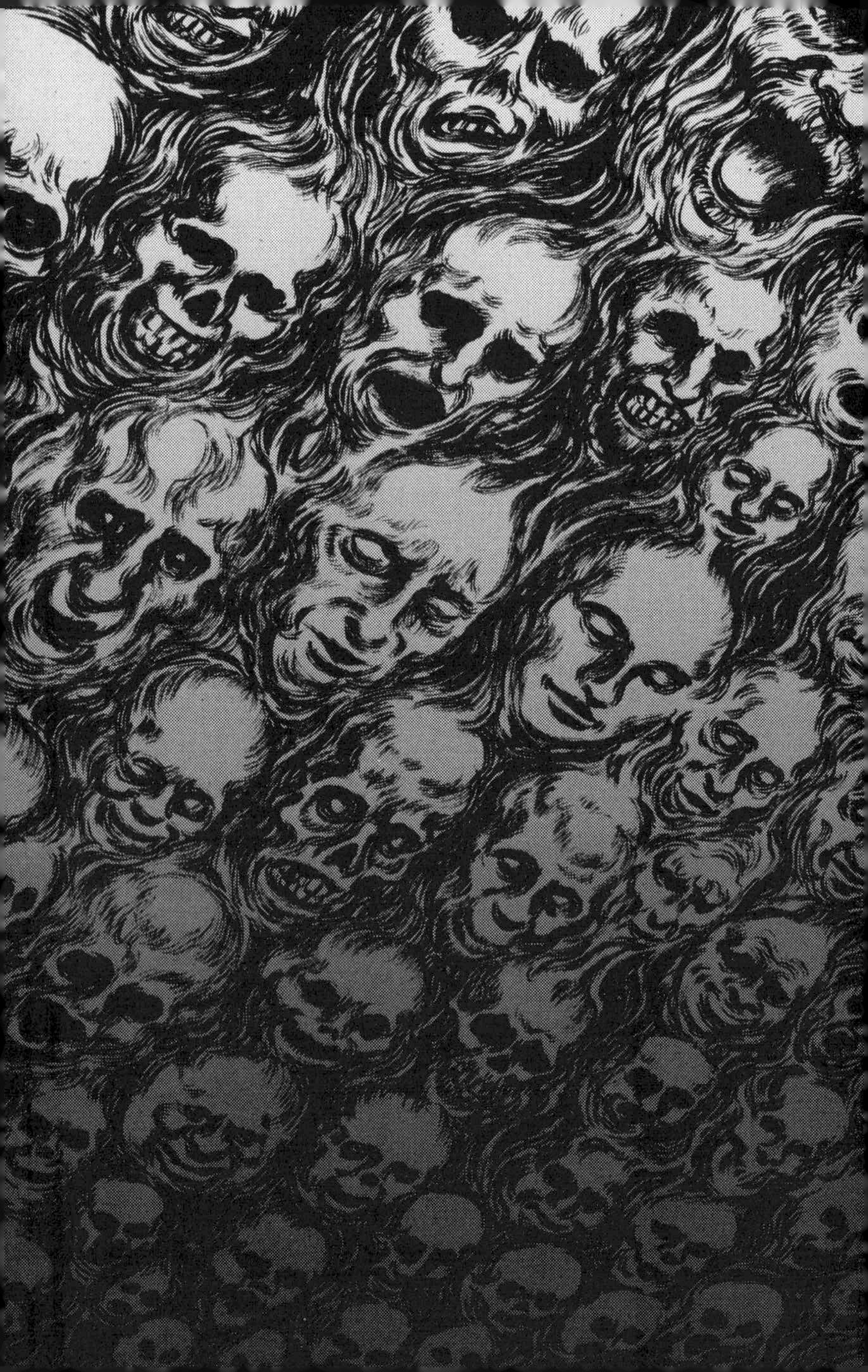

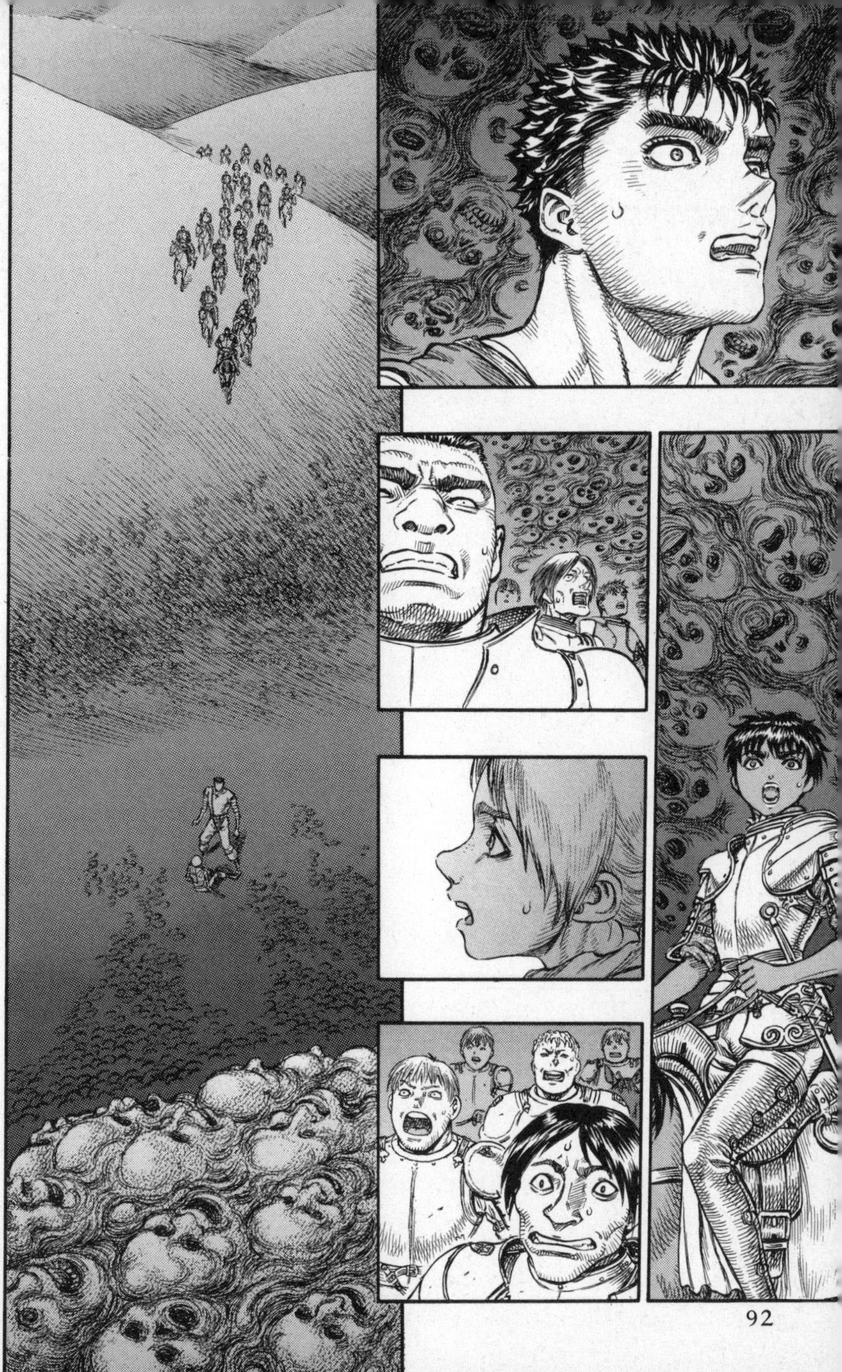

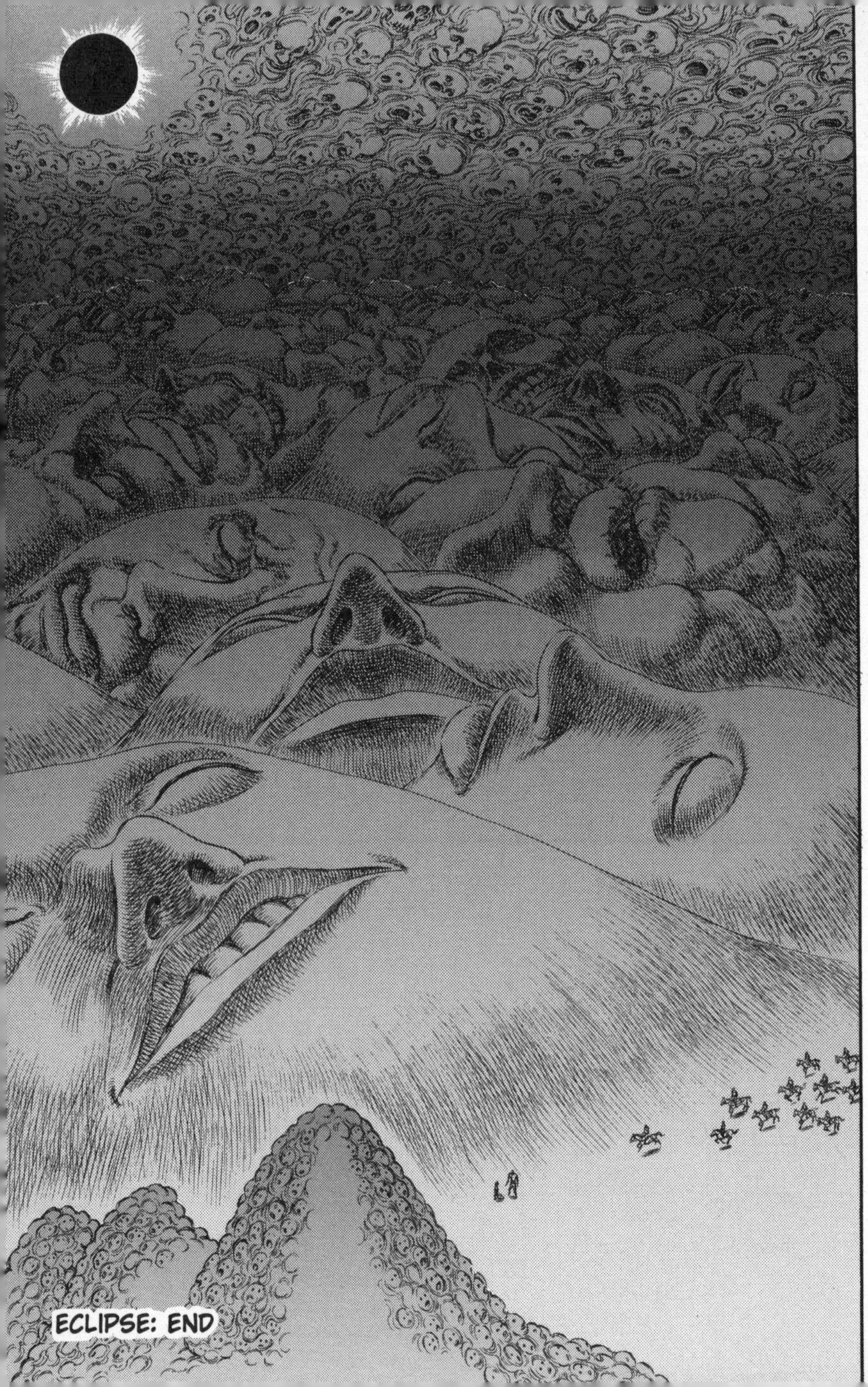
ECLIPSE: END

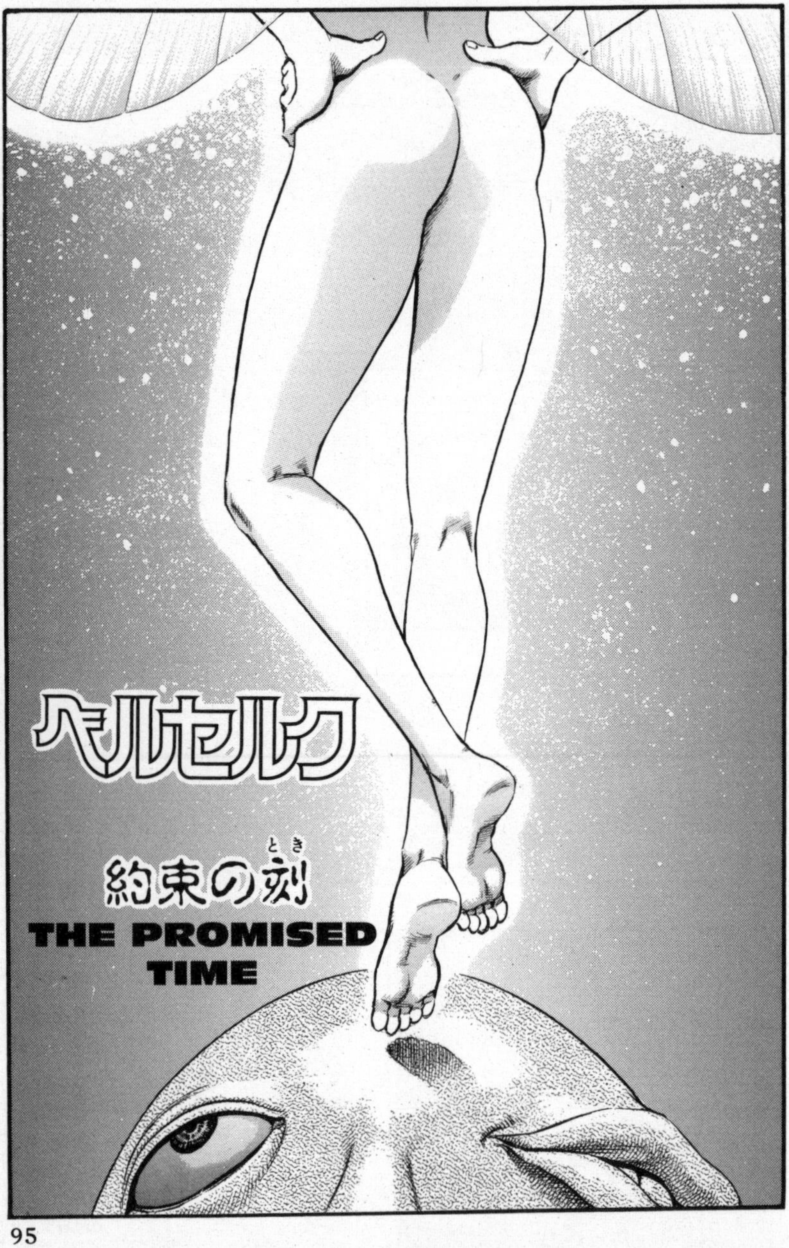
ベルセルク
約束の刻(とき)
THE PROMISED TIME

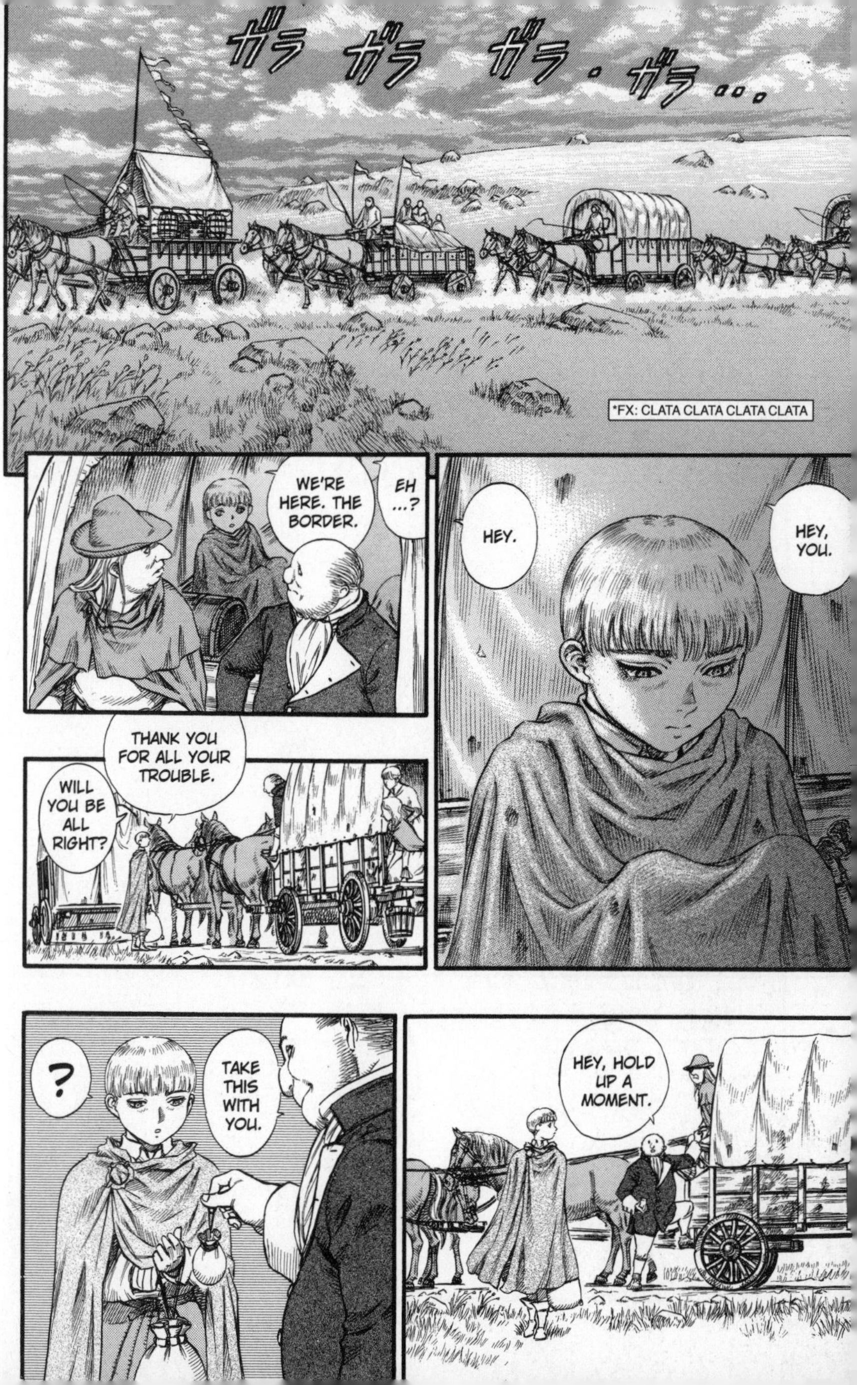
ガラ ガラ ガラ・ガラ…。
*FX: CLATA CLATA CLATA CLATA
HEY, YOU.
HEY.
EH ...?
WE'RE HERE. THE BORDER.
THANK YOU FOR ALL YOUR TROUBLE.
WILL YOU BE ALL RIGHT?
HEY, HOLD UP A MOMENT.
TAKE THIS WITH YOU.
?

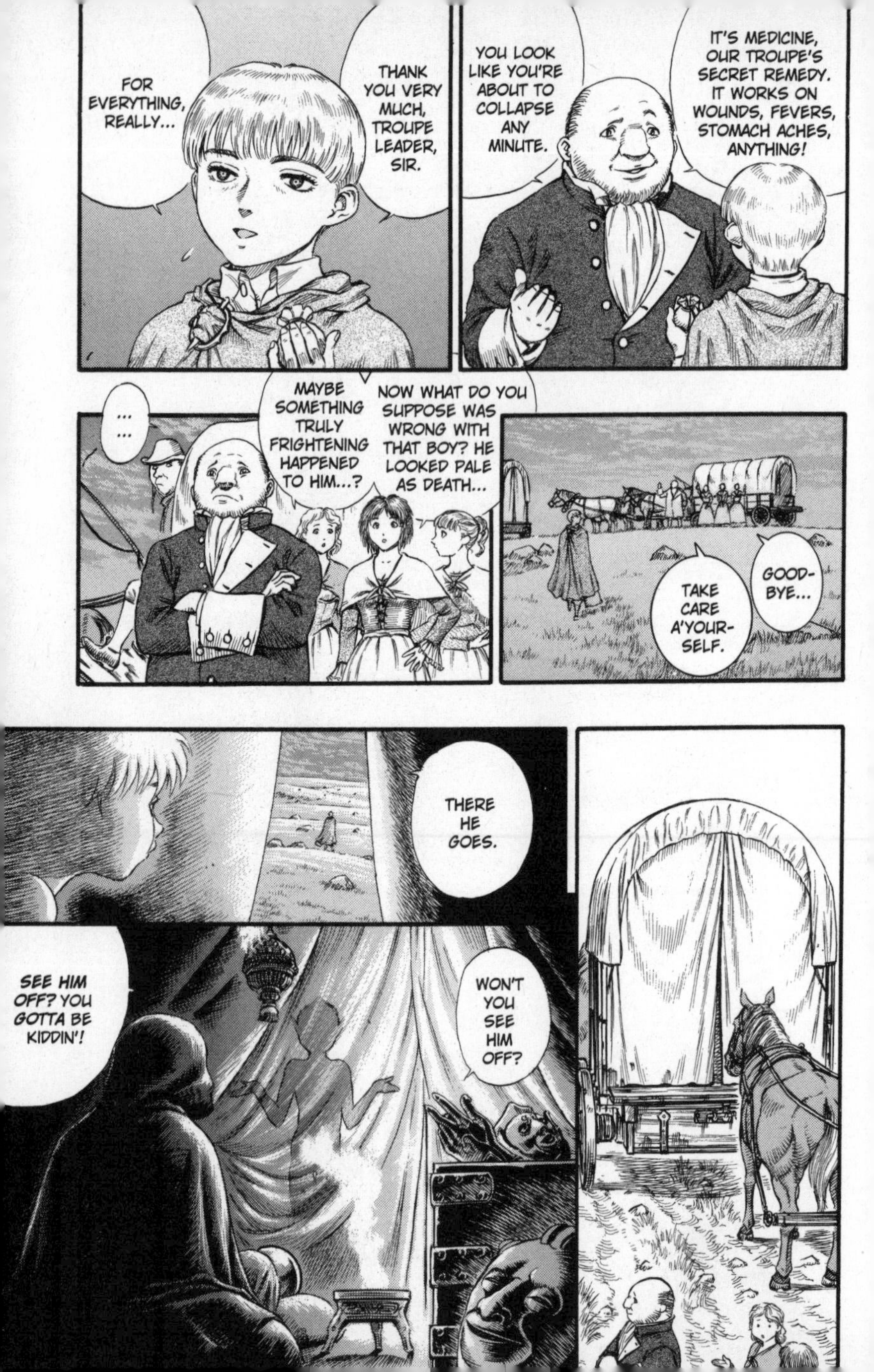
IT'S MEDICINE, OUR TROUPE'S SECRET REMEDY. IT WORKS ON WOUNDS, FEVERS, STOMACH ACHES, ANYTHING!
YOU LOOK LIKE YOU'RE ABOUT TO COLLAPSE ANY MINUTE.
THANK YOU VERY MUCH, TROUPE LEADER, SIR.
FOR EVERYTHING, REALLY...
GOOD-BYE...
TAKE CARE A'YOURSELF.
NOW WHAT DO YOU SUPPOSE WAS WRONG WITH THAT BOY? HE LOOKED PALE AS DEATH...
MAYBE SOMETHING TRULY FRIGHTENING HAPPENED TO HIM...?
... ...
THERE HE GOES.
WON'T YOU SEE HIM OFF?
SEE HIM OFF? YOU GOTTA BE KIDDIN'!

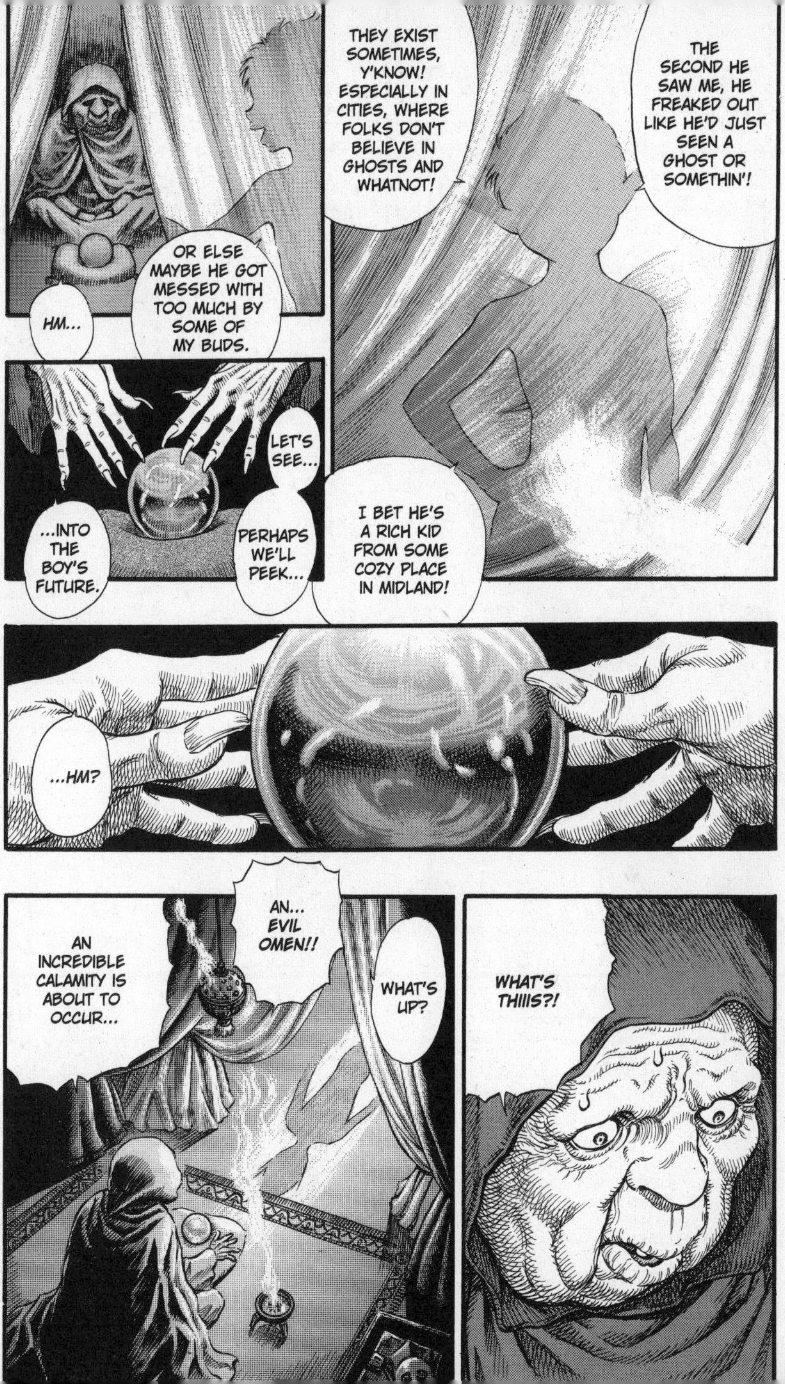
THE SECOND HE SAW ME, HE FREAKED OUT LIKE HE'D JUST SEEN A GHOST OR SOMETHIN'!
THEY EXIST SOMETIMES, Y'KNOW! ESPECIALLY IN CITIES, WHERE FOLKS DON'T BELIEVE IN GHOSTS AND WHATNOT!
OR ELSE MAYBE HE GOT MESSED WITH TOO MUCH BY SOME OF MY BUDS.
HM...
I BET HE'S A RICH KID FROM SOME COZY PLACE IN MIDLAND!
LET'S SEE...
PERHAPS WE'LL PEEK...
...INTO THE BOY'S FUTURE.
...HM?
WHAT'S THIIIS?!
WHAT'S UP?
AN... EVIL OMEN!!
AN INCREDIBLE CALAMITY IS ABOUT TO OCCUR...

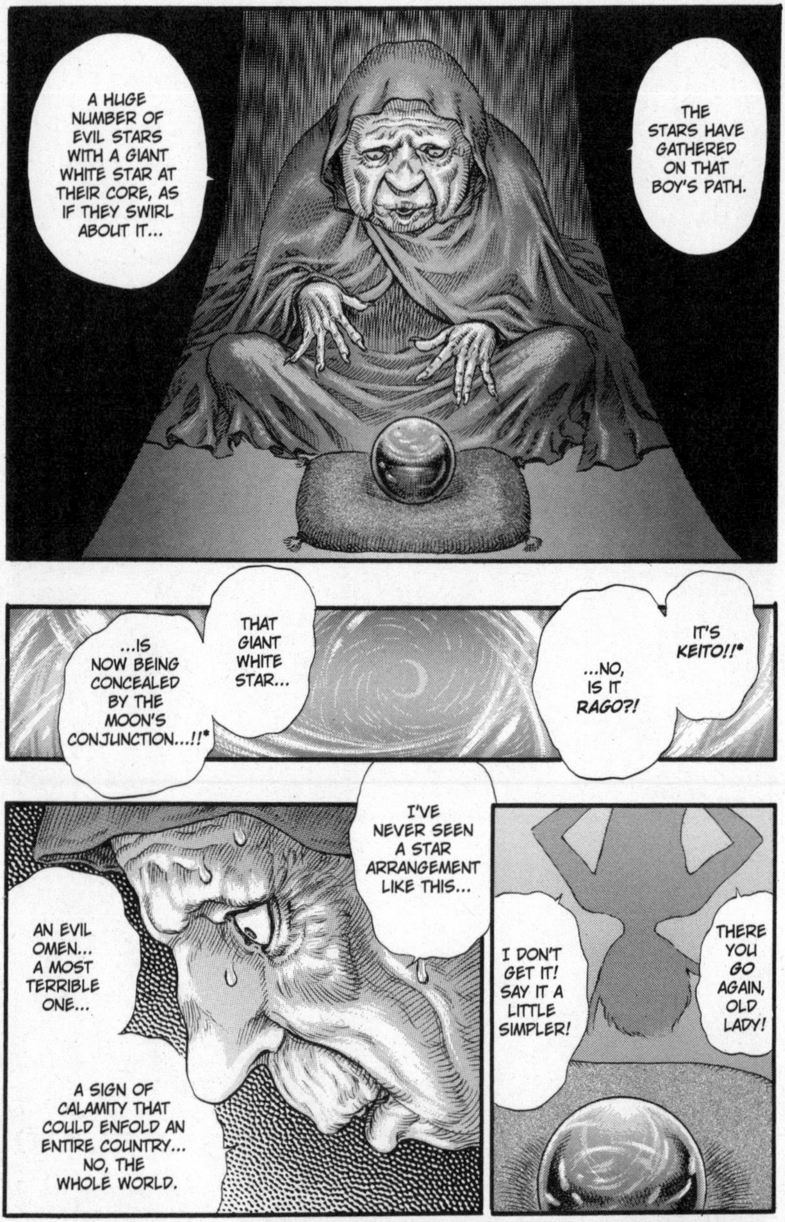
THE STARS HAVE GATHERED ON THAT BOY'S PATH.
A HUGE NUMBER OF EVIL STARS WITH A GIANT WHITE STAR AT THEIR CORE, AS IF THEY SWIRL ABOUT IT...
IT'S *KEITO!!**
...NO, IS IT *RAGO?!*
THAT GIANT WHITE STAR...
...IS NOW BEING CONCEALED BY THE MOON'S CONJUNCTION...!!*
THERE YOU GO AGAIN, OLD LADY!
I DON'T GET IT! SAY IT A LITTLE SIMPLER!
I'VE NEVER SEEN A STAR ARRANGEMENT LIKE THIS...
AN EVIL OMEN... A MOST TERRIBLE ONE...
A SIGN OF CALAMITY THAT COULD ENFOLD AN ENTIRE COUNTRY... NO, THE WHOLE WORLD.

*NOTE: CONJUNCTION IS A NEW MOON.

*NOTE: THE STAR THAT SUDDENLY APPEARS IN THE NIGHT SKY AND SCARES PEOPLE IS CALLED KEITO. THE STAR THAT STEALS LIGHT FROM THE SUN OR MOON AND CAUSES AN ECLIPSE IS CALLED RAGO. ALONG WITH OTHER IMAGINARY STARS, THEY ARE ANCIENT LEGENDS.

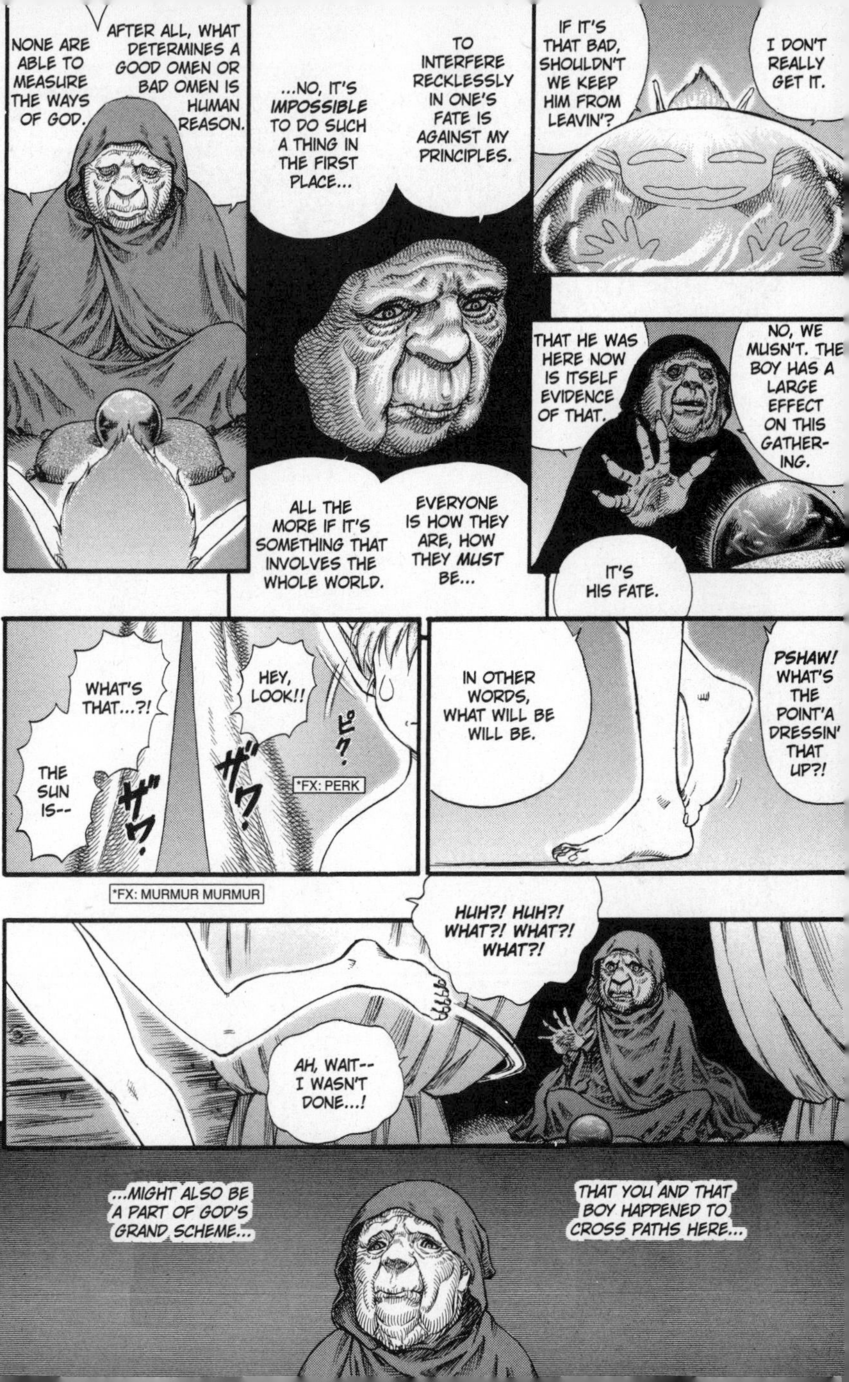
I DON'T REALLY GET IT.
IF IT'S THAT BAD, SHOULDN'T WE KEEP HIM FROM LEAVIN'?
NO, WE MUSN'T. THE BOY HAS A LARGE EFFECT ON THIS GATHERING.
THAT HE WAS HERE NOW IS ITSELF EVIDENCE OF THAT.
IT'S HIS FATE.
TO INTERFERE RECKLESSLY IN ONE'S FATE IS AGAINST MY PRINCIPLES.
...NO, IT'S *IMPOSSIBLE* TO DO SUCH A THING IN THE FIRST PLACE...
EVERYONE IS HOW THEY ARE, HOW THEY *MUST* BE...
ALL THE MORE IF IT'S SOMETHING THAT INVOLVES THE WHOLE WORLD.
AFTER ALL, WHAT DETERMINES A GOOD OMEN OR BAD OMEN IS HUMAN REASON.
NONE ARE ABLE TO MEASURE THE WAYS OF GOD.
PSHAW! WHAT'S THE POINT'A DRESSIN' THAT UP?!
IN OTHER WORDS, WHAT WILL BE WILL BE.
HEY, LOOK!!
ピク
*FX: PERK
WHAT'S THAT...?!
THE SUN IS--
ザワ
ザワ
*FX: MURMUR MURMUR
HUH?! HUH?! WHAT?! WHAT?! WHAT?!
AH, WAIT-- I WASN'T DONE...!
THAT YOU AND THAT BOY HAPPENED TO CROSS PATHS HERE...
...MIGHT ALSO BE A PART OF GOD'S GRAND SCHEME...

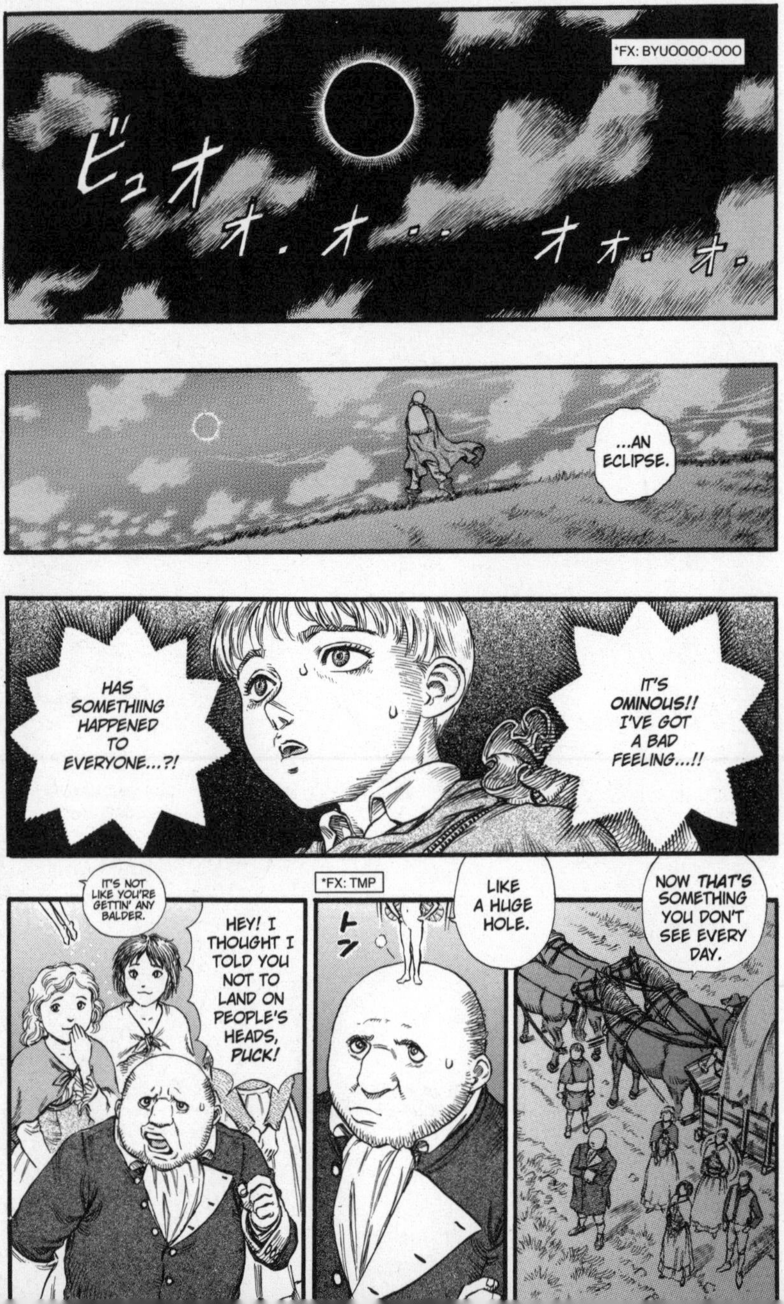
ビュオオ・オ・・オオ・オ・
*FX: BYUOOOO-OOO
...AN ECLIPSE.
IT'S OMINOUS!! I'VE GOT A BAD FEELING...!!
HAS SOMETHIING HAPPENED TO EVERYONE...?!
NOW THAT'S SOMETHING YOU DON'T SEE EVERY DAY.
LIKE A HUGE HOLE.
トッ
*FX: TMP
HEY! I THOUGHT I TOLD YOU NOT TO LAND ON PEOPLE'S HEADS, PUCK!
IT'S NOT LIKE YOU'RE GETTIN' ANY BALDER.

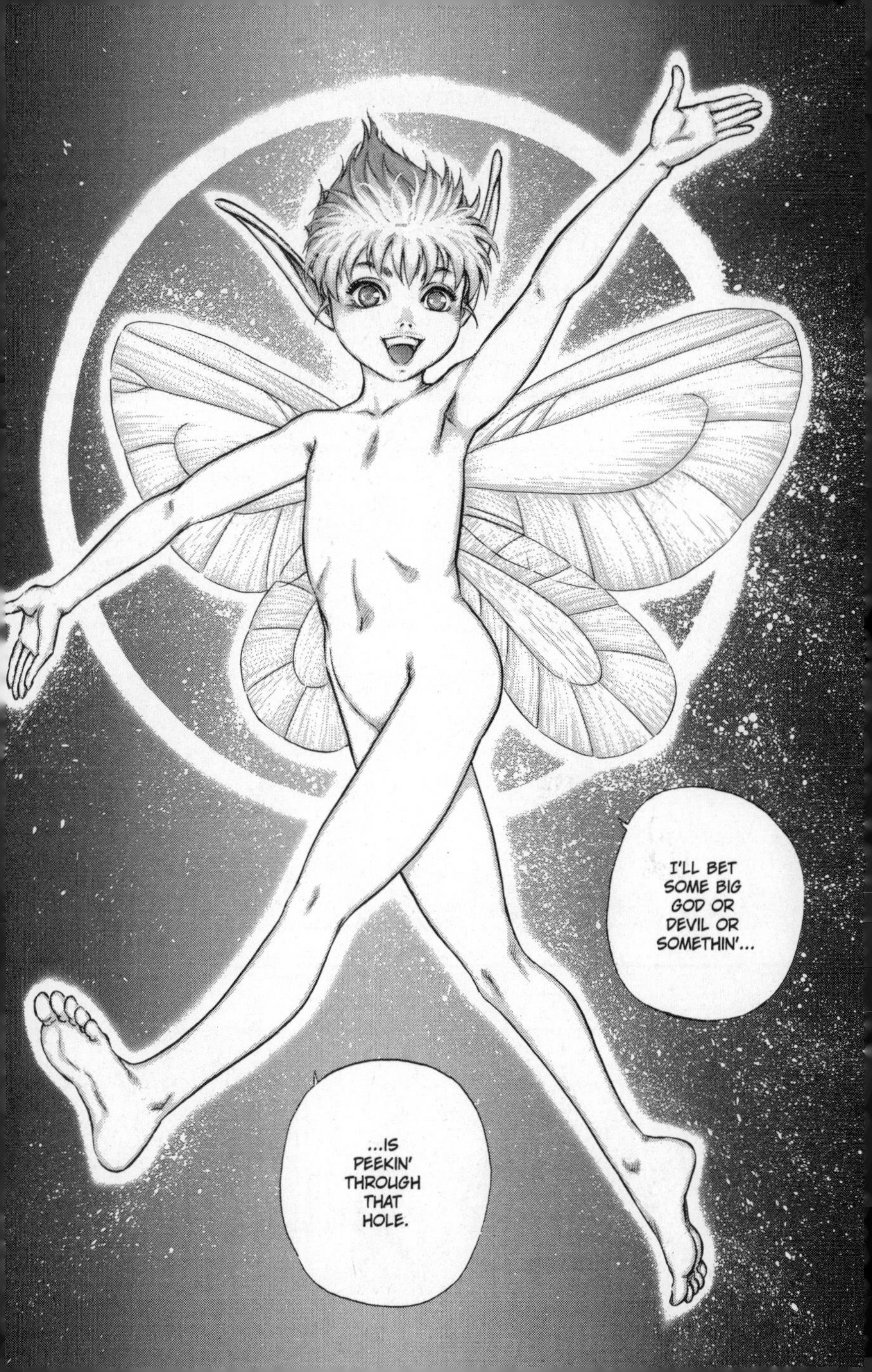
I'LL BET SOME BIG GOD OR DEVIL OR SOMETHIN'...
...IS PEEKIN' THROUGH THAT HOLE.

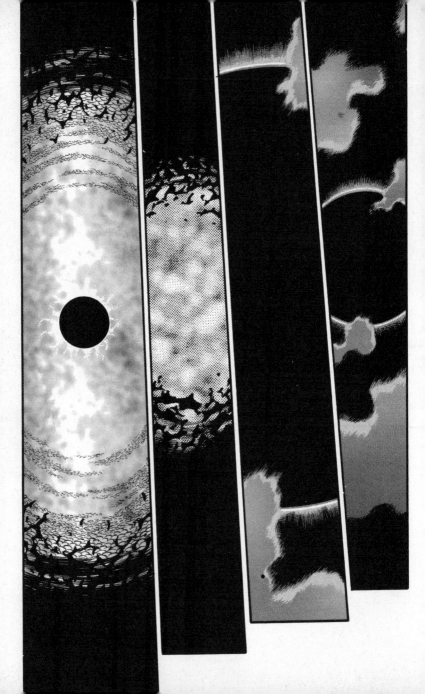

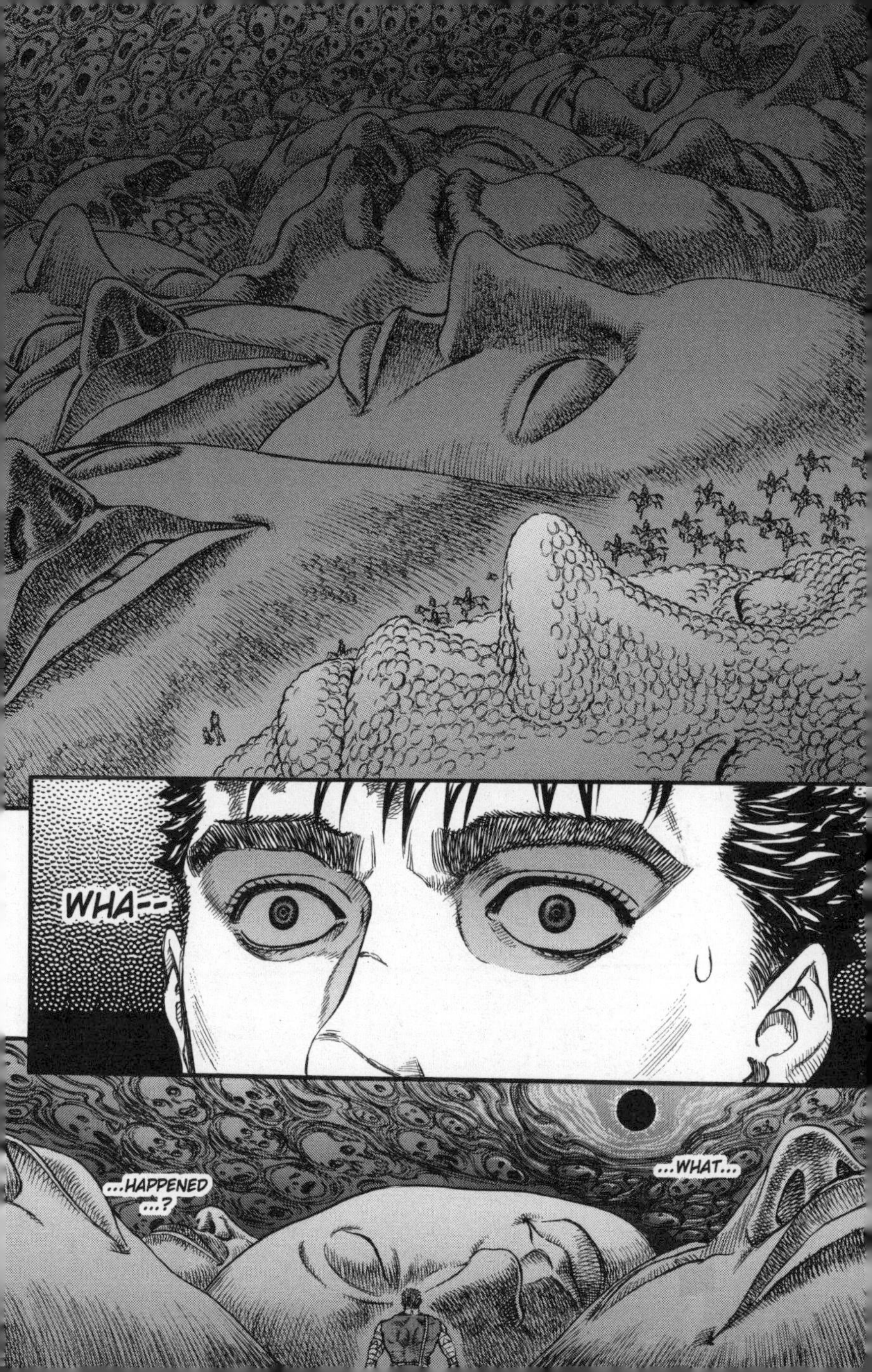
WHA--
...WHAT...
...HAPPENED ...?

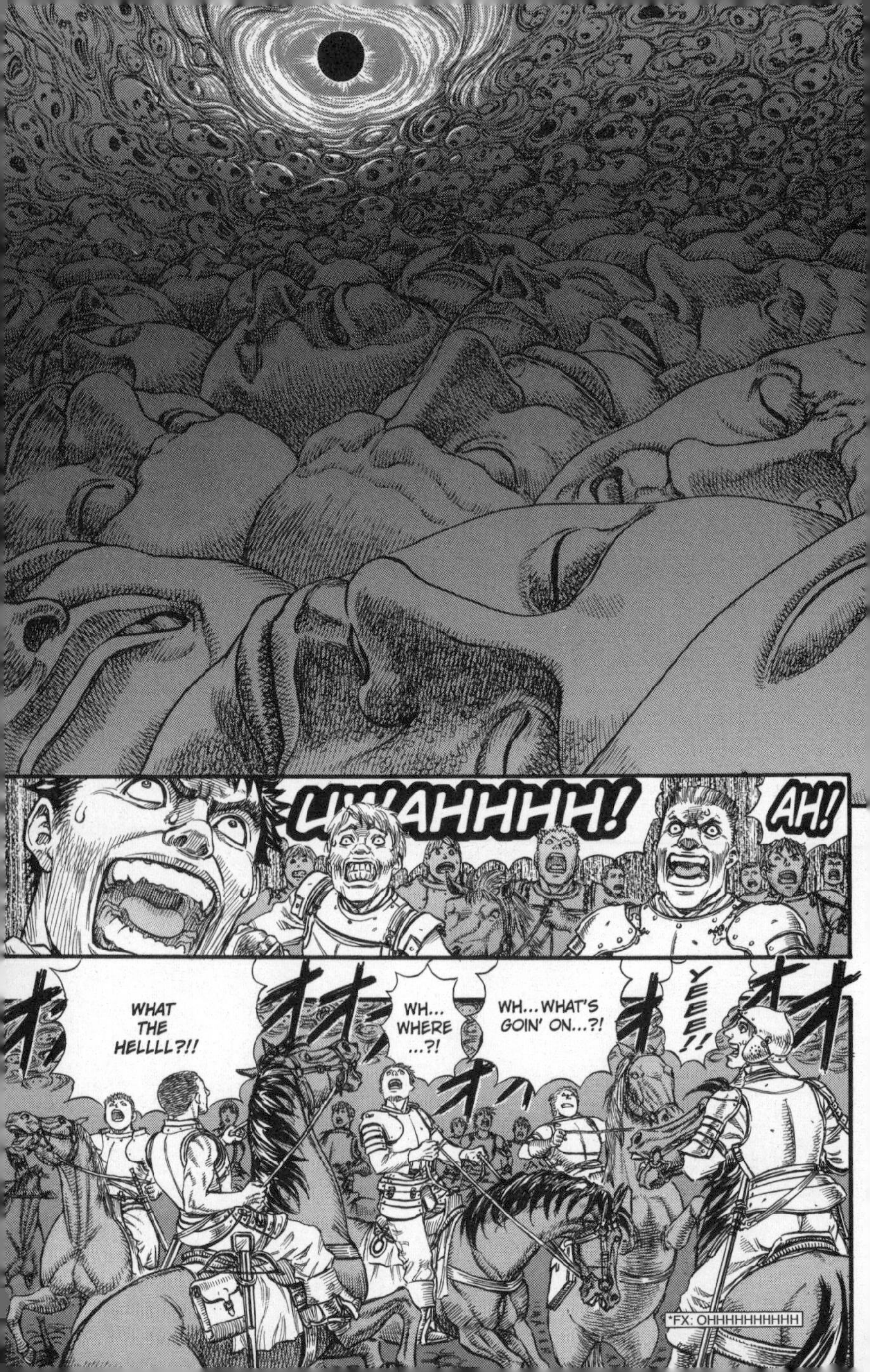
AH!
UWAHHHHH!
YEEE!!
WH...WHAT'S GOIN' ON...?!
WH... WHERE ...?!
WHAT THE HELLLL?!!
*FX: OHHHHHHHHHH

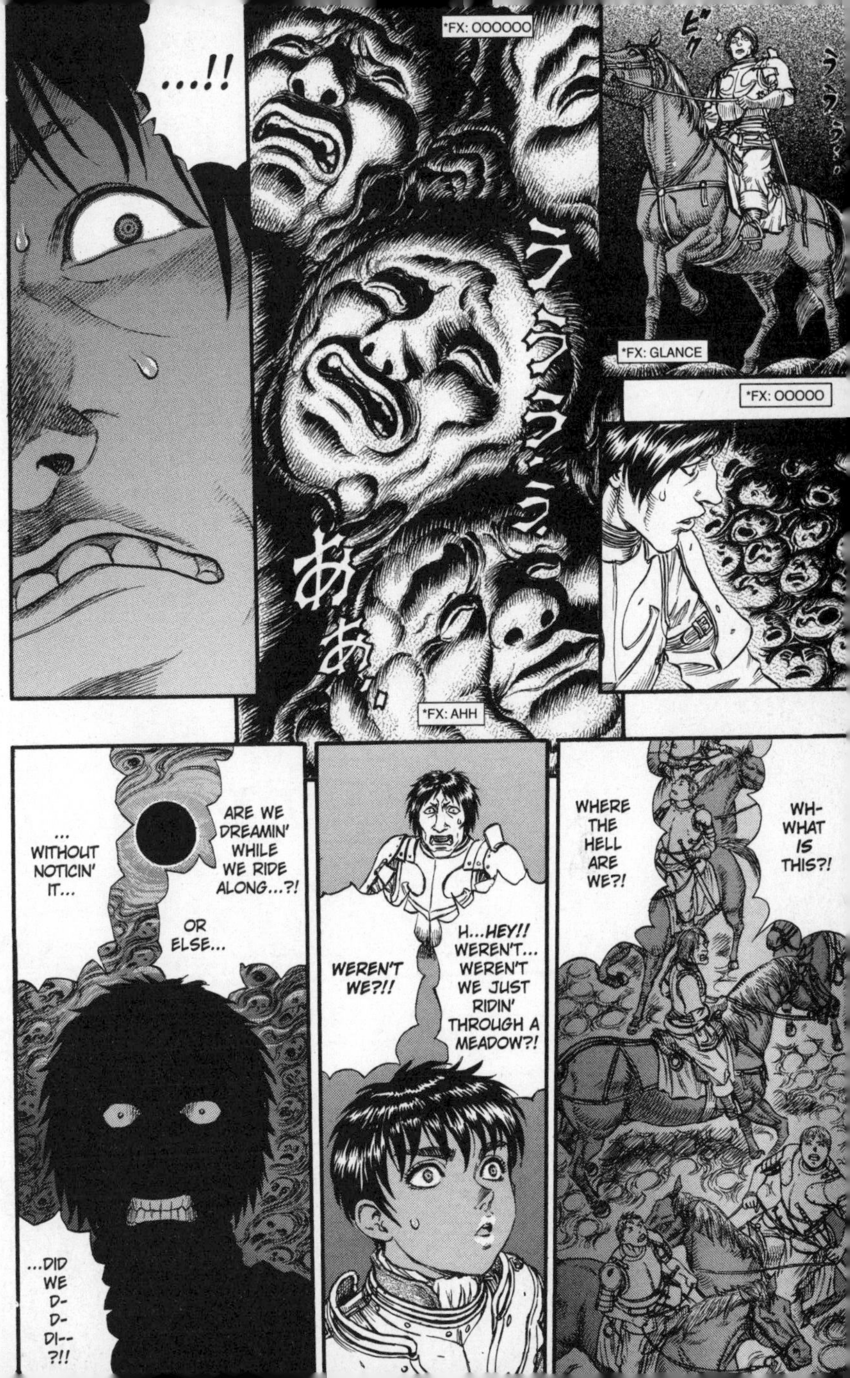

*FX: GLANCE
*FX: OOOOO
*FX: OOOOOO
*FX: AHH
...!!
WH- WHAT IS THIS?!
WHERE THE HELL ARE WE?!
H...HEY!! WEREN'T... WEREN'T WE JUST RIDIN' THROUGH A MEADOW?!
WEREN'T WE?!!
ARE WE DREAMIN' WHILE WE RIDE ALONG...?!
... WITHOUT NOTICIN' IT...
OR ELSE...
...DID WE D-D-DI--?!!

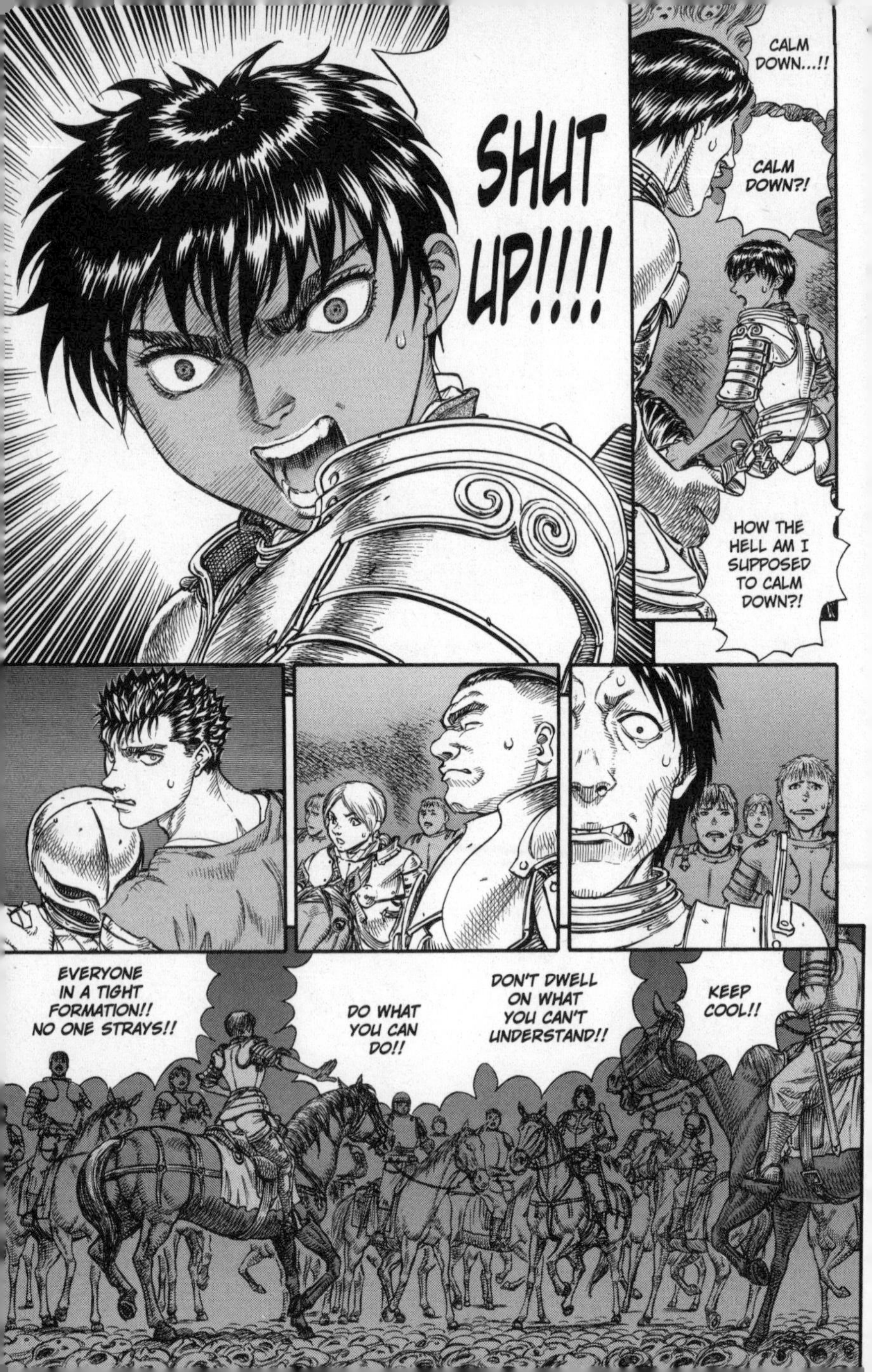
CALM DOWN...!!
CALM DOWN?!
HOW THE HELL AM I SUPPOSED TO CALM DOWN?!
SHUT UP!!!!
KEEP COOL!!
DON'T DWELL ON WHAT YOU CAN'T UNDERSTAND!!
DO WHAT YOU CAN DO!!
EVERYONE IN A TIGHT FORMATION!! NO ONE STRAYS!!

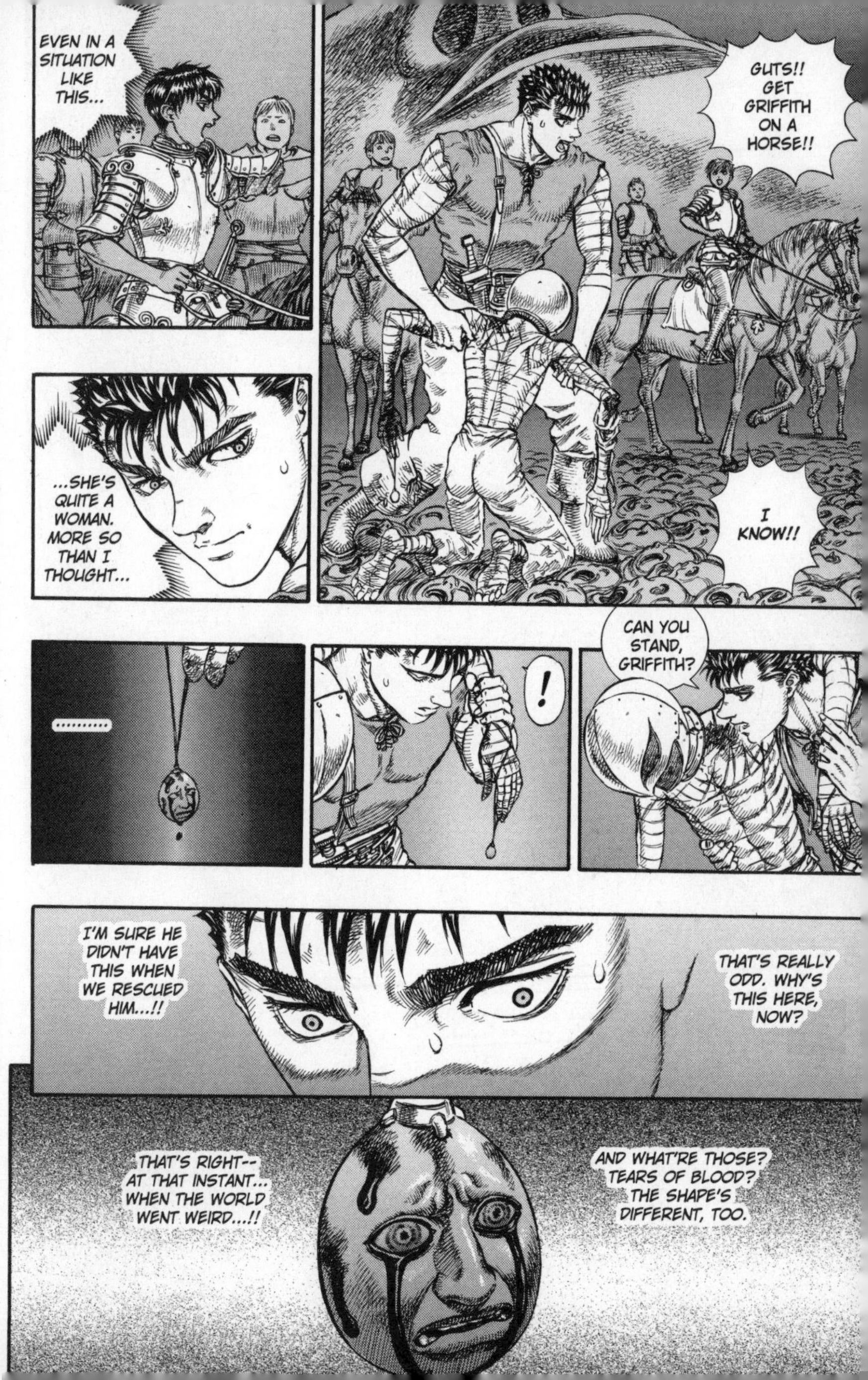
GUTS!! GET GRIFFITH ON A HORSE!!
I KNOW!!
EVEN IN A SITUATION LIKE THIS...
...SHE'S QUITE A WOMAN. MORE SO THAN I THOUGHT...
CAN YOU STAND, GRIFFITH?
!
....
THAT'S REALLY ODD. WHY'S THIS HERE, NOW?
I'M SURE HE DIDN'T HAVE THIS WHEN WE RESCUED HIM...!!
AND WHAT'RE THOSE? TEARS OF BLOOD? THE SHAPE'S DIFFERENT, TOO.
THAT'S RIGHT-- AT THAT INSTANT... WHEN THE WORLD WENT WEIRD...!!

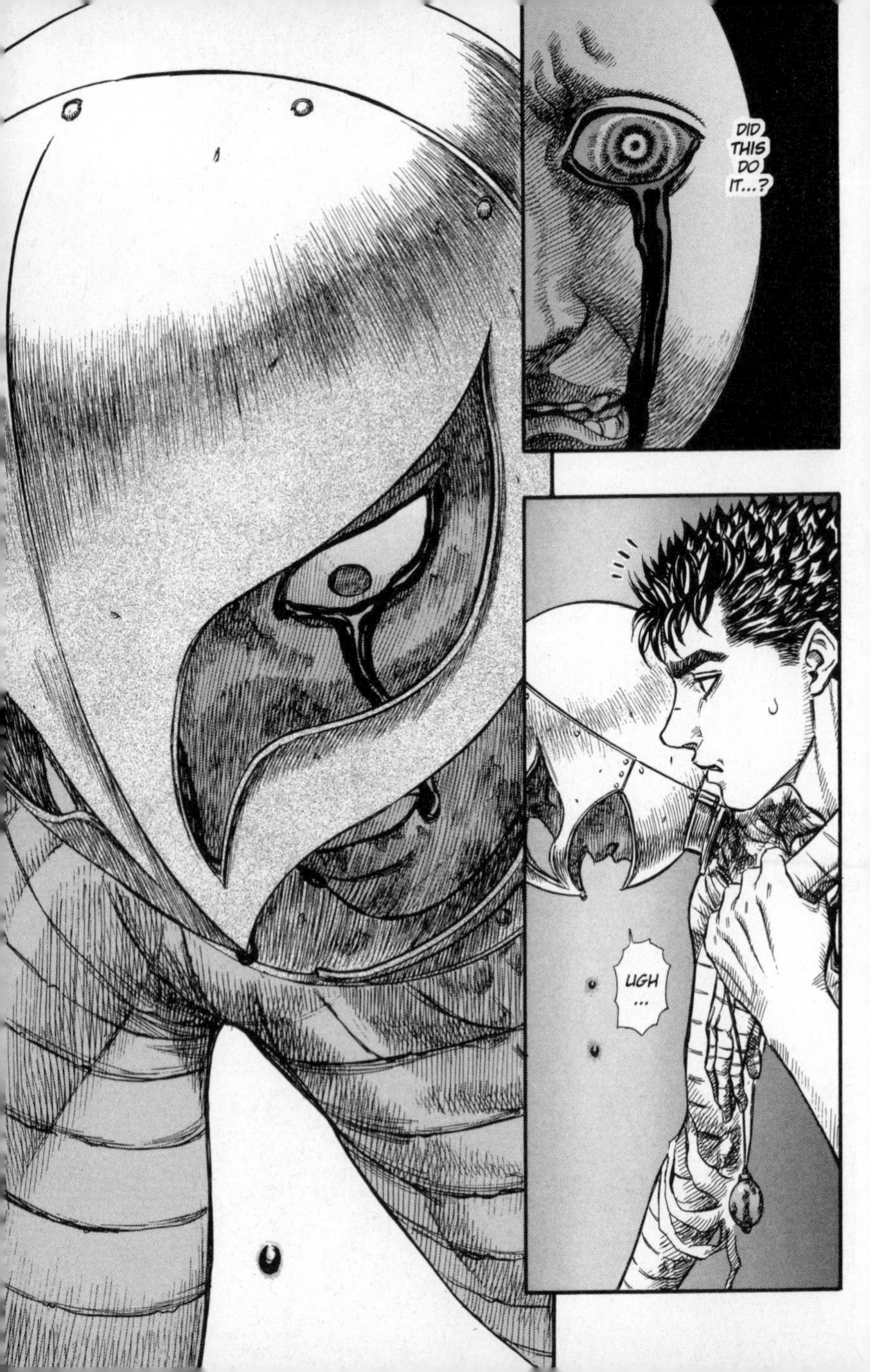
DID THIS DO IT...?
UGH ...

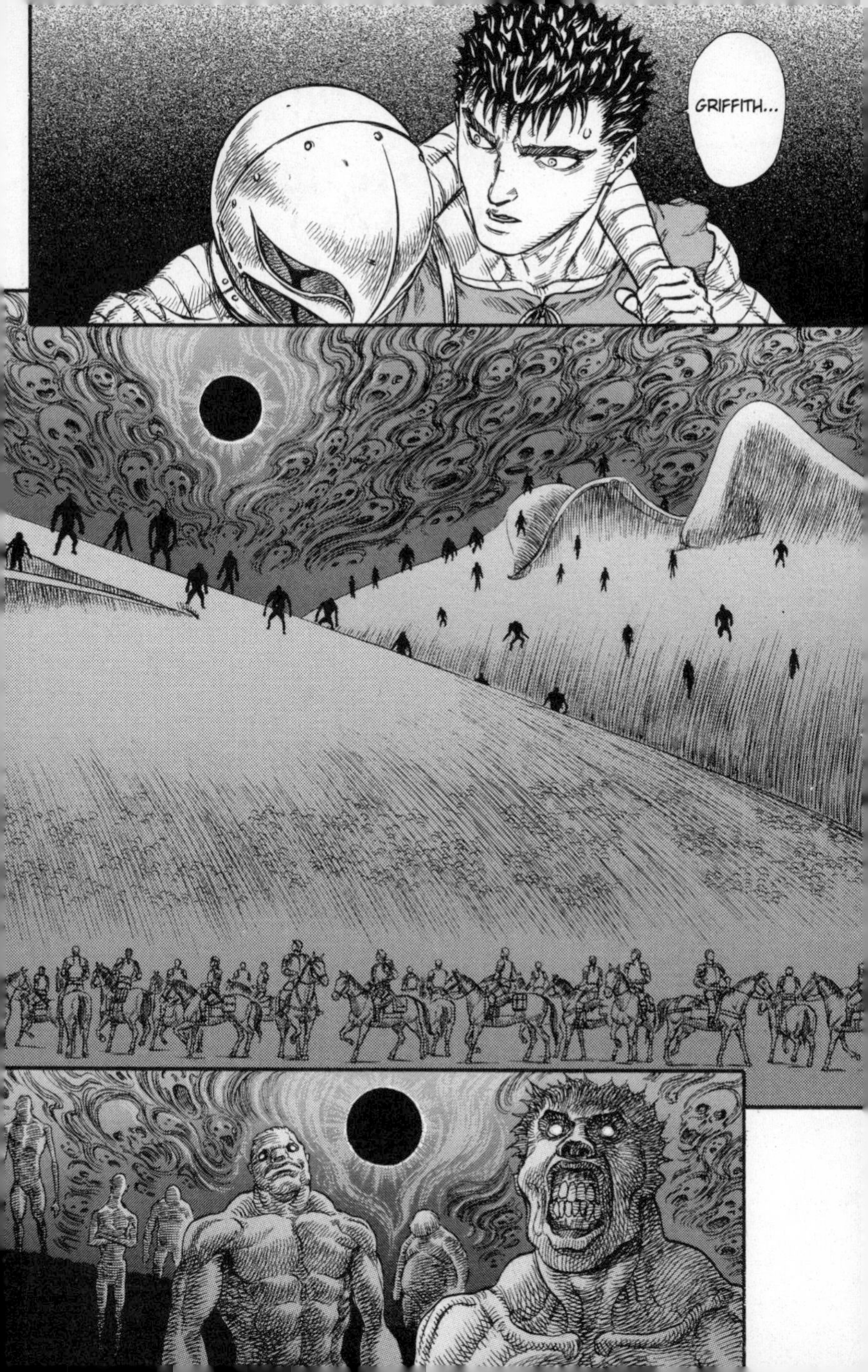
GRIFFITH...

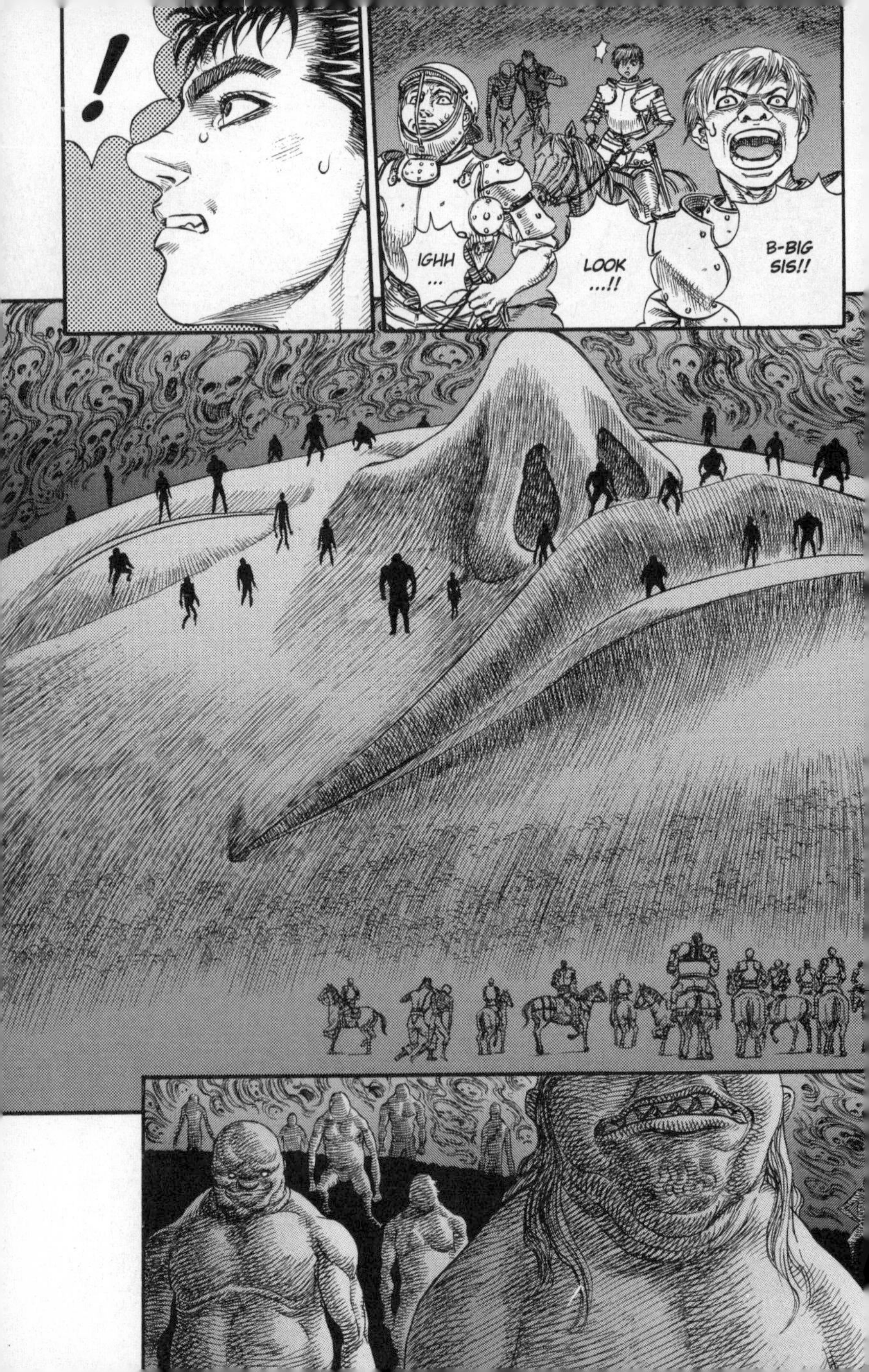
B-BIG SIS!!
LOOK ...!!
IGHH ...
!

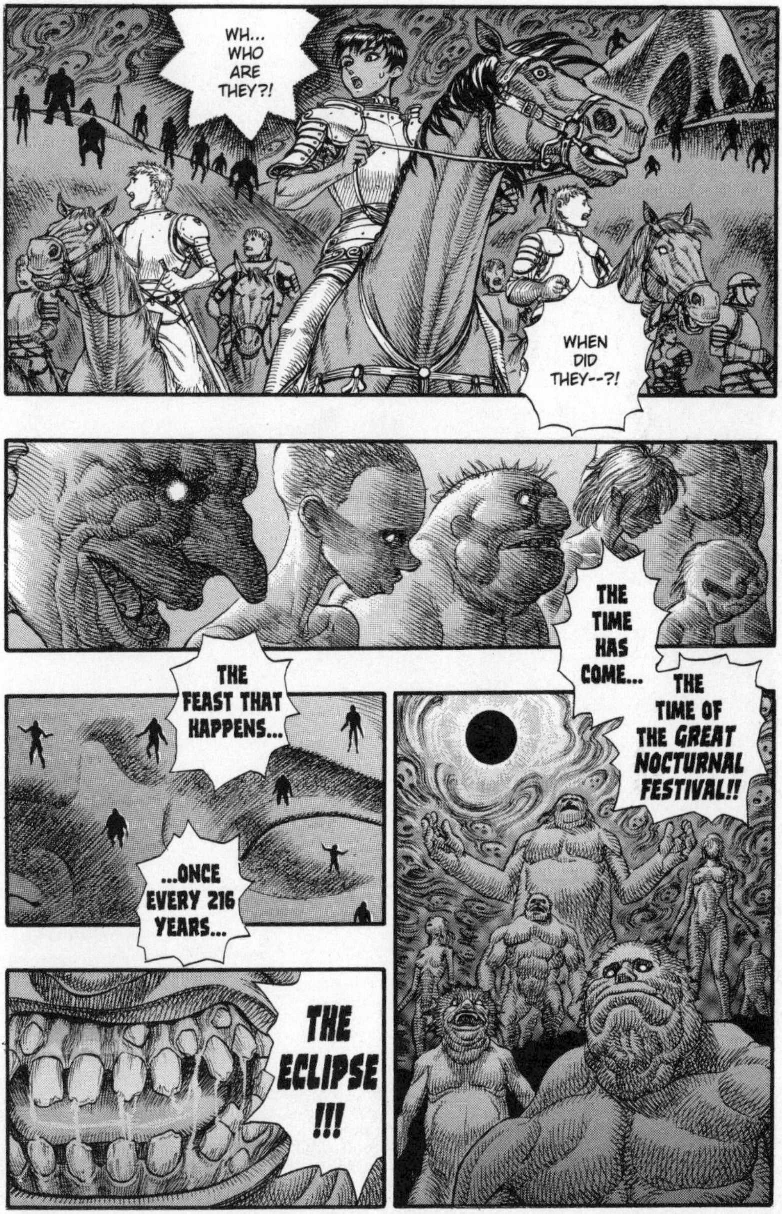
WH... WHO ARE THEY?!
WHEN DID THEY--?!
THE TIME HAS COME...
THE TIME OF THE GREAT NOCTURNAL FESTIVAL!!
THE FEAST THAT HAPPENS...
...ONCE EVERY 216 YEARS...
THE ECLIPSE !!!

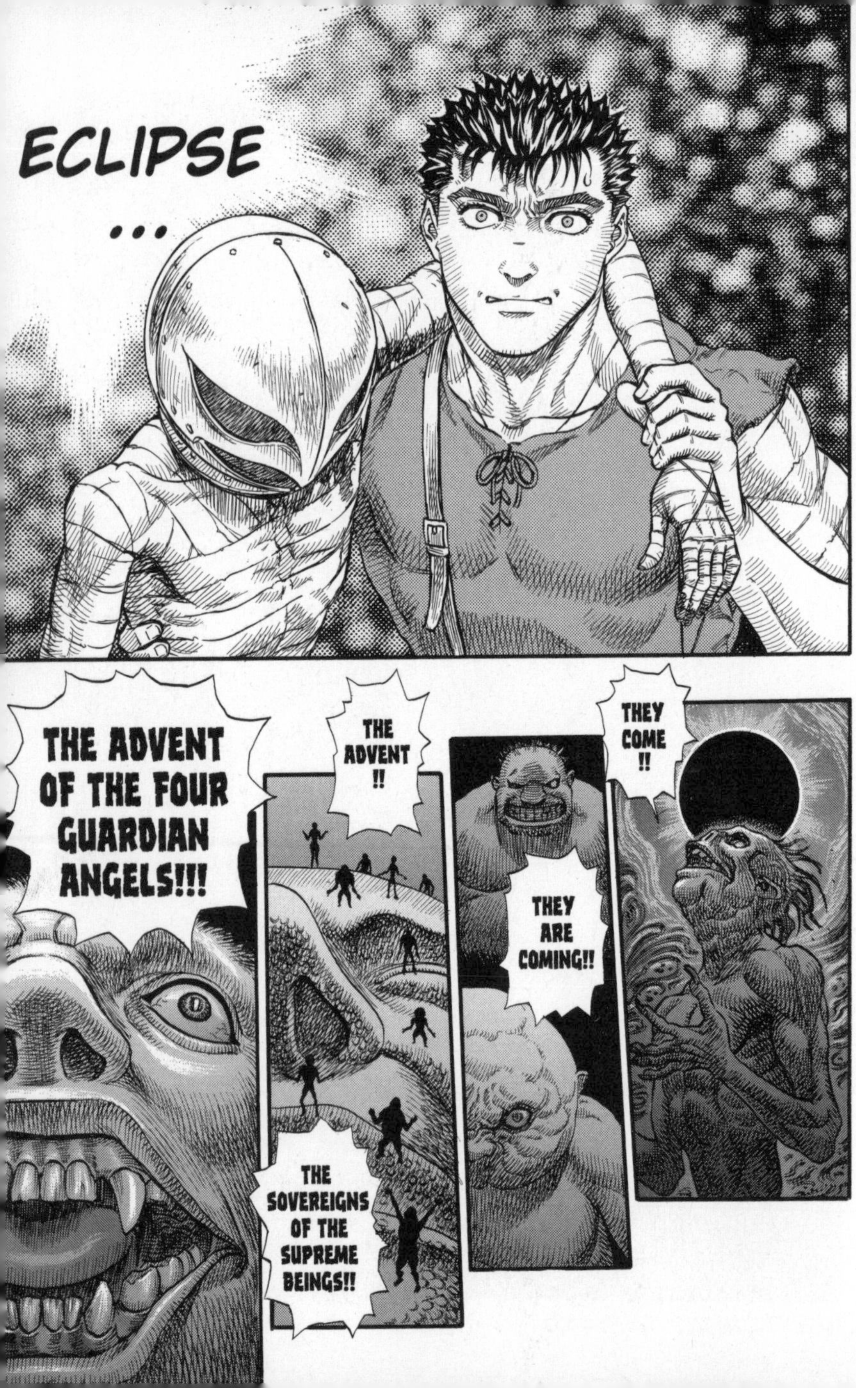
ECLIPSE ...
THEY COME !!
THEY ARE COMING!!
THE ADVENT !!
THE SOVEREIGNS OF THE SUPREME BEINGS!!
THE ADVENT OF THE FOUR GUARDIAN ANGELS!!!

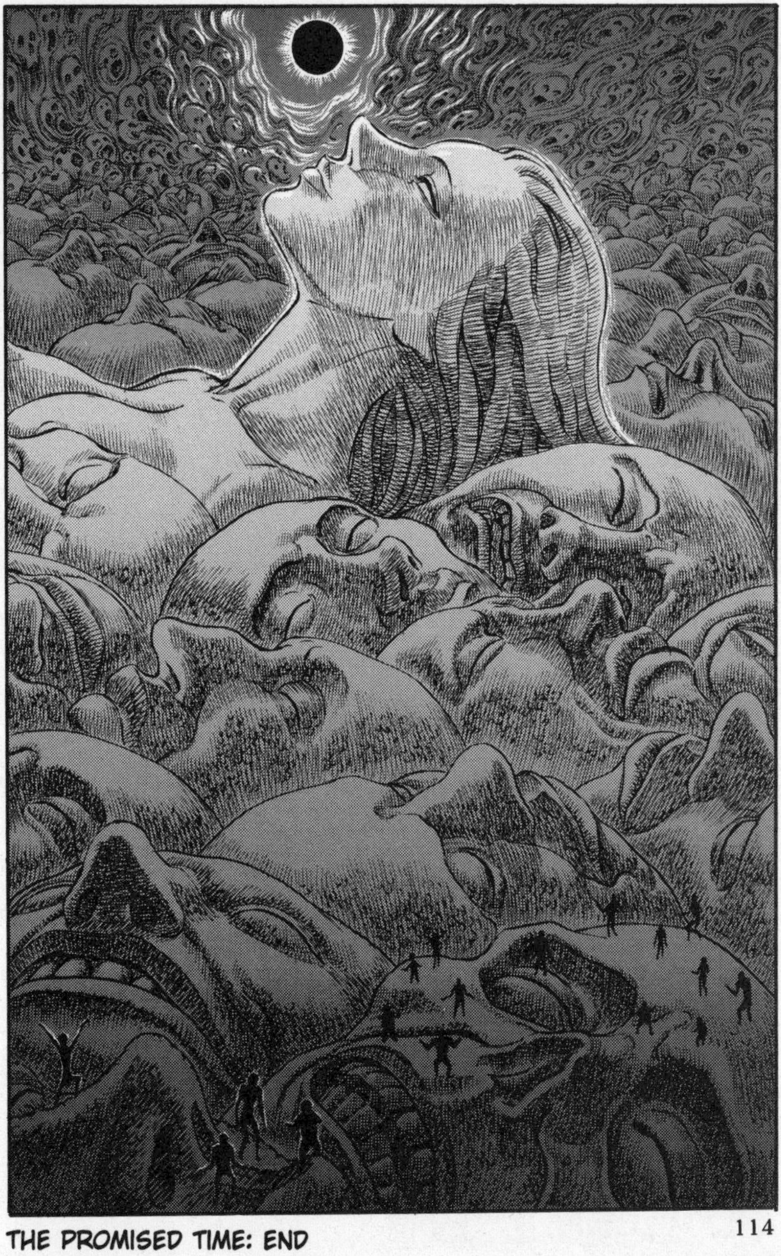

THE PROMISED TIME: END

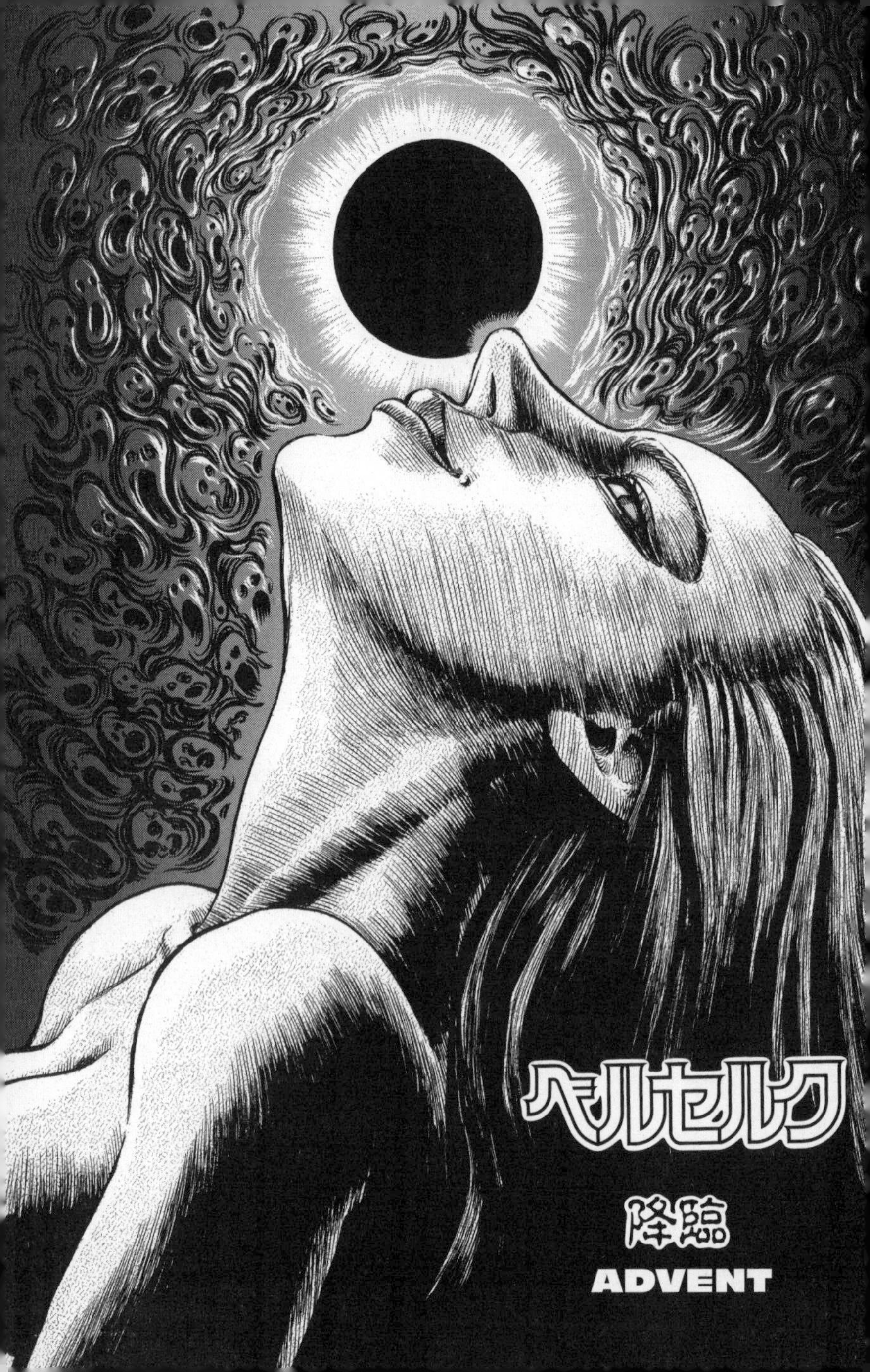
ベルセルク
降臨
ADVENT

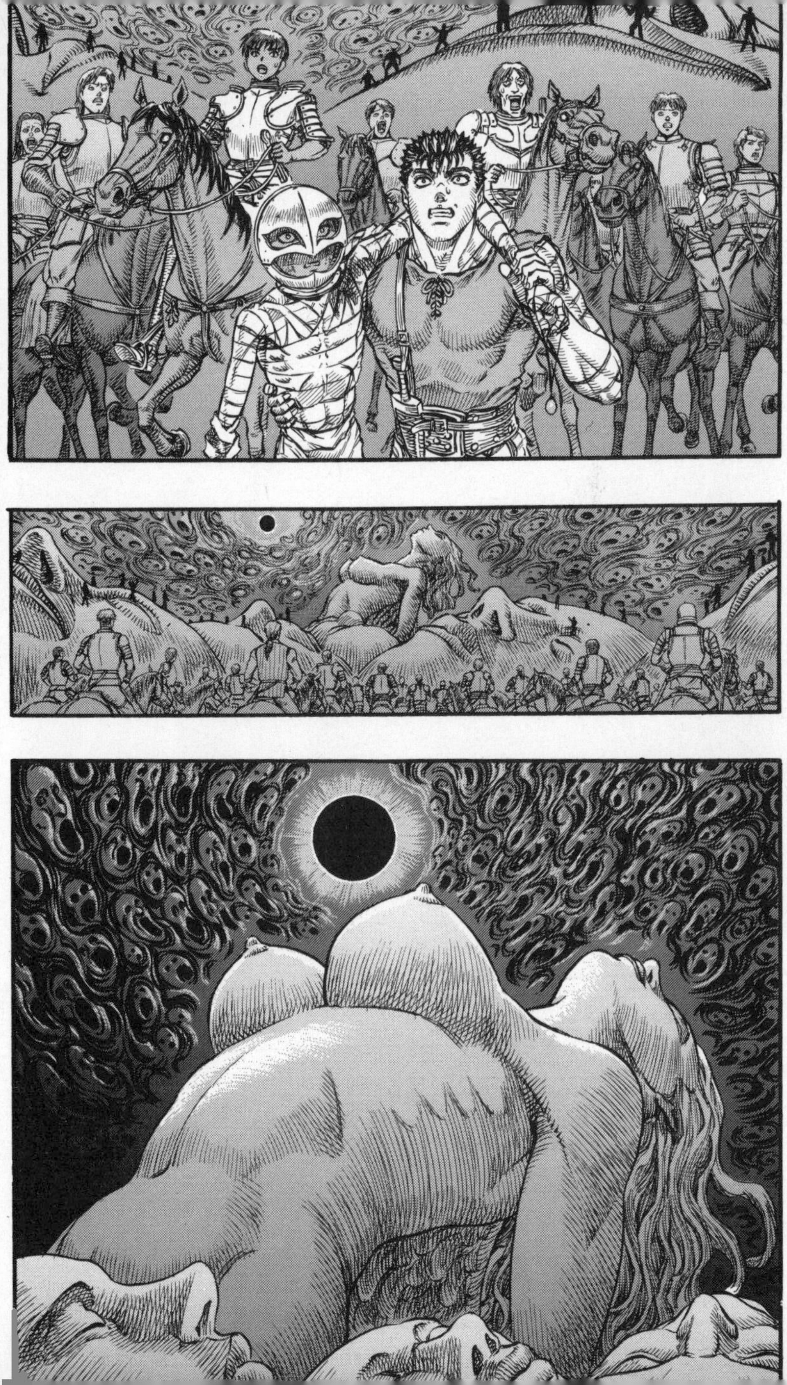

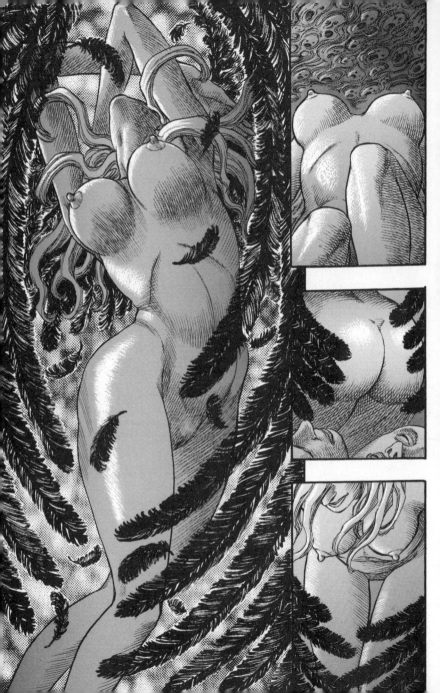

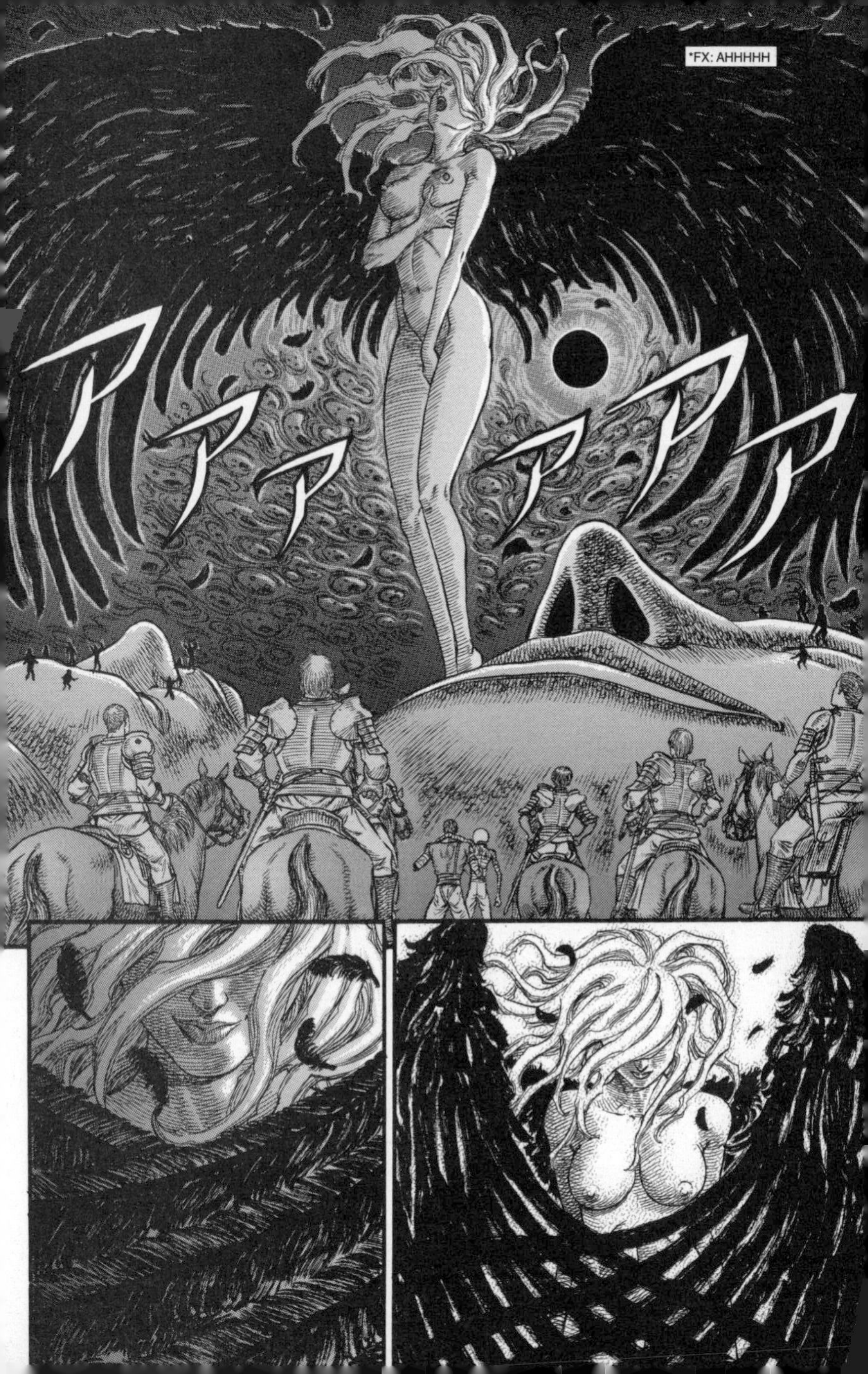
*FX: AHHHHH

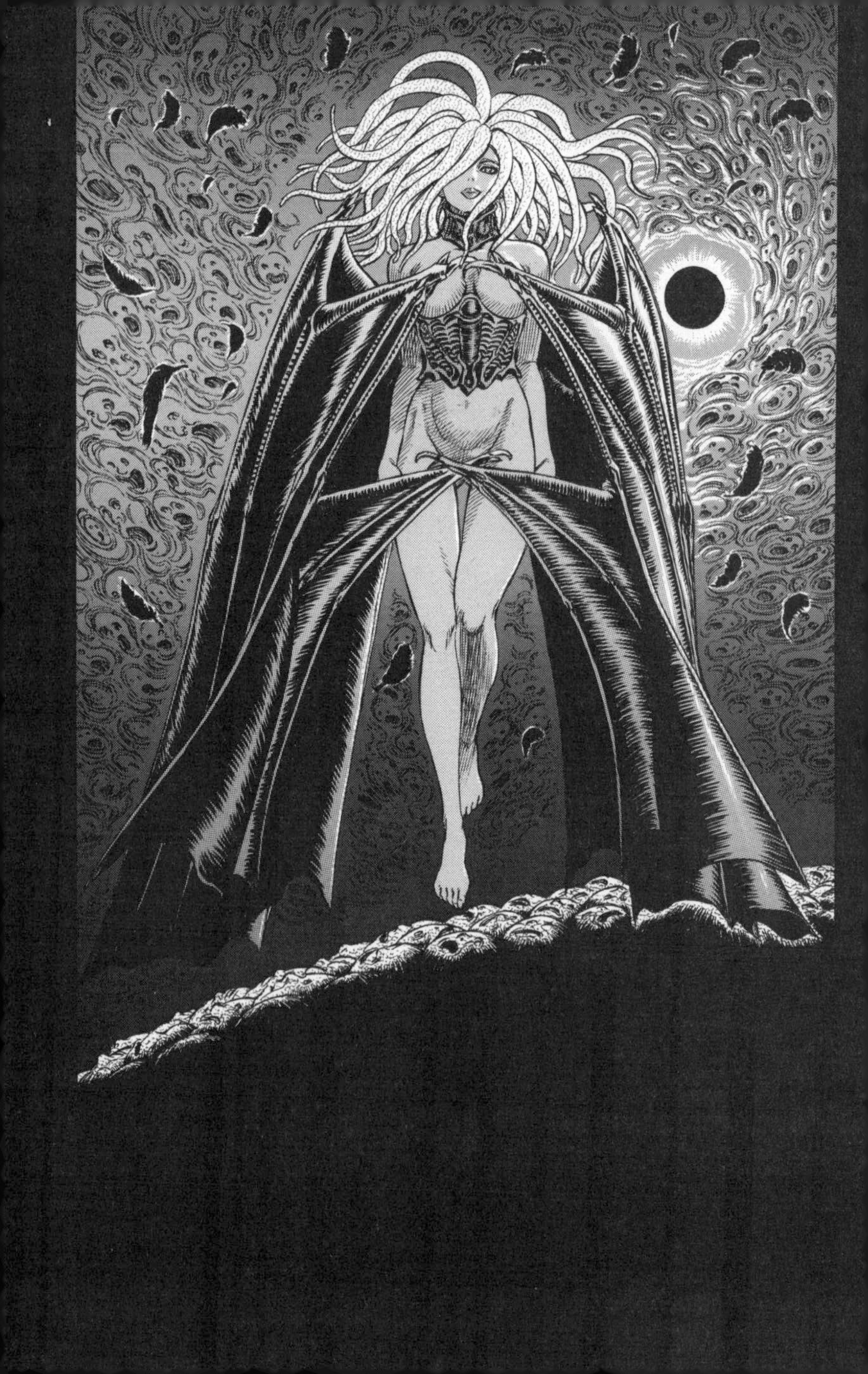

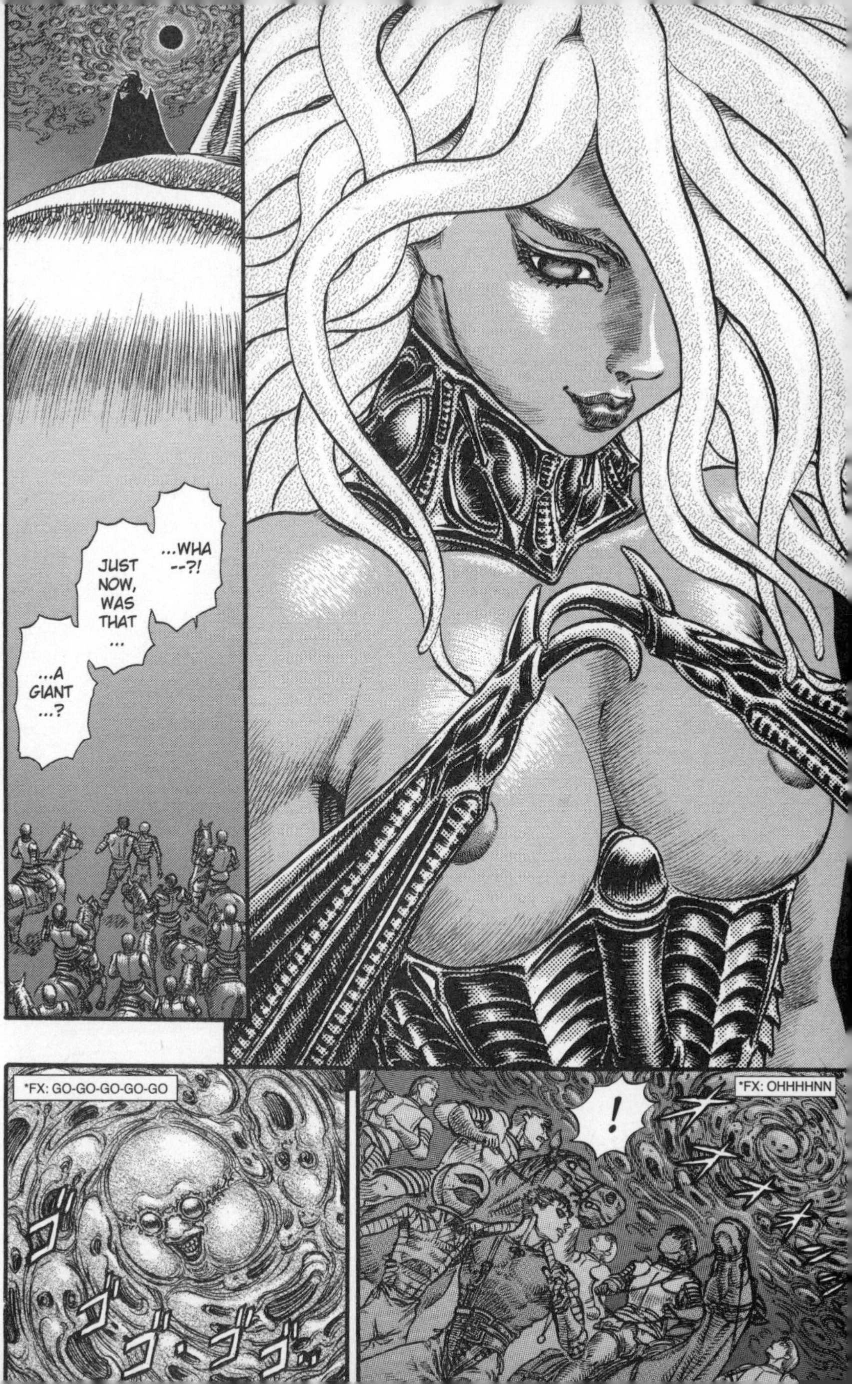
...WHA --?!
JUST NOW, WAS THAT ...
...A GIANT ...?
*FX: OHHHHNN
!
*FX: GO-GO-GO-GO-GO

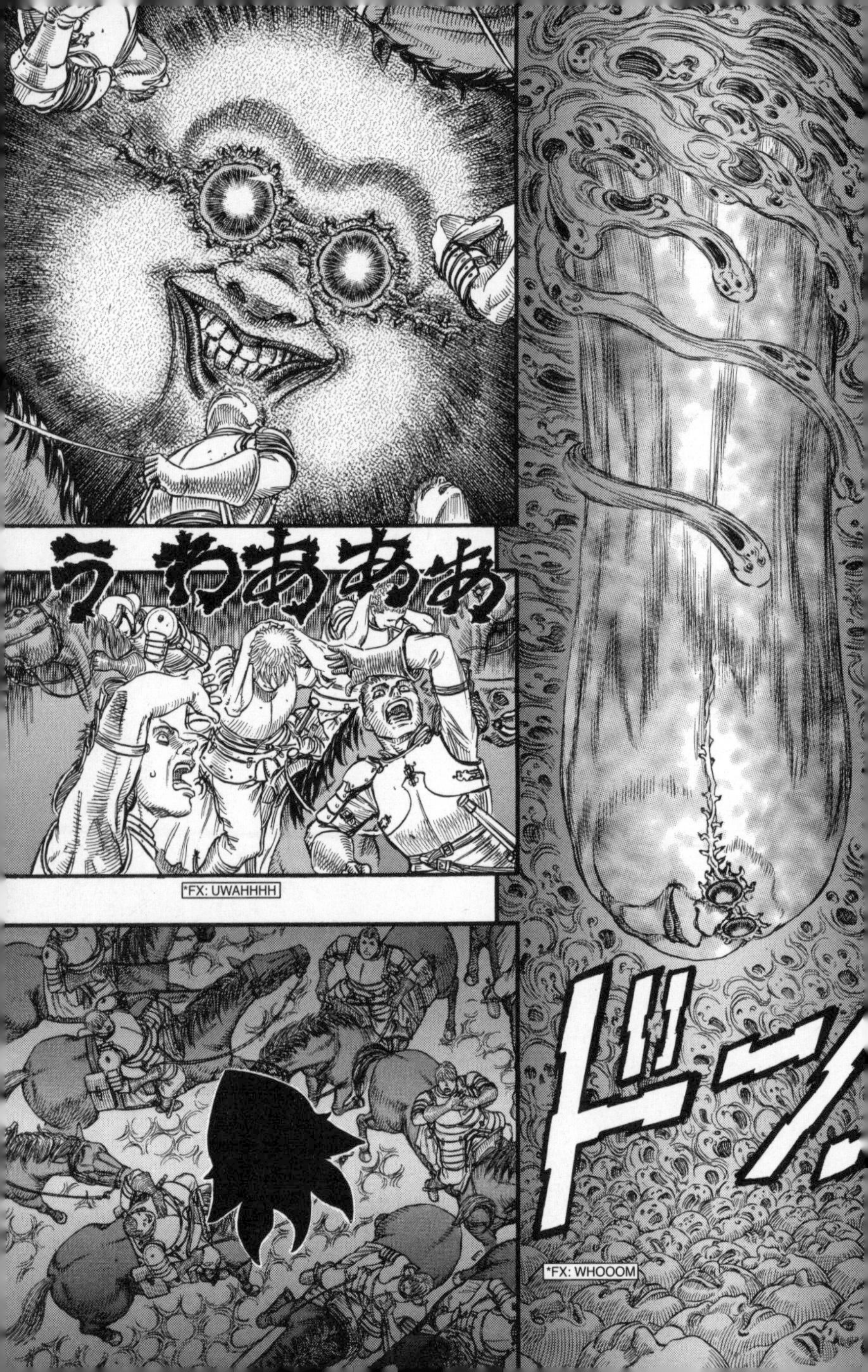
ドン
*FX: WHOOOM
うわあああ
*FX: UWAHHHH

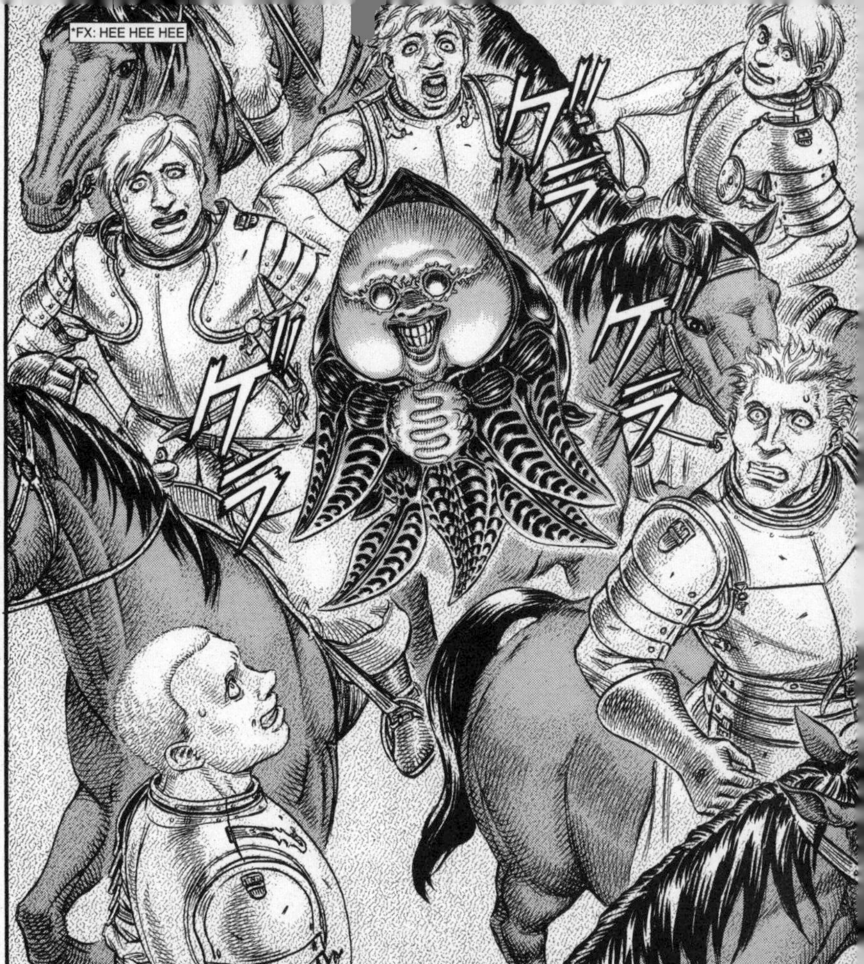
*FX: HEE HEE HEE
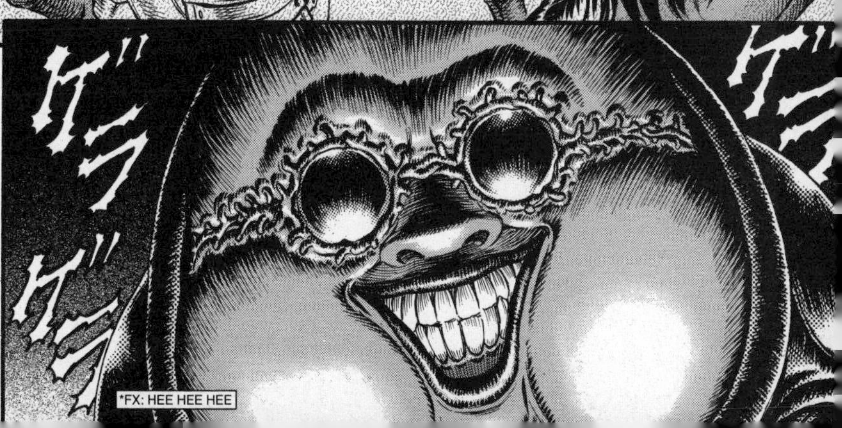
*FX: HEE HEE HEE

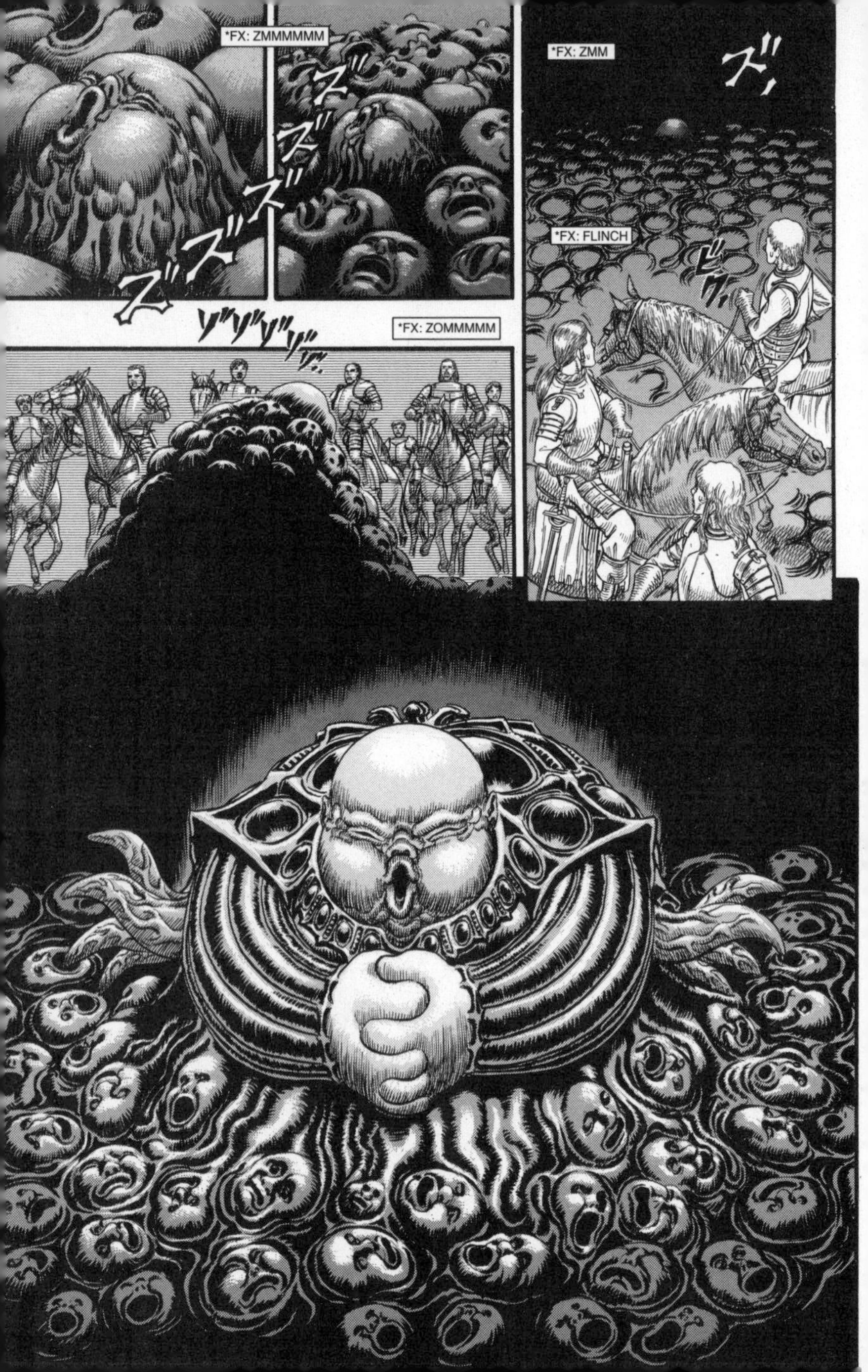
*FX: ZMM
*FX: FLINCH
*FX: ZMMMMMM
*FX: ZOMMMMM

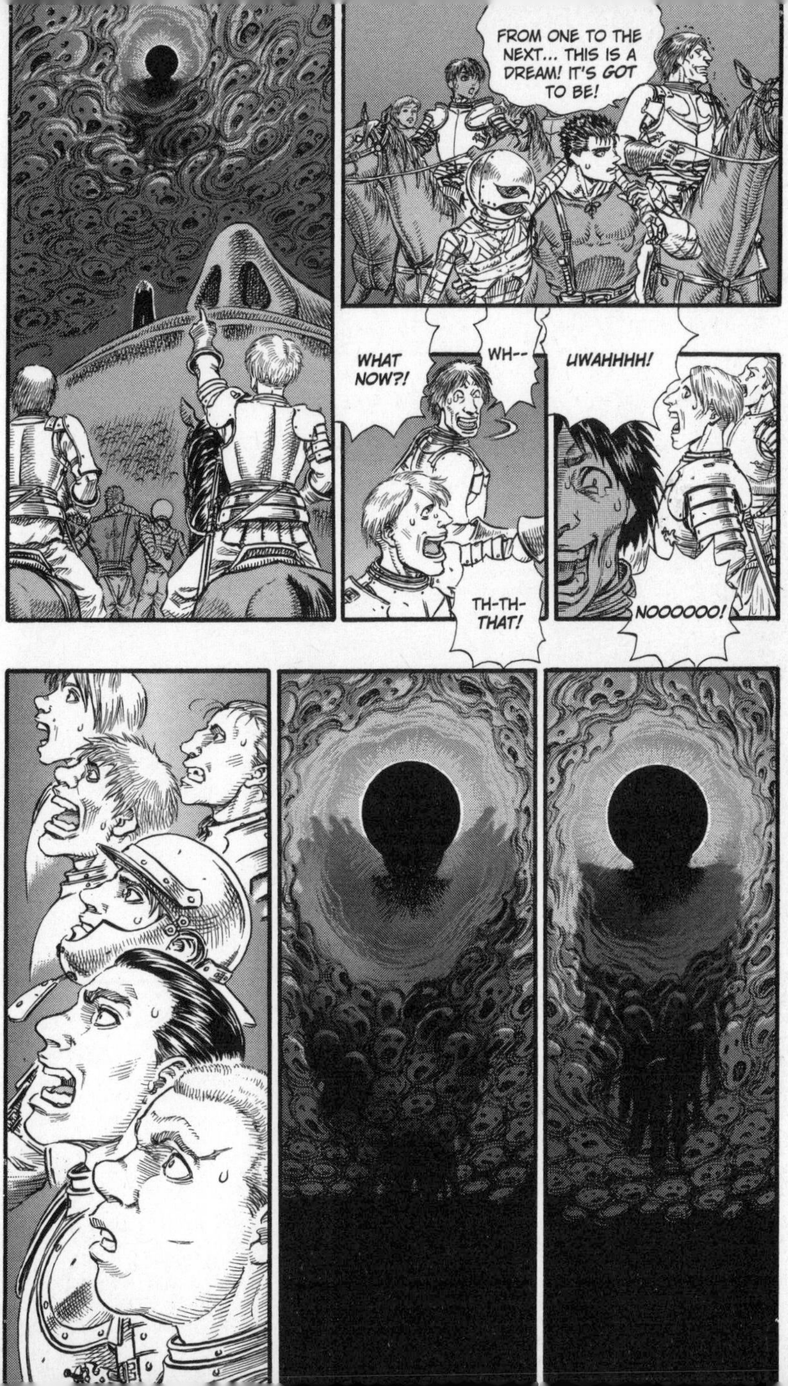
FROM ONE TO THE NEXT... THIS IS A DREAM! IT'S GOT TO BE!
UWAHHHH!
NOOOOOO!
WH--
WHAT NOW?!
TH-TH-THAT!

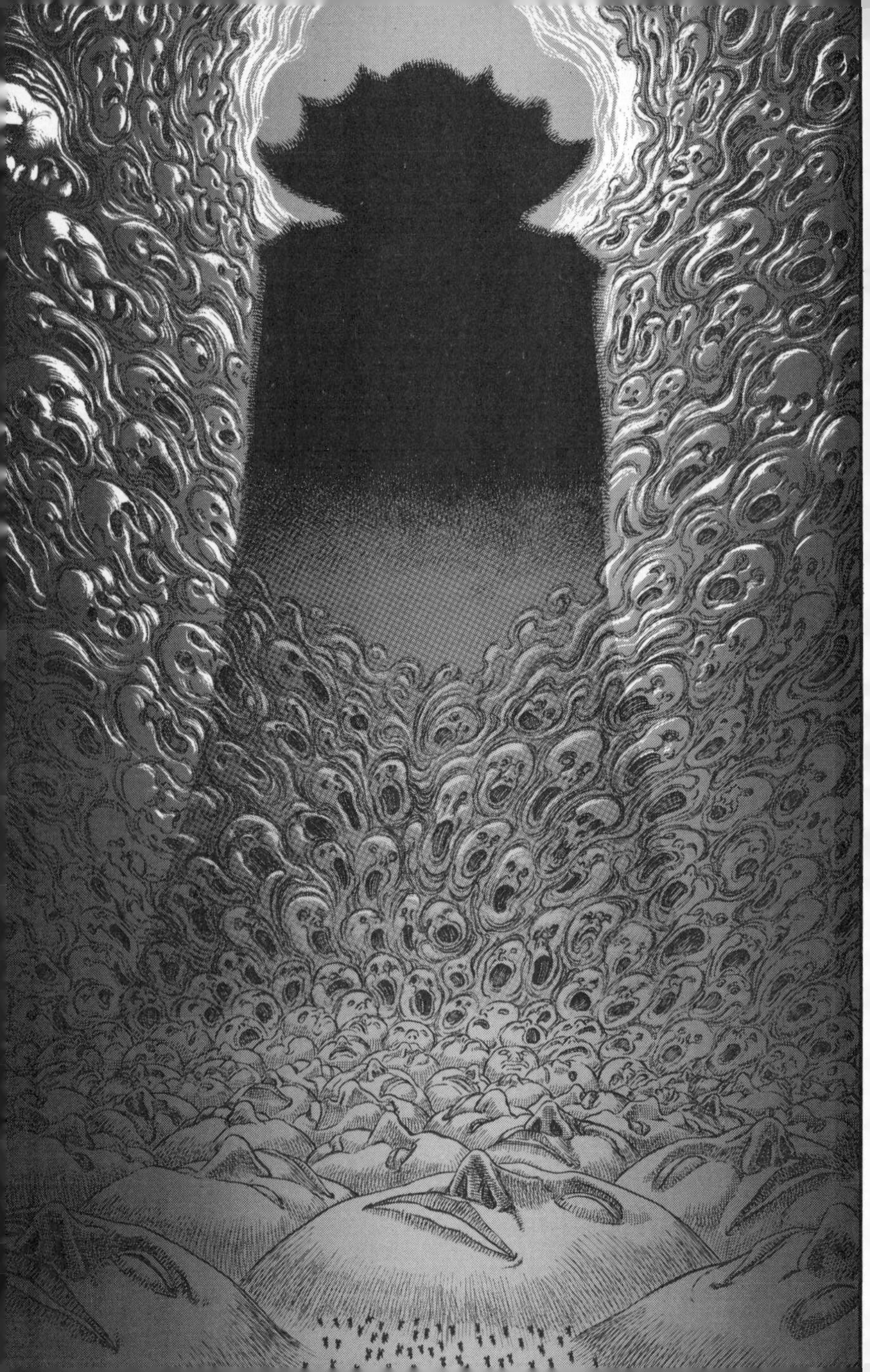

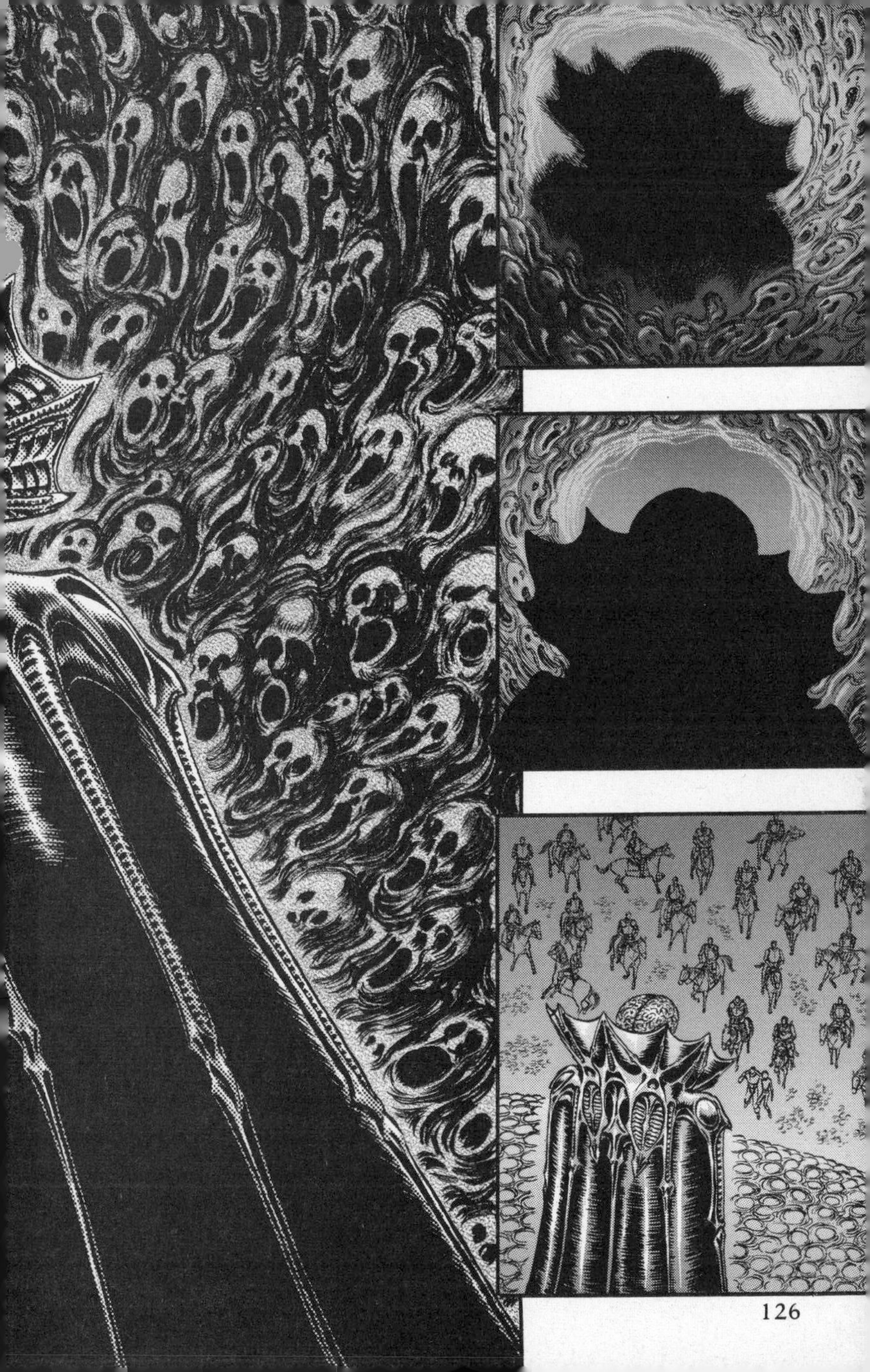

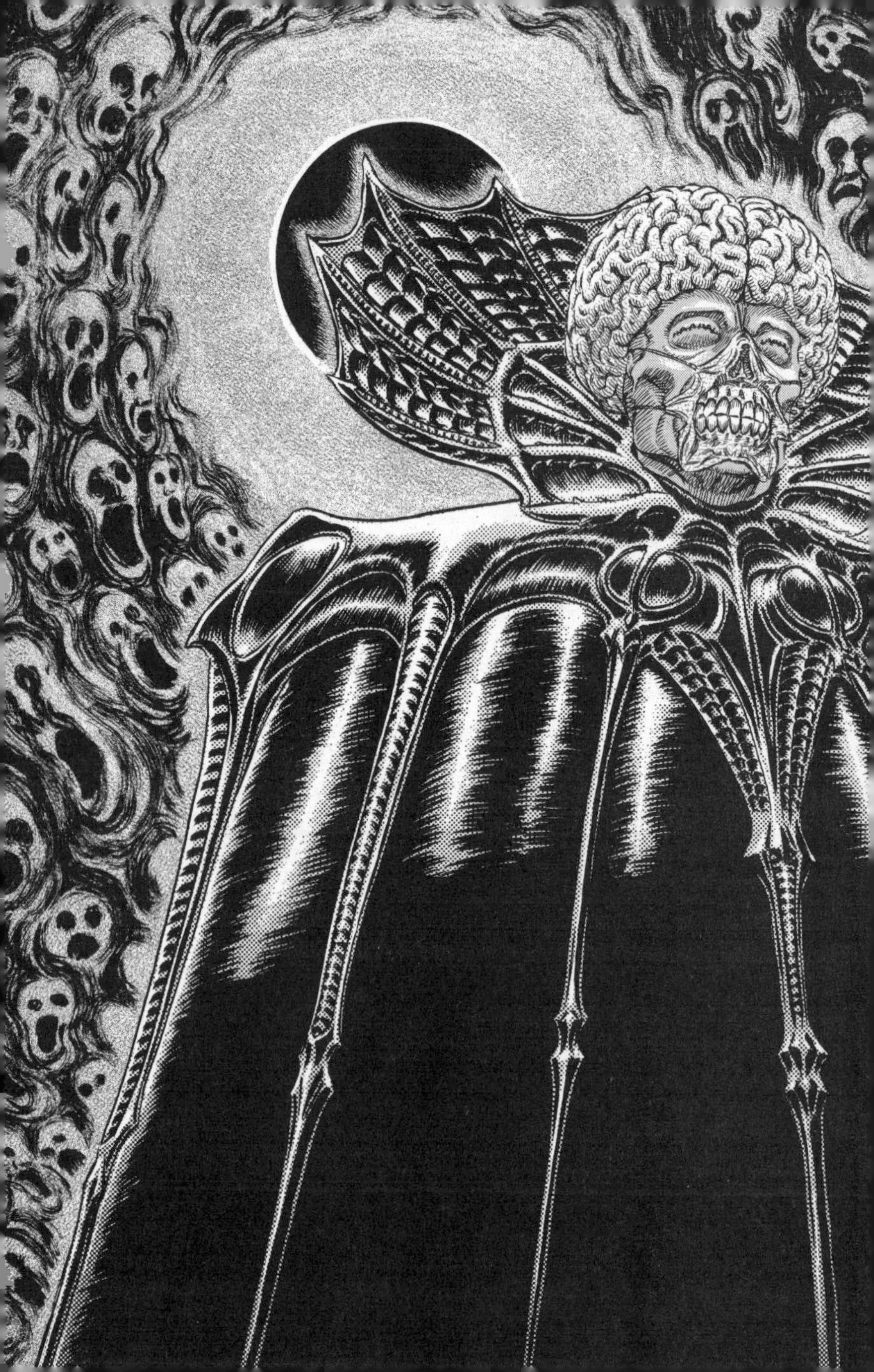

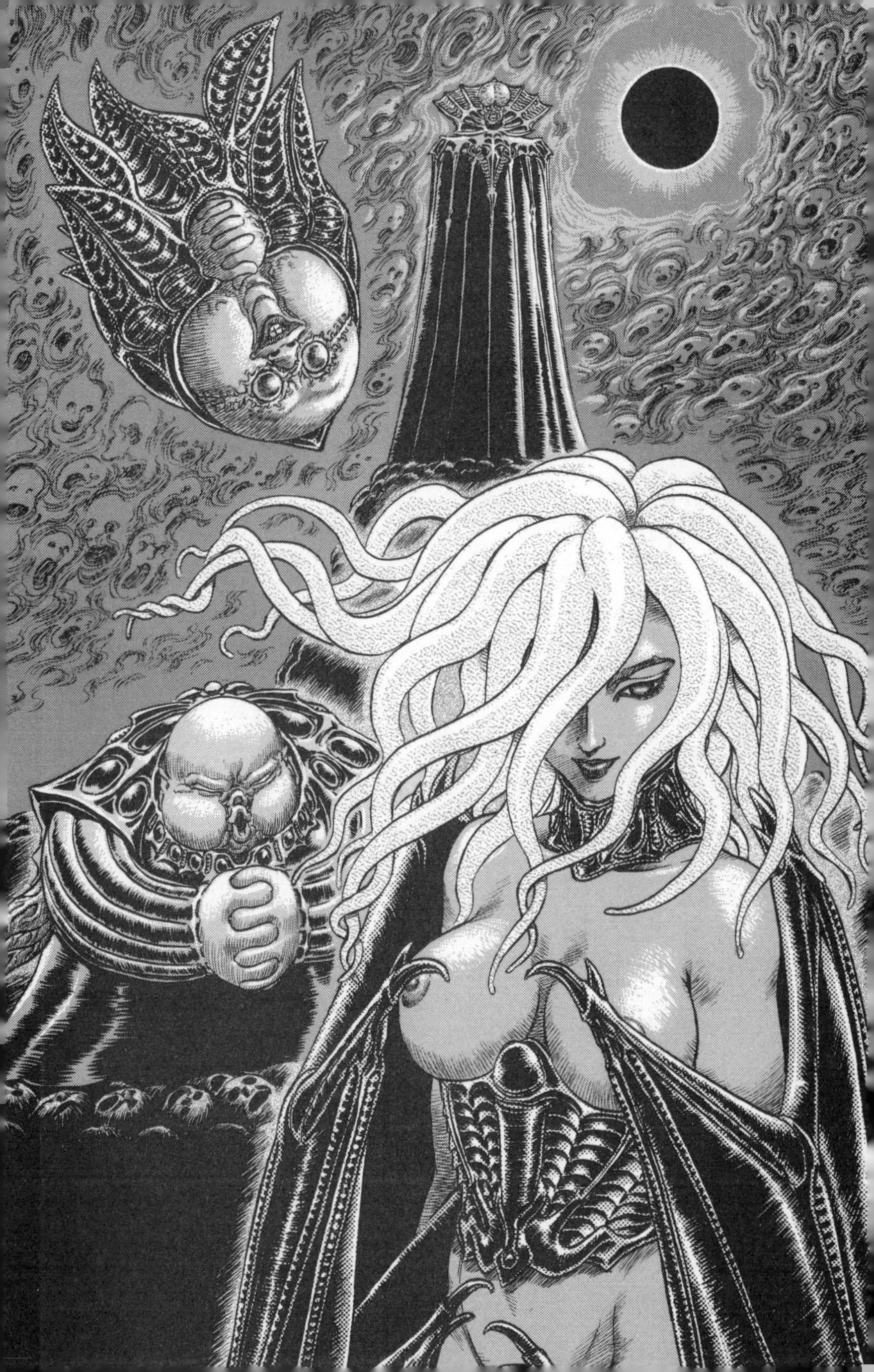

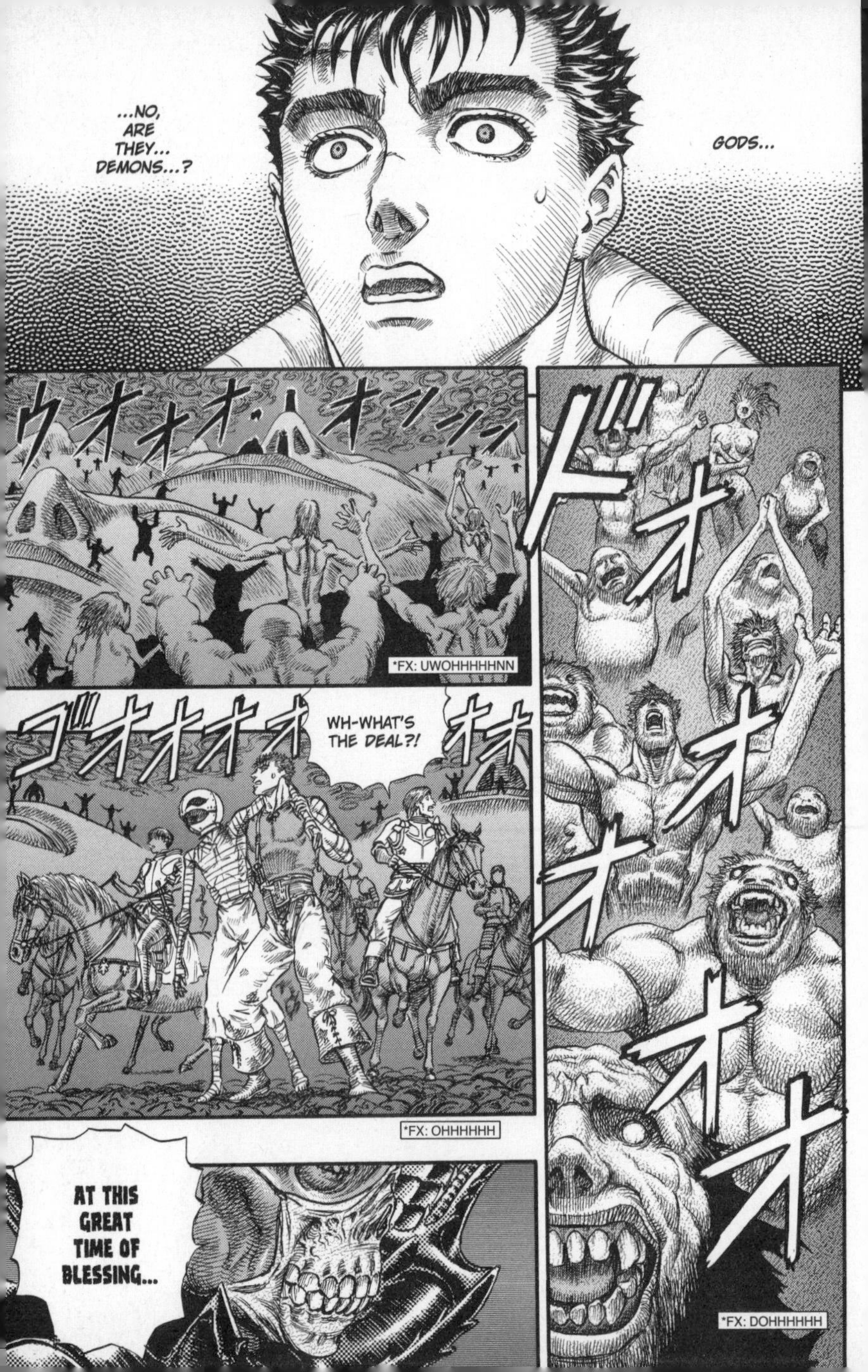
GODS...
...NO, ARE THEY... DEMONS...?
ドオオオ
*FX: DOHHHHHH
ウオオオ・オンンンン
*FX: UWOHHHHHNN
ゴオオオオオ
WH-WHAT'S THE DEAL?!
オオ
*FX: OHHHHHH
AT THIS GREAT TIME OF BLESSING...

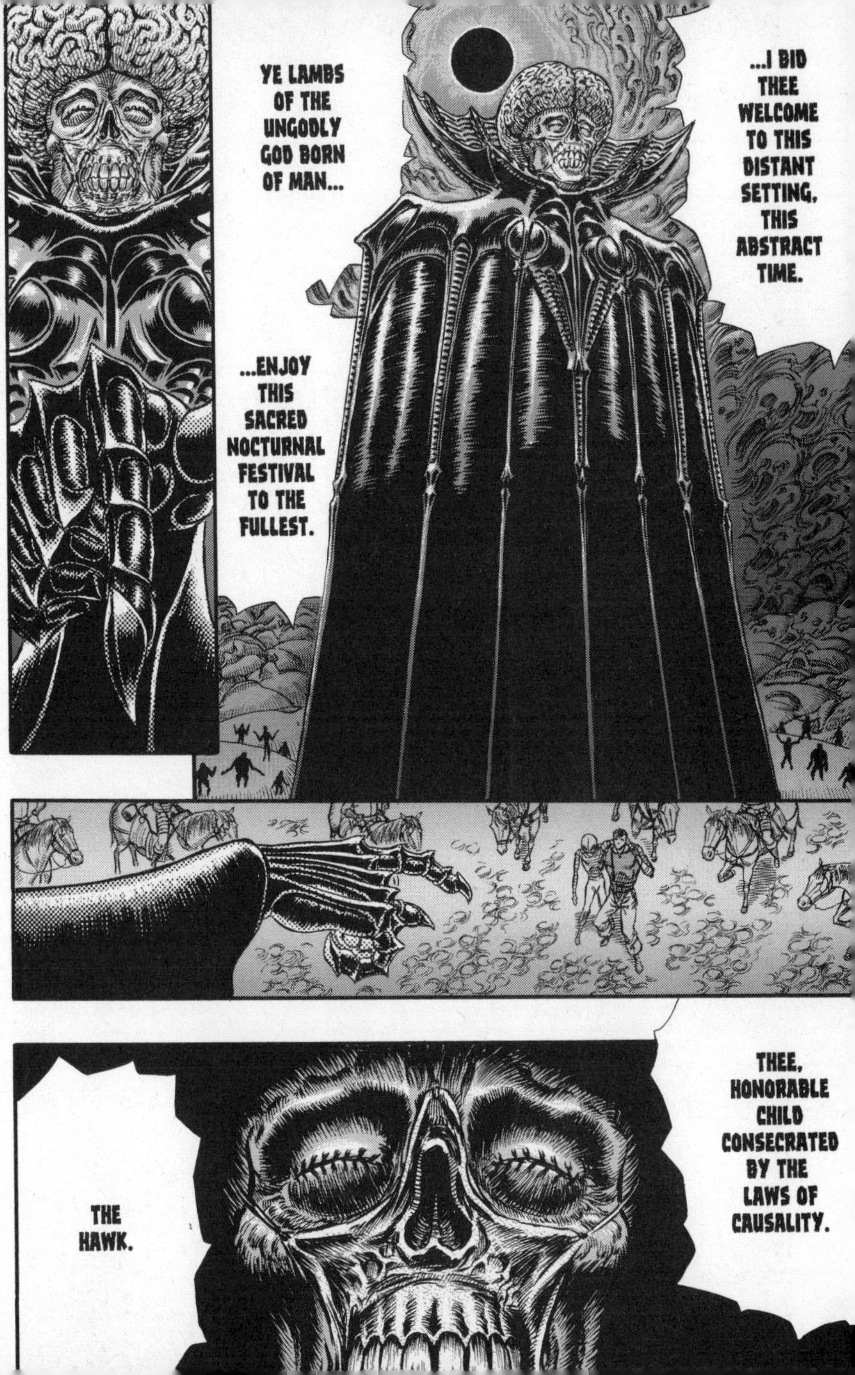
YE LAMBS OF THE UNGODLY GOD BORN OF MAN...
...I BID THEE WELCOME TO THIS DISTANT SETTING, THIS ABSTRACT TIME.
...ENJOY THIS SACRED NOCTURNAL FESTIVAL TO THE FULLEST.
THEE, HONORABLE CHILD CONSECRATED BY THE LAWS OF CAUSALITY.
THE HAWK.

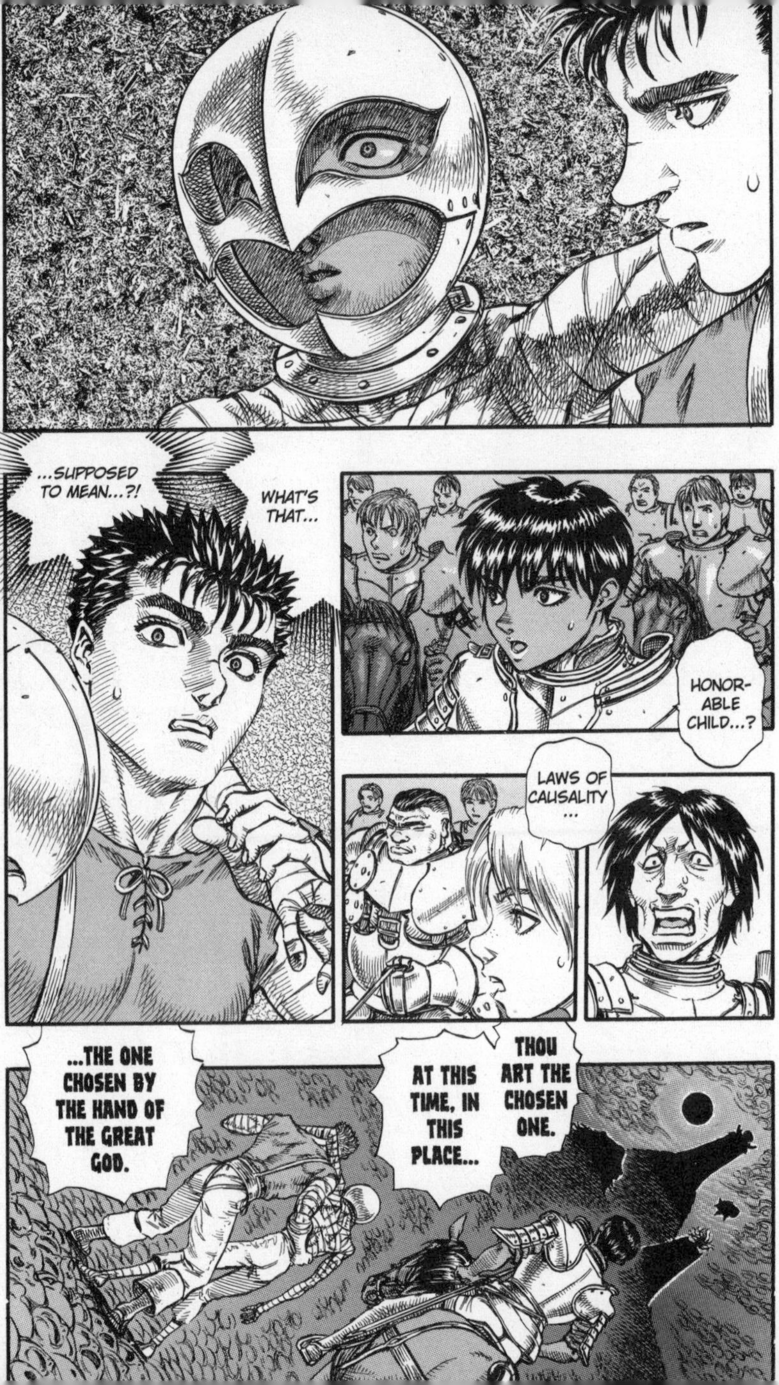
HONOR-ABLE CHILD...?
LAWS OF CAUSALITY ...
WHAT'S THAT...
...SUPPOSED TO MEAN...?!
THOU ART THE CHOSEN ONE.
AT THIS TIME, IN THIS PLACE...
...THE ONE CHOSEN BY THE HAND OF THE GREAT GOD.

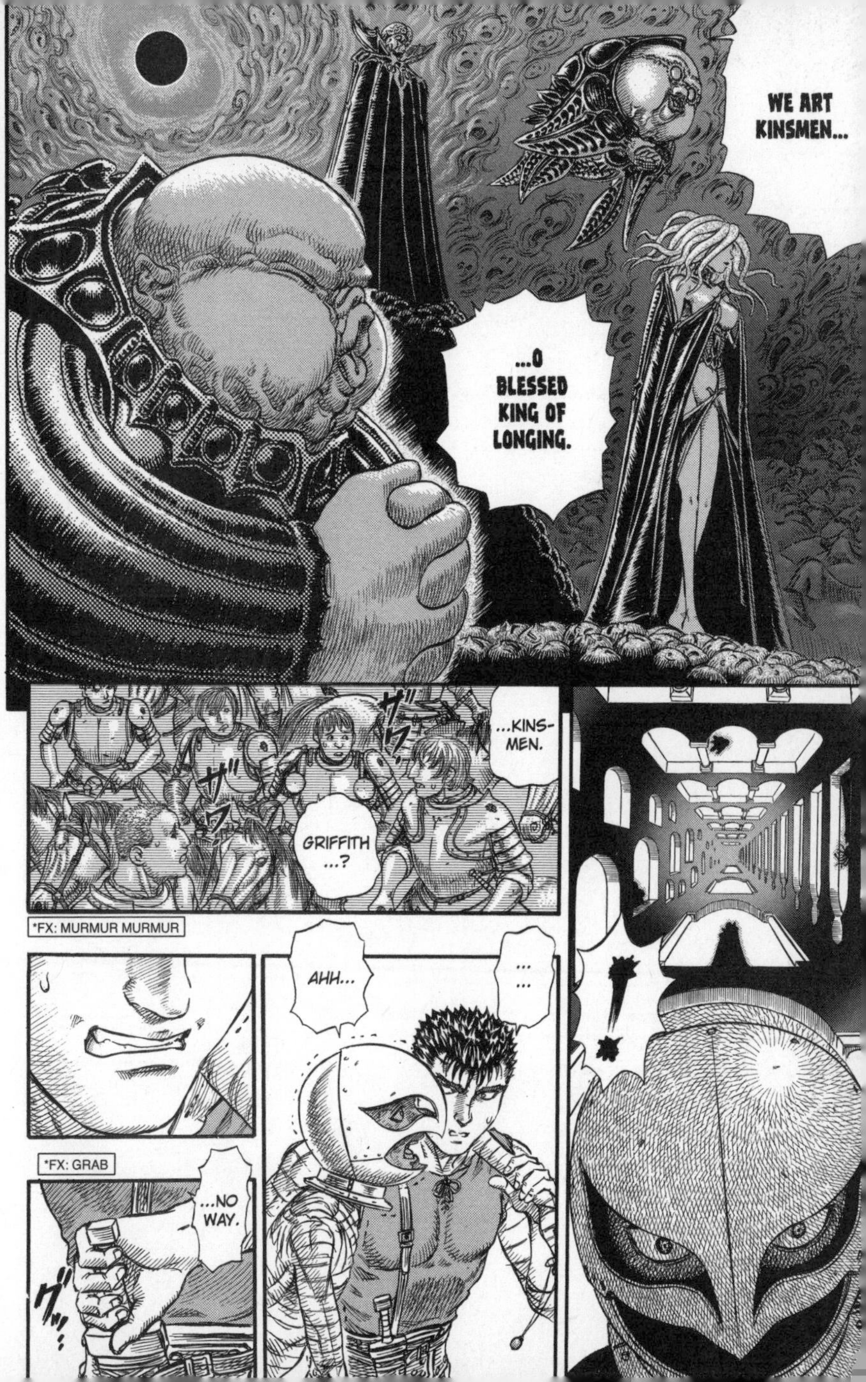
WE ART KINSMEN...
...O BLESSED KING OF LONGING.
...KINSMEN.
GRIFFITH ...?
*FX: MURMUR MURMUR
!!
... ...
AHH...
...NO WAY.
*FX: GRAB

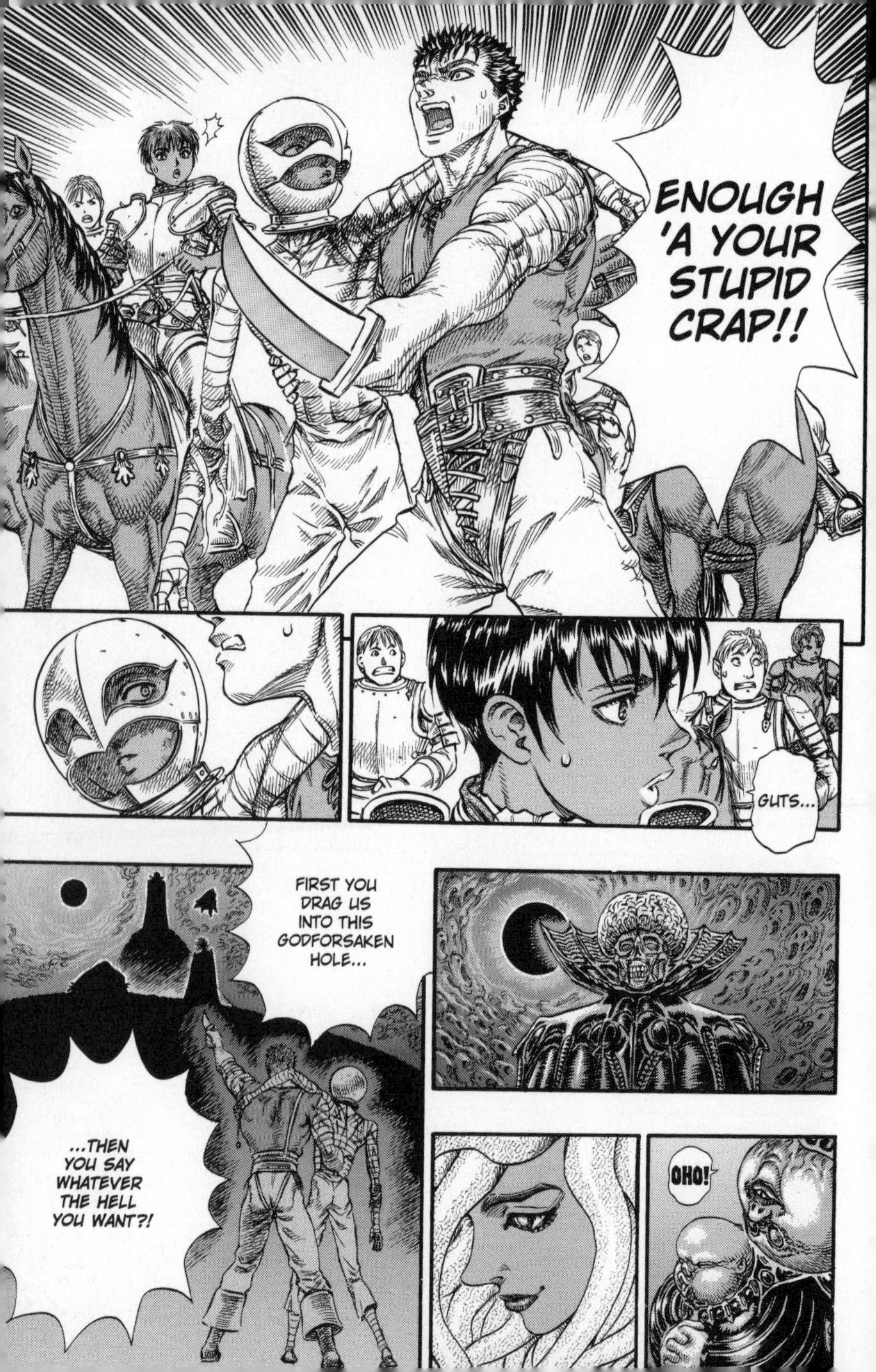
ENOUGH 'A YOUR STUPID CRAP!!
GUTS...
OHO!
FIRST YOU DRAG US INTO THIS GODFORSAKEN HOLE...
...THEN YOU SAY WHATEVER THE HELL YOU WANT?!

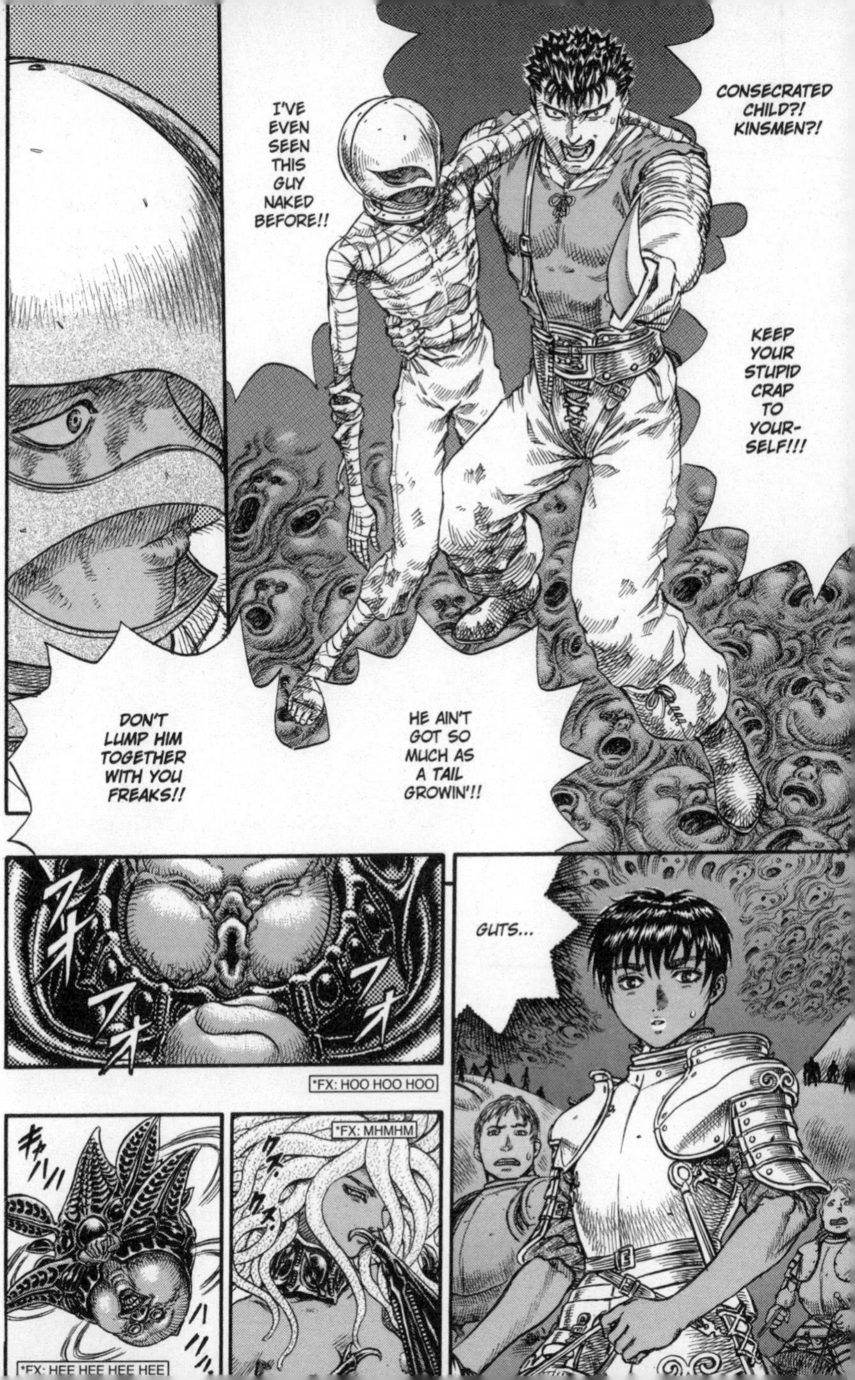

CONSECRATED CHILD?! KINSMEN?!
KEEP YOUR STUPID CRAP TO YOUR-SELF!!!
I'VE EVEN SEEN THIS GUY NAKED BEFORE!!
HE AIN'T GOT SO MUCH AS A TAIL GROWIN'!!
DON'T LUMP HIM TOGETHER WITH YOU FREAKS!!
GUTS...
*FX: HOO HOO HOO
*FX: MHMHM
*FX: HEE HEE HEE HEE

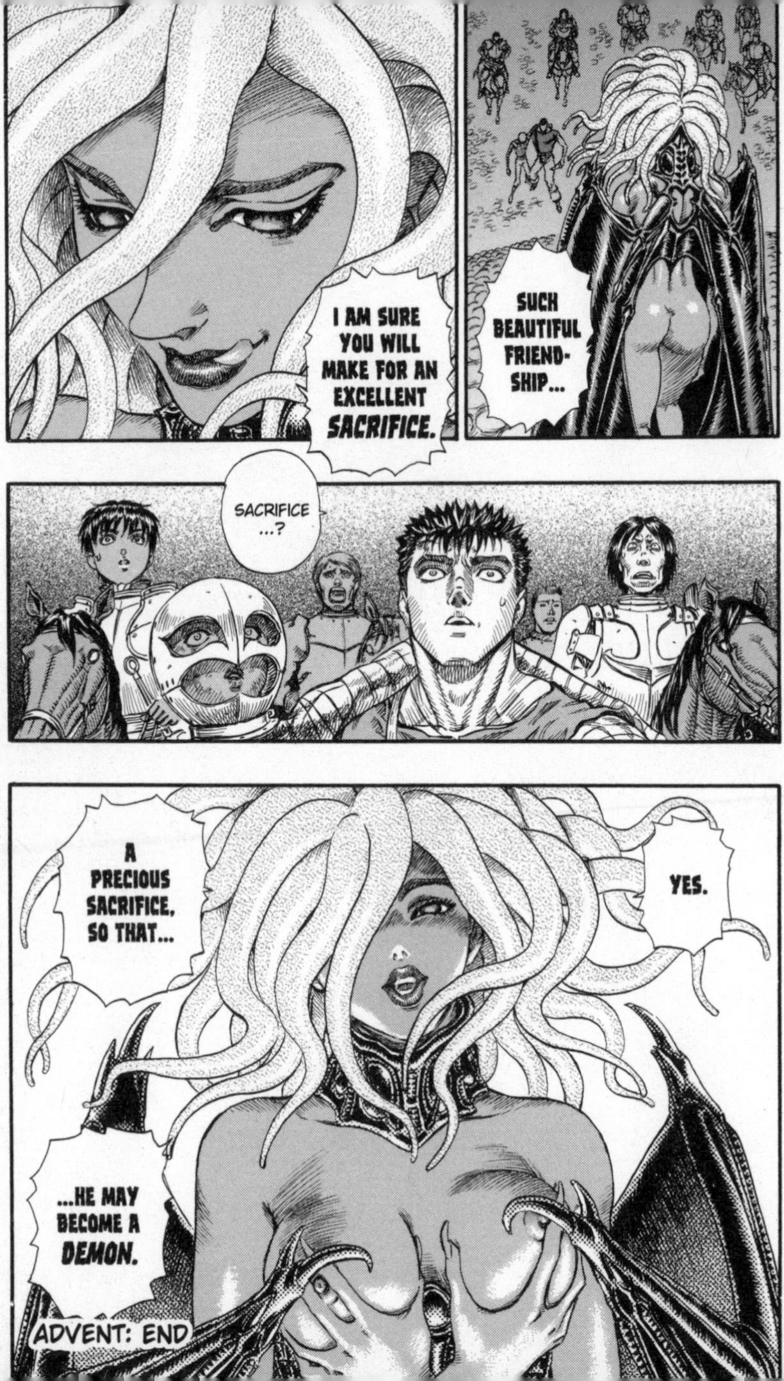
SUCH BEAUTIFUL FRIEND-SHIP...
I AM SURE YOU WILL MAKE FOR AN EXCELLENT SACRIFICE.
SACRIFICE ...?
YES.
A PRECIOUS SACRIFICE, SO THAT...
...HE MAY BECOME A DEMON.
ADVENT: END

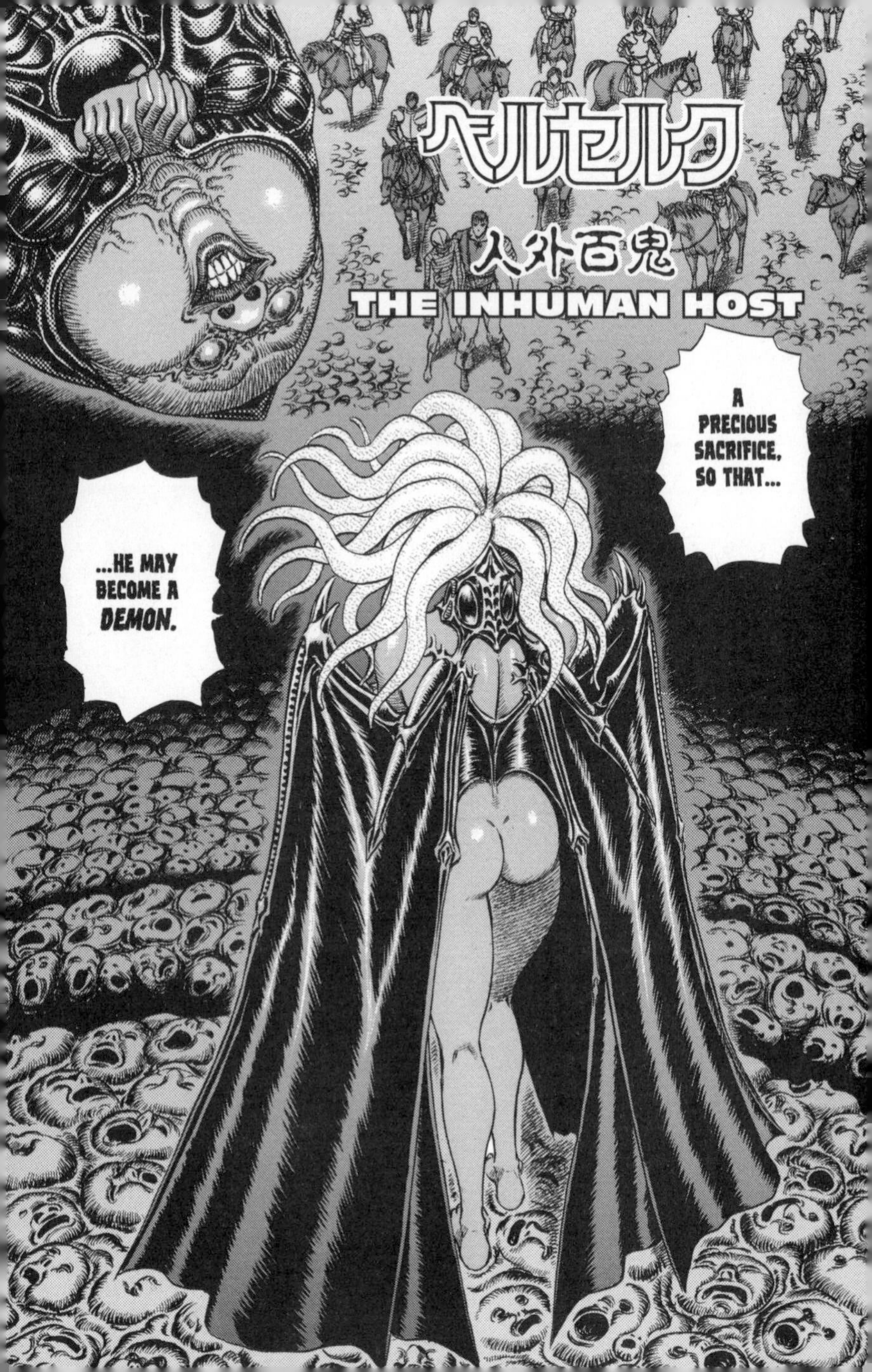
ベルセルク
人外百鬼
THE INHUMAN HOST
A PRECIOUS SACRIFICE, SO THAT...
...HE MAY BECOME A DEMON.

A SACRIFICE ...?

...DEMON ...

FROM THE MOMENT YOU TOOK POSSESSION OF THAT *CRIMSON BEHELIT*, YOU HAD THE QUALITIES TO BECOME A DEMON.

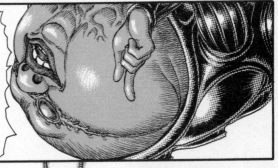

...
...!!

!

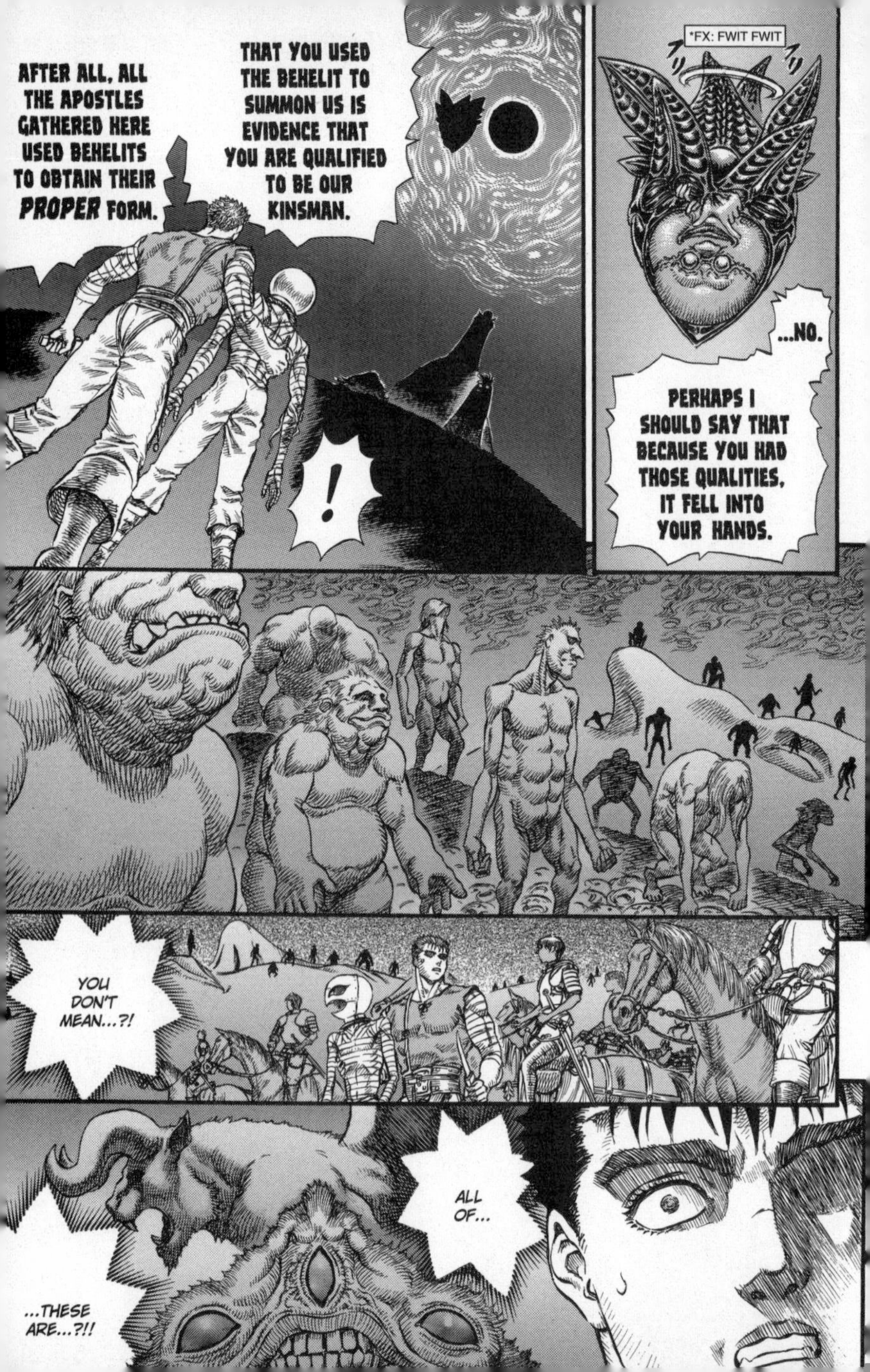
AFTER ALL, ALL THE APOSTLES GATHERED HERE USED BEHELITS TO OBTAIN THEIR *PROPER* FORM.
THAT YOU USED THE BEHELIT TO SUMMON US IS EVIDENCE THAT YOU ARE QUALIFIED TO BE OUR KINSMAN.
!
*FX: FWIT FWIT
...NO.
PERHAPS I SHOULD SAY THAT BECAUSE YOU HAD THOSE QUALITIES, IT FELL INTO YOUR HANDS.
YOU DON'T MEAN...?!
ALL OF...
...THESE ARE...?!!

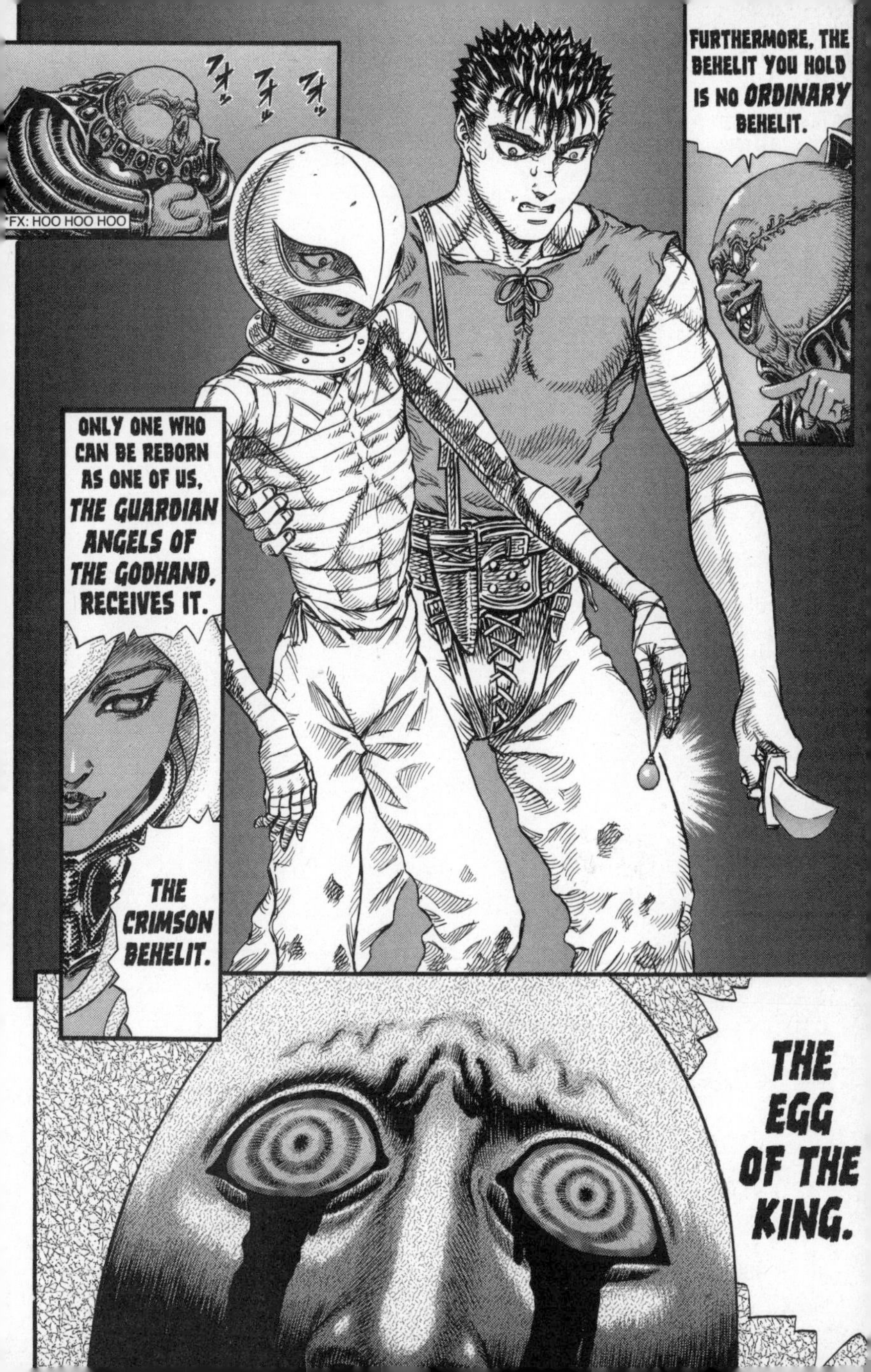
FURTHERMORE, THE BEHELIT YOU HOLD IS NO *ORDINARY* BEHELIT.
FX: HOO HOO HOO
ONLY ONE WHO CAN BE REBORN AS ONE OF US, *THE GUARDIAN ANGELS OF THE GODHAND,* RECEIVES IT.
THE CRIMSON BEHELIT.
THE EGG OF THE KING.

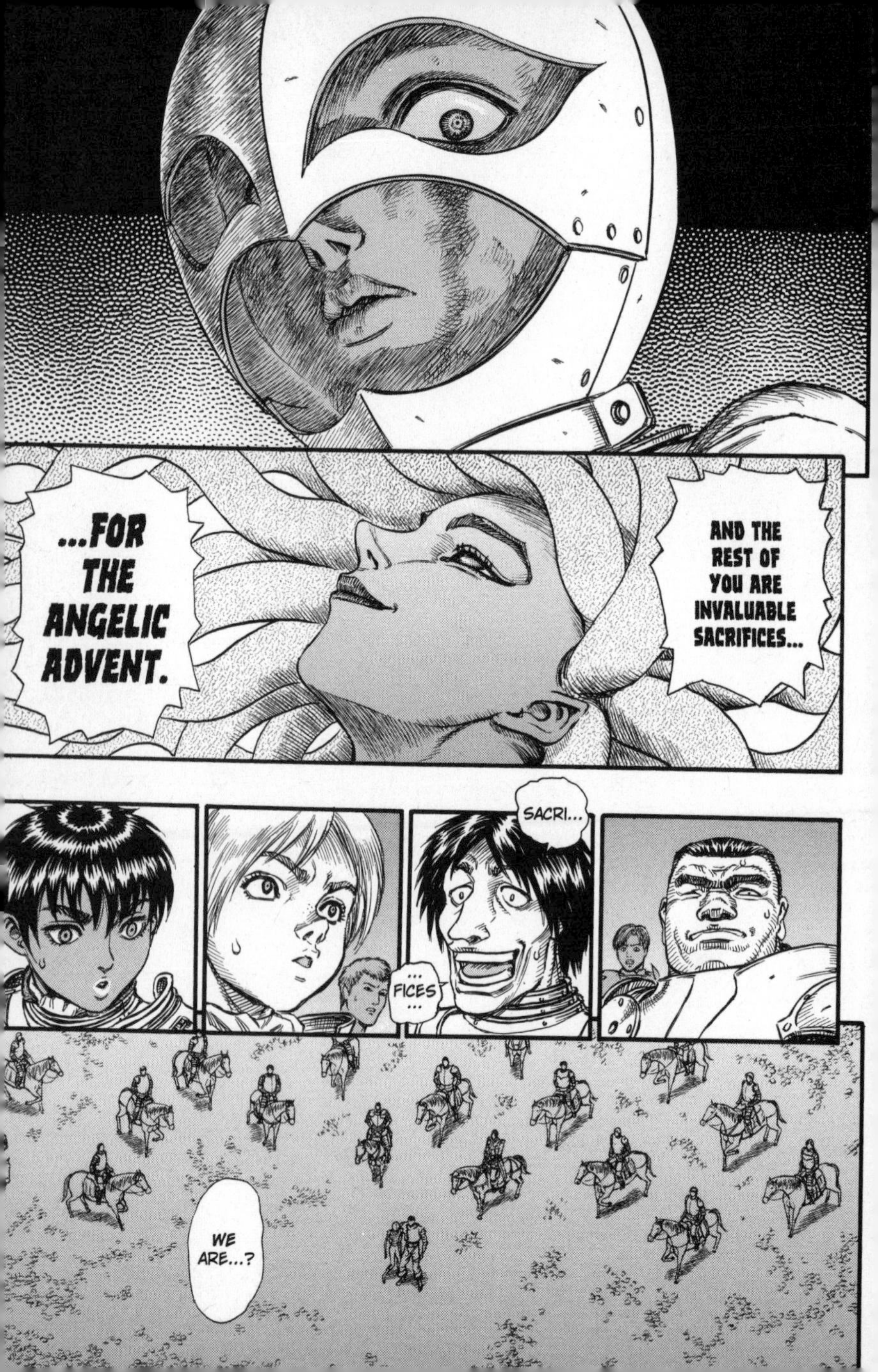
AND THE REST OF YOU ARE INVALUABLE SACRIFICES...
...FOR THE ANGELIC ADVENT.
SACRI...
...FICES...
WE ARE...?

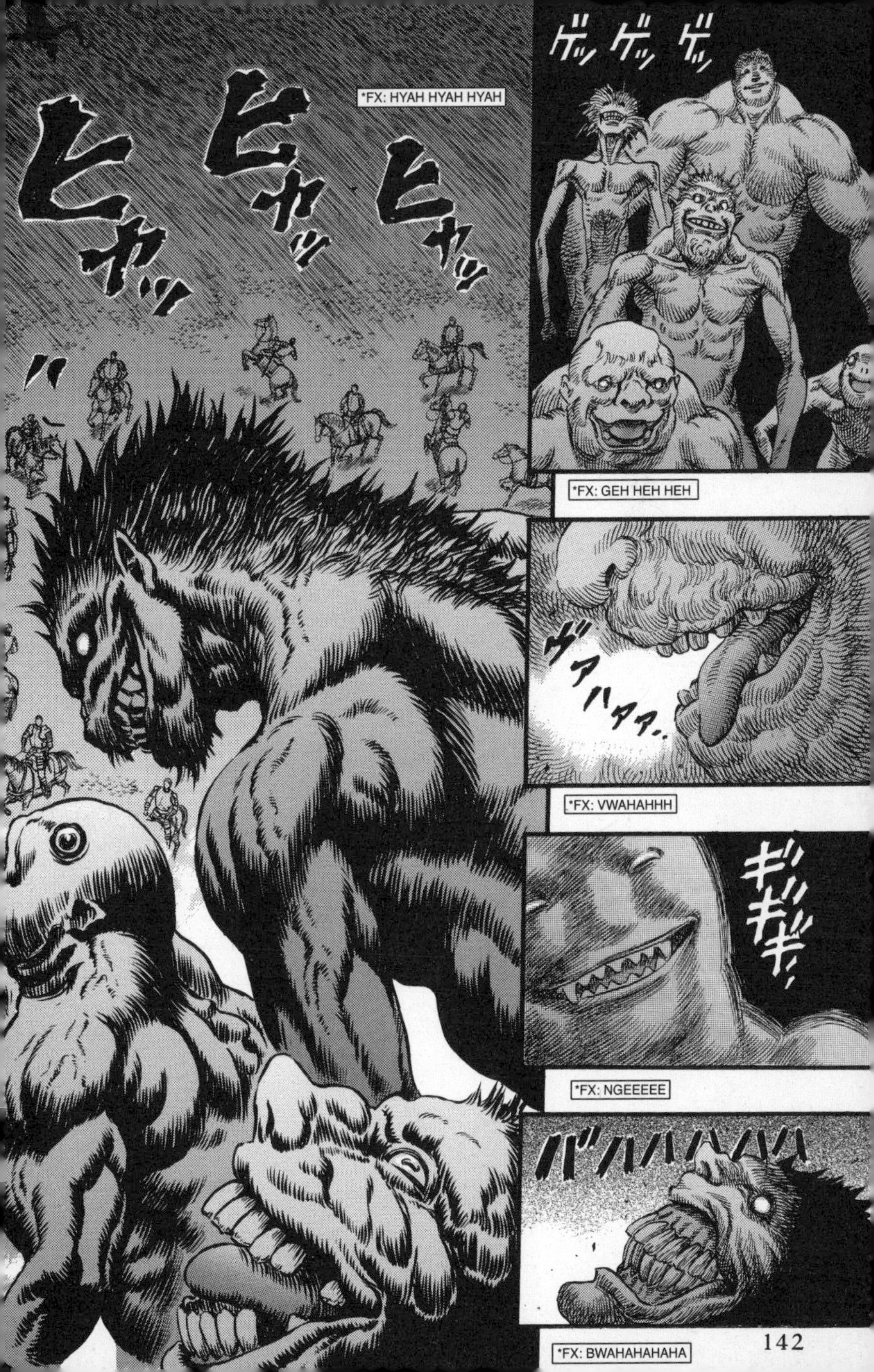
*FX: GEH HEH HEH
*FX: VWAHAHHH
*FX: NGEEEEE
*FX: BWAHAHAHAHA
*FX: HYAH HYAH HYAH

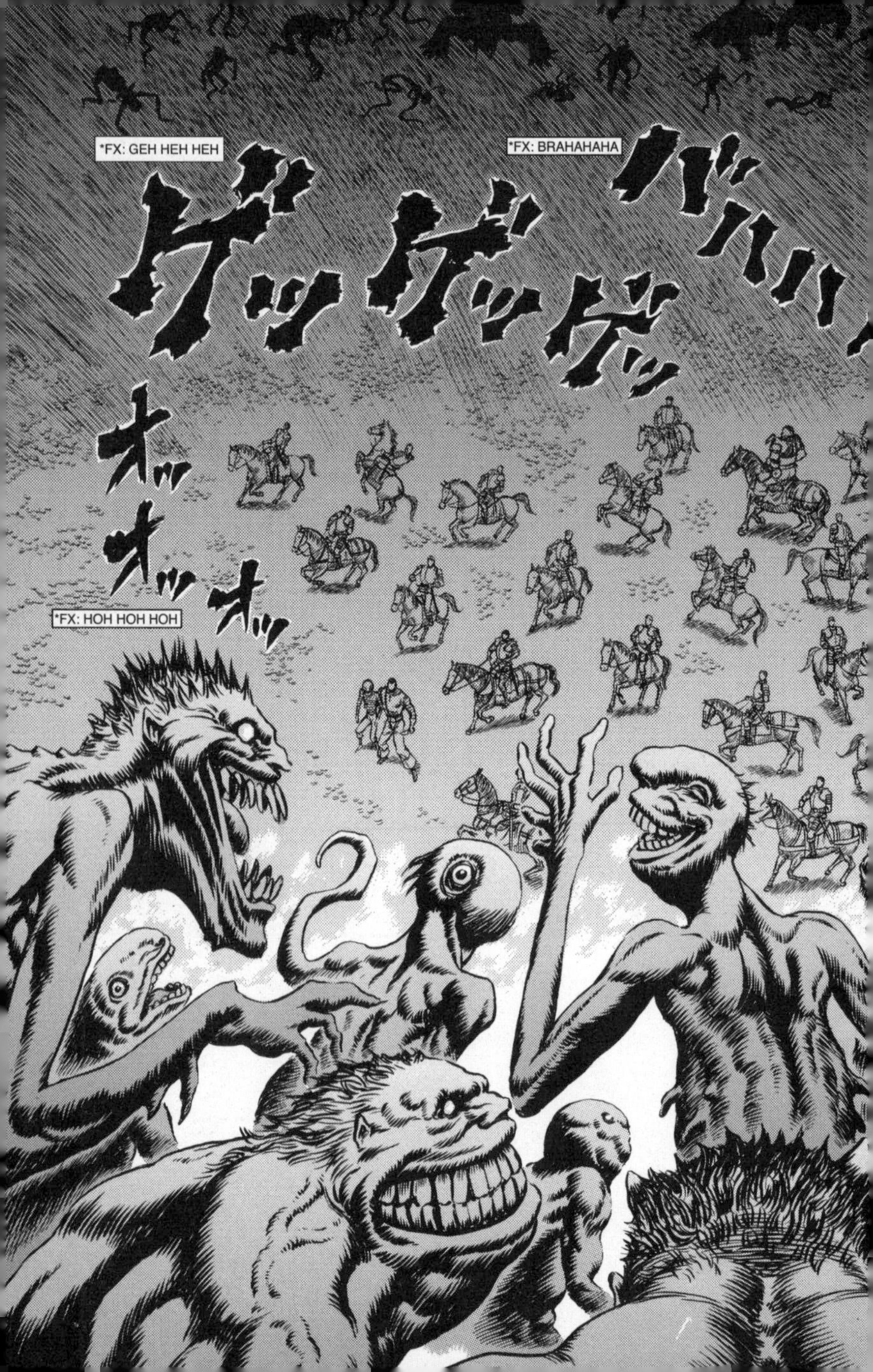
*FX: BRAHAHAHA
*FX: GEH HEH HEH
*FX: HOH HOH HOH

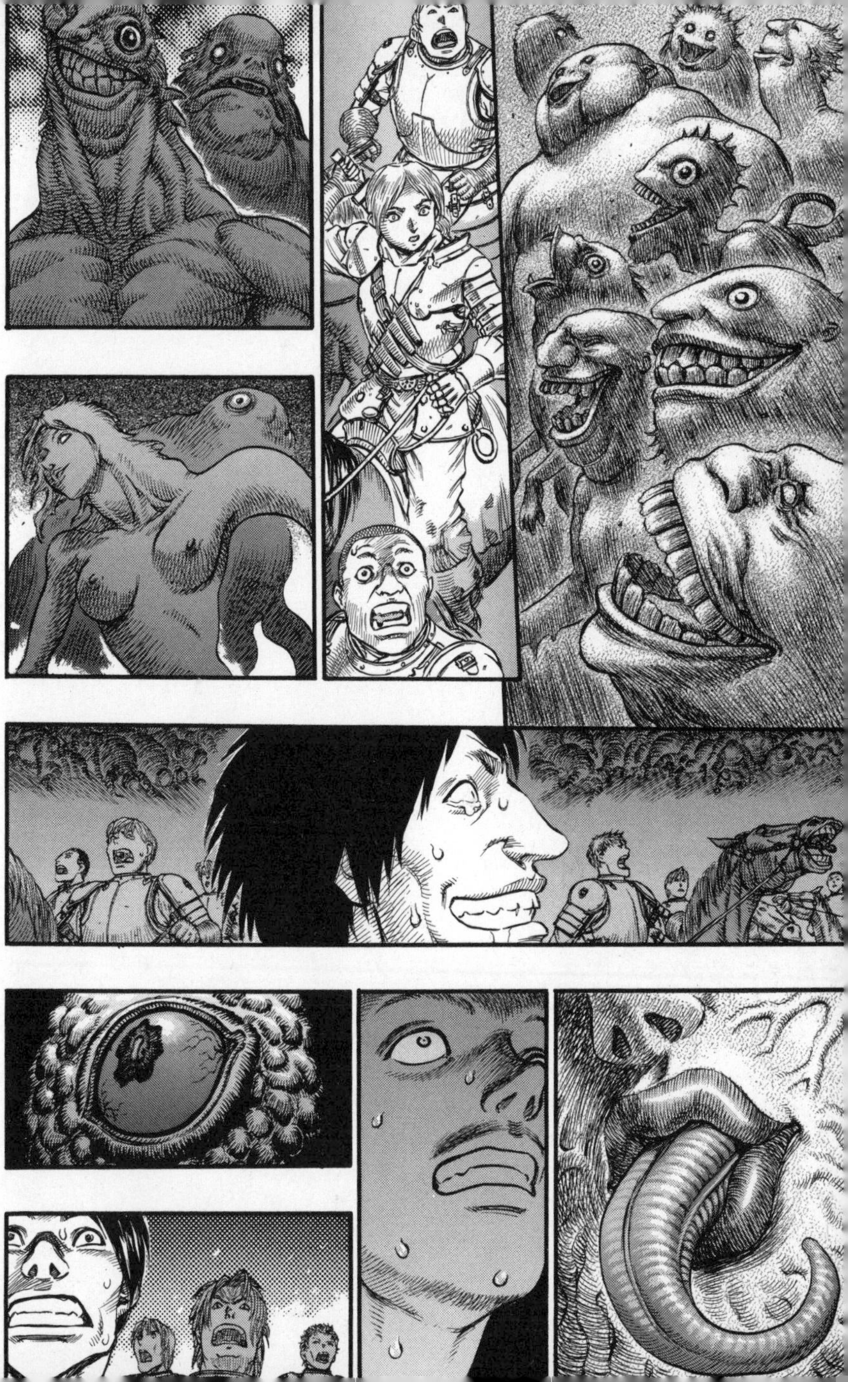

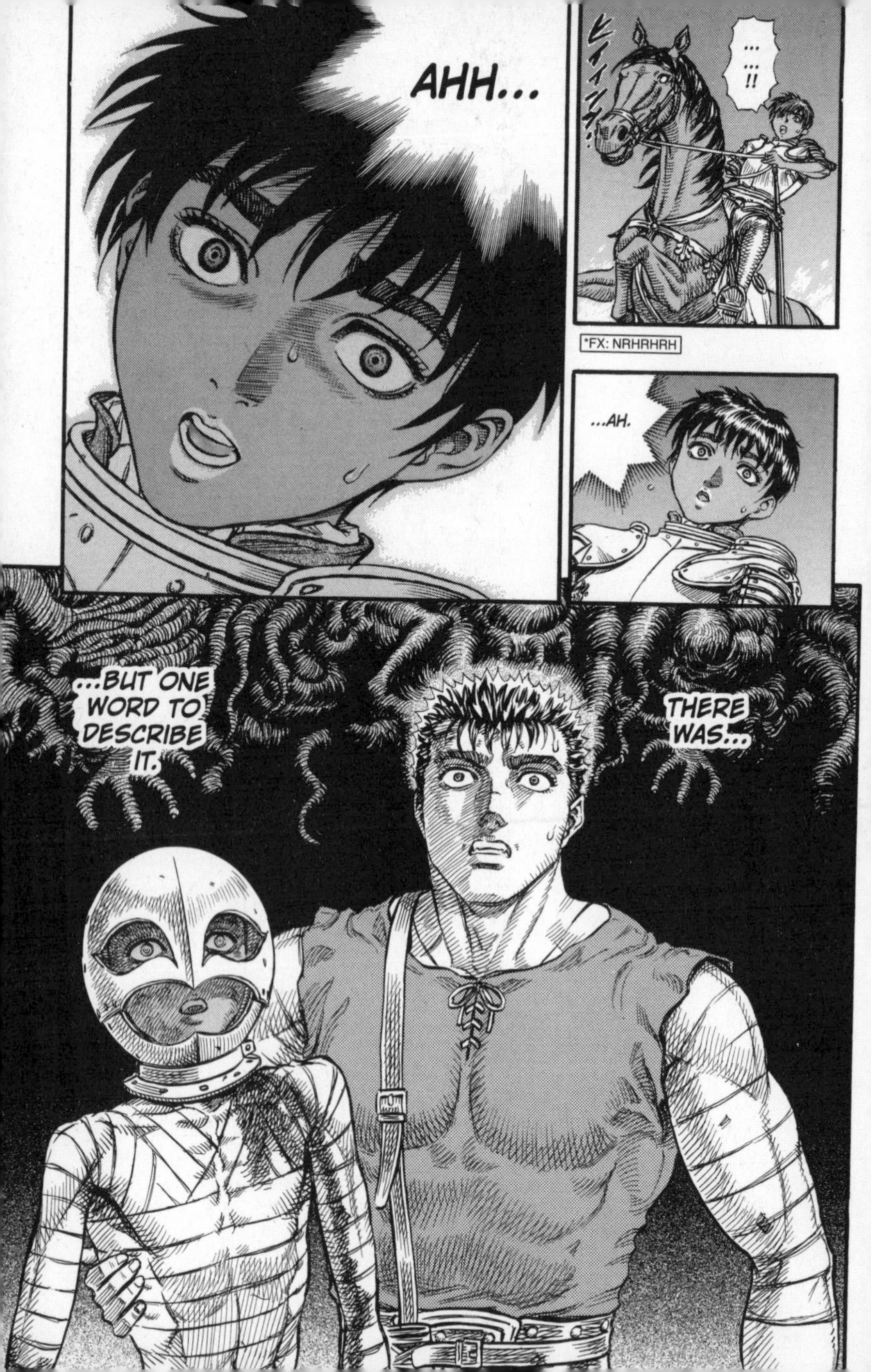

... ... !!
*FX: NRHRHRH
...AH.
AHH...
THERE WAS...
...BUT ONE WORD TO DESCRIBE IT.

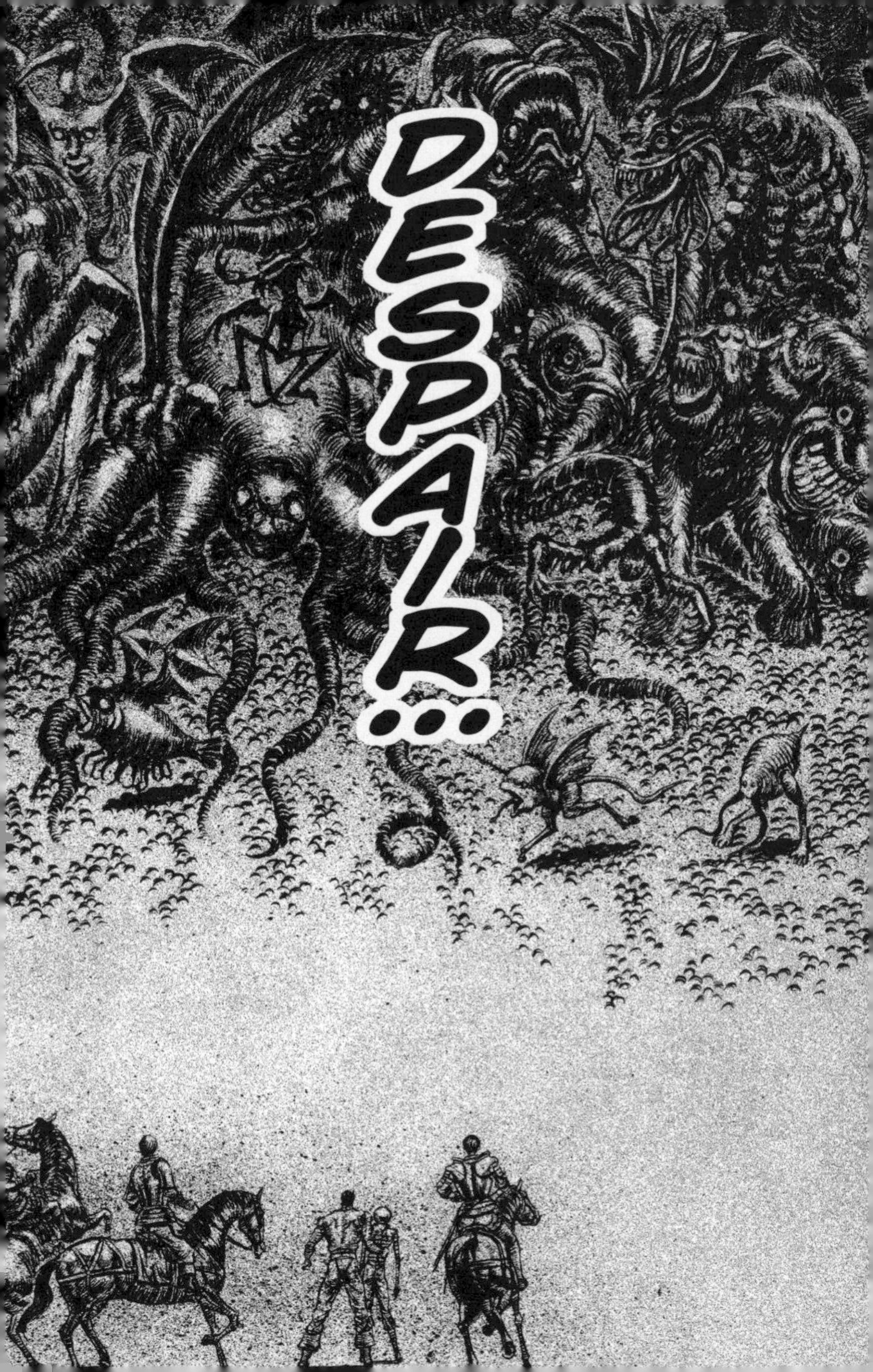
DESPAIR...

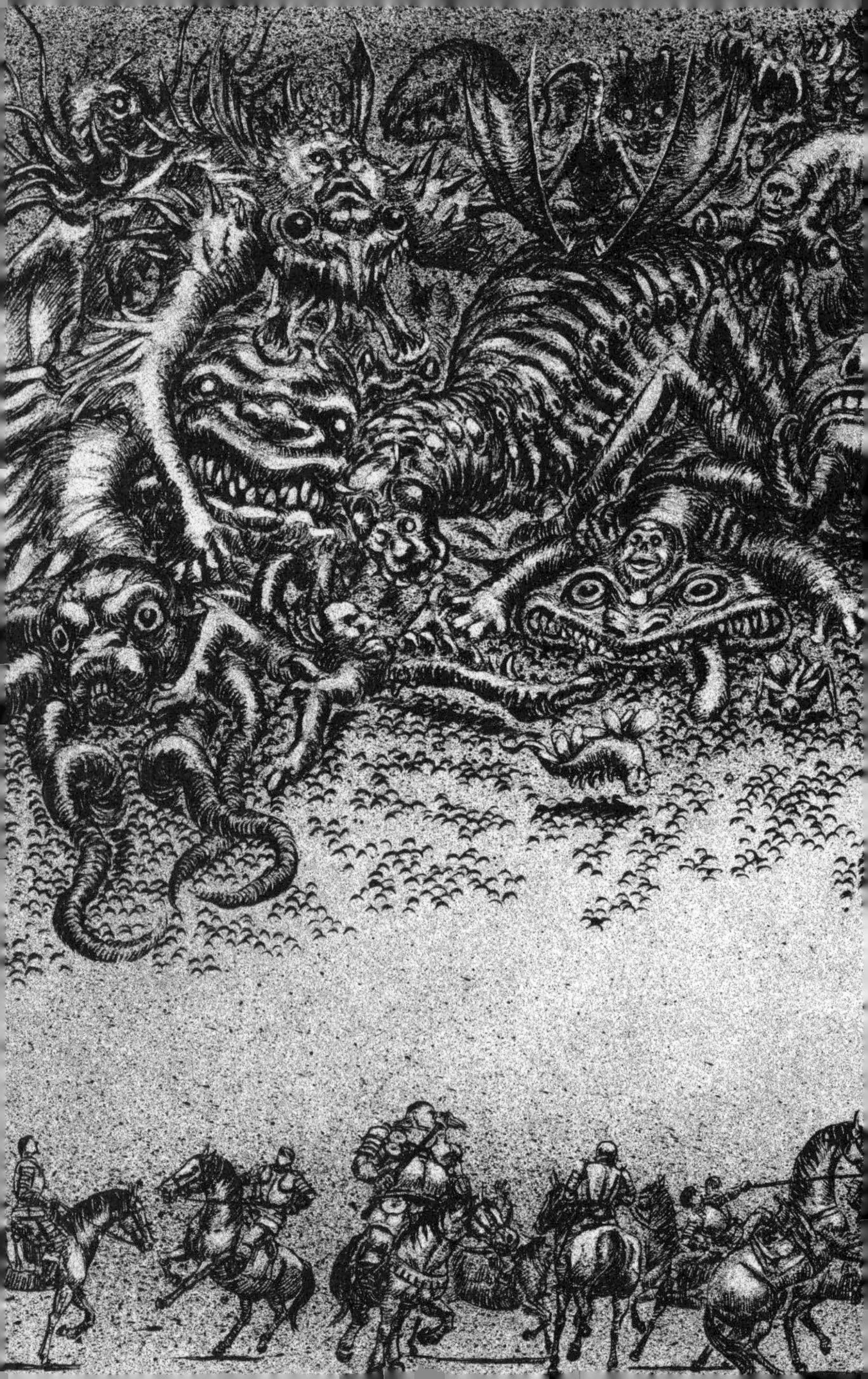

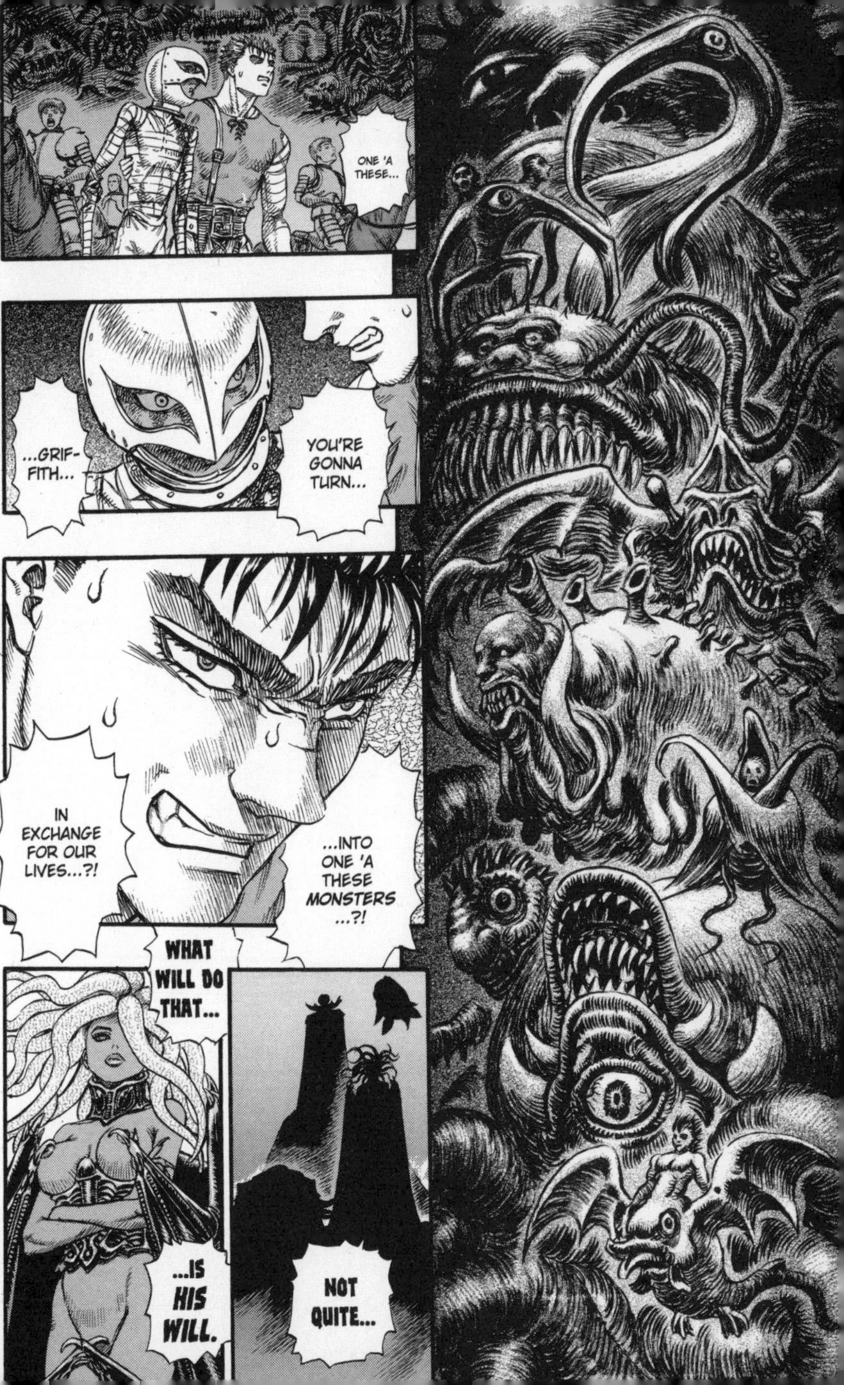

ONE 'A THESE...
YOU'RE GONNA TURN...
...GRIF-FITH...
...INTO ONE 'A THESE MONSTERS ...?!
IN EXCHANGE FOR OUR LIVES...?!
NOT QUITE...
WHAT WILL DO THAT...
...IS HIS WILL.

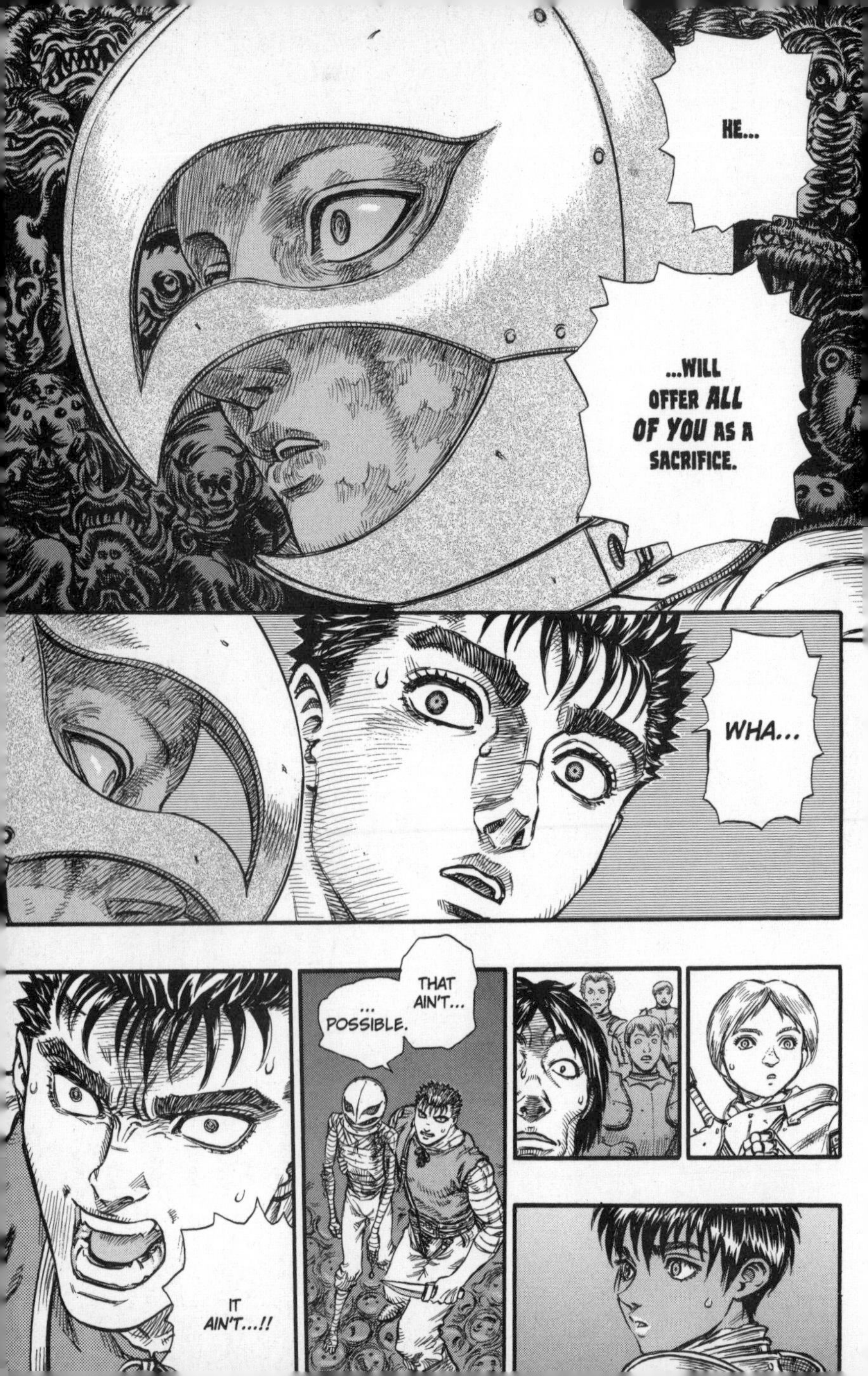
HE...
...WILL OFFER ALL OF YOU AS A SACRIFICE.
WHA...
THAT AIN'T...
... POSSIBLE.
IT AIN'T...!!

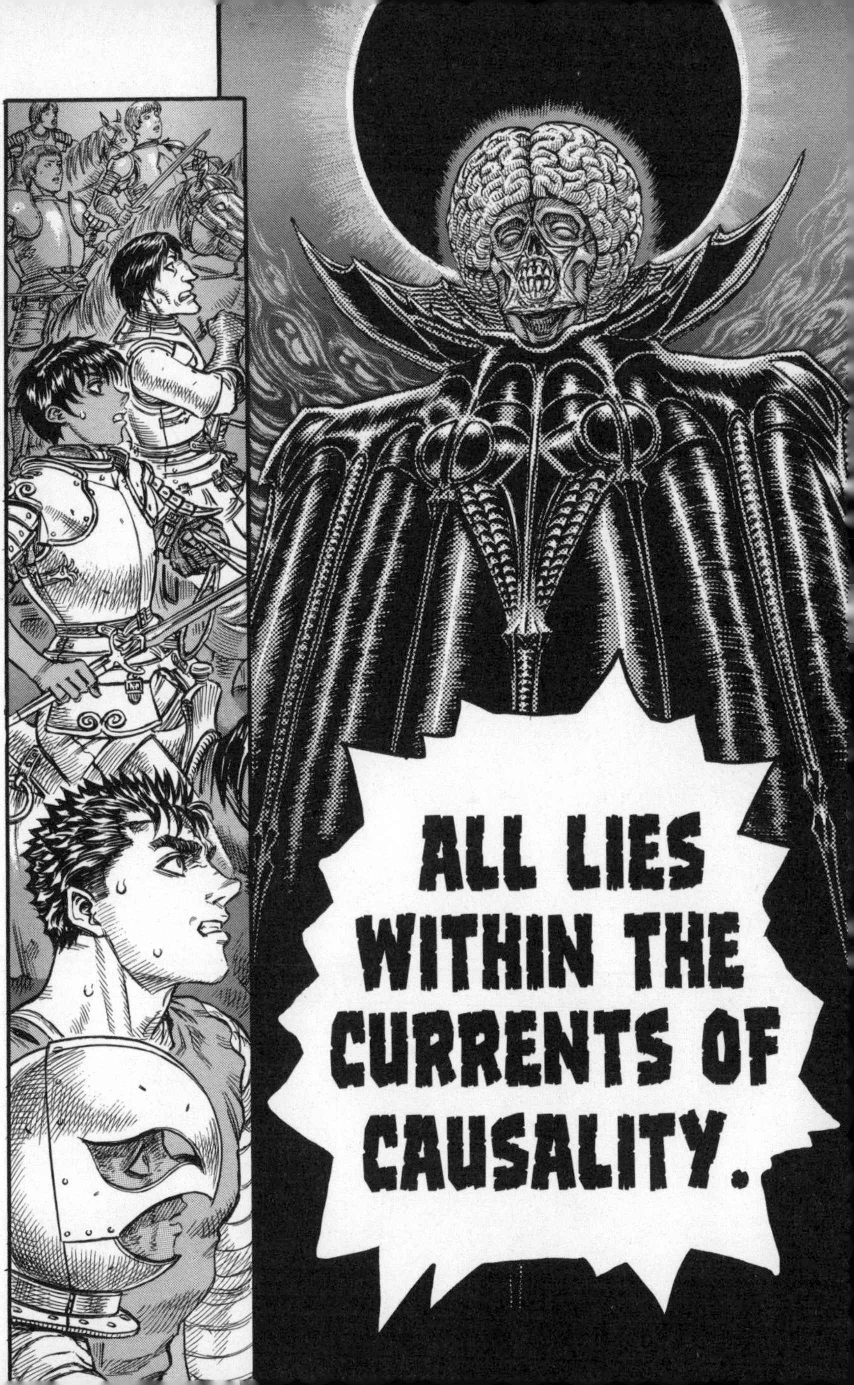
ALL LIES WITHIN THE CURRENTS OF CAUSALITY.

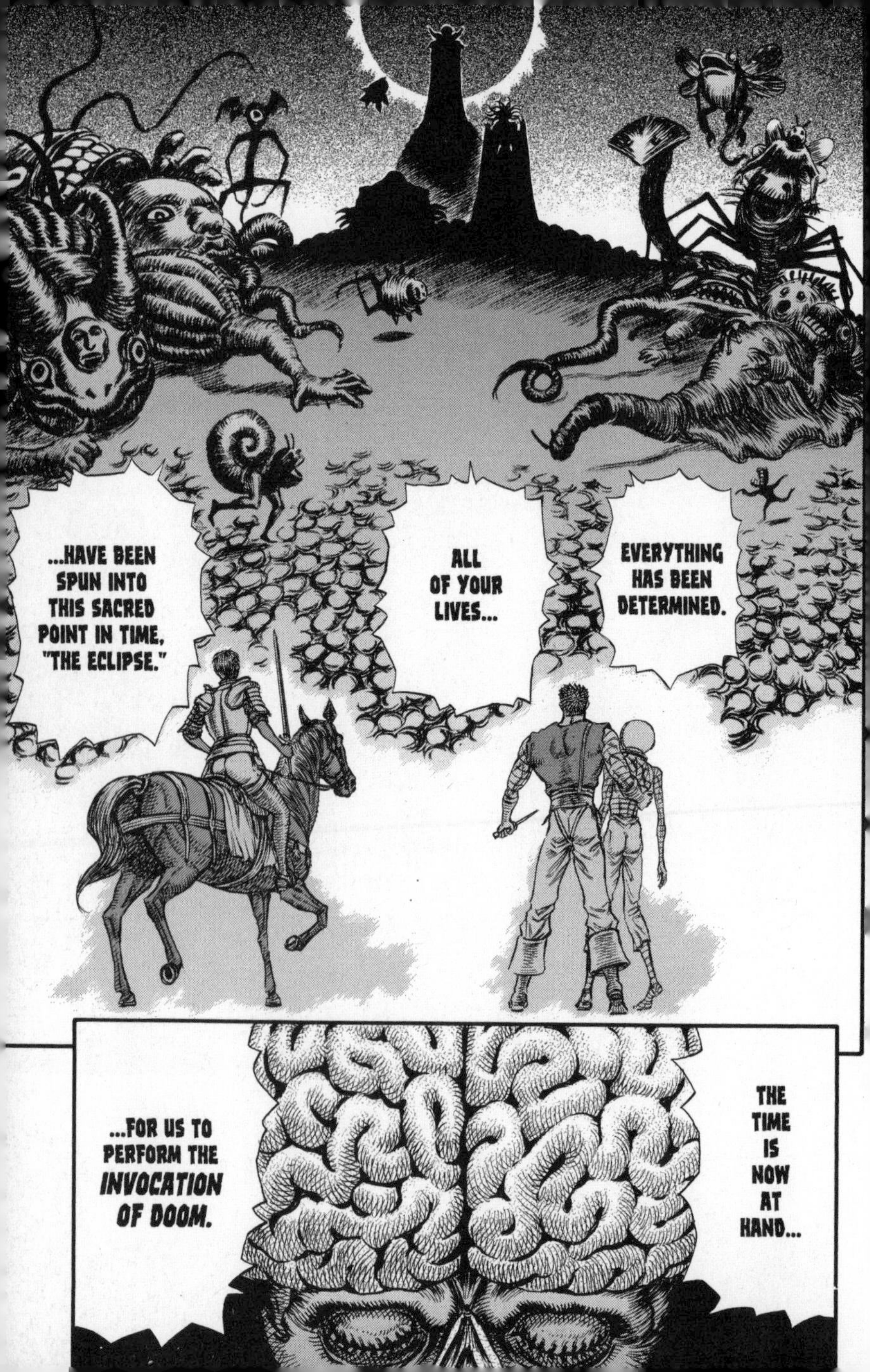
EVERYTHING HAS BEEN DETERMINED.
ALL OF YOUR LIVES...
...HAVE BEEN SPUN INTO THIS SACRED POINT IN TIME, "THE ECLIPSE."
THE TIME IS NOW AT HAND...
...FOR US TO PERFORM THE *INVOCATION OF DOOM.*

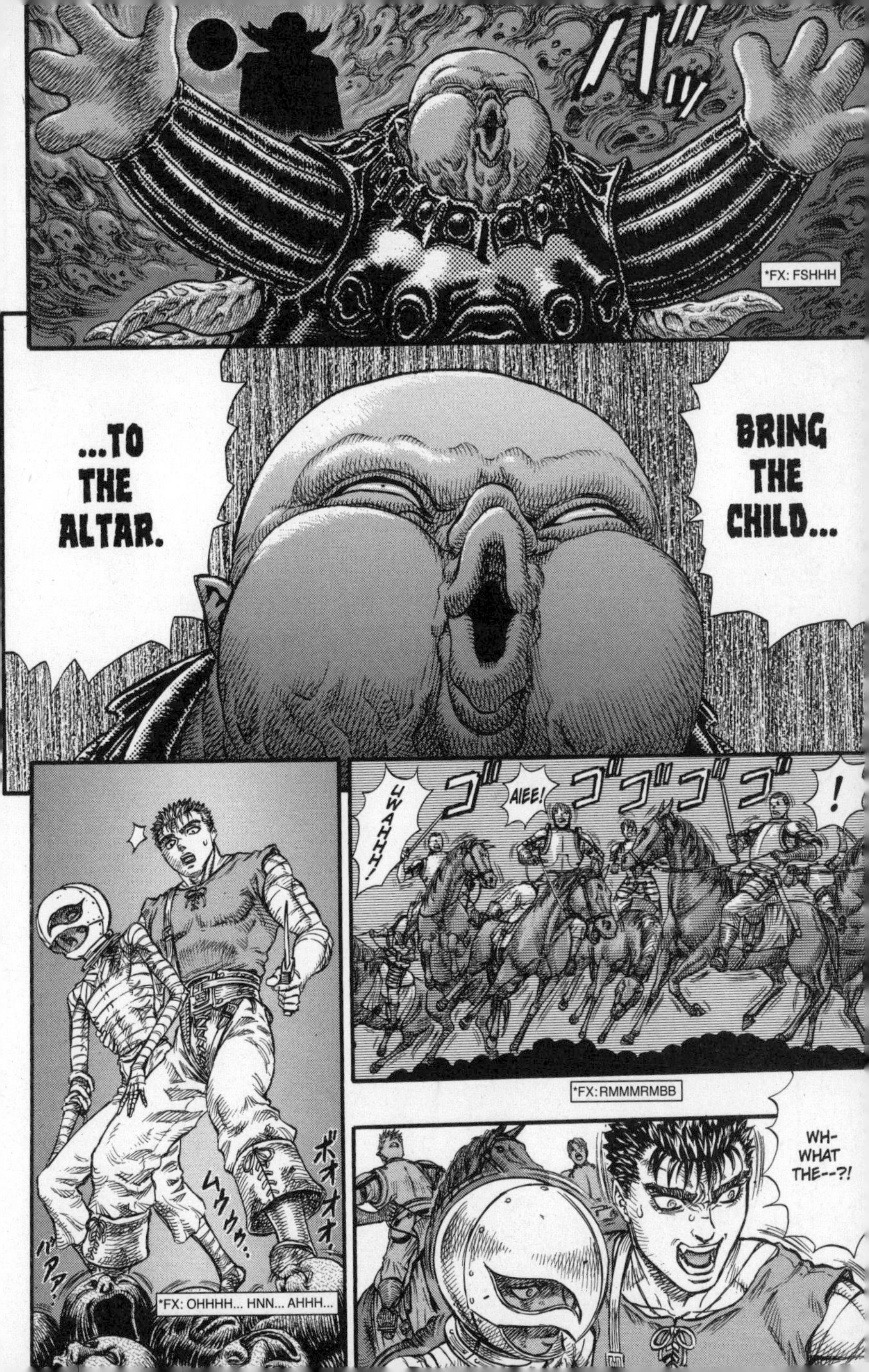
*FX: FSHHH
BRING THE CHILD...
...TO THE ALTAR.
!
AIEE!
UWAHHH!
*FX: RMMMRMBB
WH- WHAT THE--?!
*FX: OHHHH... HNN... AHHH...

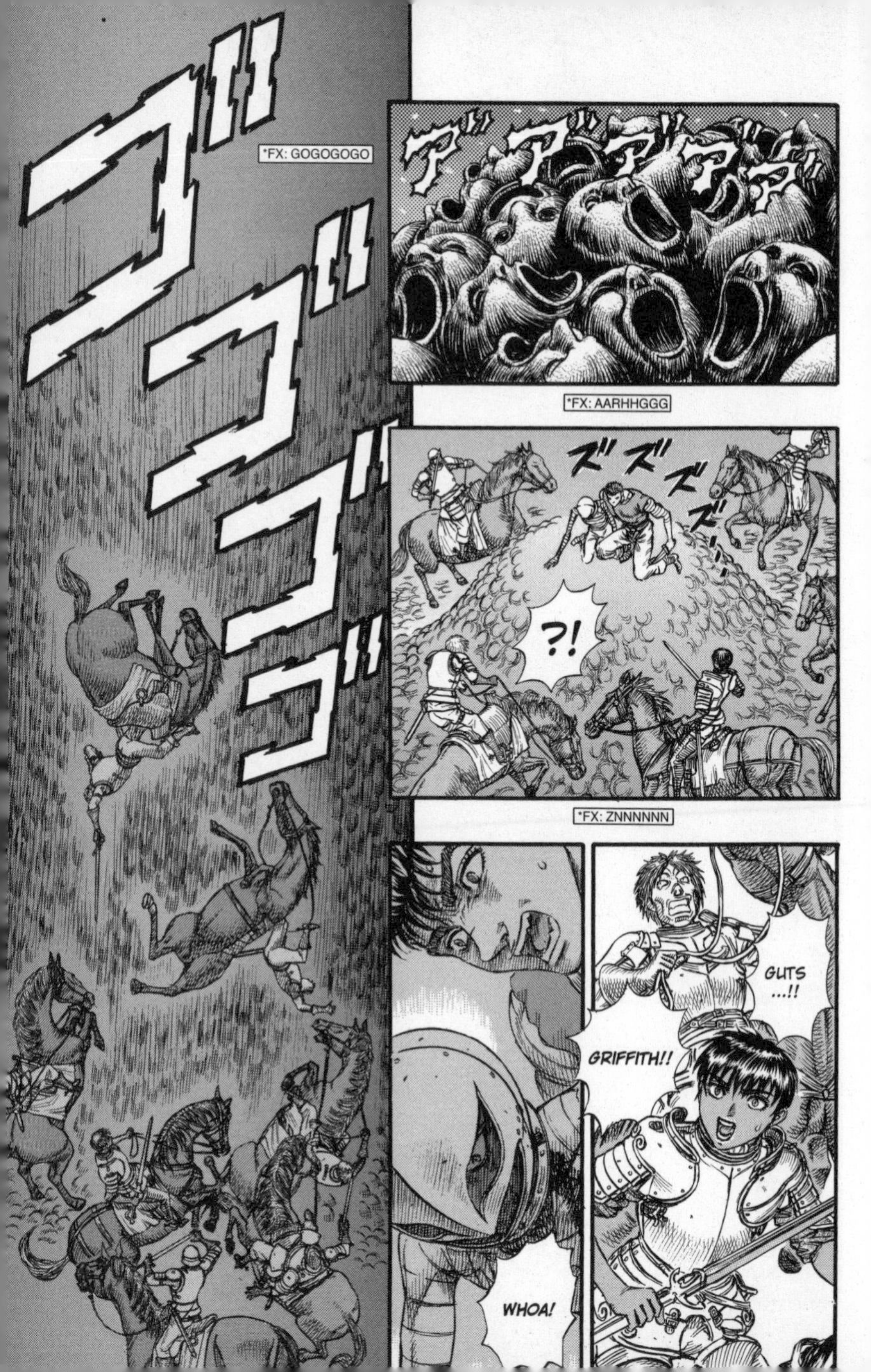
*FX: AARHHGGG
?!
*FX: ZNNNNNN
GUTS ...!!
GRIFFITH!!
WHOA!
*FX: GOGOGOGO

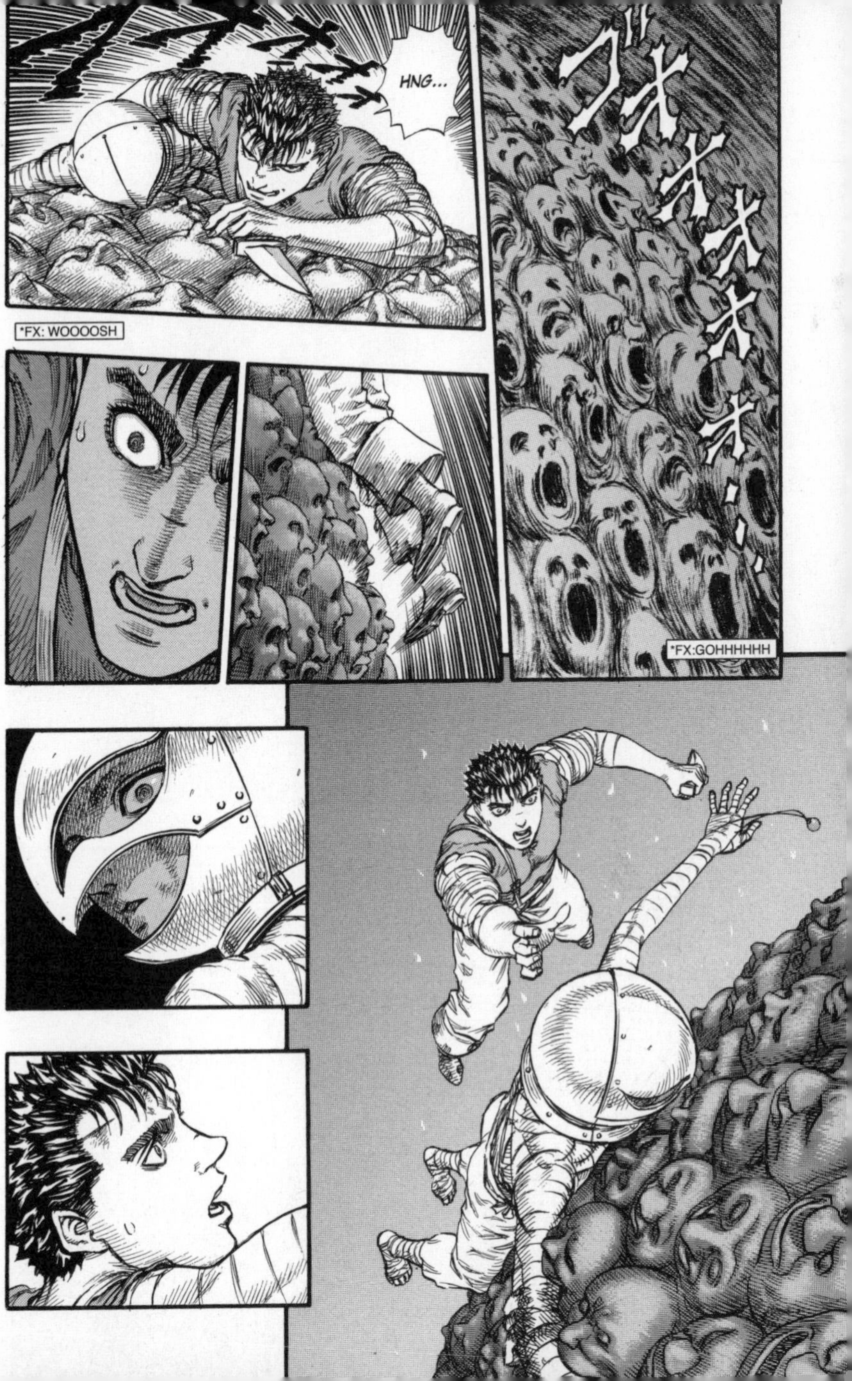
*FX:GOHHHHHH
HNG...
*FX: WOOOOSH

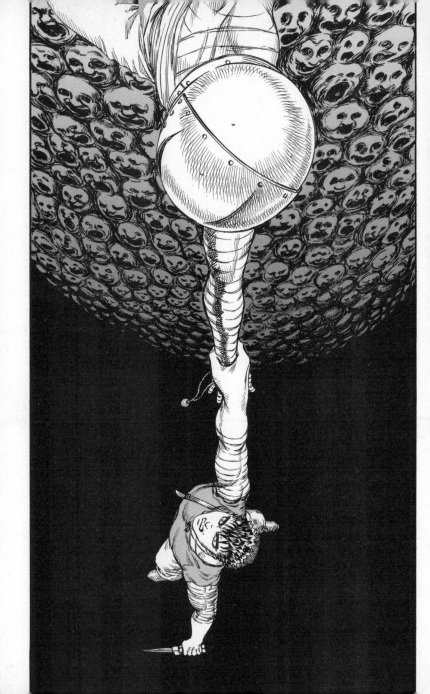

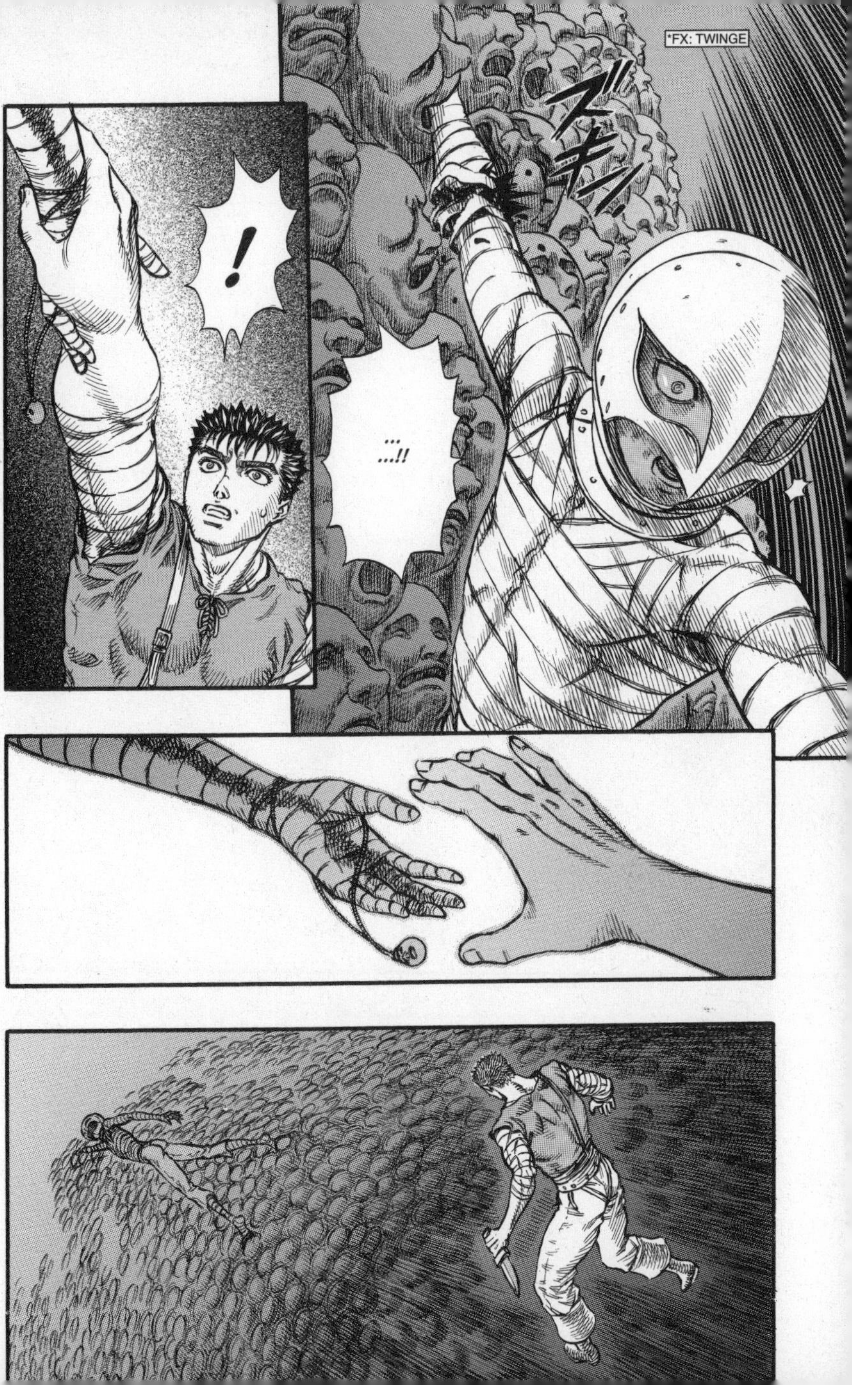
*FX: TWINGE
ズキン
...
...!!
!

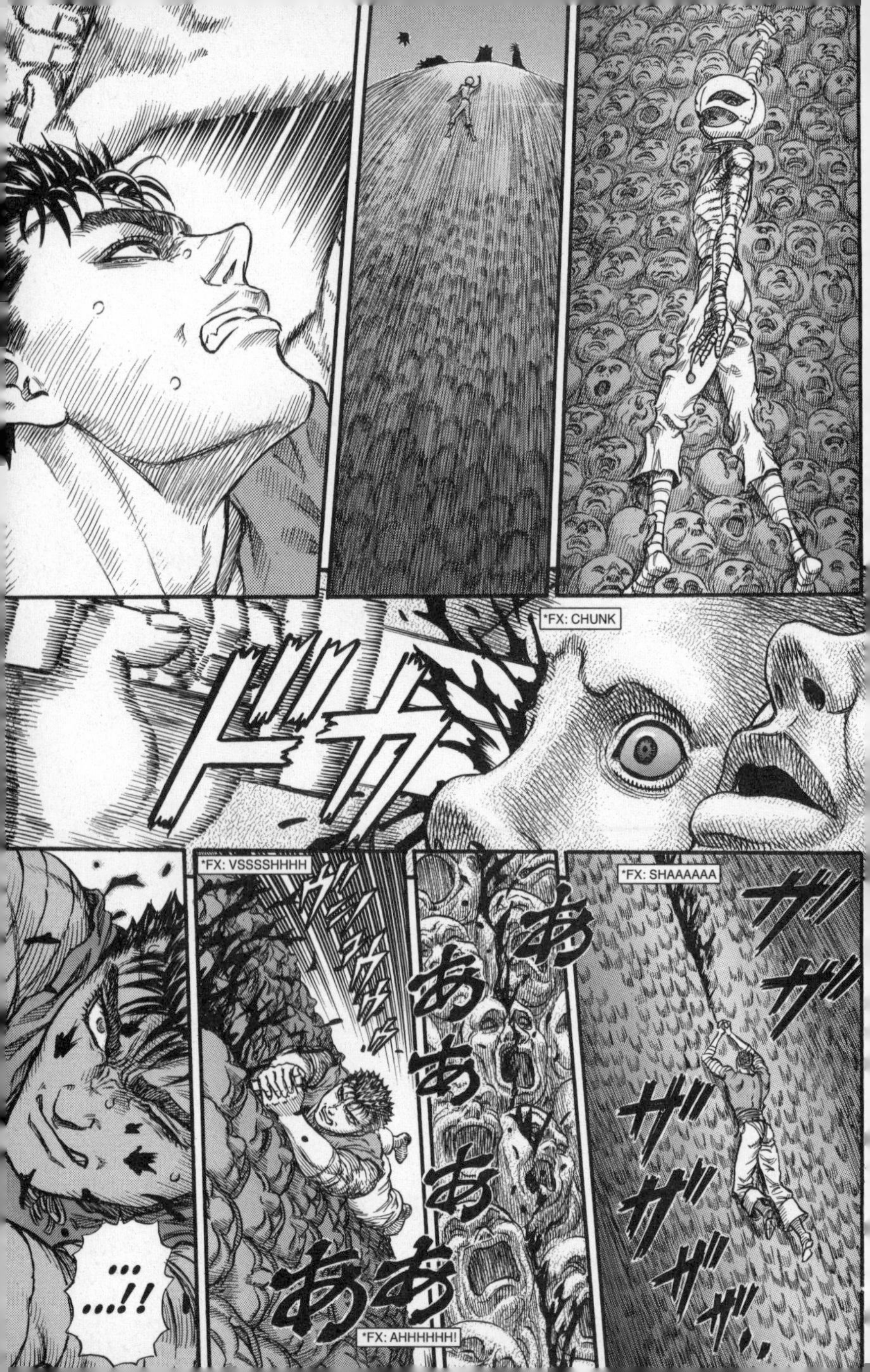
*FX: CHUNK
*FX: SHAAAAAA
*FX: AHHHHHH!
*FX: VSSSSHHHH
... ...!!

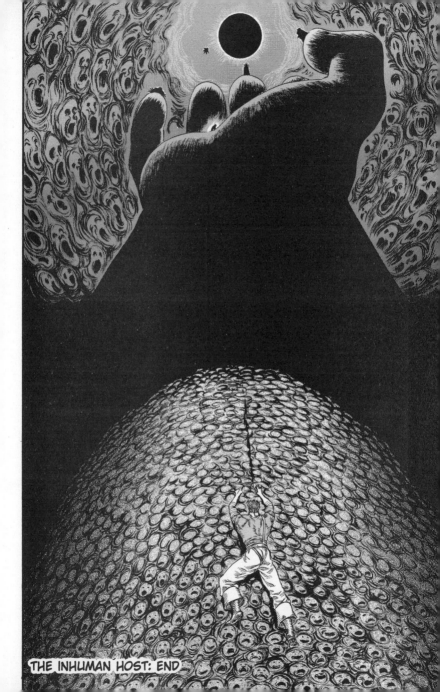

THE INHUMAN HOST: END

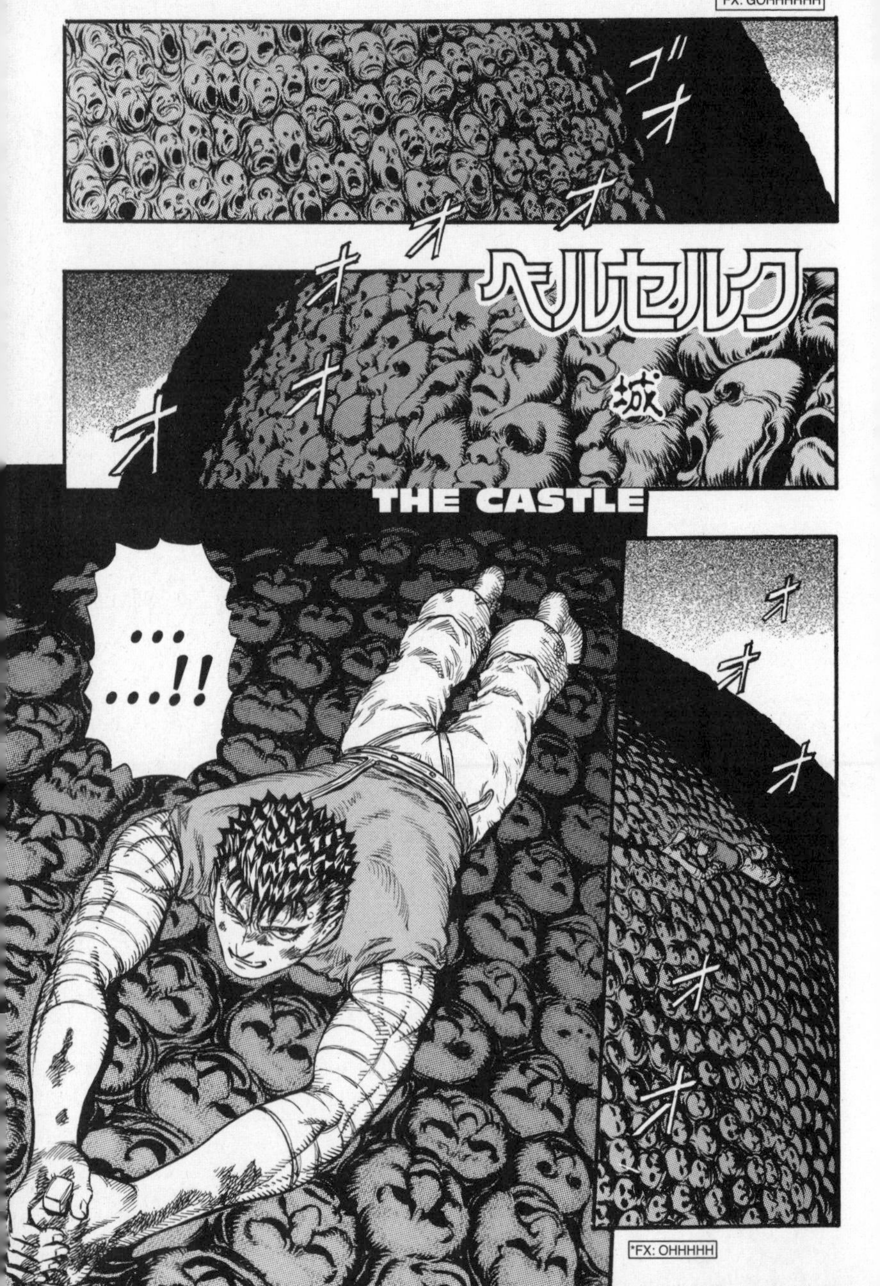
*FX: GOHHHHHH
ゴオオオオオオ
ベルセルク
城
THE CASTLE
オオオオオオ
*FX: OHHHHH
...
...!!

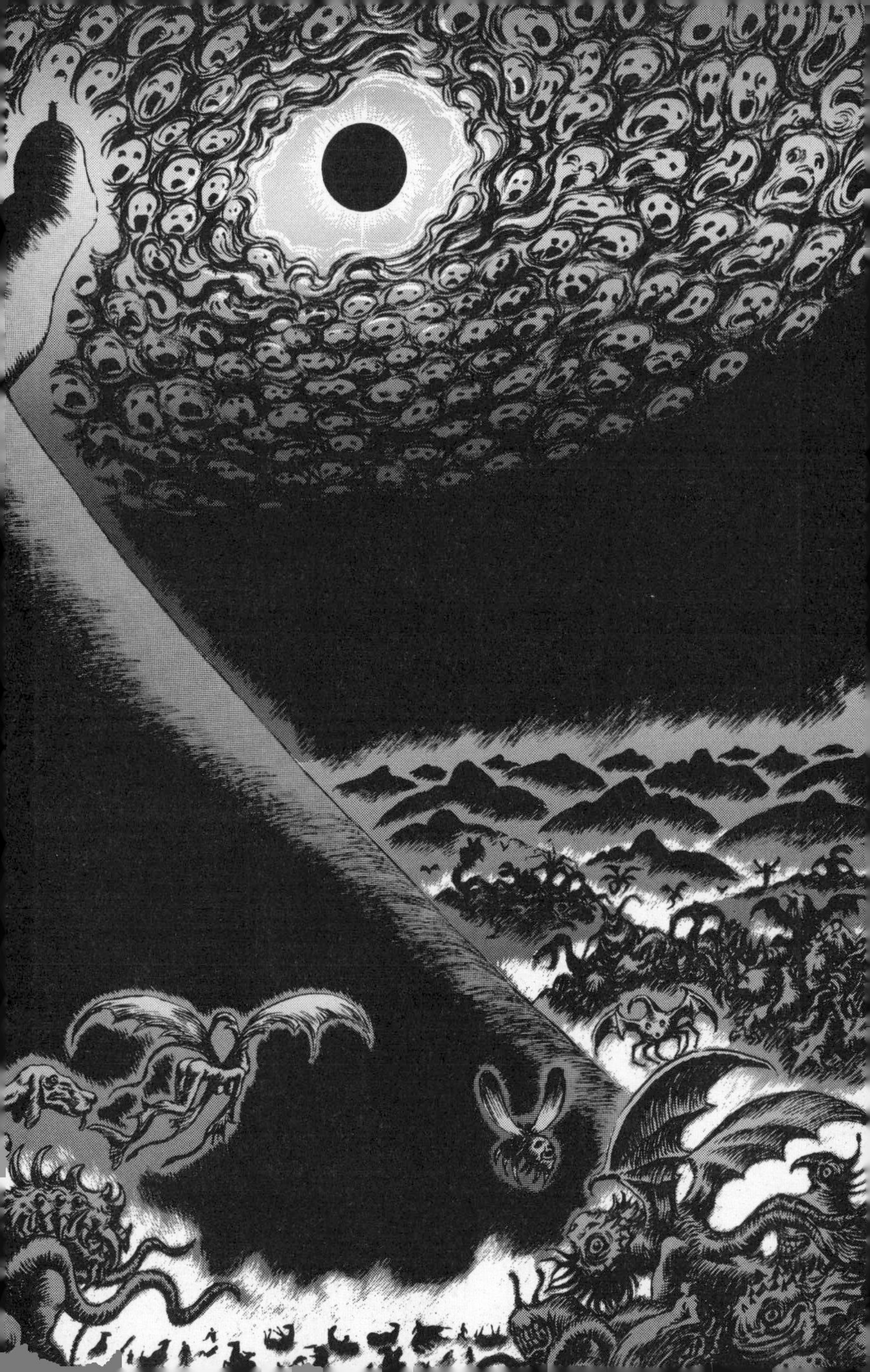

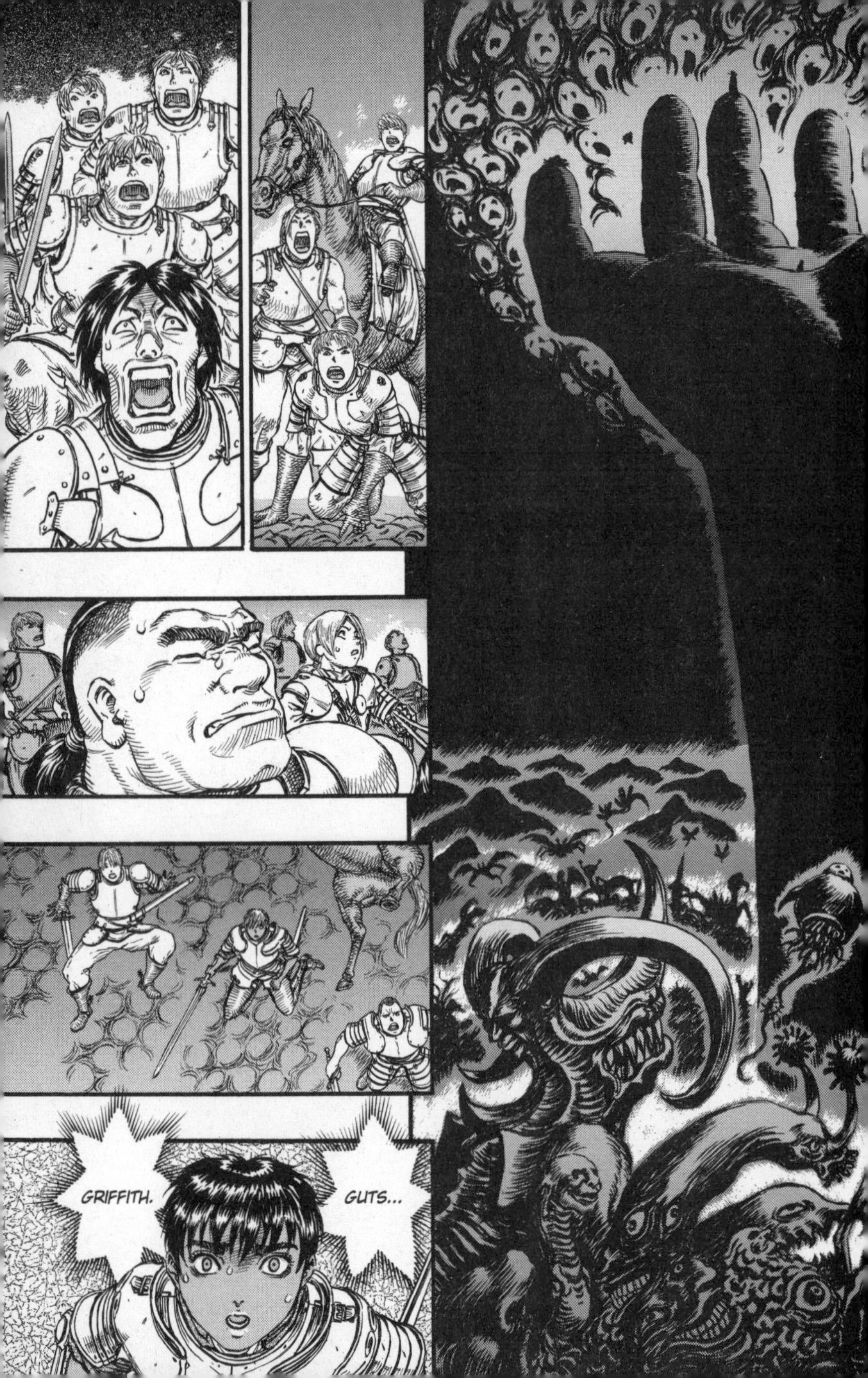
GUTS...
GRIFFITH.

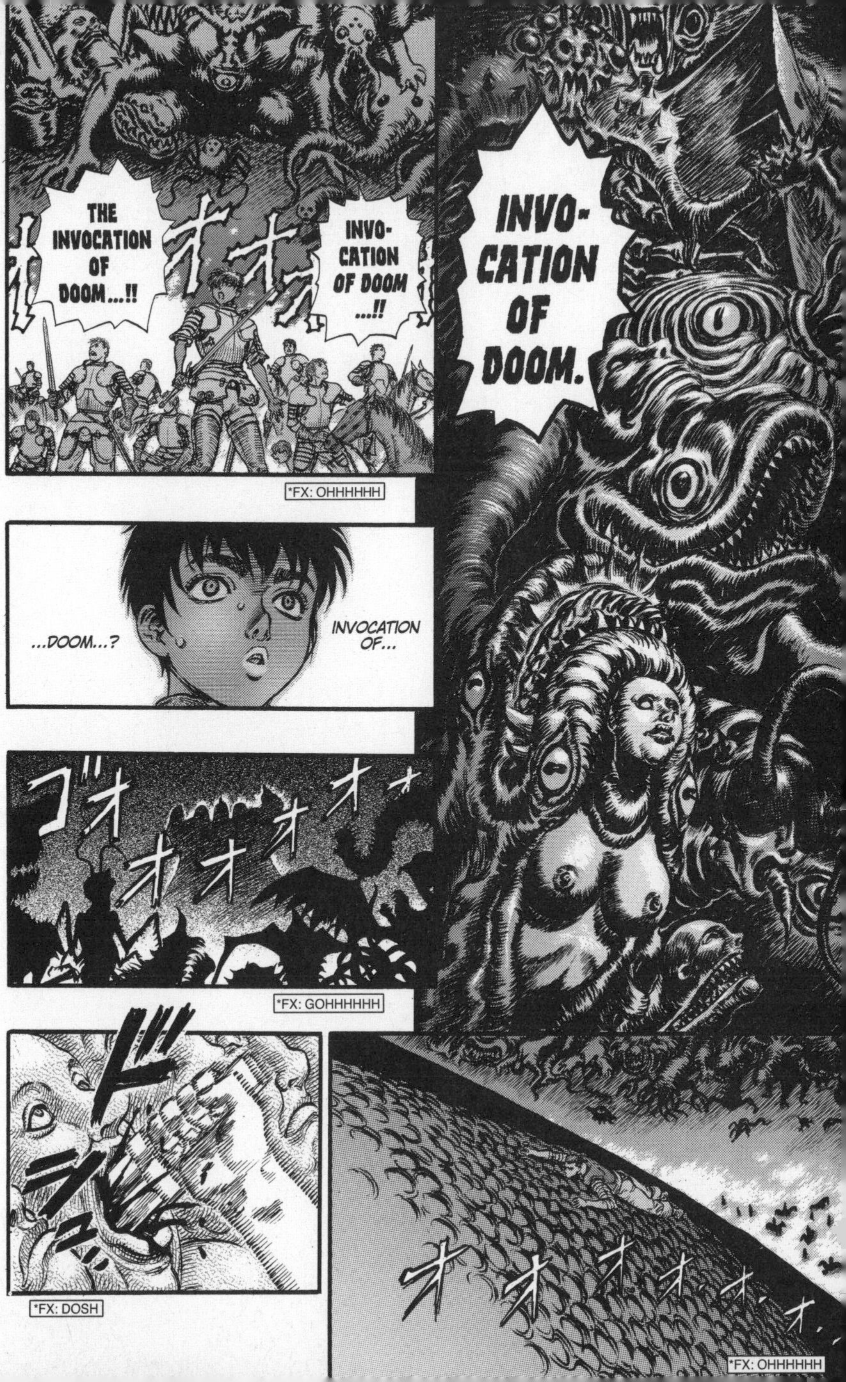
INVO-CATION OF DOOM.
INVO-CATION OF DOOM ...!!
THE INVOCATION OF DOOM...!!
*FX: OHHHHHH
INVOCATION OF...
...DOOM...?
*FX: GOHHHHHH
*FX: OHHHHHH
*FX: DOSH

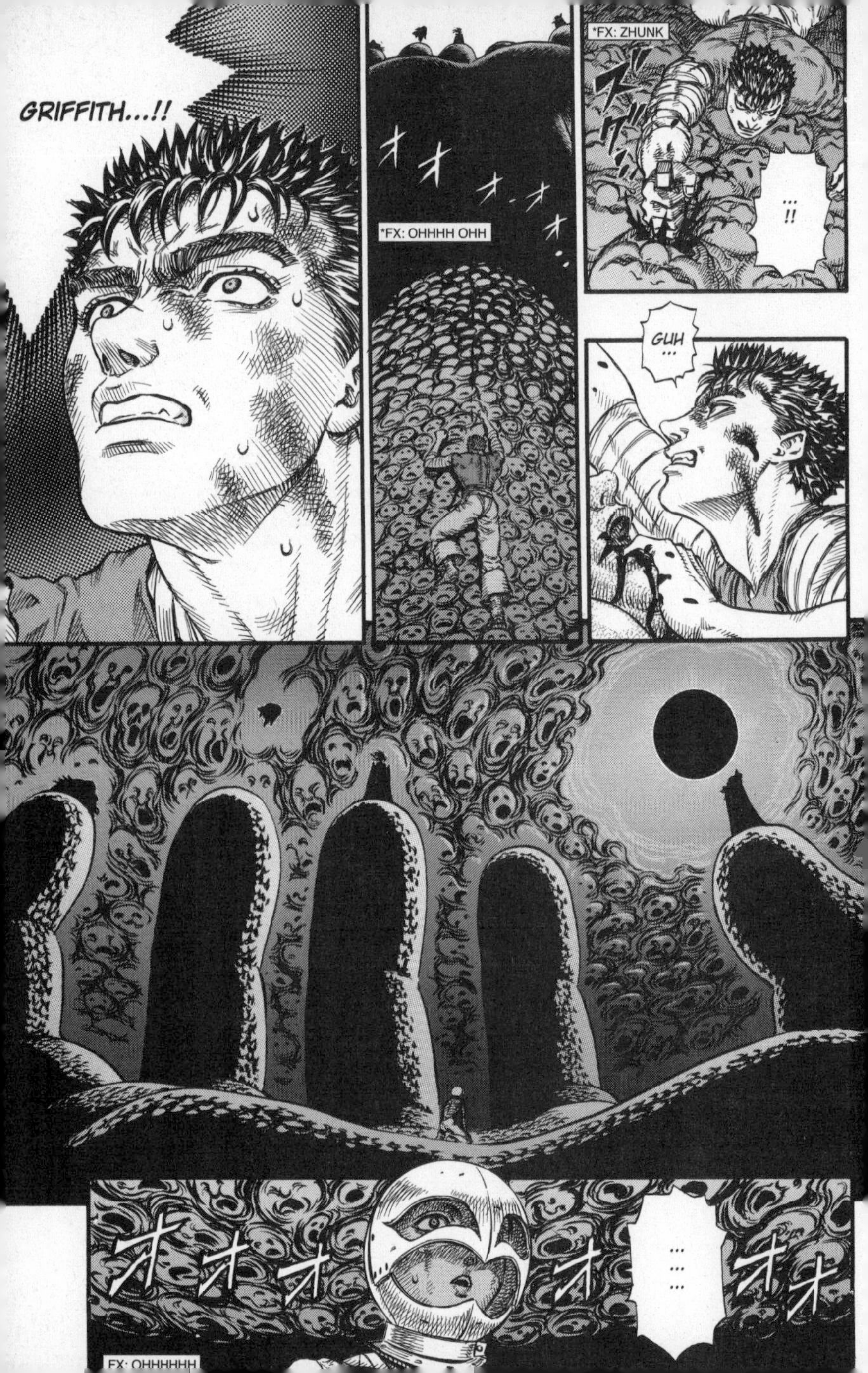

*FX: ZHUNK
...!!
GUH ...
オオオ・オオ・
*FX: OHHHH OHH
GRIFFITH...!!
オオオ
...
...
...
オオオ
FX: OHHHHHH

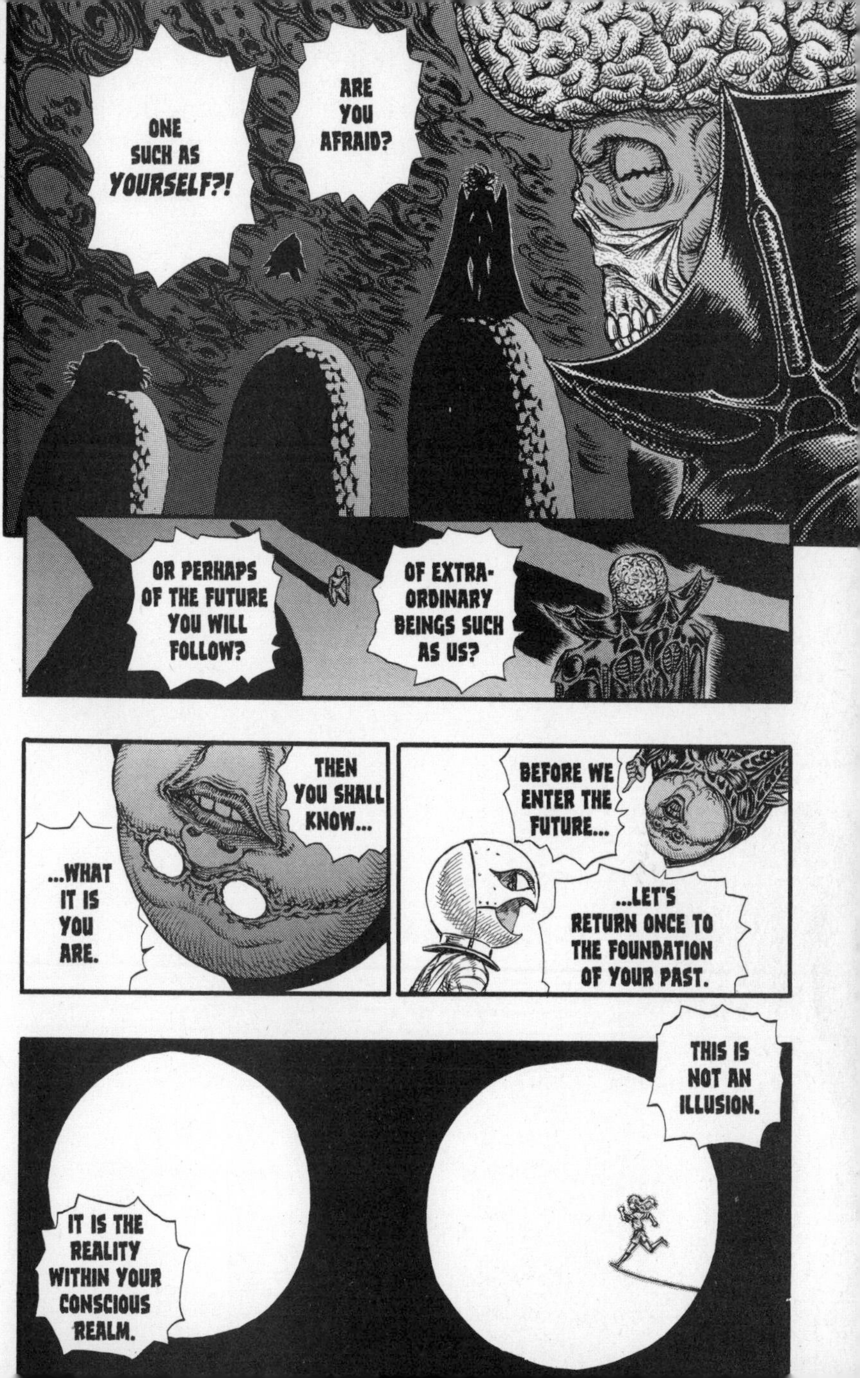
ARE YOU AFRAID?
ONE SUCH AS *YOURSELF*?!
OF EXTRA-ORDINARY BEINGS SUCH AS US?
OR PERHAPS OF THE FUTURE YOU WILL FOLLOW?
BEFORE WE ENTER THE FUTURE...
...LET'S RETURN ONCE TO THE FOUNDATION OF YOUR PAST.
THEN YOU SHALL KNOW...
...WHAT IT IS YOU ARE.
THIS IS NOT AN ILLUSION.
IT IS THE REALITY WITHIN YOUR CONSCIOUS REALM.

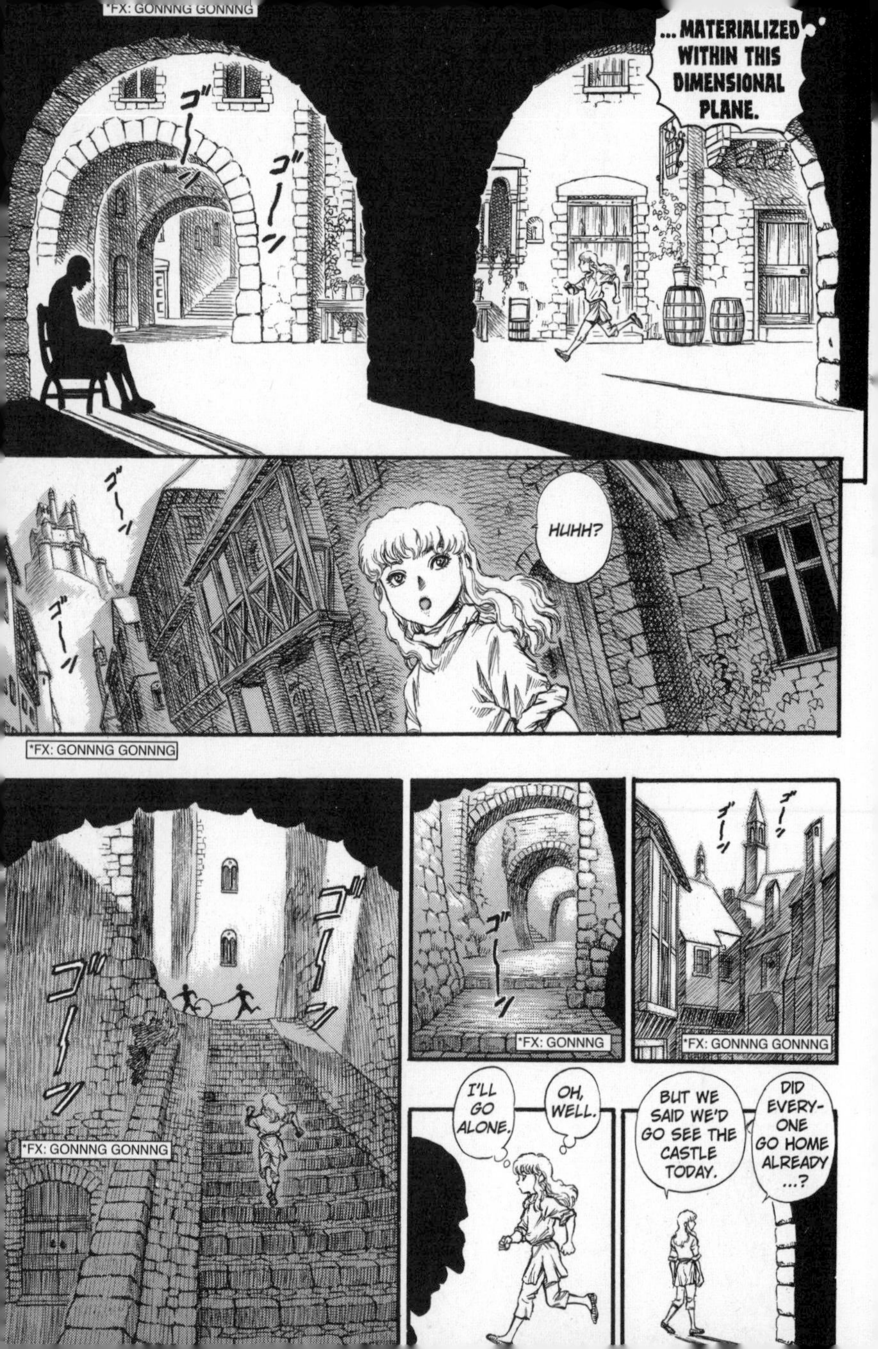
... MATERIALIZED WITHIN THIS DIMENSIONAL PLANE.
*FX: GONNNG GONNNG
HUHH?
*FX: GONNNG GONNNG
*FX: GONNNG GONNNG
*FX: GONNNG
DID EVERYONE GO HOME ALREADY ...?
BUT WE SAID WE'D GO SEE THE CASTLE TODAY.
OH, WELL.
I'LL GO ALONE.
*FX: GONNNG GONNNG

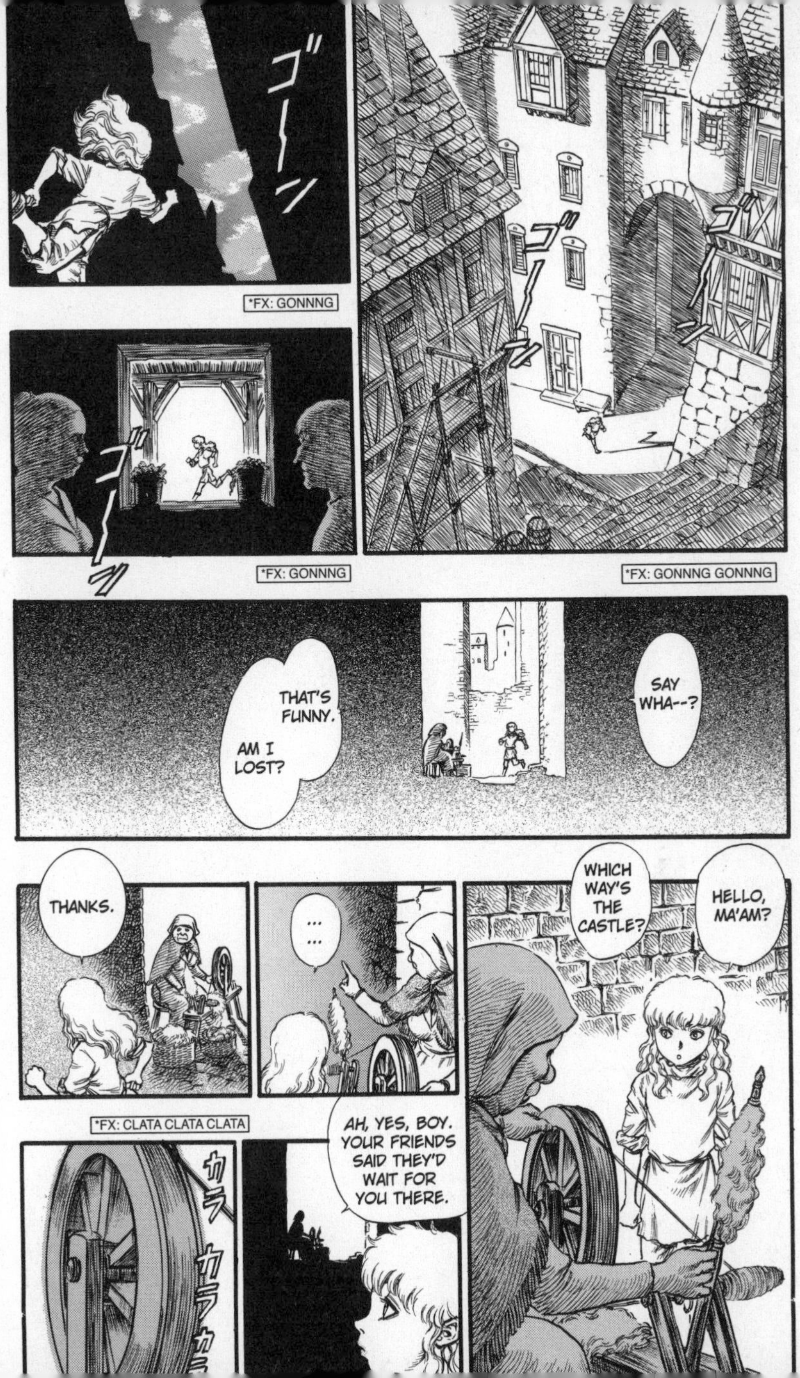
*FX: GONNNG GONNNG
*FX: GONNNG
*FX: GONNNG
SAY WHA--?
THAT'S FUNNY.
AM I LOST?
HELLO, MA'AM?
WHICH WAY'S THE CASTLE?
AH, YES, BOY. YOUR FRIENDS SAID THEY'D WAIT FOR YOU THERE.
... ...
THANKS.
*FX: CLATA CLATA CLATA

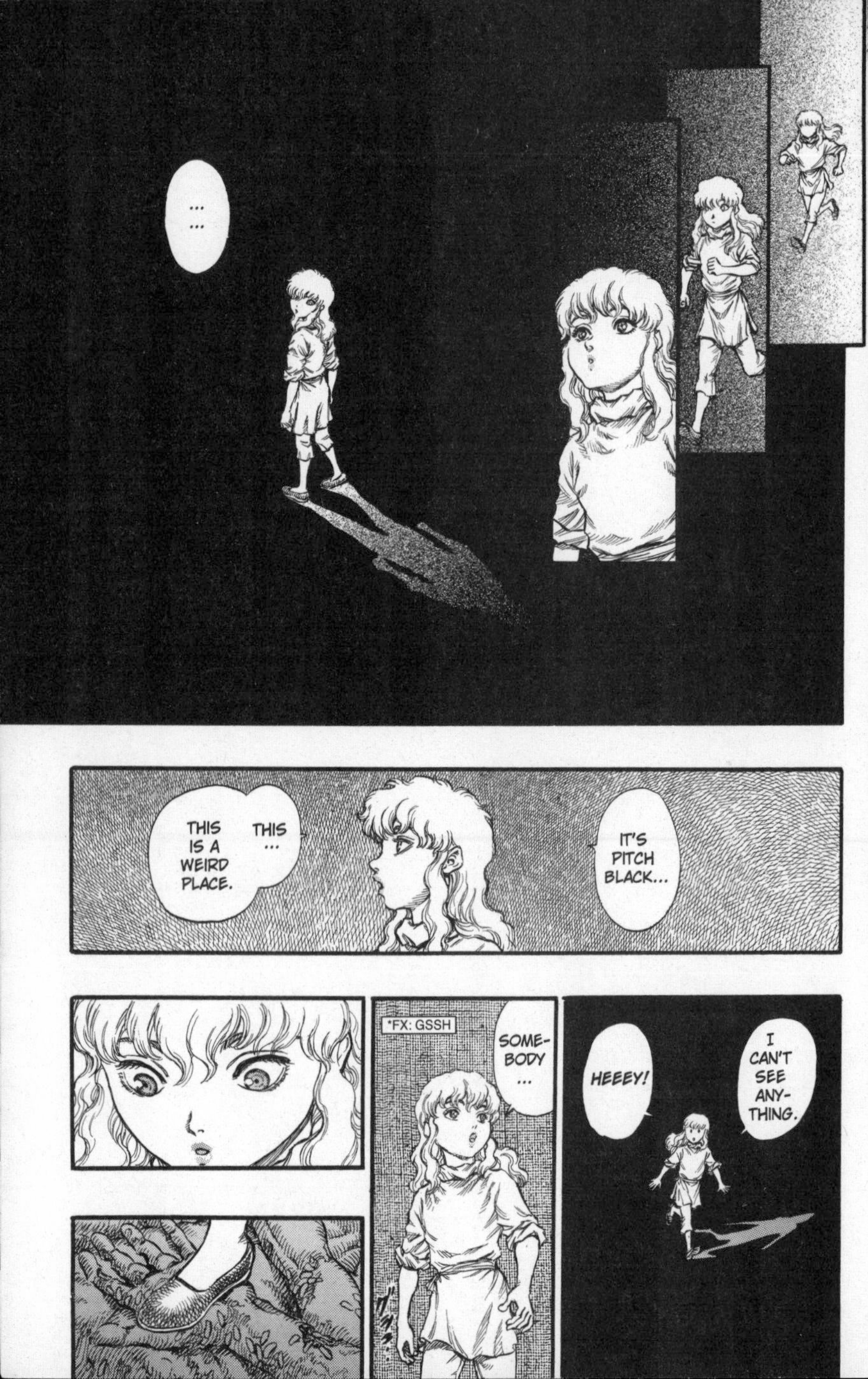
......
IT'S PITCH BLACK...
THIS ...
THIS IS A WEIRD PLACE.
I CAN'T SEE ANY-THING.
HEEEY!
SOME-BODY ...
*FX: GSSH

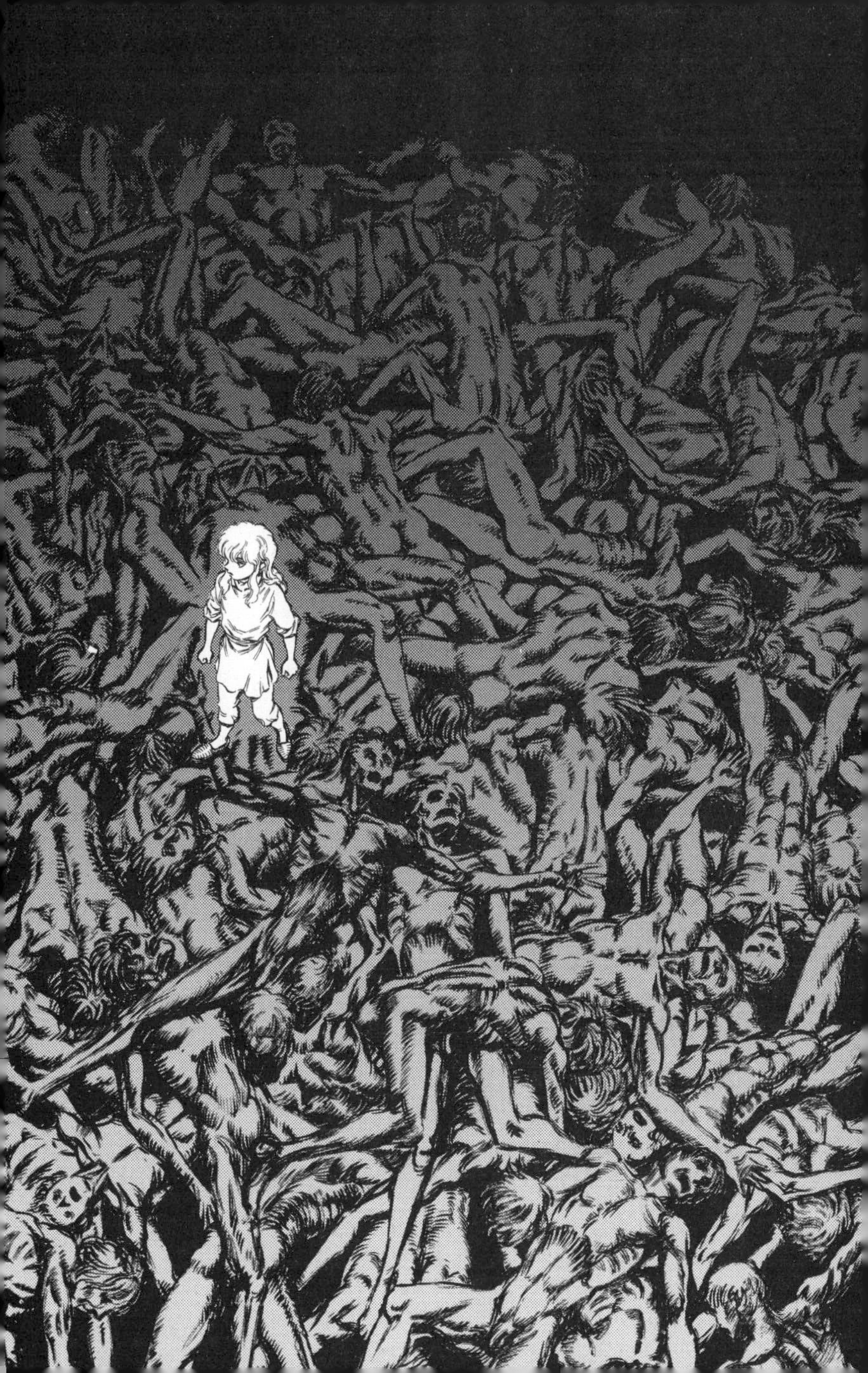

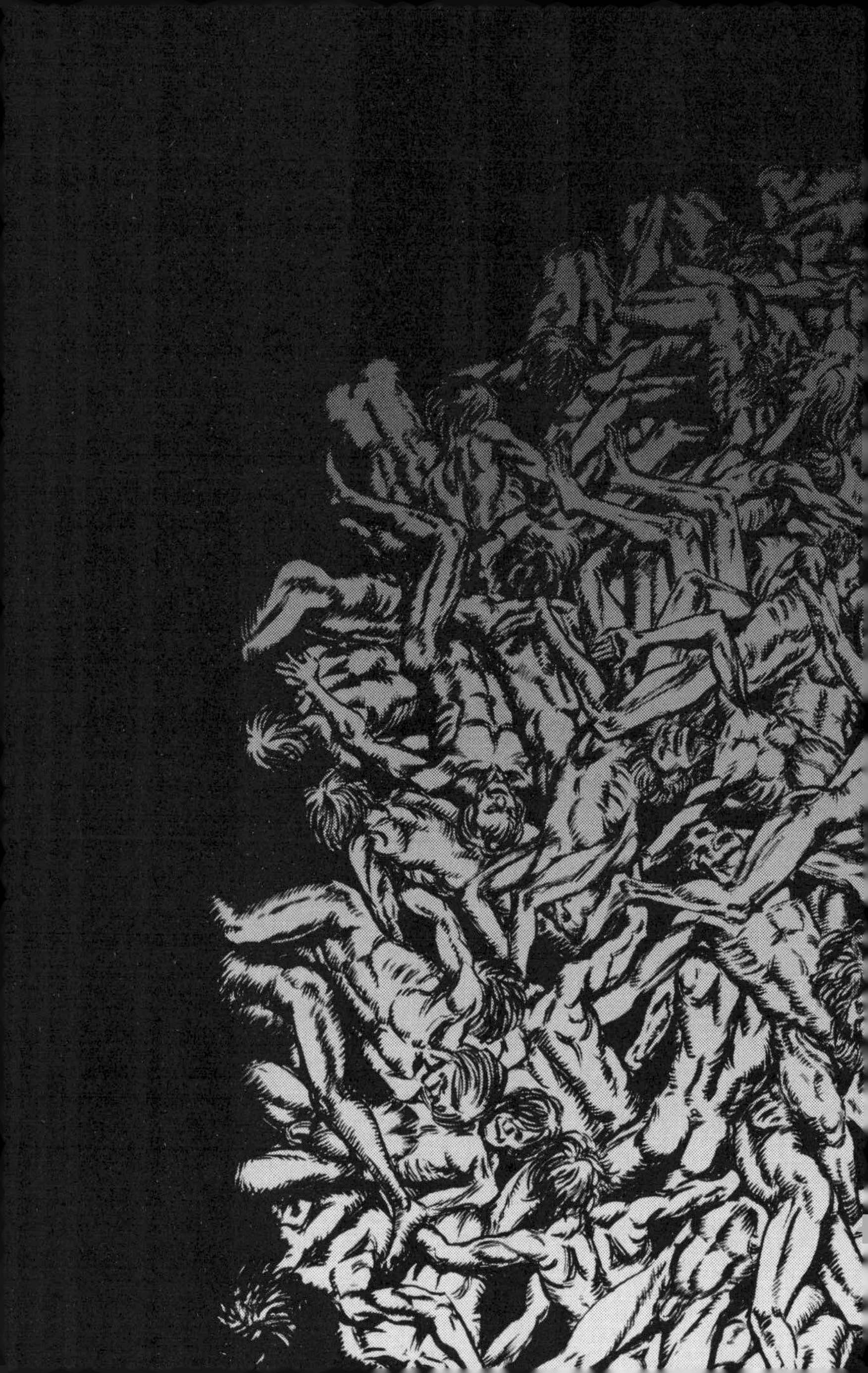

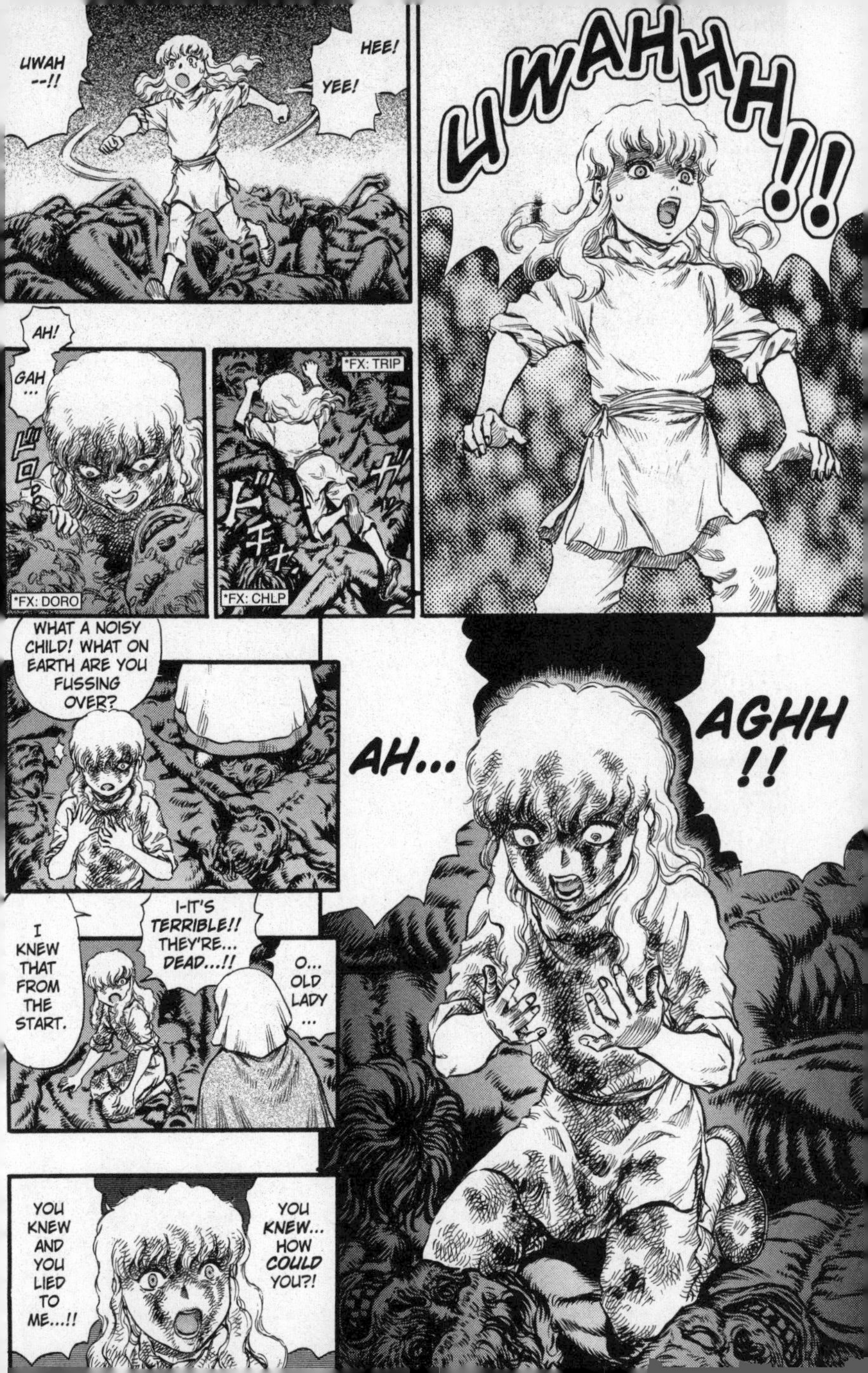

UWAHHH!!
HEE! YEE!
UWAH --!!
*FX: TRIP
*FX: CHLP
AH! GAH...
*FX: DORO
AH... AGHH!!
WHAT A NOISY CHILD! WHAT ON EARTH ARE YOU FUSSING OVER?
O... OLD LADY...
I-IT'S TERRIBLE!! THEY'RE... DEAD...!!
I KNEW THAT FROM THE START.
YOU KNEW... HOW COULD YOU?!
YOU KNEW AND YOU LIED TO ME...!!

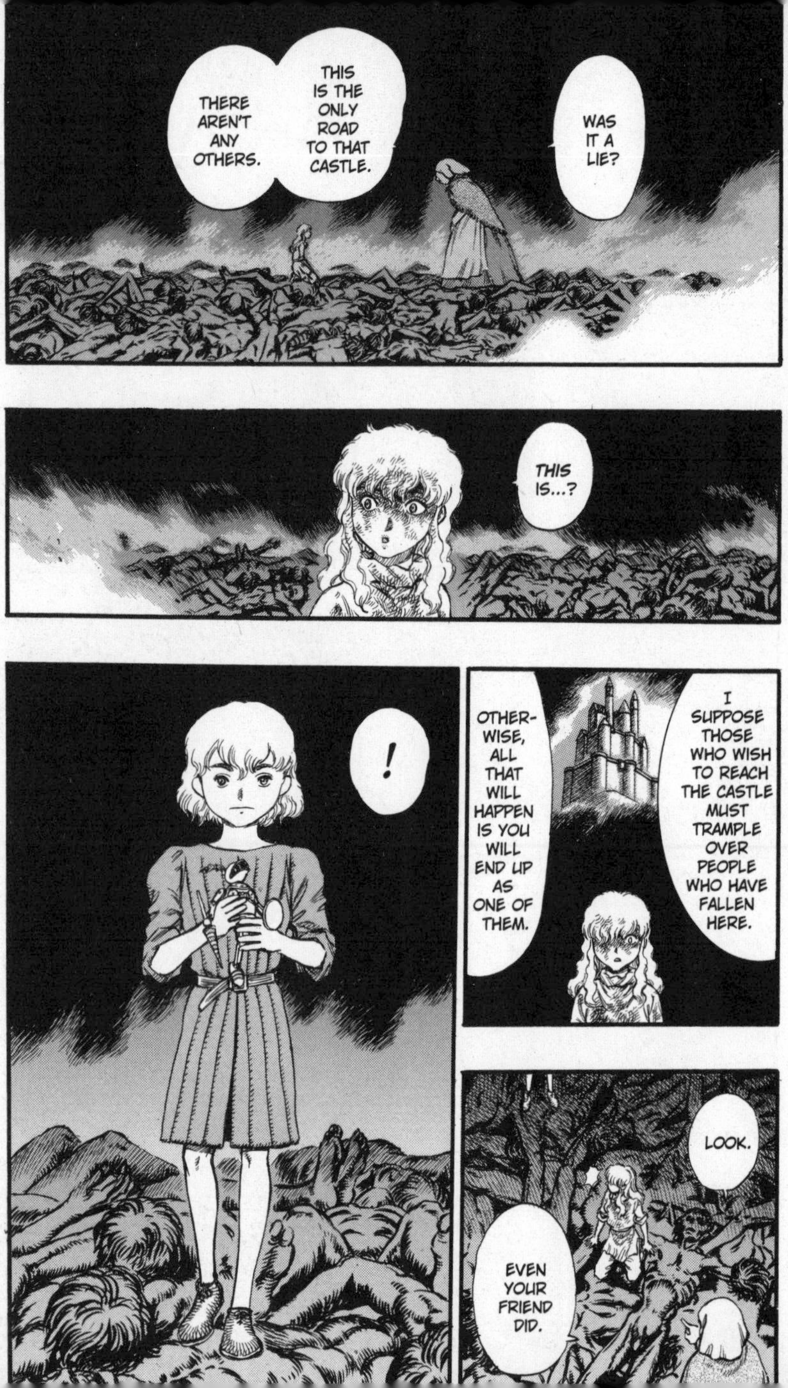
WAS IT A LIE?
THIS IS THE ONLY ROAD TO THAT CASTLE.
THERE AREN'T ANY OTHERS.
THIS IS...?
I SUPPOSE THOSE WHO WISH TO REACH THE CASTLE MUST TRAMPLE OVER PEOPLE WHO HAVE FALLEN HERE.
OTHER-WISE, ALL THAT WILL HAPPEN IS YOU WILL END UP AS ONE OF THEM.
LOOK.
EVEN YOUR FRIEND DID.
!

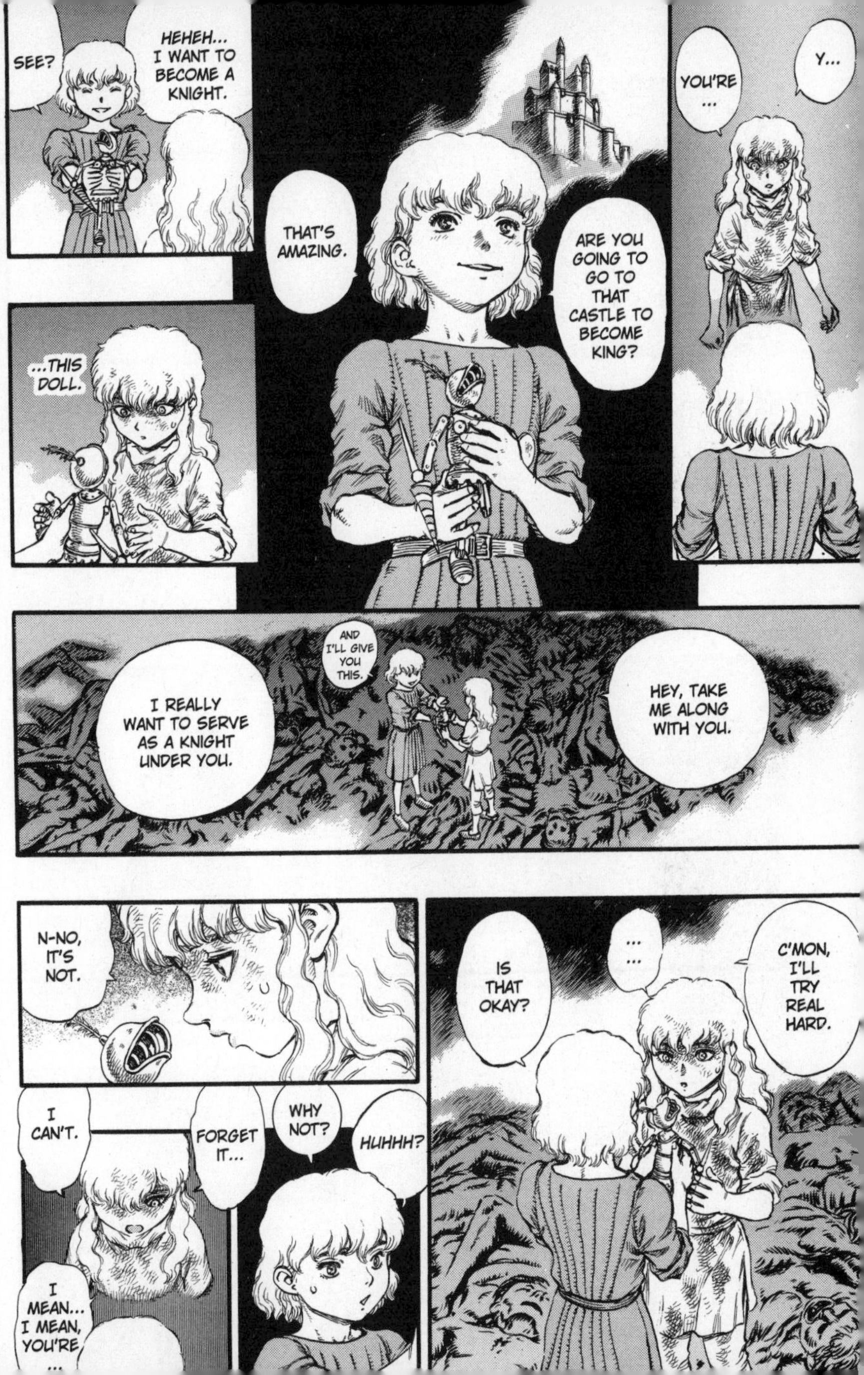
Y...
YOU'RE ...
ARE YOU GOING TO GO TO THAT CASTLE TO BECOME KING?
THAT'S AMAZING.
HEHEH... I WANT TO BECOME A KNIGHT.
SEE?
...THIS DOLL.
HEY, TAKE ME ALONG WITH YOU.
AND I'LL GIVE YOU THIS.
I REALLY WANT TO SERVE AS A KNIGHT UNDER YOU.
C'MON, I'LL TRY REAL HARD.
... ...
IS THAT OKAY?
N-NO, IT'S NOT.
HUHHH?
WHY NOT?
FORGET IT...
I CAN'T.
I MEAN... I MEAN, YOU'RE ...

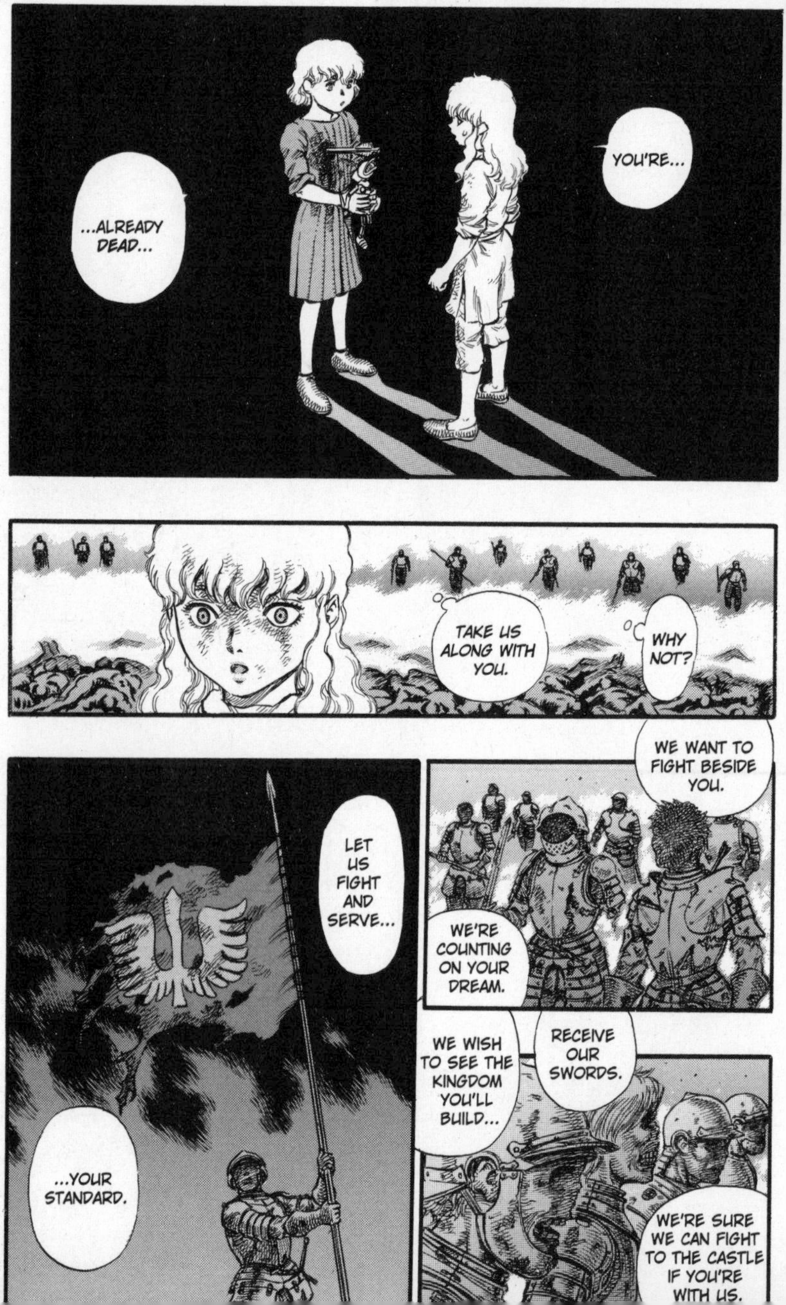
YOU'RE...
...ALREADY DEAD...
WHY NOT?
TAKE US ALONG WITH YOU.
WE WANT TO FIGHT BESIDE YOU.
WE'RE COUNTING ON YOUR DREAM.
RECEIVE OUR SWORDS.
WE WISH TO SEE THE KINGDOM YOU'LL BUILD...
WE'RE SURE WE CAN FIGHT TO THE CASTLE IF YOU'RE WITH US.
LET US FIGHT AND SERVE...
...YOUR STANDARD.

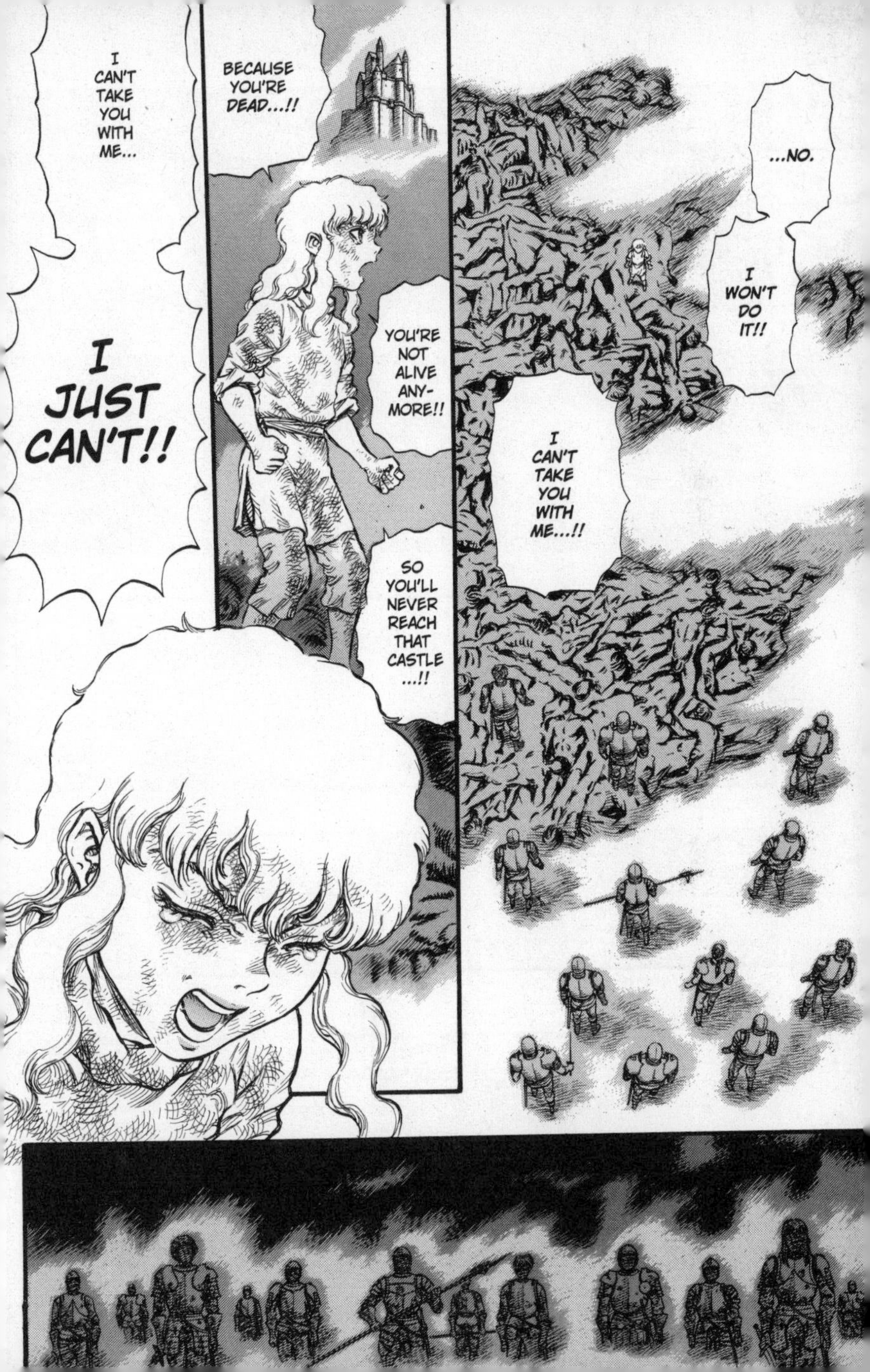
...NO.
I WON'T DO IT!!
I CAN'T TAKE YOU WITH ME...!!
BECAUSE YOU'RE DEAD...!!
YOU'RE NOT ALIVE ANYMORE!!
SO YOU'LL NEVER REACH THAT CASTLE...!!
I CAN'T TAKE YOU WITH ME...
I JUST CAN'T!!

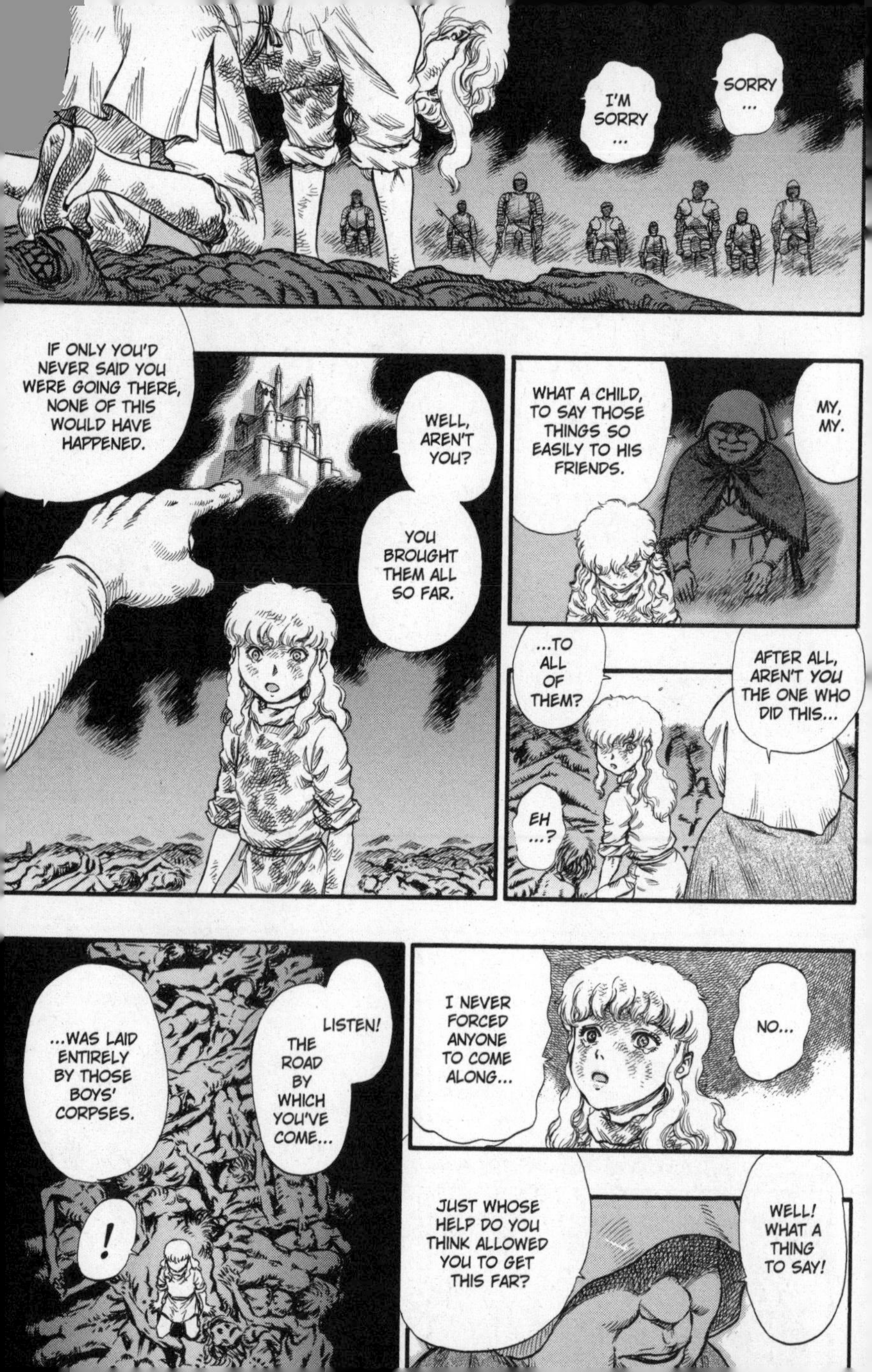

SORRY ...
I'M SORRY ...
MY, MY.
WHAT A CHILD, TO SAY THOSE THINGS SO EASILY TO HIS FRIENDS.
AFTER ALL, AREN'T YOU THE ONE WHO DID THIS...
...TO ALL OF THEM?
EH ...?
WELL, AREN'T YOU?
YOU BROUGHT THEM ALL SO FAR.
IF ONLY YOU'D NEVER SAID YOU WERE GOING THERE, NONE OF THIS WOULD HAVE HAPPENED.
NO...
I NEVER FORCED ANYONE TO COME ALONG...
WELL! WHAT A THING TO SAY!
JUST WHOSE HELP DO YOU THINK ALLOWED YOU TO GET THIS FAR?
LISTEN! THE ROAD BY WHICH YOU'VE COME...
...WAS LAID ENTIRELY BY THOSE BOYS' CORPSES.
!

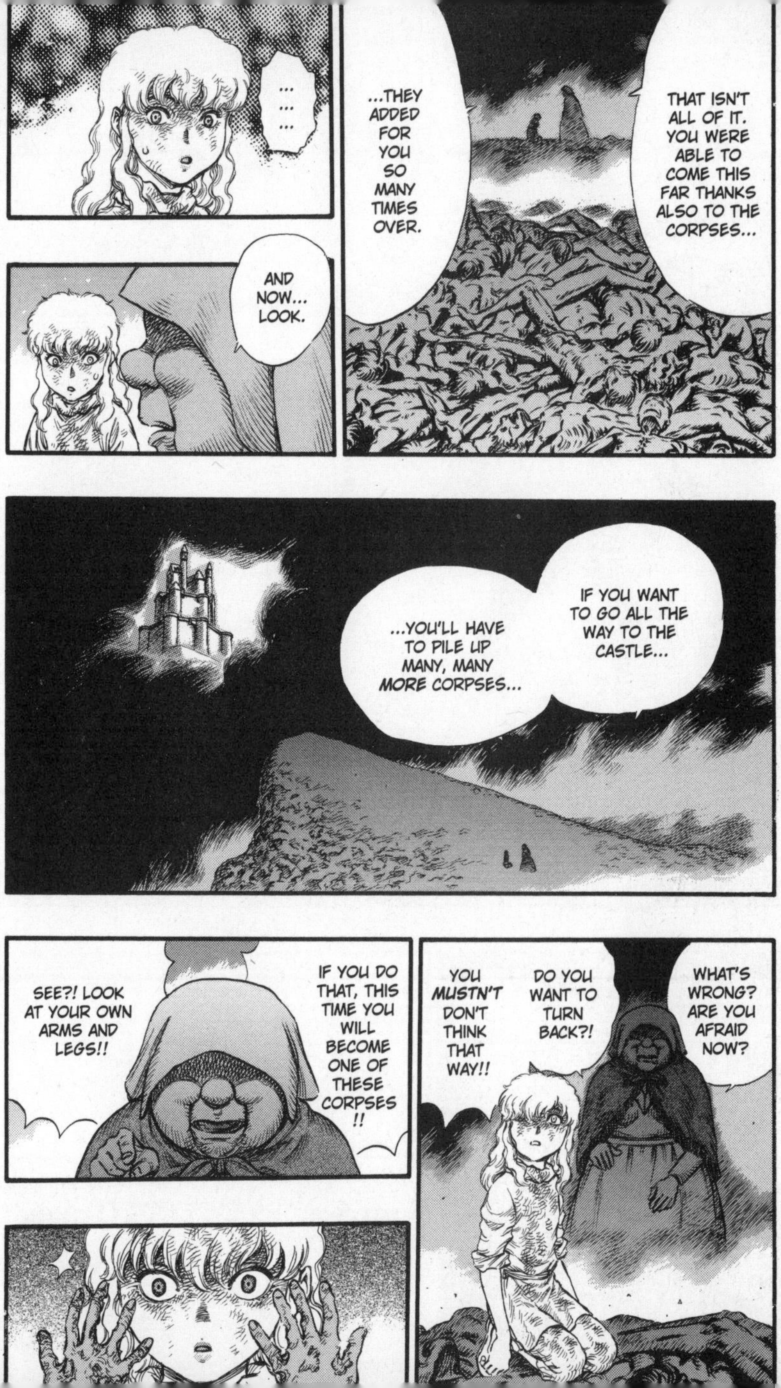
THAT ISN'T ALL OF IT. YOU WERE ABLE TO COME THIS FAR THANKS ALSO TO THE CORPSES...
...THEY ADDED FOR YOU SO MANY TIMES OVER.
... ...
AND NOW... LOOK.
IF YOU WANT TO GO ALL THE WAY TO THE CASTLE...
...YOU'LL HAVE TO PILE UP MANY, MANY MORE CORPSES...
WHAT'S WRONG? ARE YOU AFRAID NOW?
DO YOU WANT TO TURN BACK?!
YOU MUSTN'T DON'T THINK THAT WAY!!
IF YOU DO THAT, THIS TIME YOU WILL BECOME ONE OF THESE CORPSES!!
SEE?! LOOK AT YOUR OWN ARMS AND LEGS!!

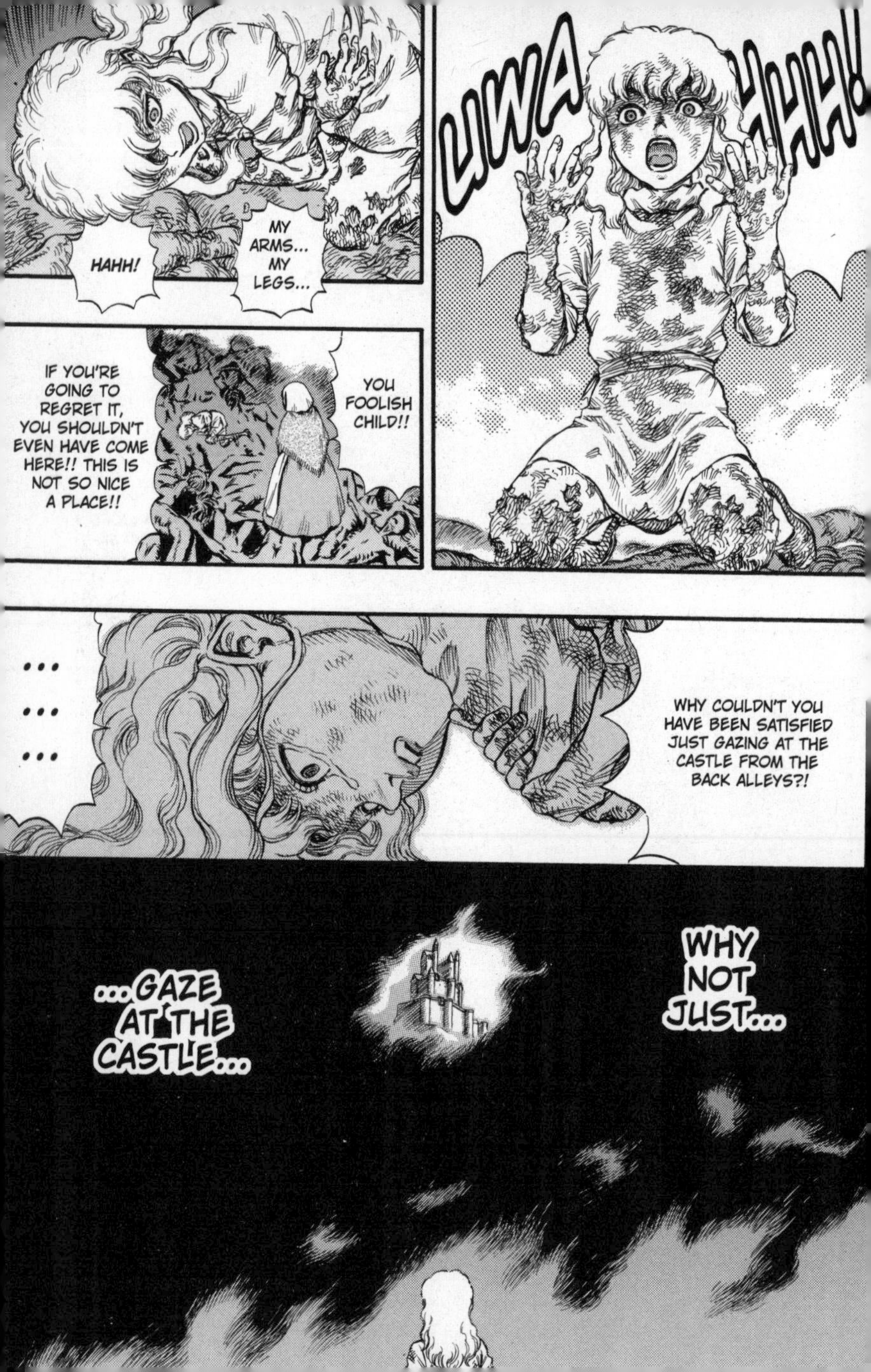
UWAHHHH!
MY ARMS... MY LEGS...
HAHH!
YOU FOOLISH CHILD!!
IF YOU'RE GOING TO REGRET IT, YOU SHOULDN'T EVEN HAVE COME HERE!! THIS IS NOT SO NICE A PLACE!!
WHY COULDN'T YOU HAVE BEEN SATISFIED JUST GAZING AT THE CASTLE FROM THE BACK ALLEYS?!
...
...
...
WHY NOT JUST...
...GAZE AT THE CASTLE...

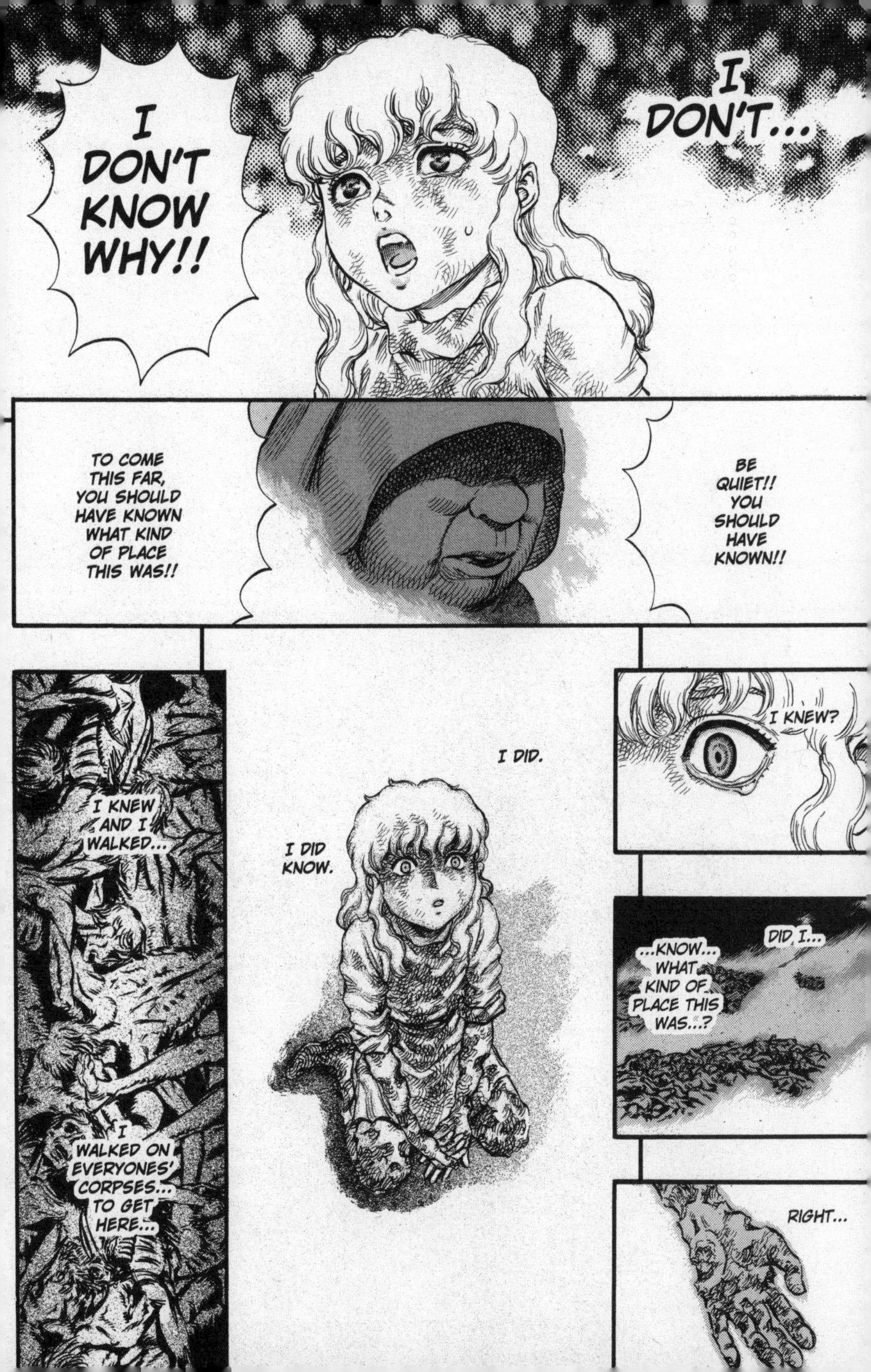
I DON'T...
I DON'T KNOW WHY!!
BE QUIET!! YOU SHOULD HAVE KNOWN!!
TO COME THIS FAR, YOU SHOULD HAVE KNOWN WHAT KIND OF PLACE THIS WAS!!
I KNEW?
DID I...
...KNOW... WHAT KIND OF PLACE THIS WAS...?
RIGHT...
I DID.
I DID KNOW.
I KNEW AND I WALKED...
I WALKED ON EVERYONES' CORPSES... TO GET HERE...

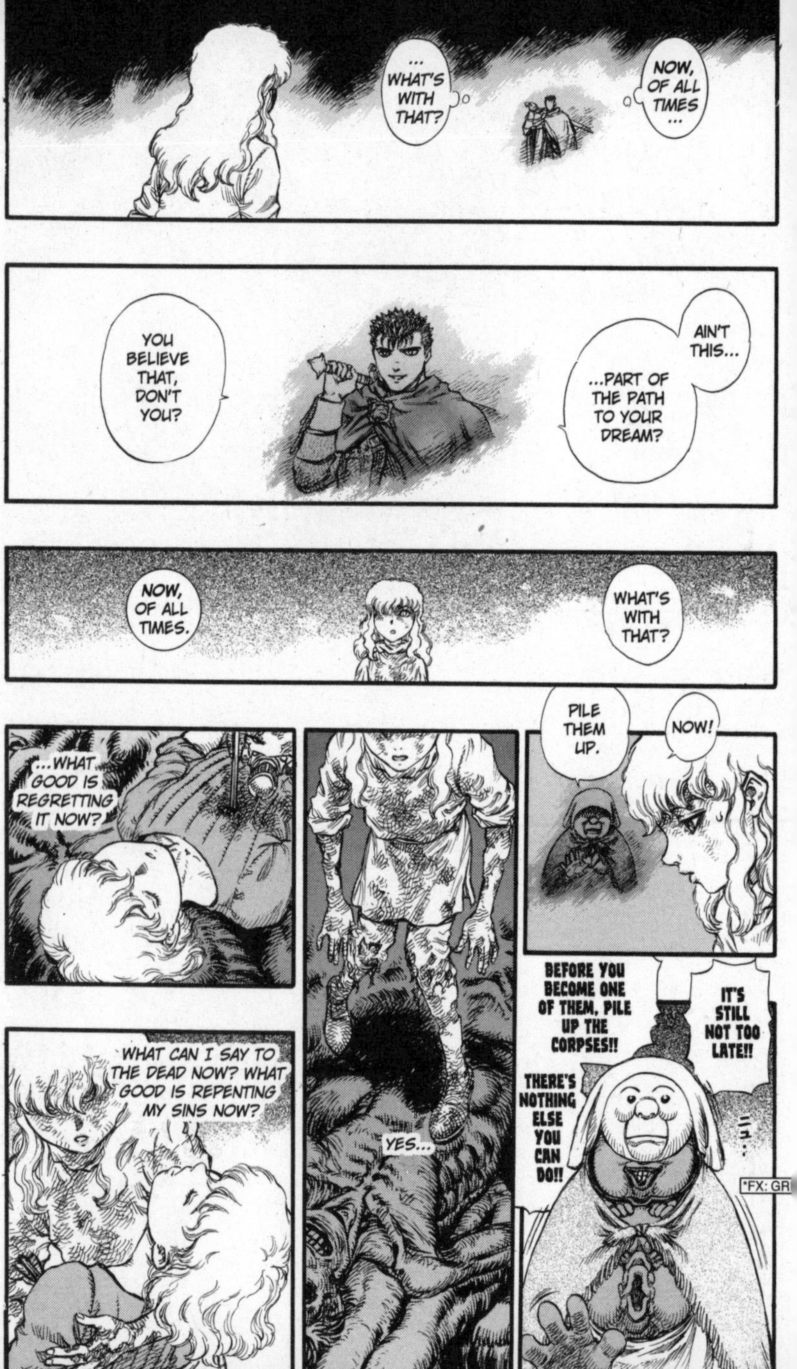
NOW, OF ALL TIMES ...
... WHAT'S WITH THAT?
AIN'T THIS...
...PART OF THE PATH TO YOUR DREAM?
YOU BELIEVE THAT, DON'T YOU?
WHAT'S WITH THAT?
NOW, OF ALL TIMES.
NOW!
PILE THEM UP.
IT'S STILL NOT TOO LATE!!
BEFORE YOU BECOME ONE OF THEM, PILE UP THE CORPSES!!
THERE'S NOTHING ELSE YOU CAN DO!!
*FX: GR
YES...
...WHAT GOOD IS REGRETTING IT NOW?
WHAT CAN I SAY TO THE DEAD NOW? WHAT GOOD IS REPENTING MY SINS NOW?

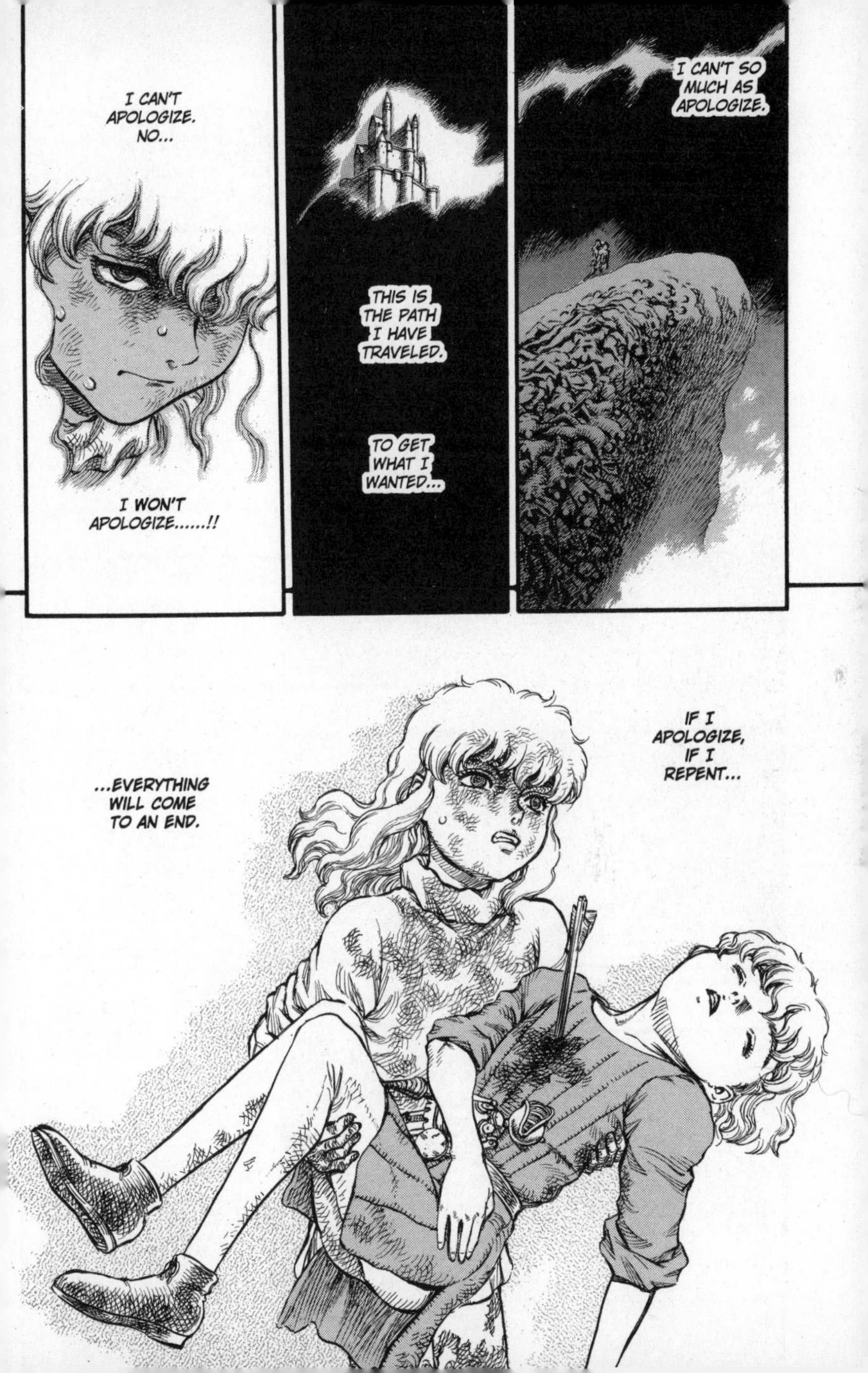
I CAN'T SO MUCH AS APOLOGIZE.
THIS IS THE PATH I HAVE TRAVELED.
TO GET WHAT I WANTED...
I CAN'T APOLOGIZE. NO...
I WON'T APOLOGIZE......!!
IF I APOLOGIZE, IF I REPENT...
...EVERYTHING WILL COME TO AN END.

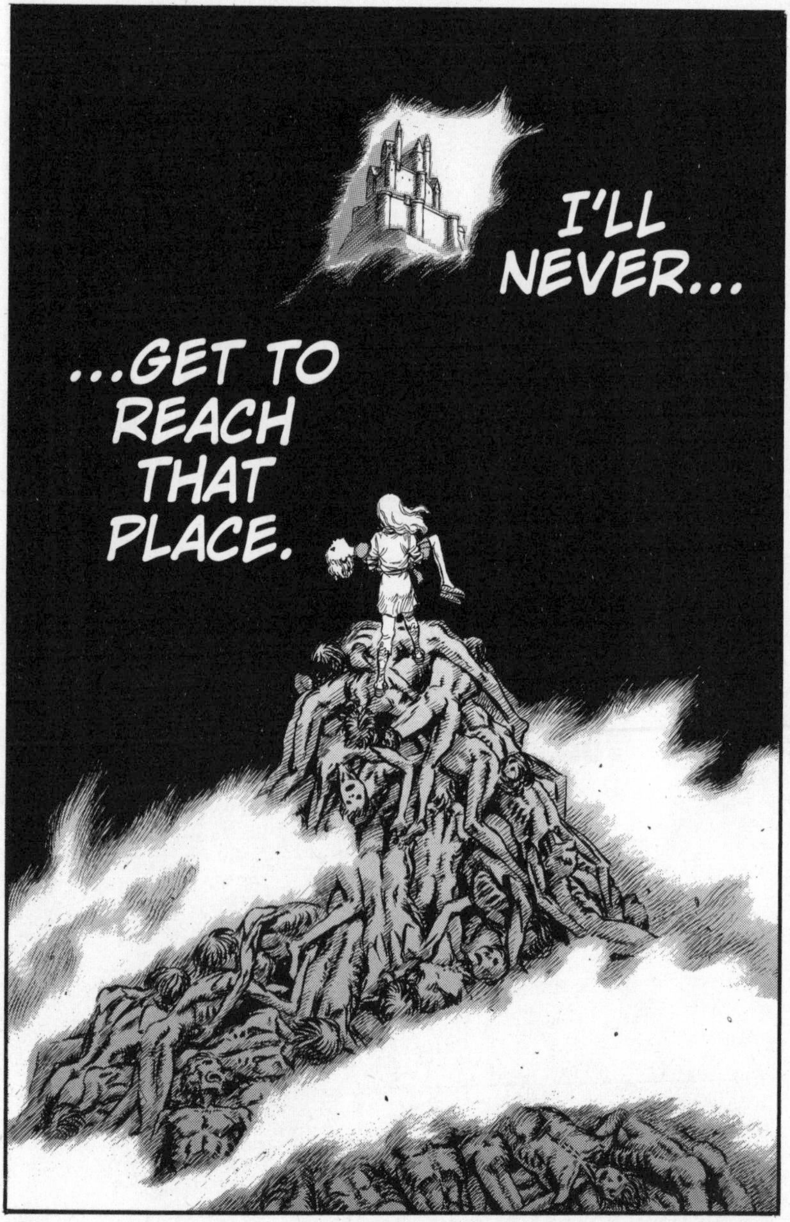
I'LL NEVER...
...GET TO REACH THAT PLACE.

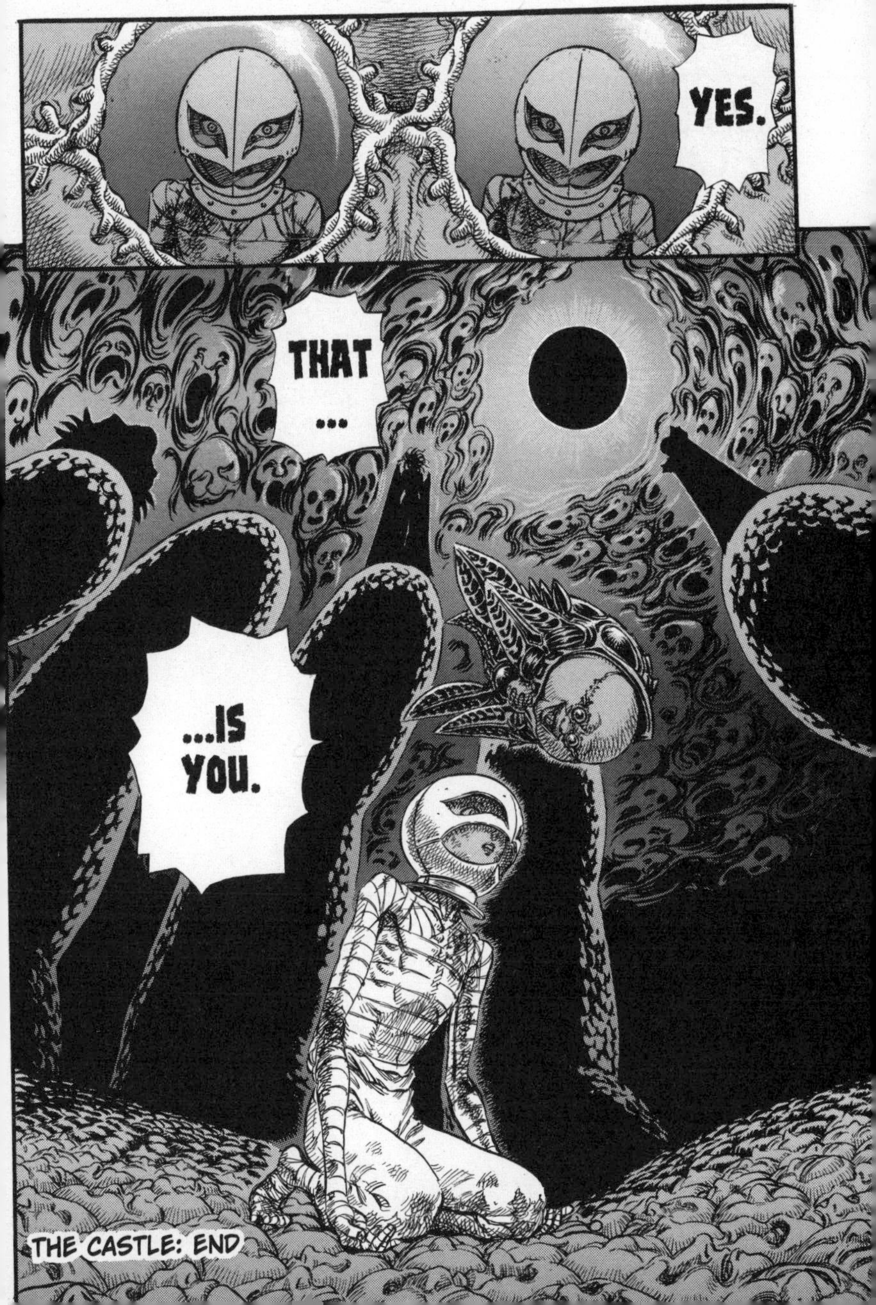
YES.
THAT ...
...IS YOU.
THE CASTLE: END

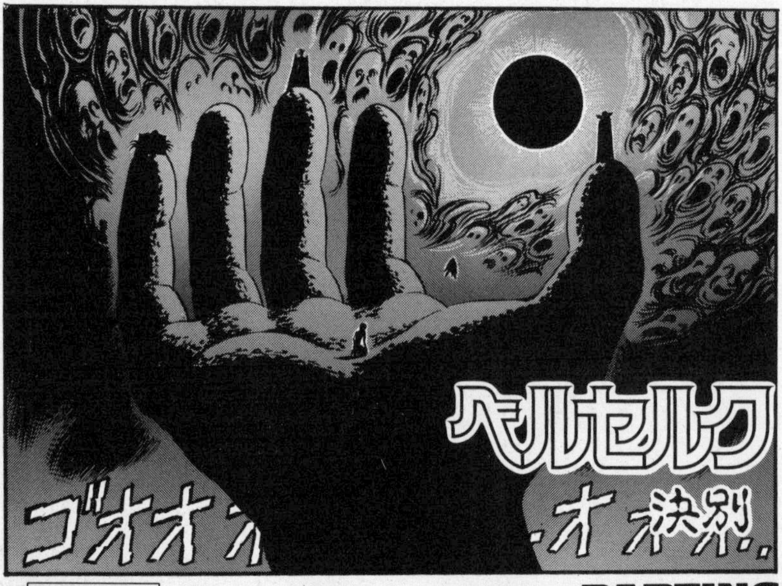
ベルセルク
決別

*FX: GOHHHH OHHH

PARTING

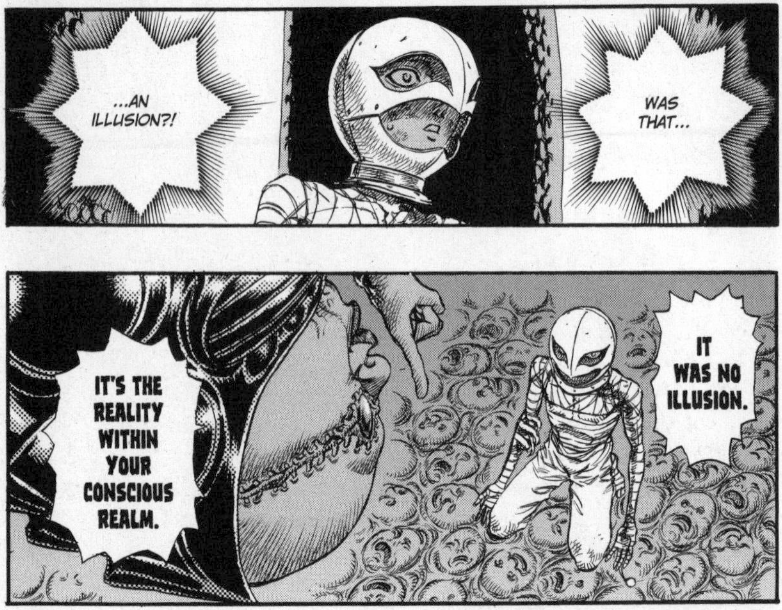
WAS THAT...
...AN ILLUSION?!
IT WAS NO ILLUSION.
IT'S THE REALITY WITHIN YOUR CONSCIOUS REALM.

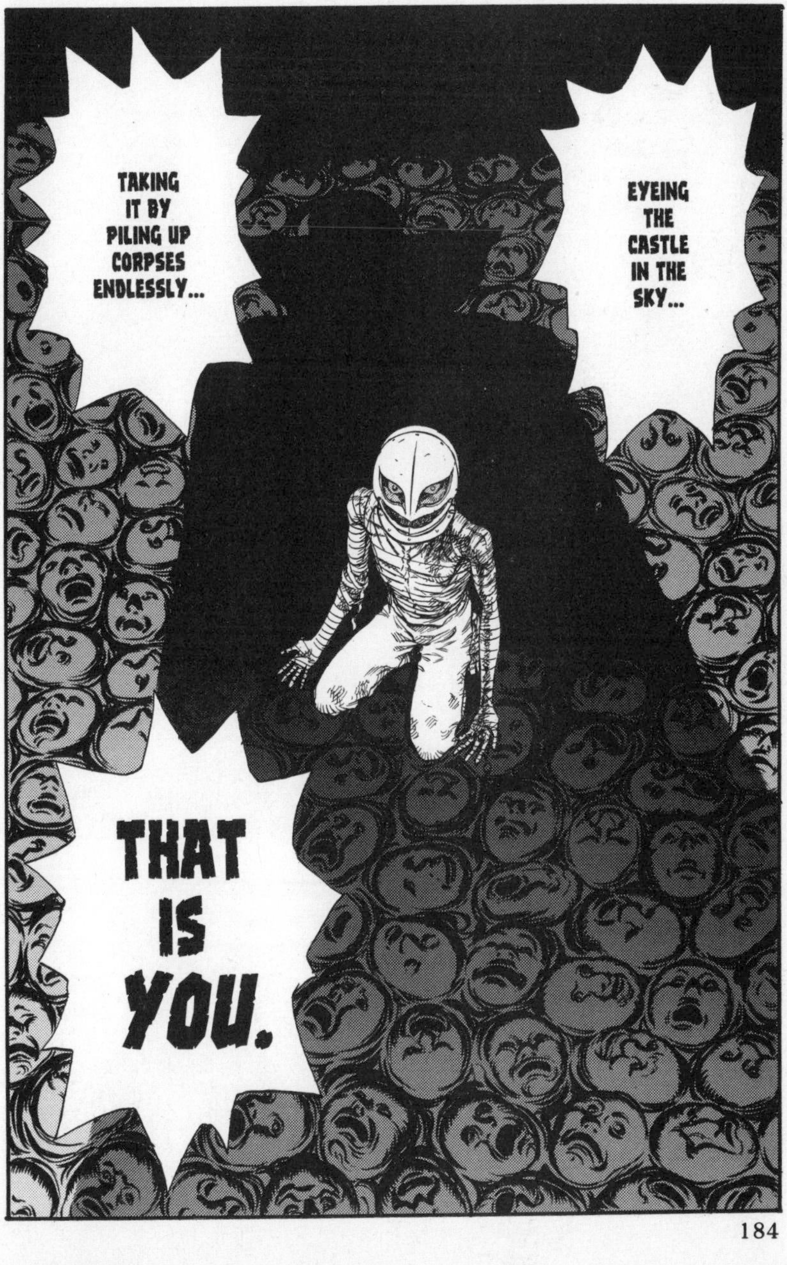
EYEING THE CASTLE IN THE SKY...
TAKING IT BY PILING UP CORPSES ENDLESSLY...
THAT IS YOU.

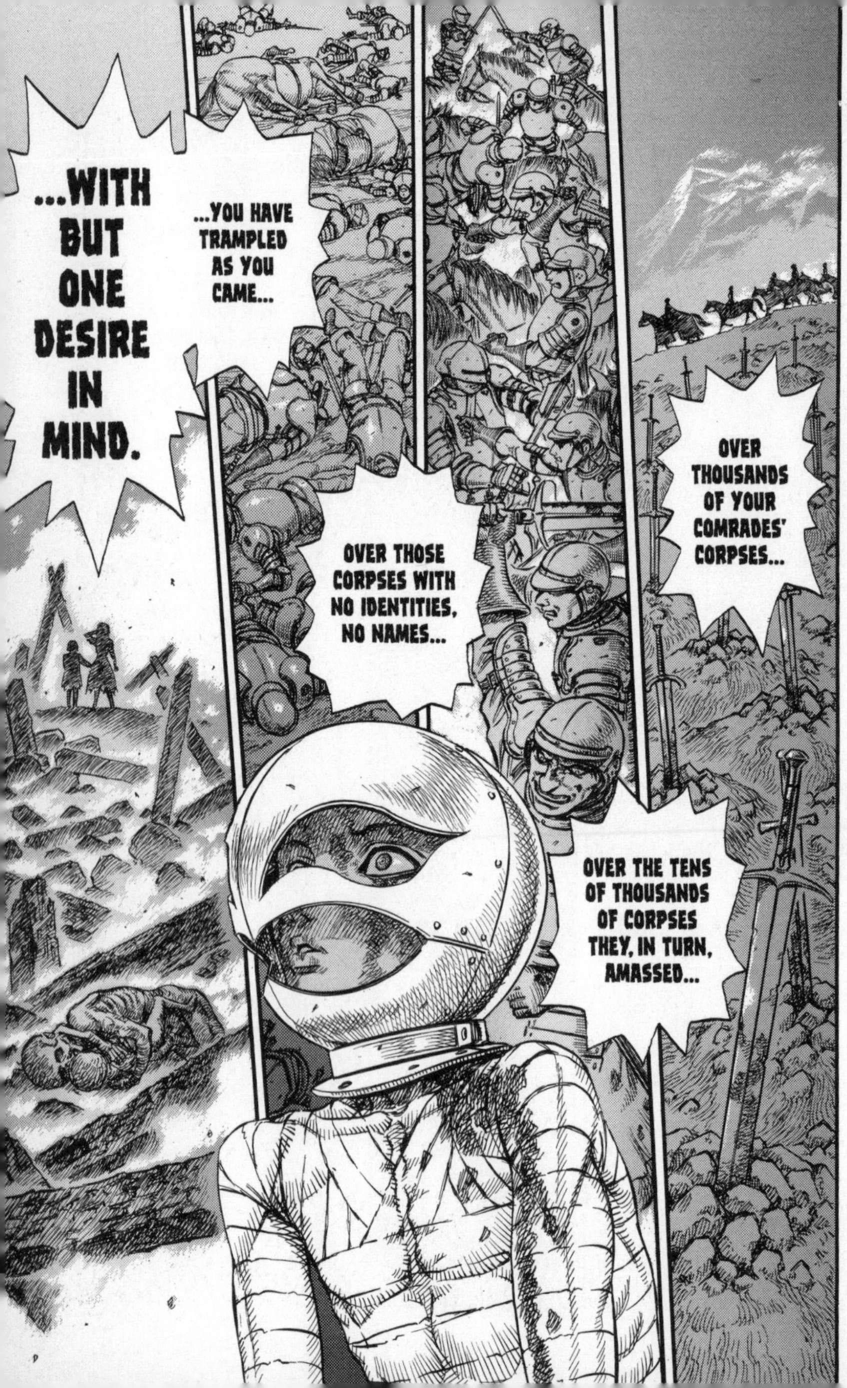
OVER THOUSANDS OF YOUR COMRADES' CORPSES...
OVER THE TENS OF THOUSANDS OF CORPSES THEY, IN TURN, AMASSED...
OVER THOSE CORPSES WITH NO IDENTITIES, NO NAMES...
...YOU HAVE TRAMPLED AS YOU CAME...
...WITH BUT ONE DESIRE IN MIND.

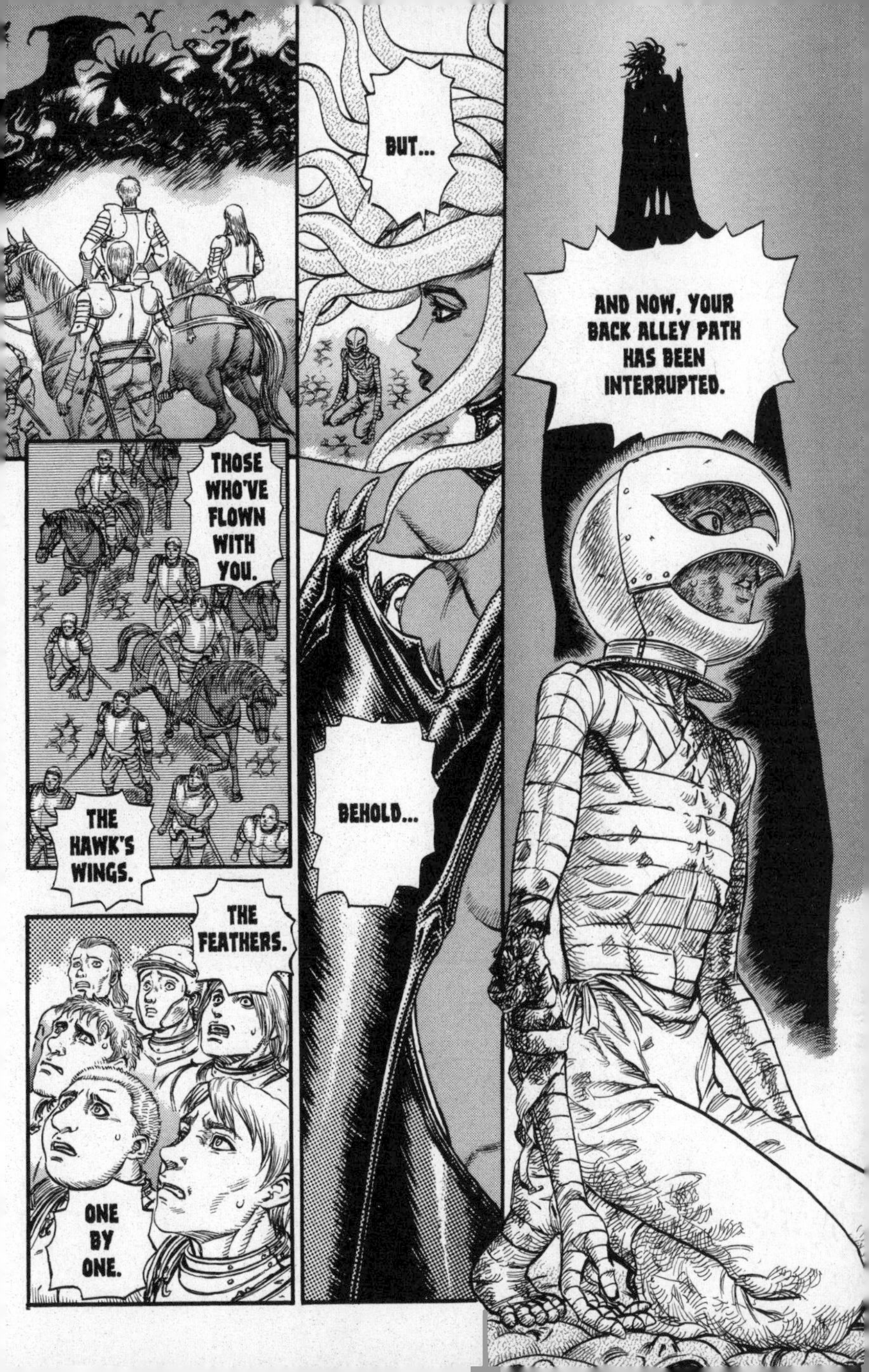
AND NOW, YOUR BACK ALLEY PATH HAS BEEN INTERRUPTED.
BUT...
BEHOLD...
THOSE WHO'VE FLOWN WITH YOU.
THE HAWK'S WINGS.
THE FEATHERS.
ONE BY ONE.

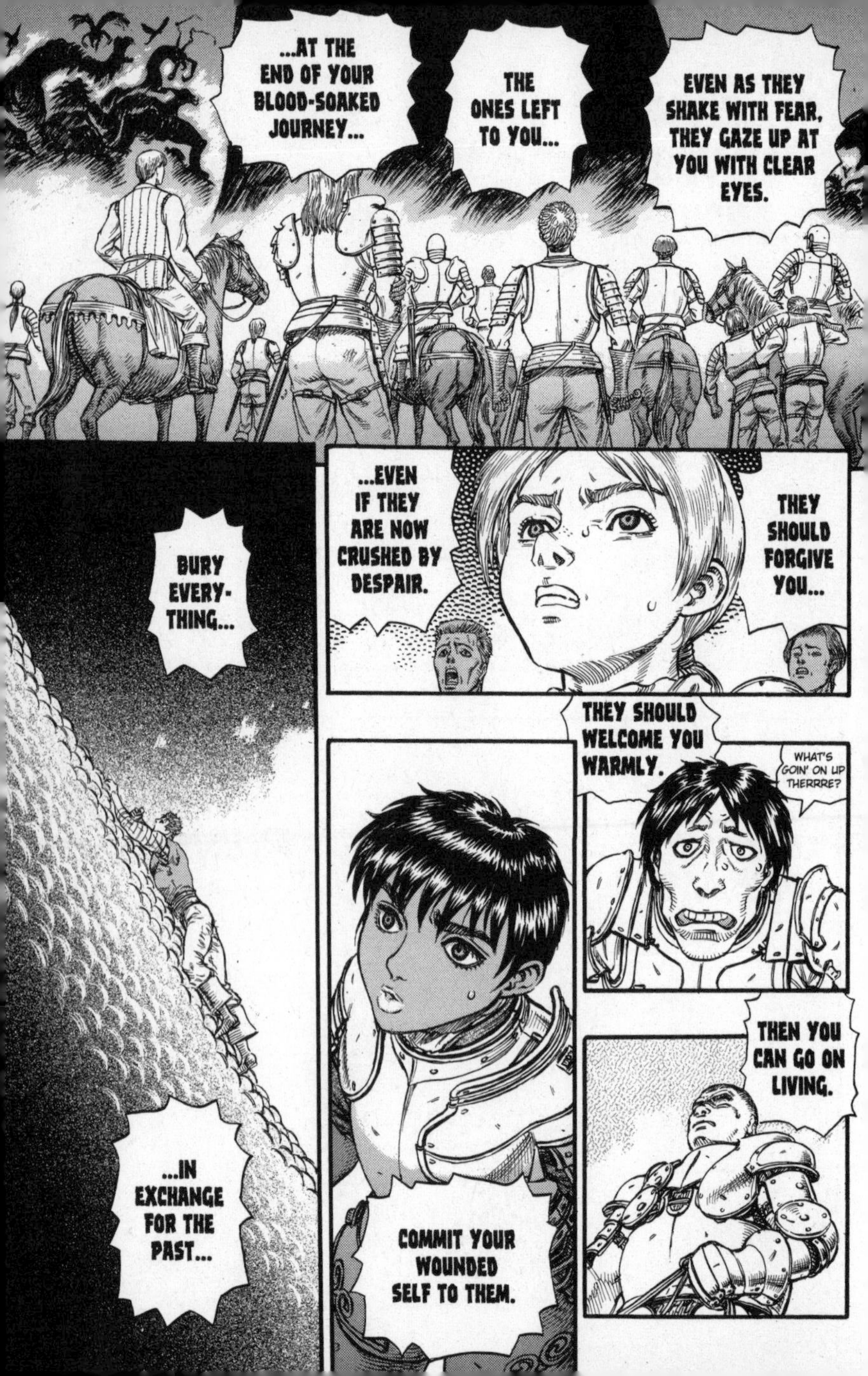
...AT THE END OF YOUR BLOOD-SOAKED JOURNEY...
THE ONES LEFT TO YOU...
EVEN AS THEY SHAKE WITH FEAR, THEY GAZE UP AT YOU WITH CLEAR EYES.
BURY EVERY-THING...
...IN EXCHANGE FOR THE PAST...
...EVEN IF THEY ARE NOW CRUSHED BY DESPAIR.
THEY SHOULD FORGIVE YOU...
THEY SHOULD WELCOME YOU WARMLY.
COMMIT YOUR WOUNDED SELF TO THEM.
WHAT'S GOIN' ON UP THERRRE?
THEN YOU CAN GO ON LIVING.

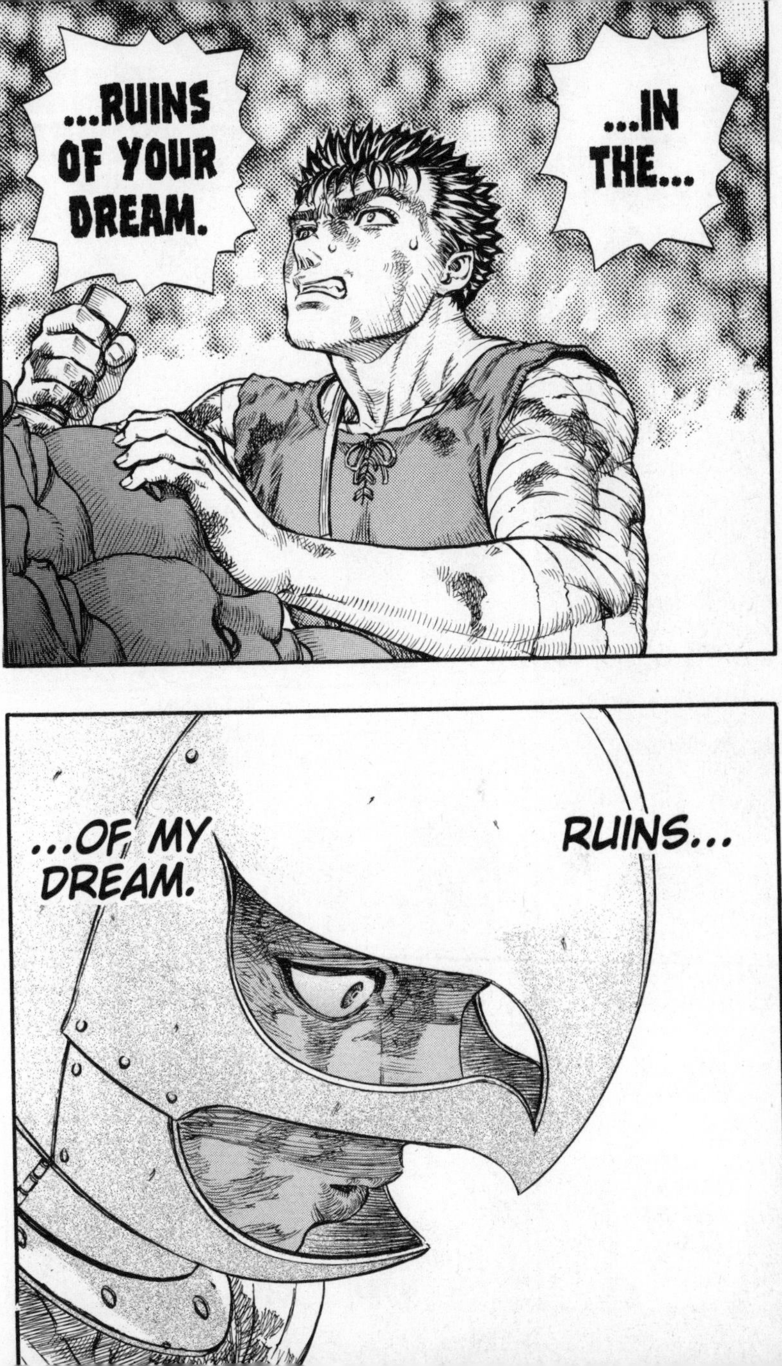
...IN THE...
...RUINS OF YOUR DREAM.
RUINS...
...OF MY DREAM.

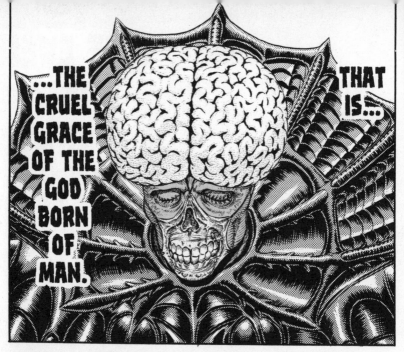

...THE CRUEL GRACE OF THE GOD BORN OF MAN.

THAT IS...

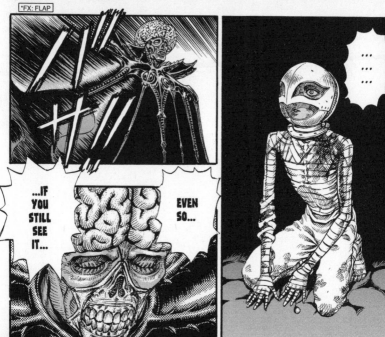

...IF YOU STILL SEE IT...

EVEN SO...

...
...
...

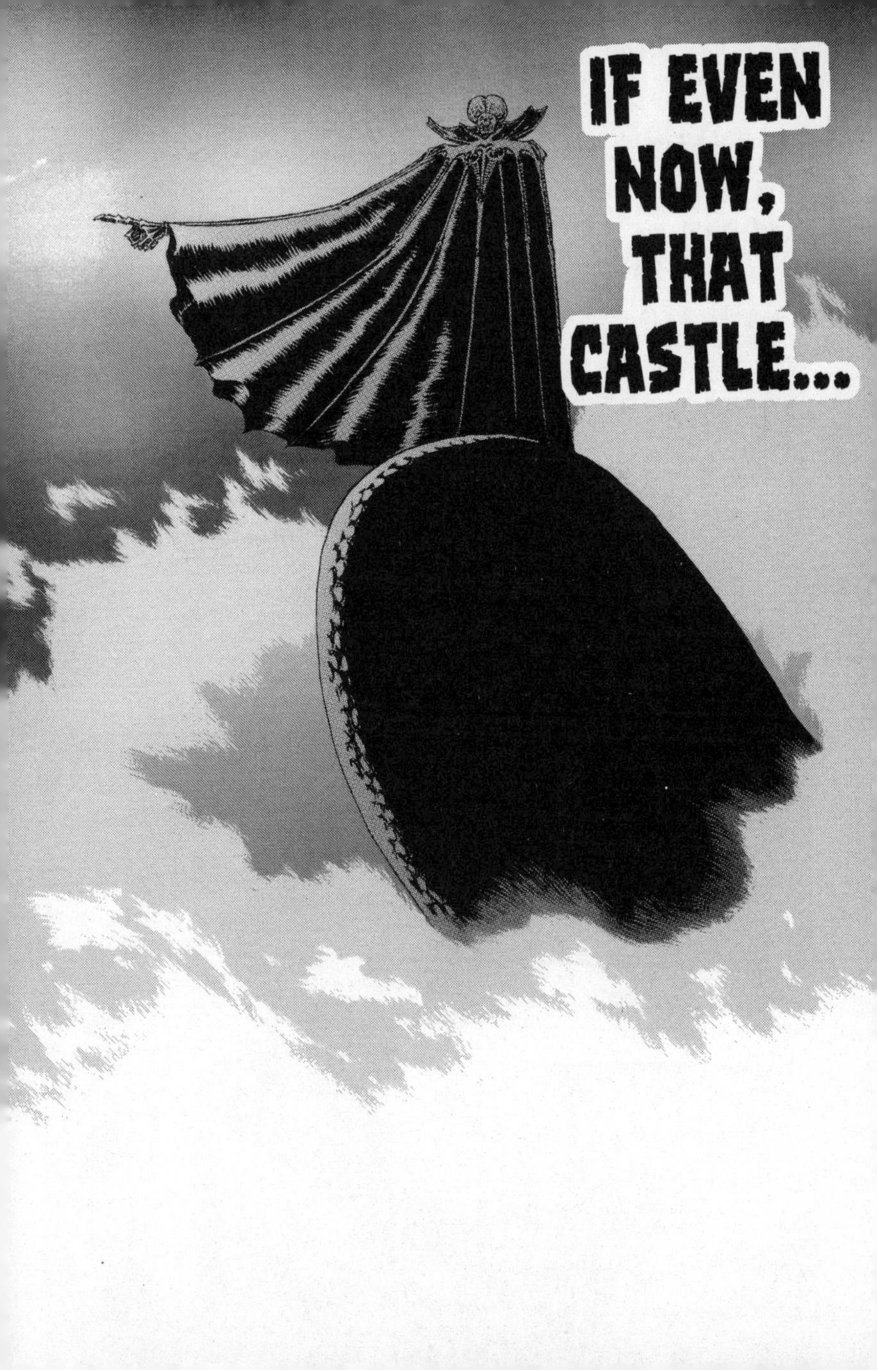
IF EVEN NOW, THAT CASTLE...

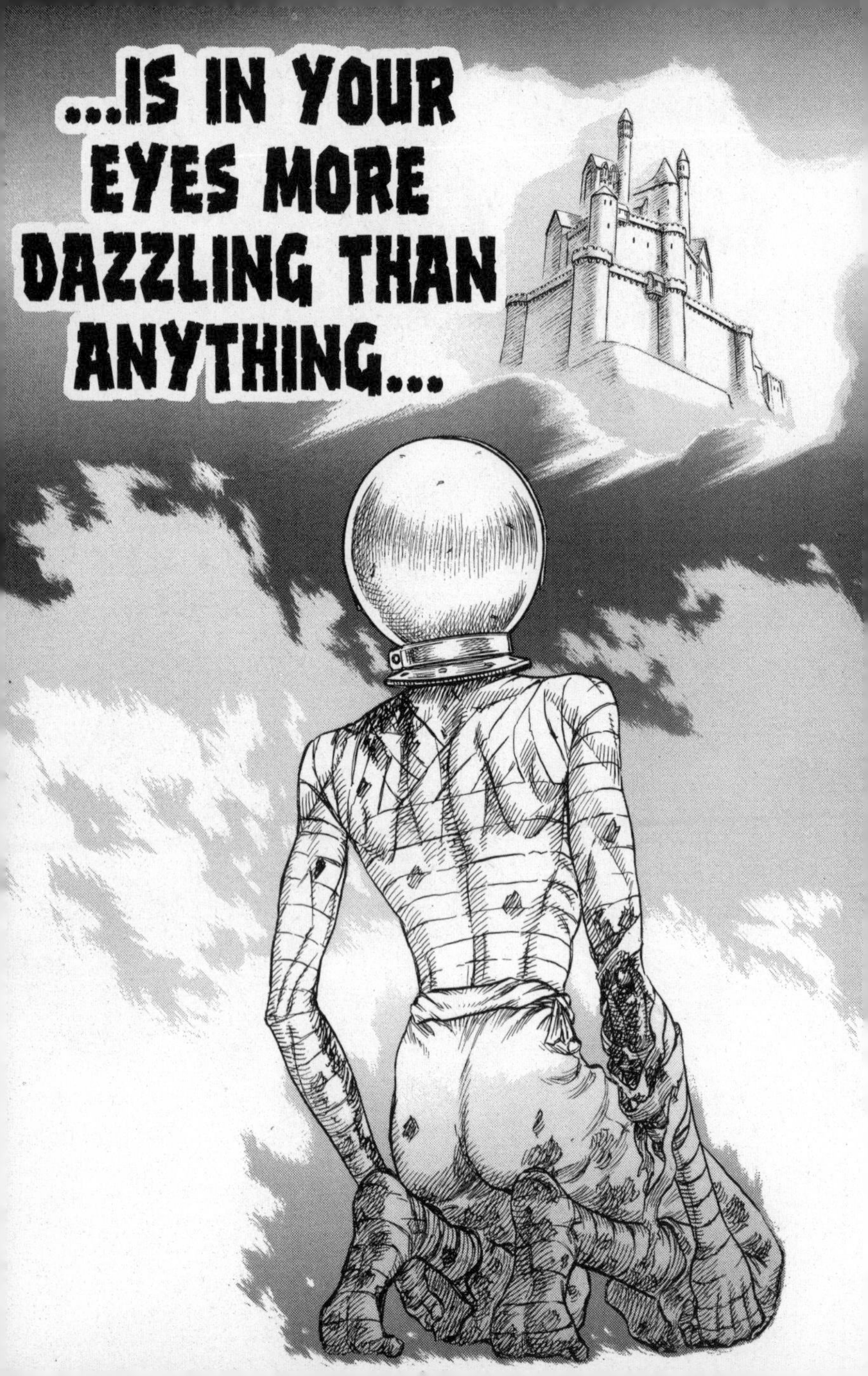
...IS IN YOUR EYES MORE DAZZLING THAN ANYTHING...

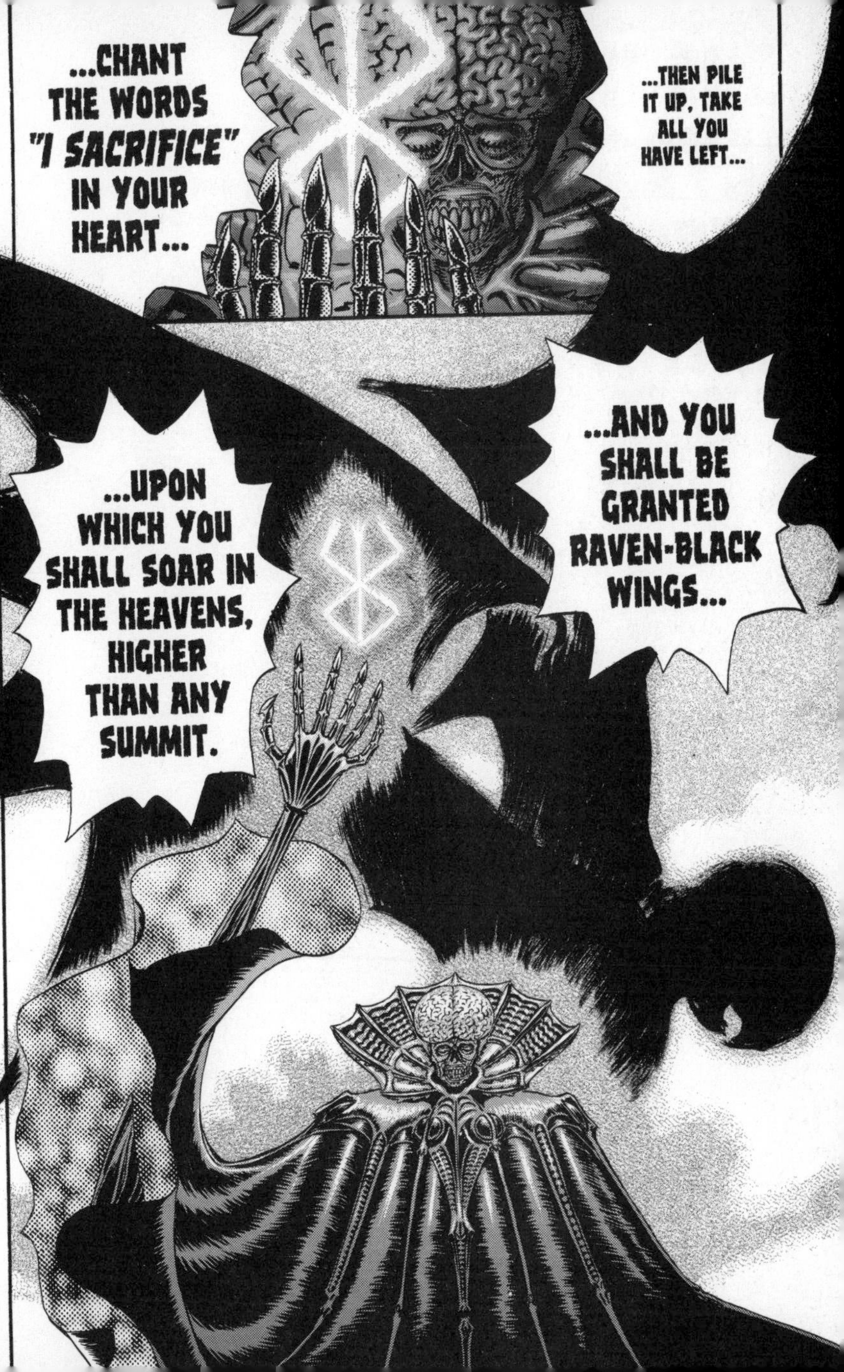
...THEN PILE IT UP, TAKE ALL YOU HAVE LEFT...
...CHANT THE WORDS "I SACRIFICE" IN YOUR HEART...
...AND YOU SHALL BE GRANTED RAVEN-BLACK WINGS...
...UPON WHICH YOU SHALL SOAR IN THE HEAVENS, HIGHER THAN ANY SUMMIT.

*FX: HAHH HAHH

GRIFFITH!!

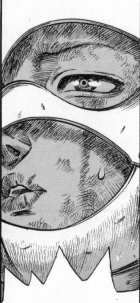

IF IT BE REASON THAT DESTINY TRANSCEND HUMAN INTELLECT AND MAKE PLAYTHINGS OF CHILDREN...

...IT IS CAUSE AND EFFECT THAT A CHILD BEAR HIS EVIL AND CONFRONT DESTINY.

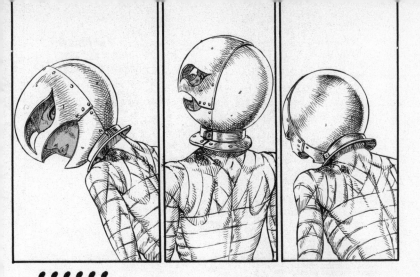

・・・・・・
YES.

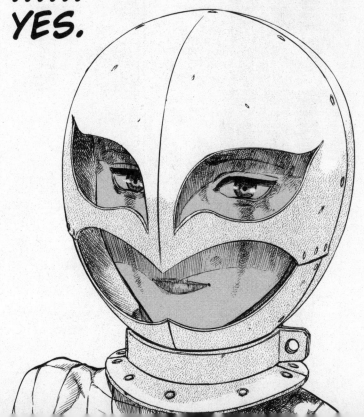

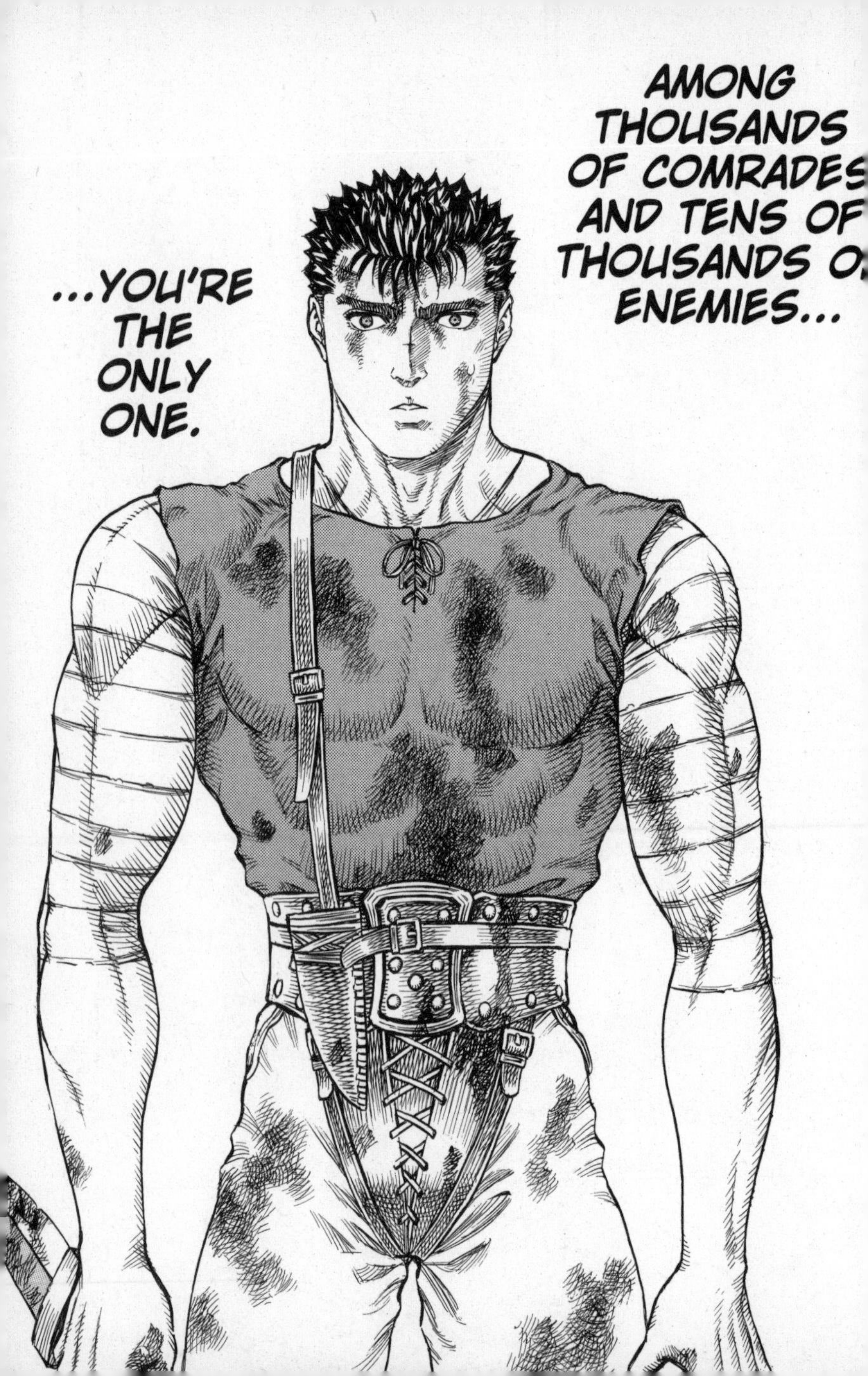
AMONG THOUSANDS OF COMRADES AND TENS OF THOUSANDS O ENEMIES...
...YOU'RE THE ONLY ONE.

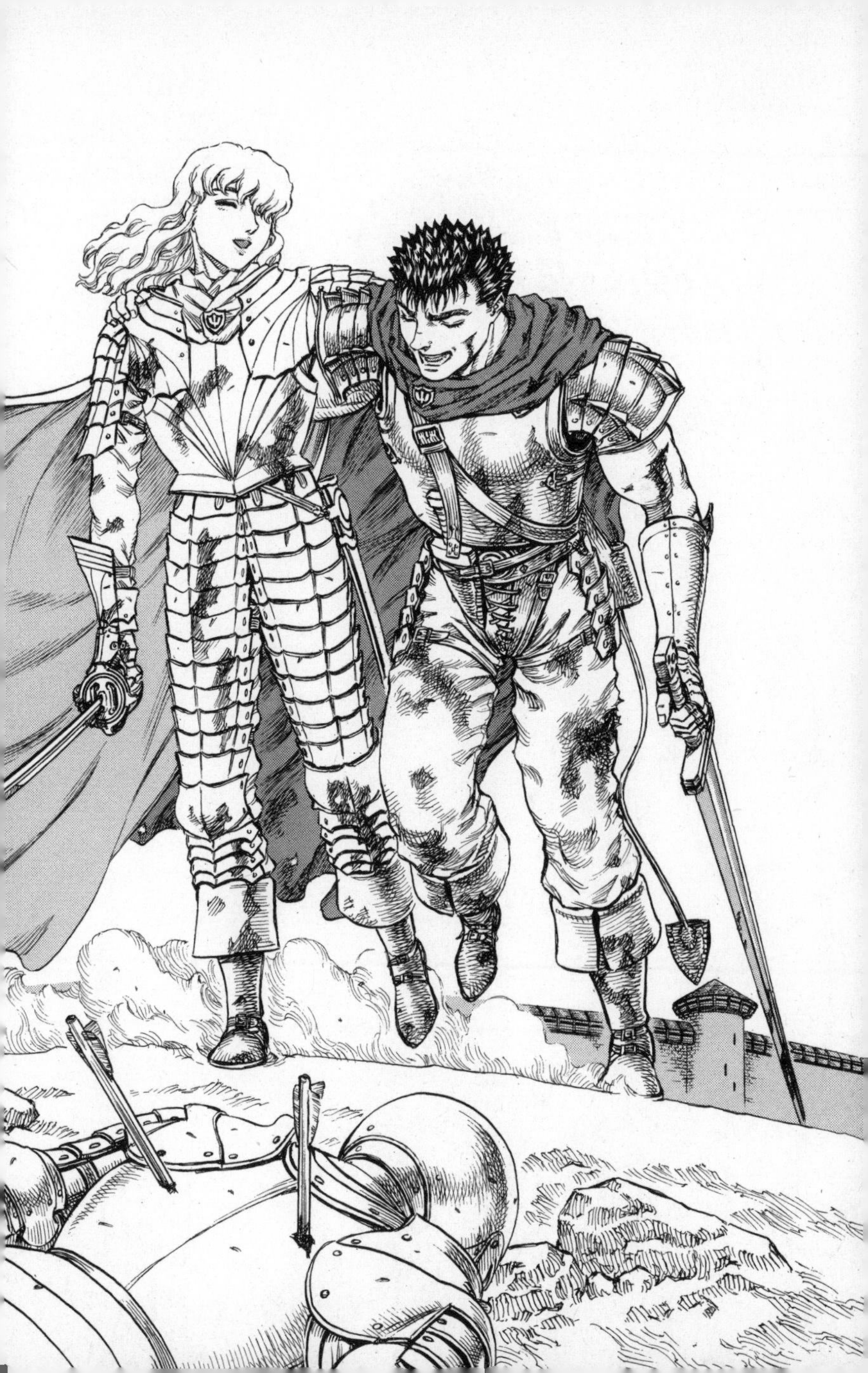

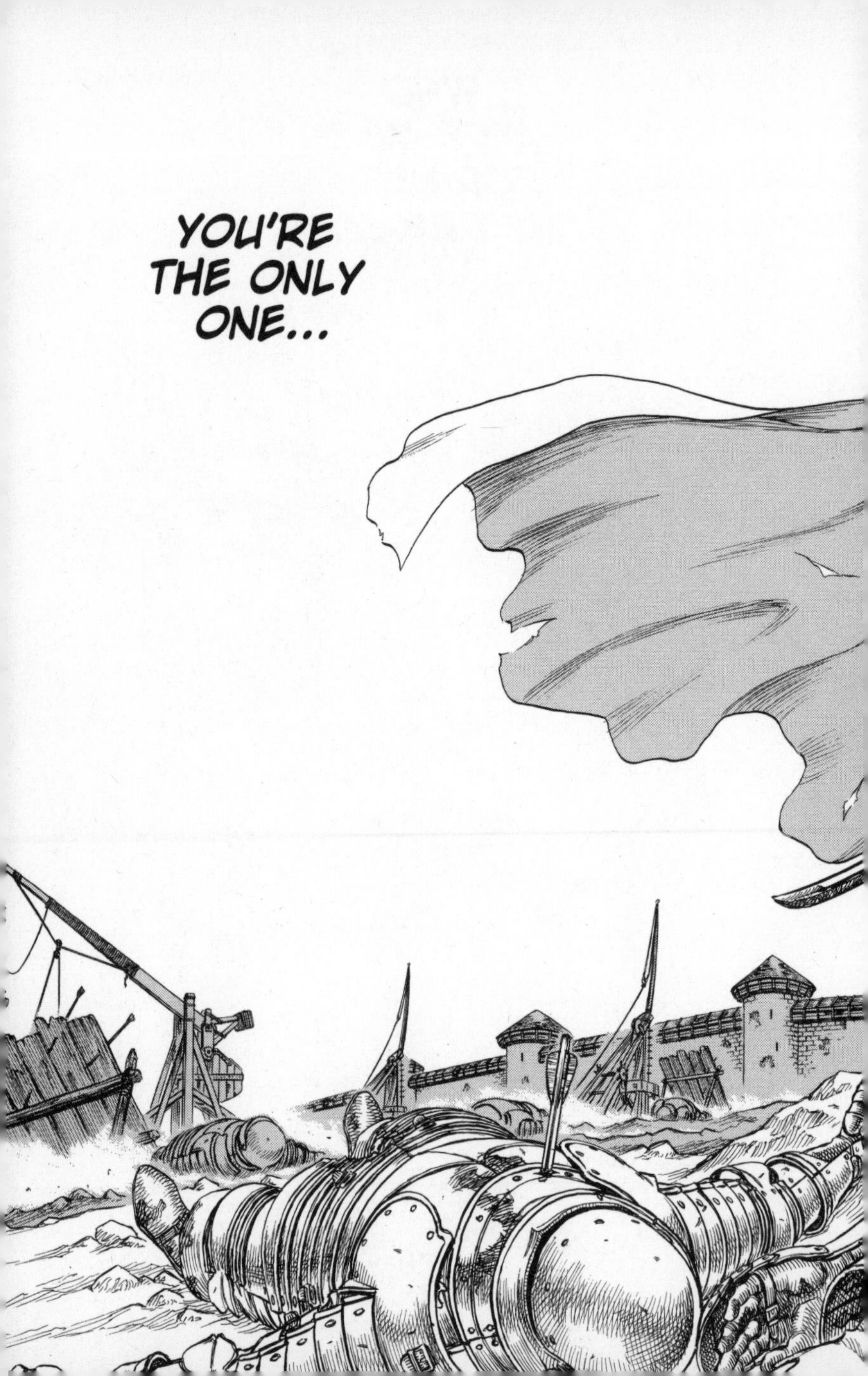
YOU'RE THE ONLY ONE...

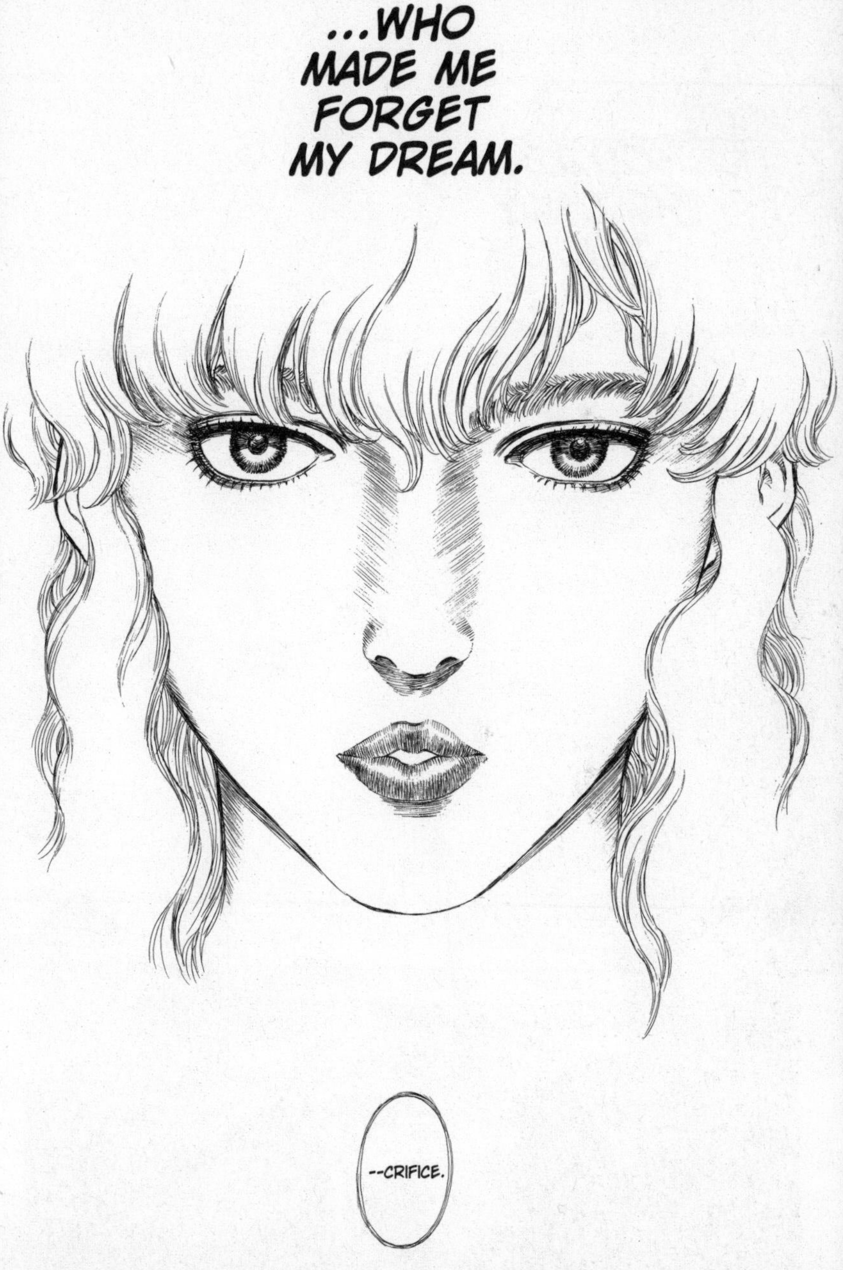
...WHO MADE ME FORGET MY DREAM.
--CRIFICE.

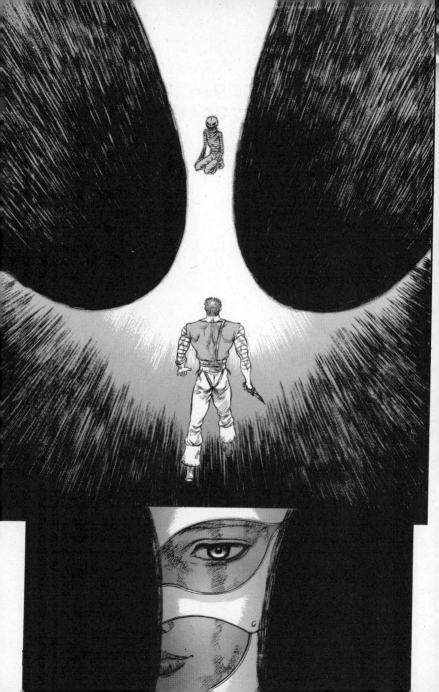

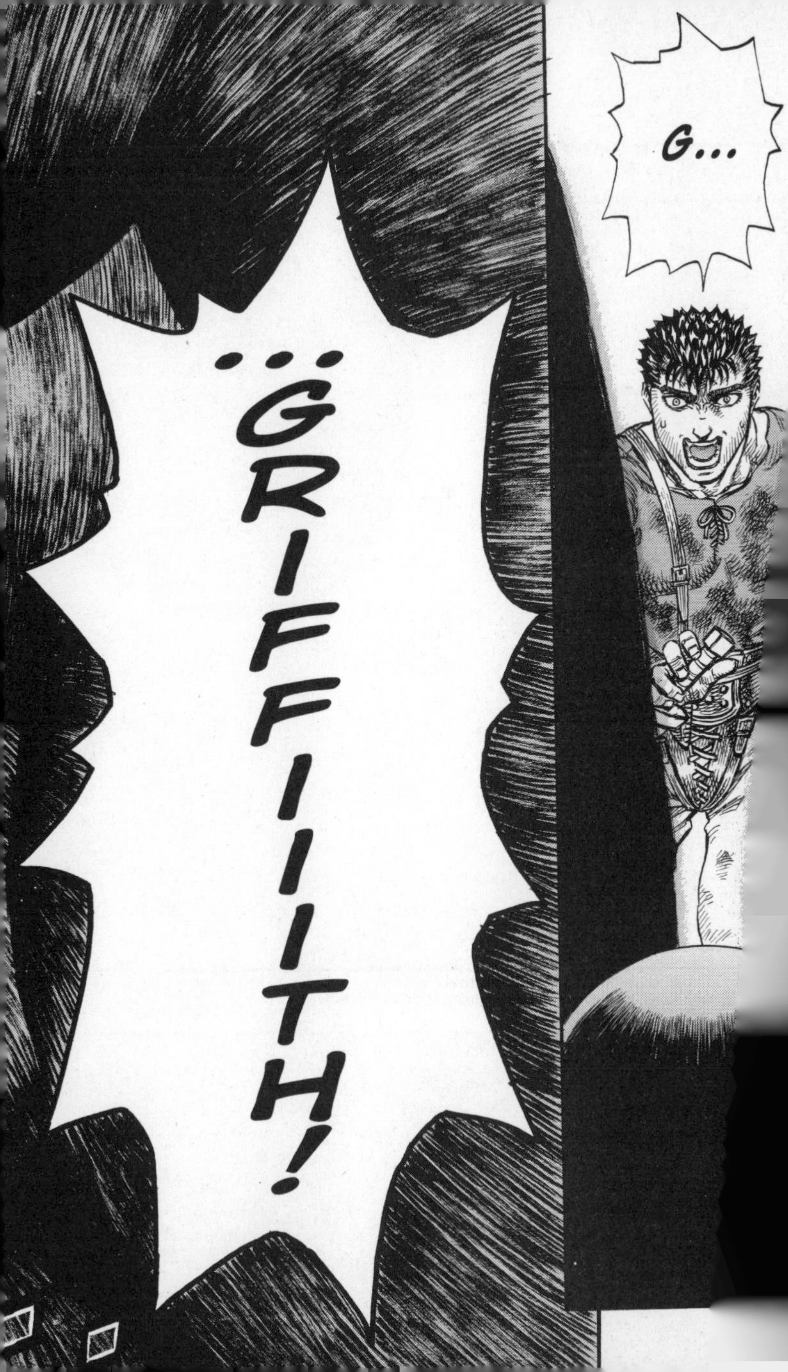
G...
...GRIFFITH!

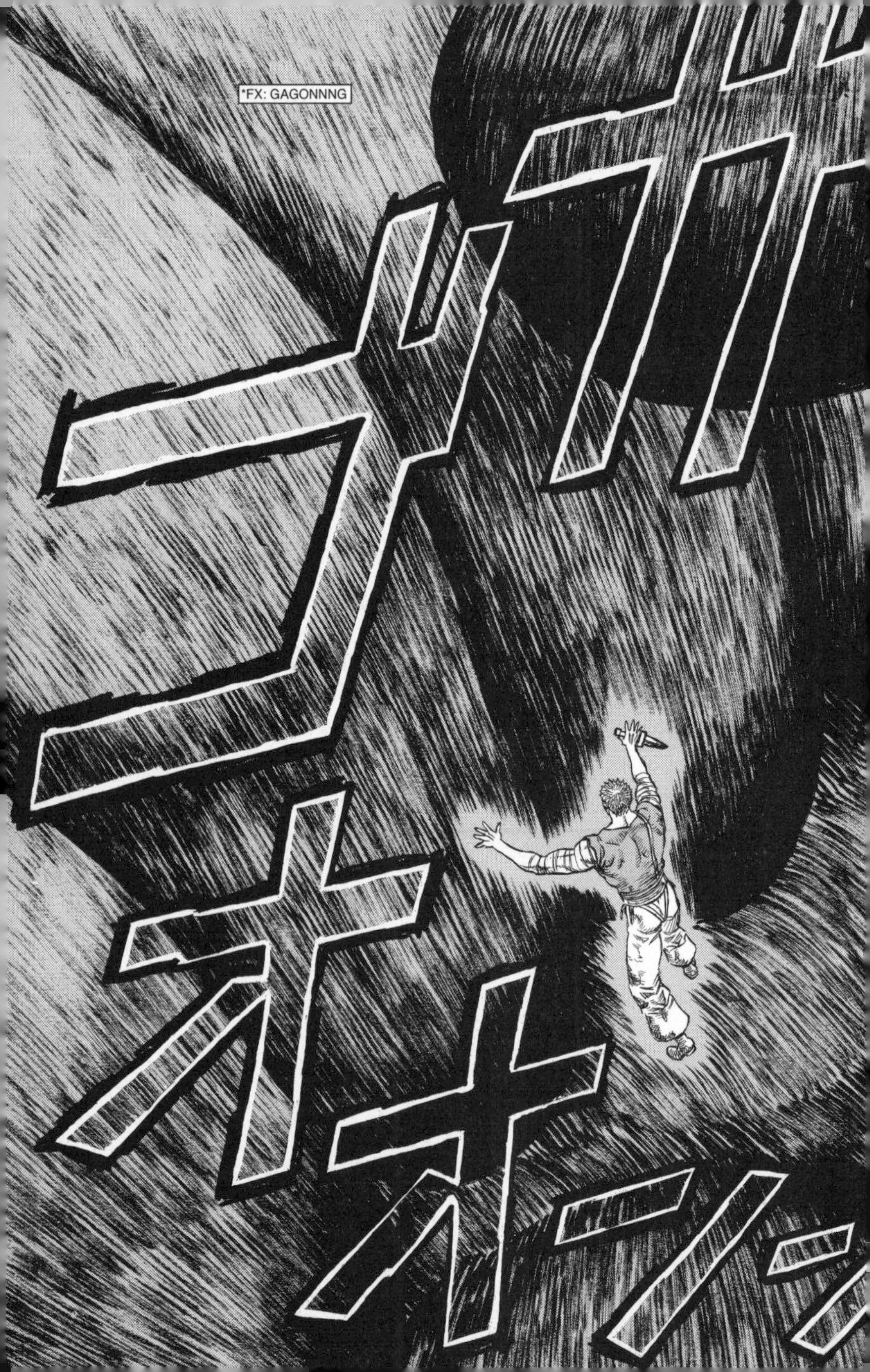
*FX: GAGONNNG

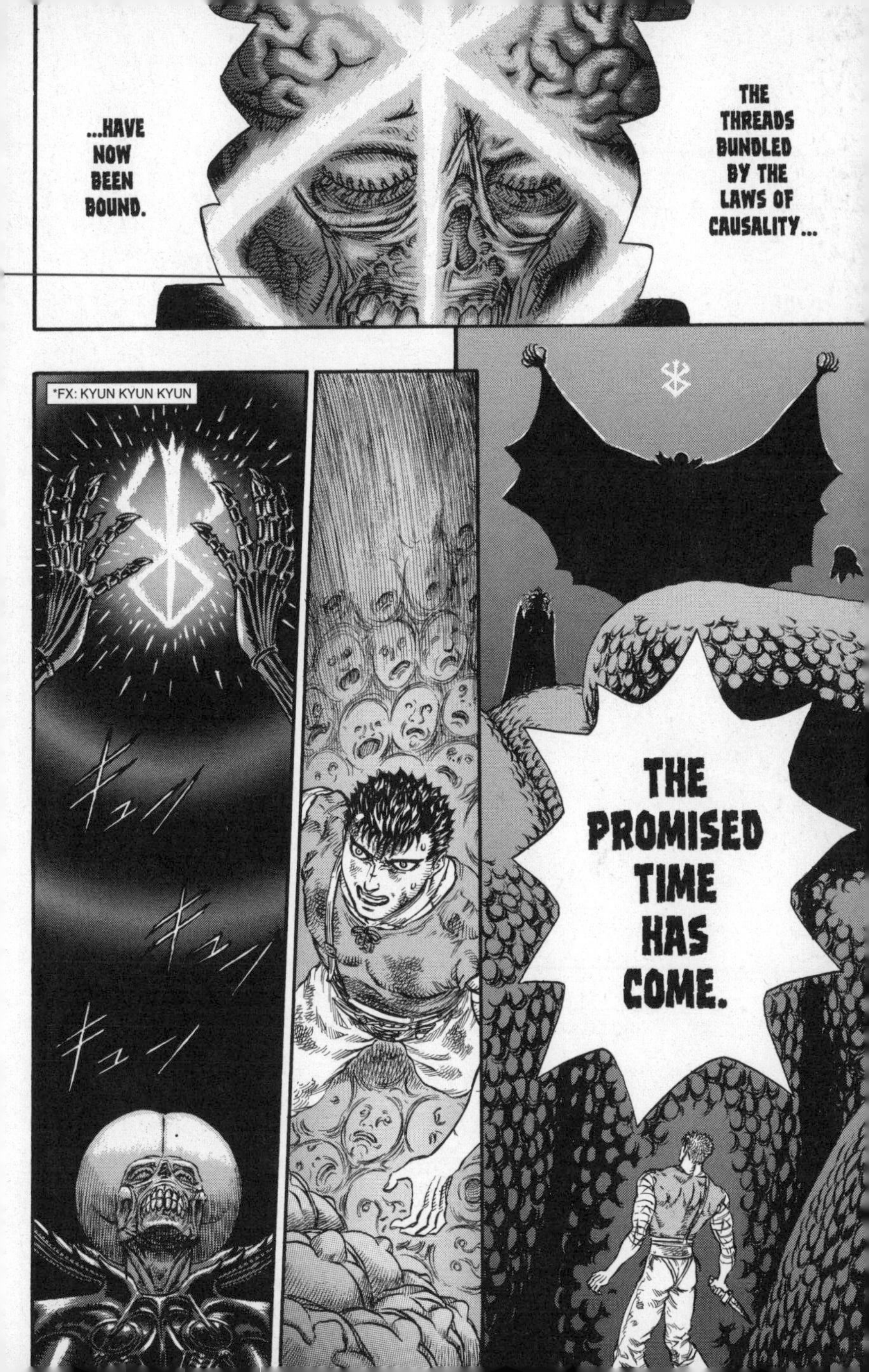
THE THREADS BUNDLED BY THE LAWS OF CAUSALITY...
...HAVE NOW BEEN BOUND.
THE PROMISED TIME HAS COME.
*FX: KYUN KYUN KYUN
キュン
キュン
キュン

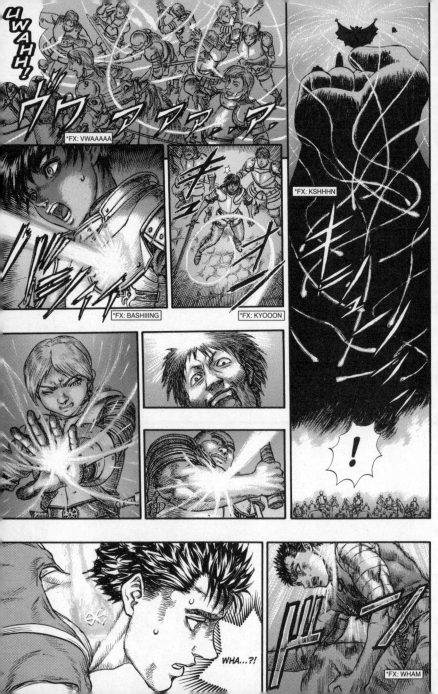

UWAHH!

*FX: VWAAAAA

*FX: BASHIIING

*FX: KYOOON

*FX: KSHHHN

!

WHA...?!

*FX: WHAM

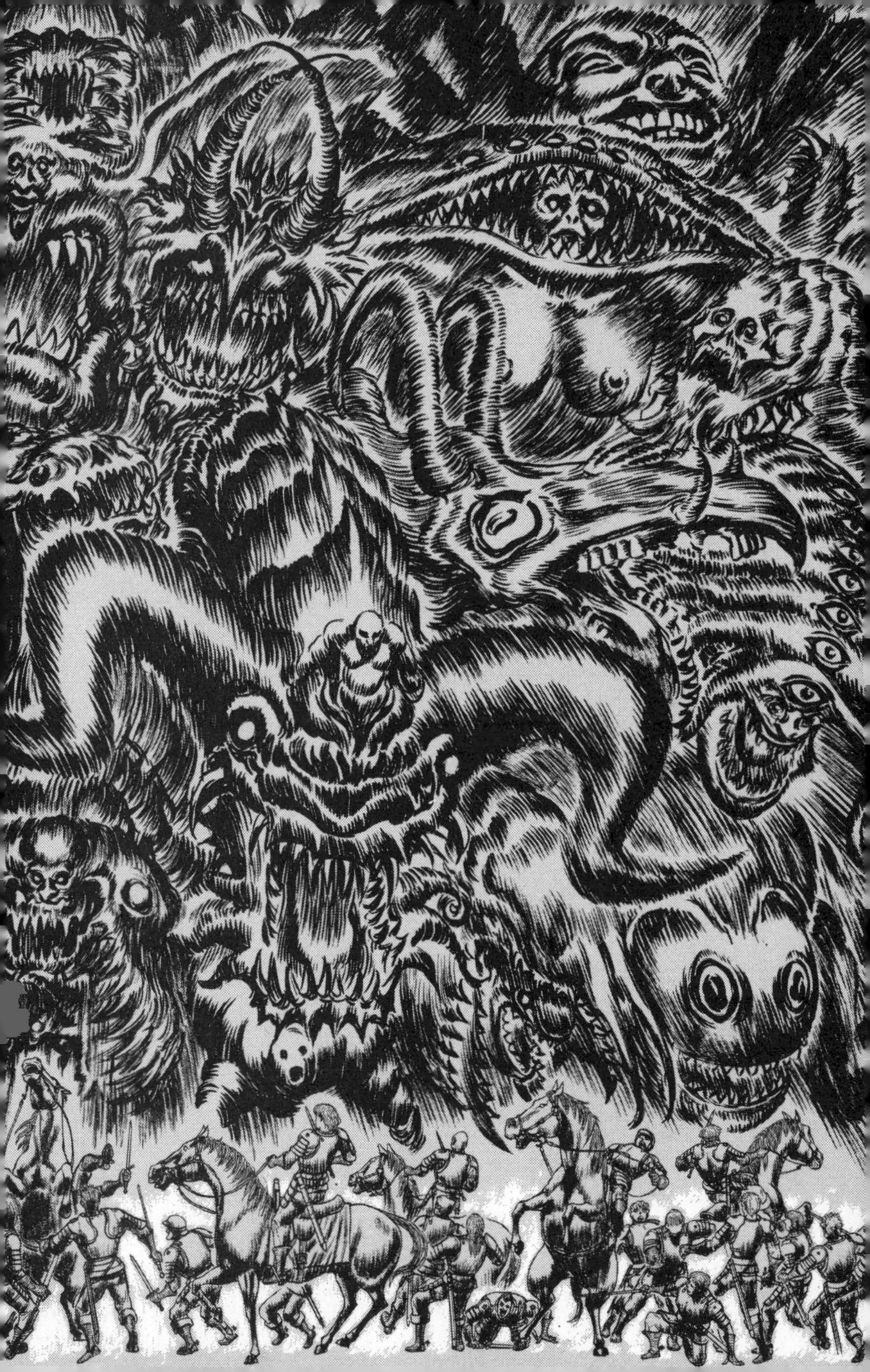

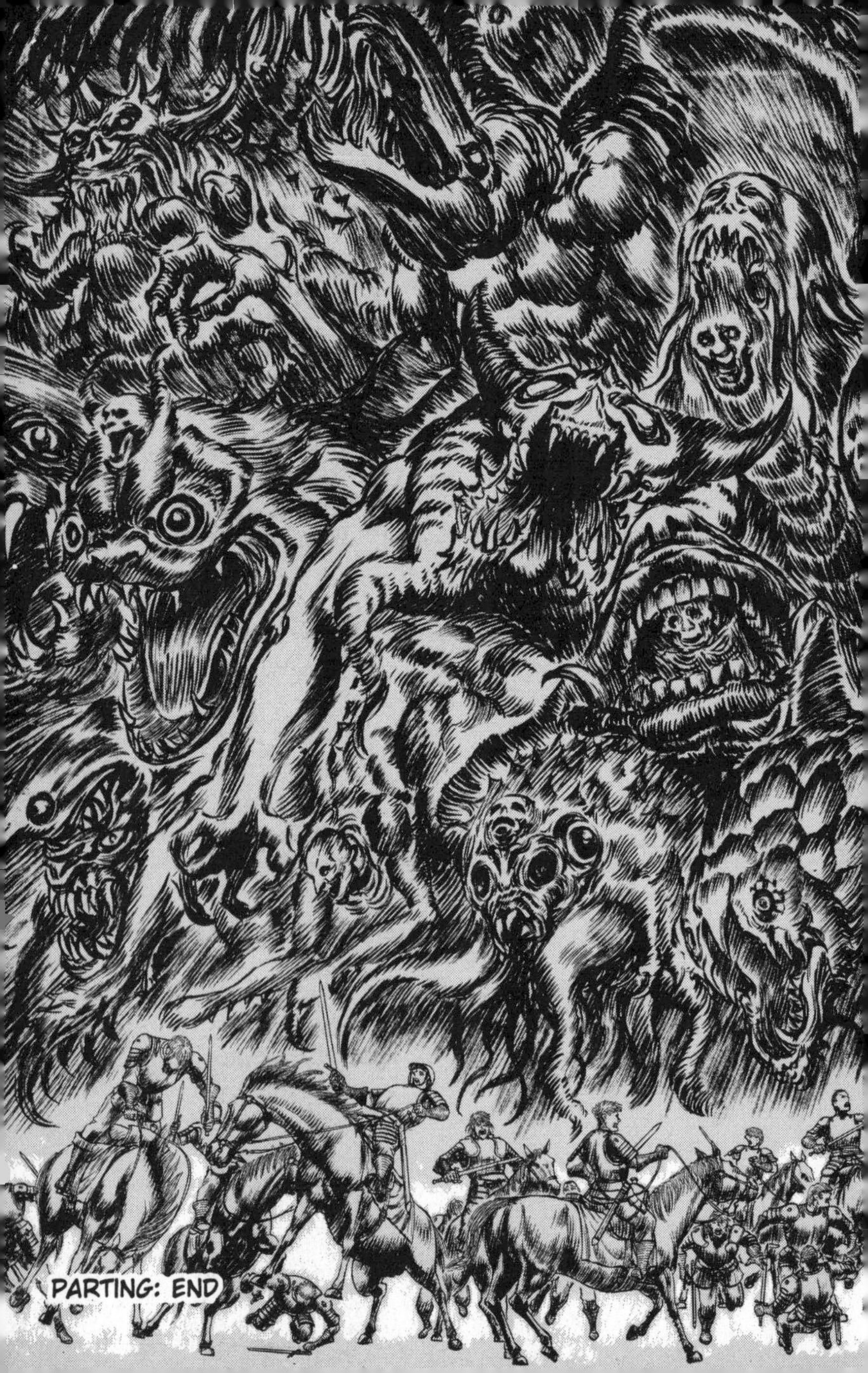
PARTING: END

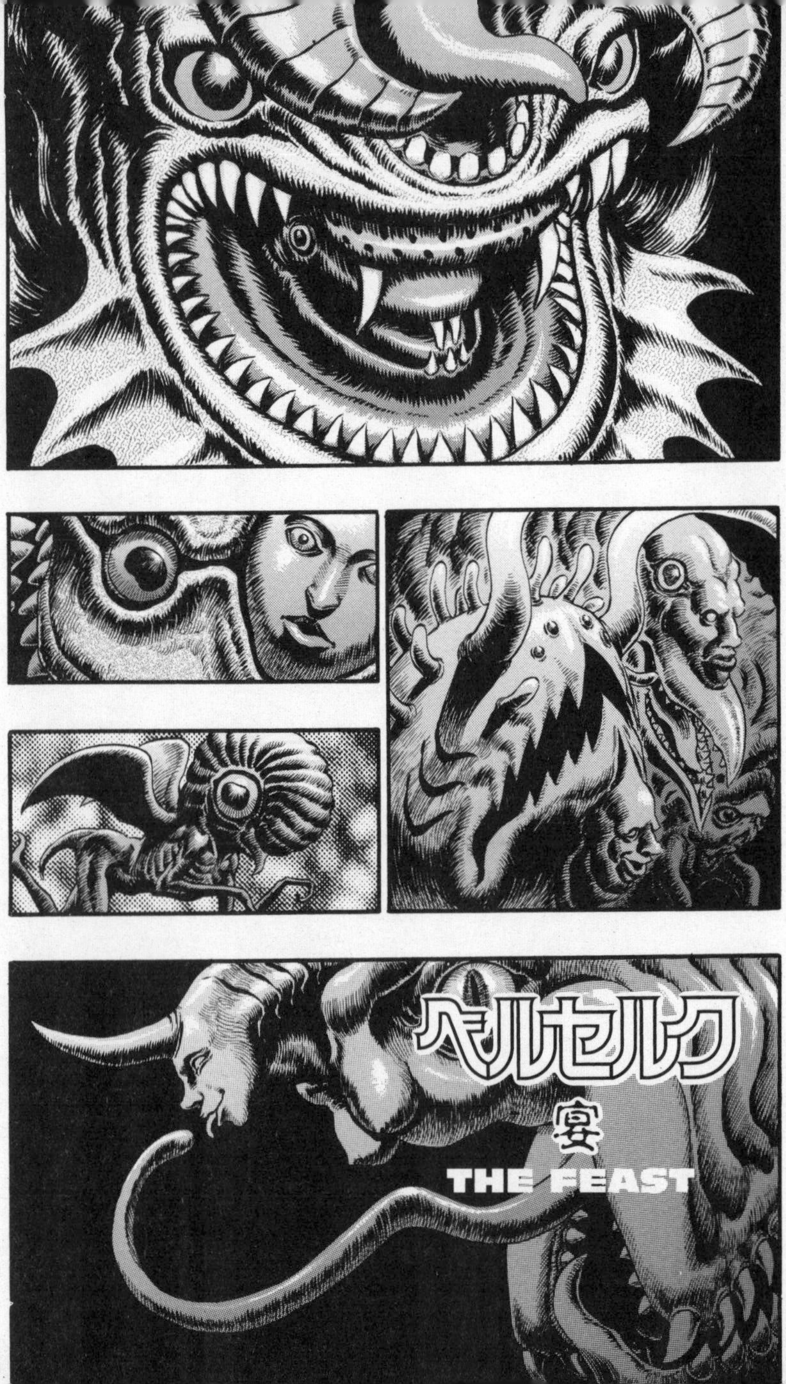
ベルセルク
宴
THE FEAST

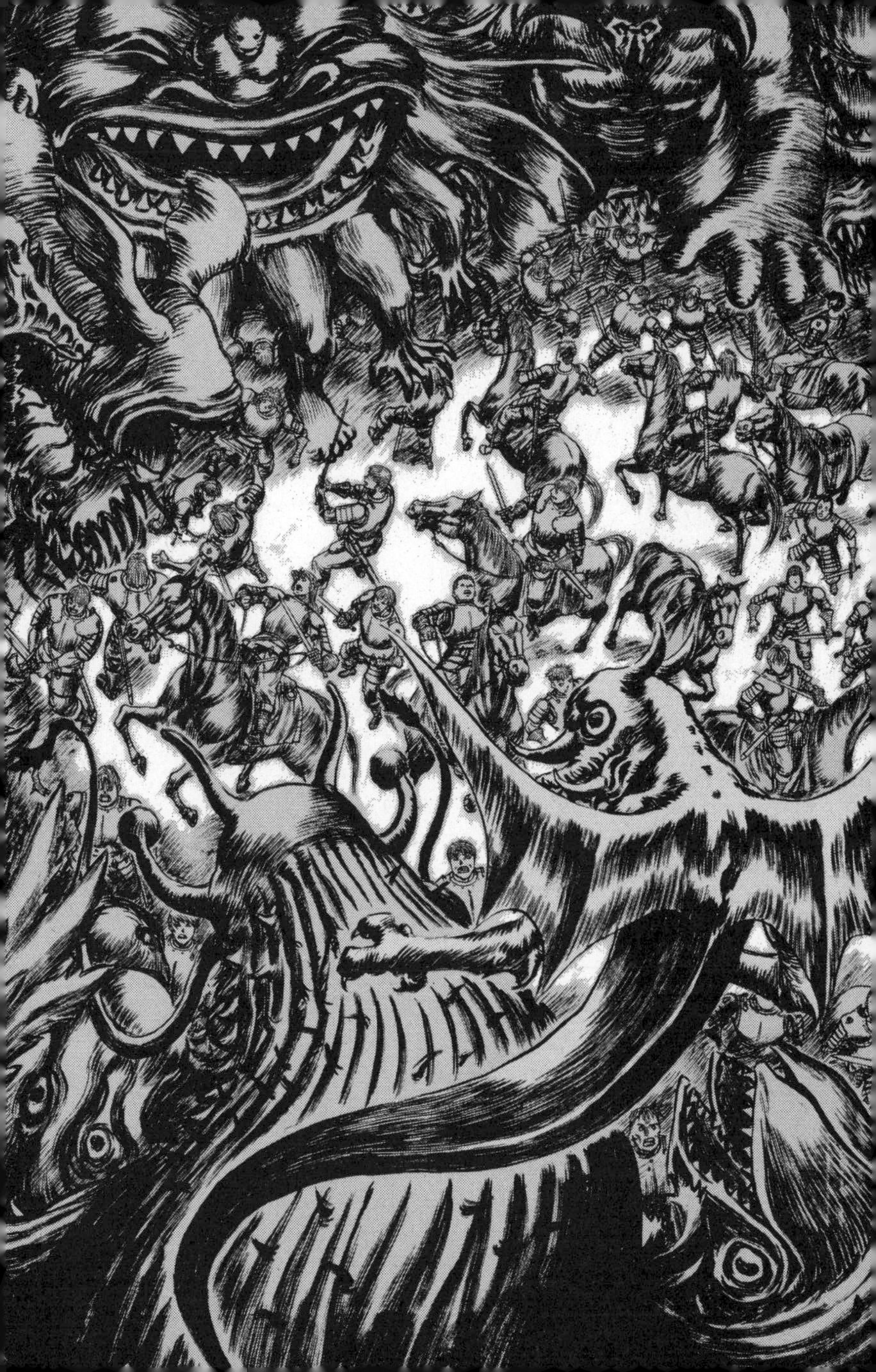

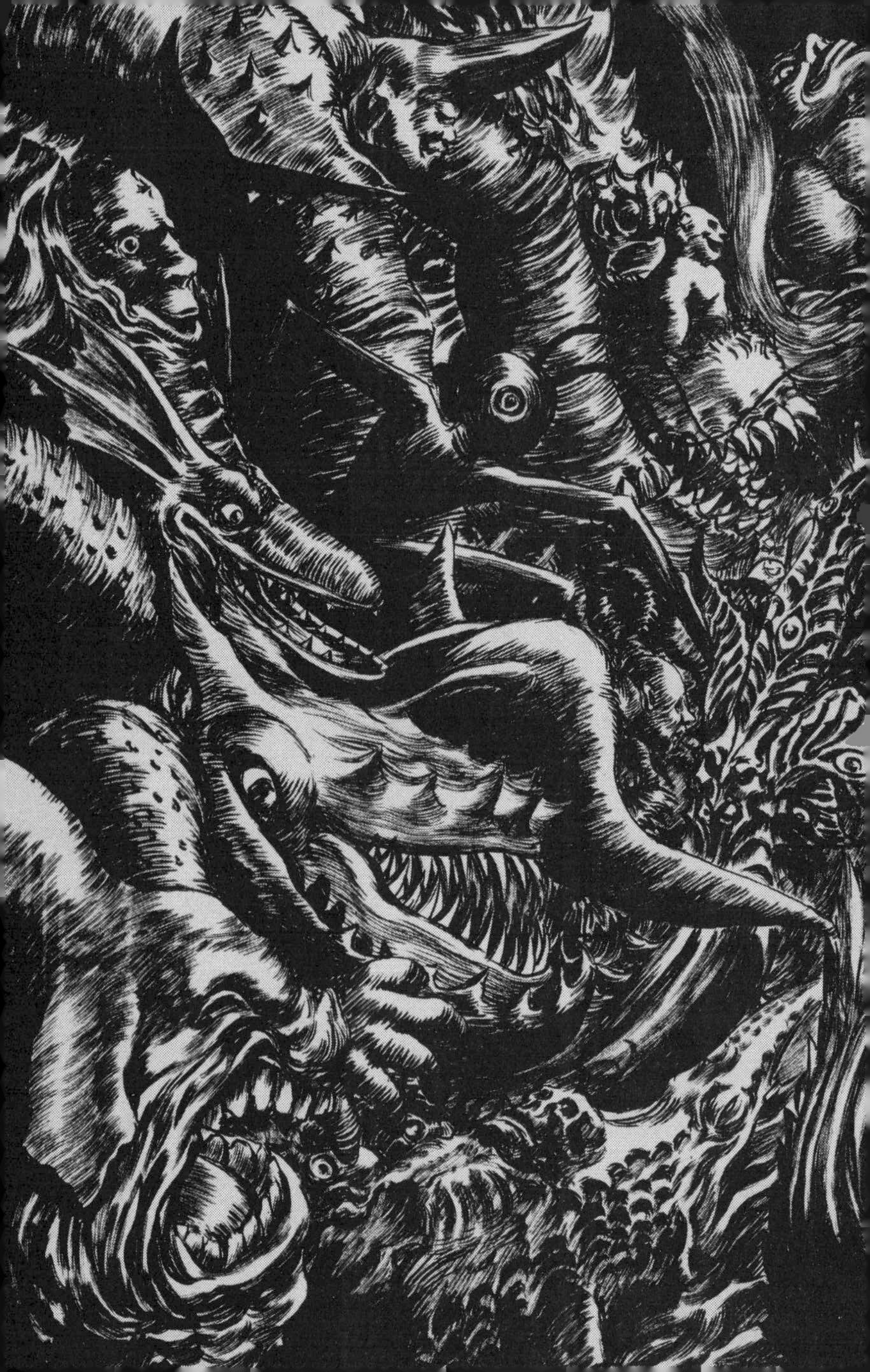

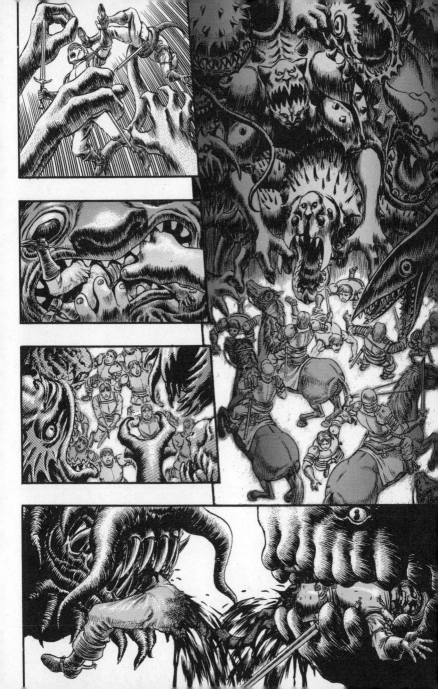

A
UNILATERAL
SLAUGHTER.

A
MASSACRE.

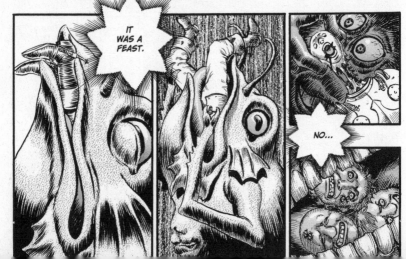

IT
WAS A
FEAST.

NO...

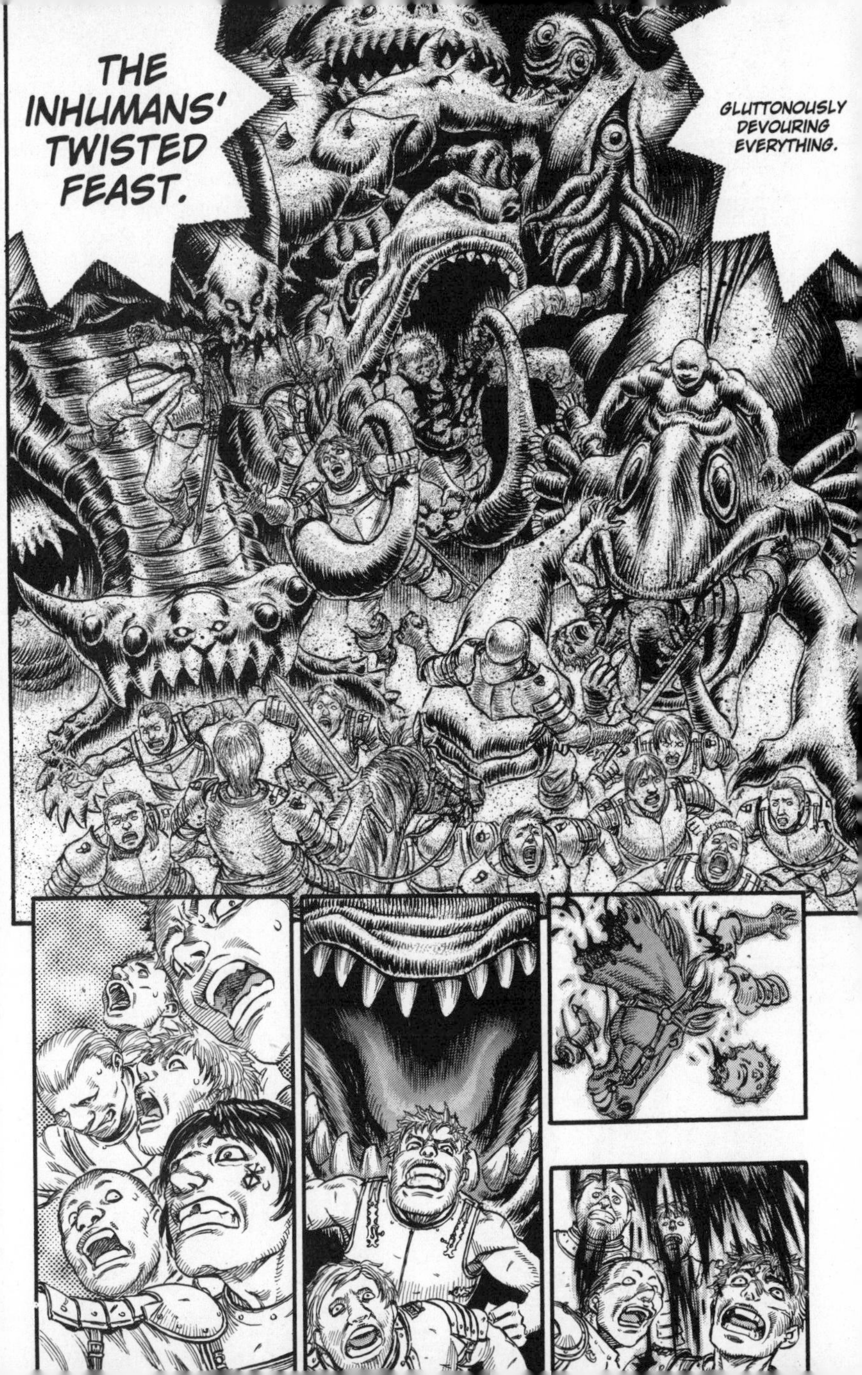
THE INHUMANS' TWISTED FEAST.
GLUTTONOUSLY DEVOURING EVERYTHING.

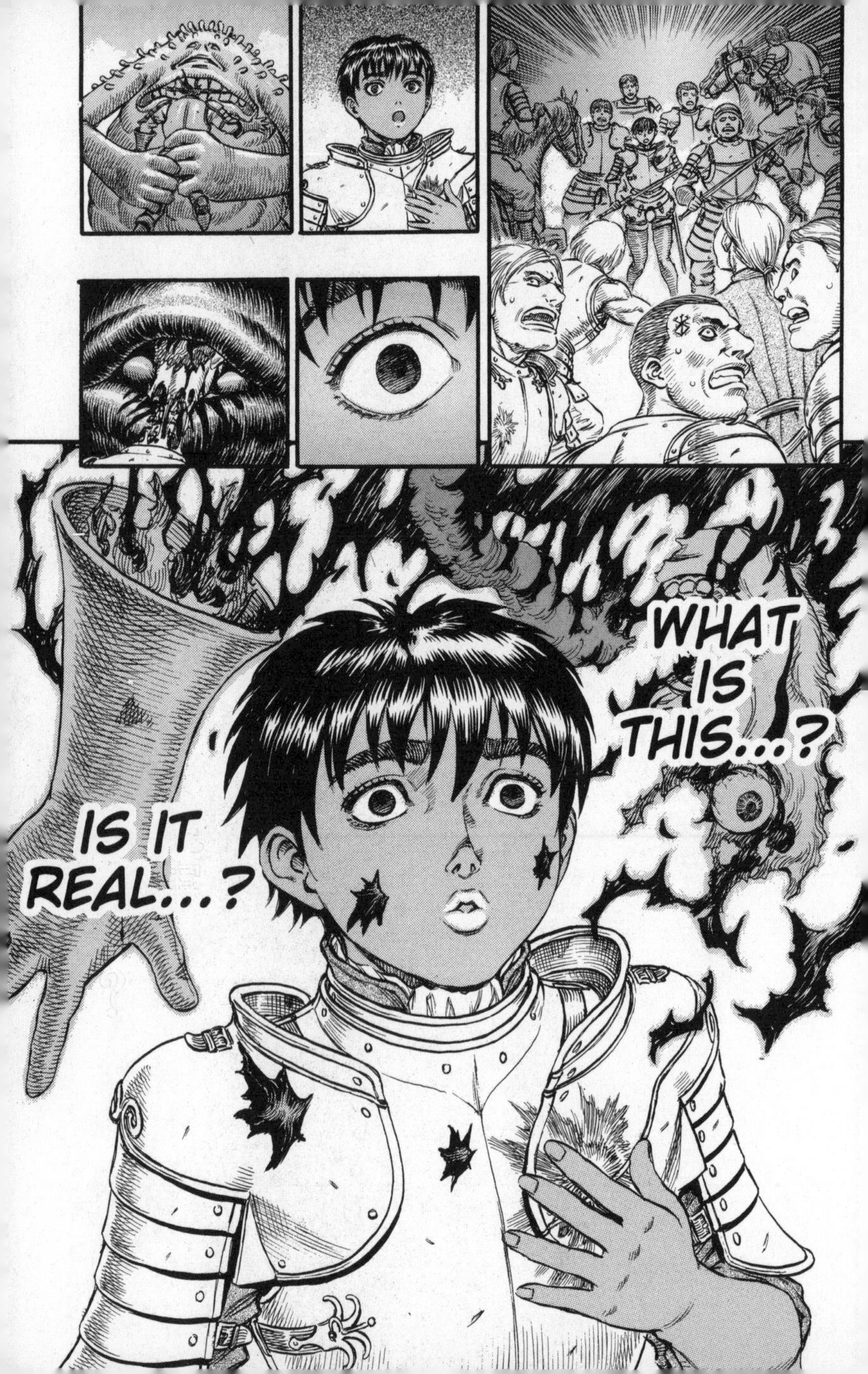
WHAT IS THIS...?
IS IT REAL...?

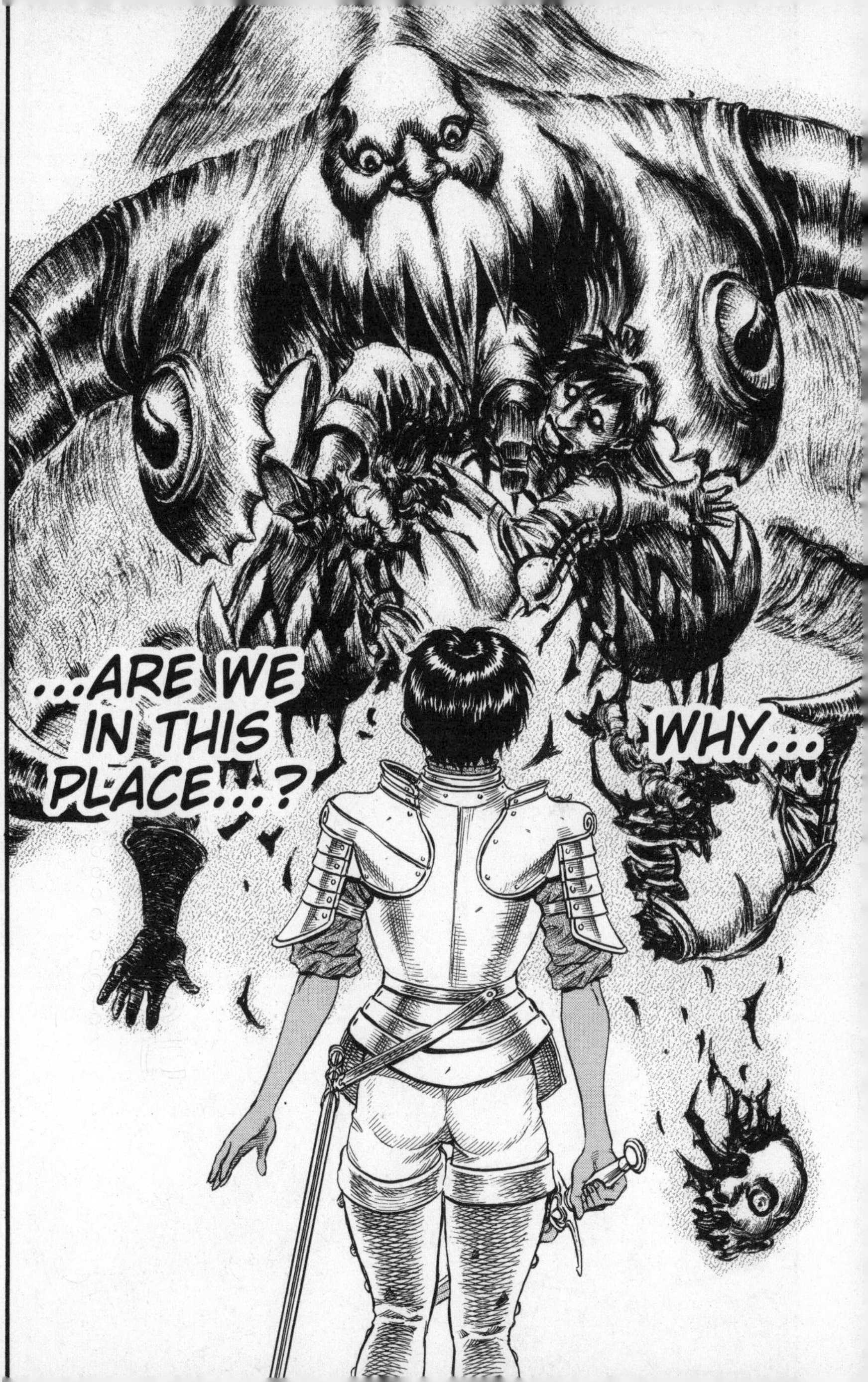
WHY...
...ARE WE IN THIS PLACE...?

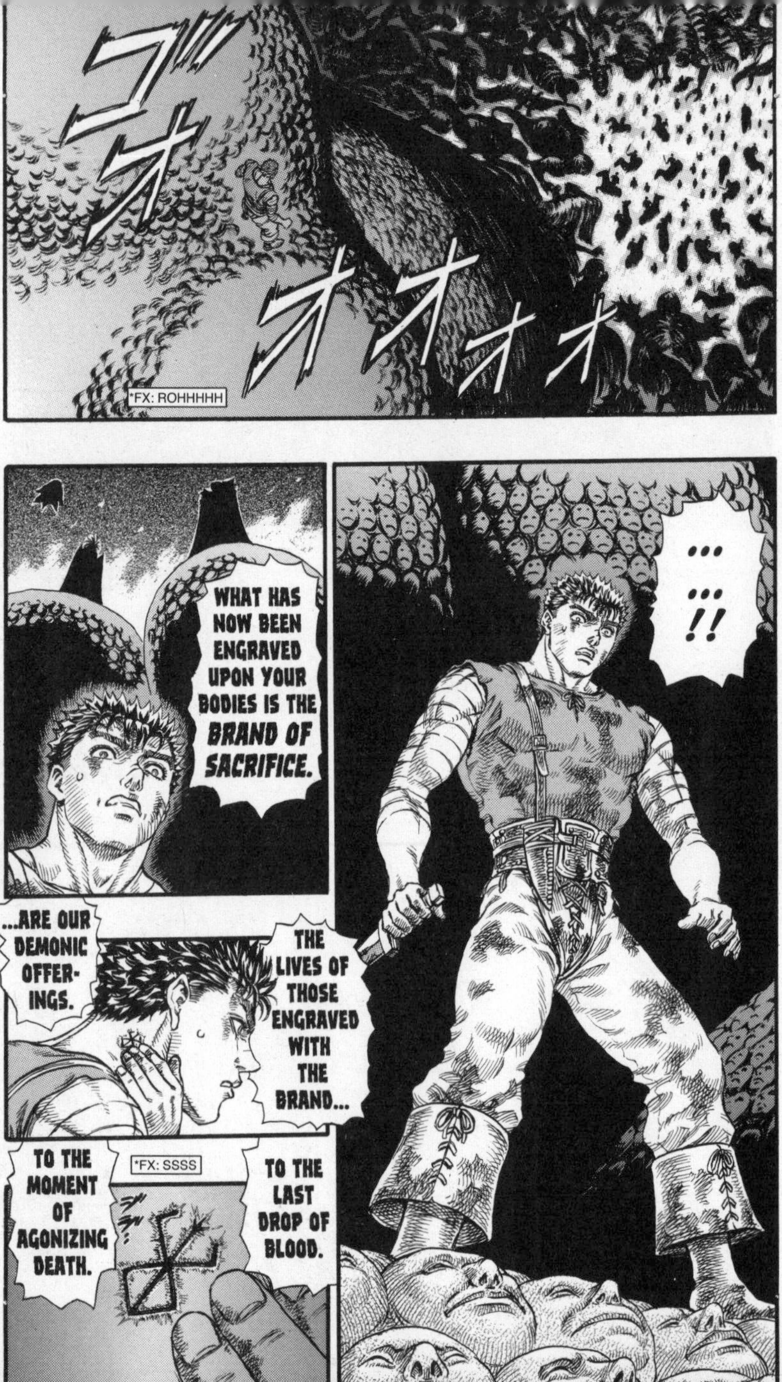
*FX: ROHHHHH
... ... !!
WHAT HAS NOW BEEN ENGRAVED UPON YOUR BODIES IS THE BRAND OF SACRIFICE.
THE LIVES OF THOSE ENGRAVED WITH THE BRAND...
...ARE OUR DEMONIC OFFER-INGS.
TO THE LAST DROP OF BLOOD.
*FX: SSSS
TO THE MOMENT OF AGONIZING DEATH.

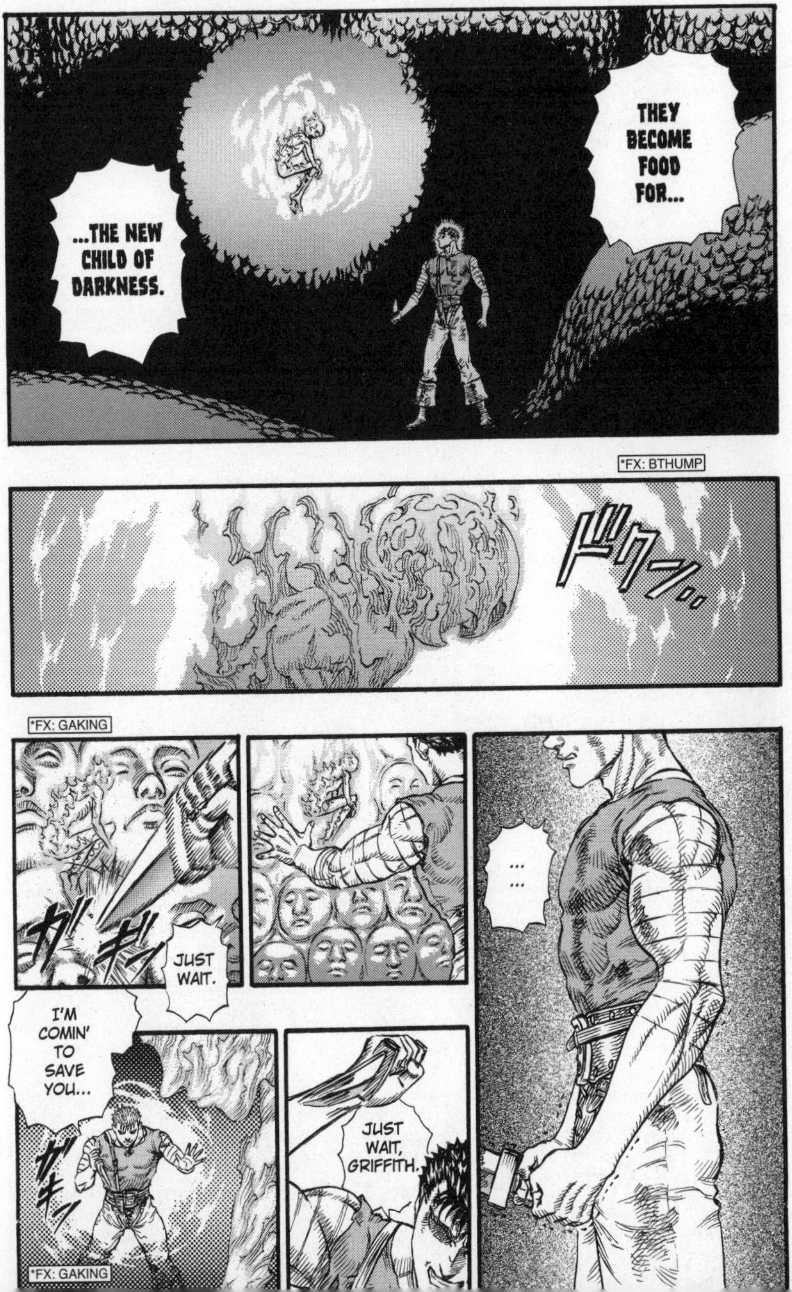
THEY BECOME FOOD FOR...
...THE NEW CHILD OF DARKNESS.
*FX: BTHUMP
ドクン
... ...
*FX: GAKING
JUST WAIT.
JUST WAIT, GRIFFITH.
I'M COMIN' TO SAVE YOU...
*FX: GAKING

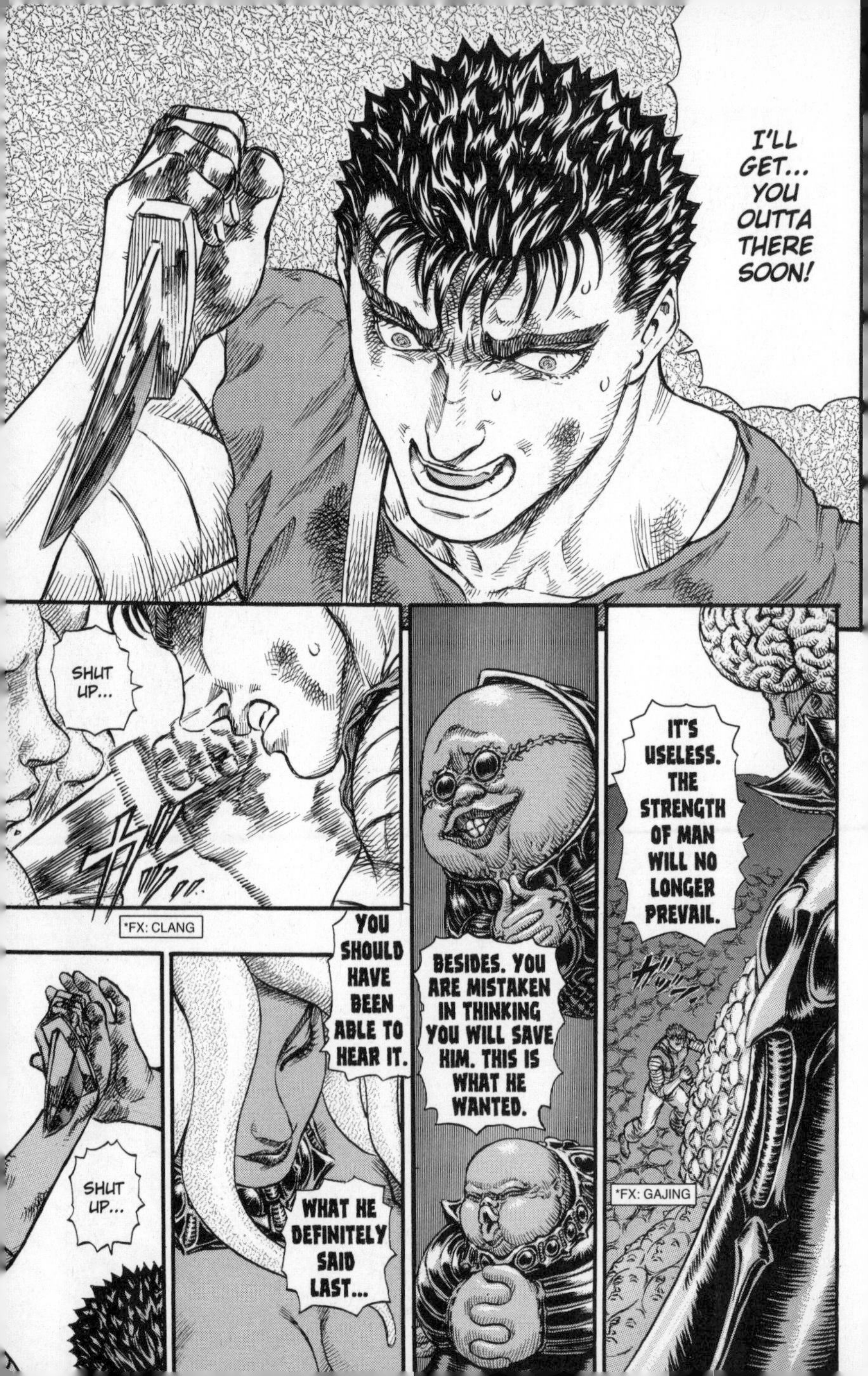
I'LL GET... YOU OUTTA THERE SOON!
IT'S USELESS. THE STRENGTH OF MAN WILL NO LONGER PREVAIL.
*FX: GAJING
BESIDES. YOU ARE MISTAKEN IN THINKING YOU WILL SAVE HIM. THIS IS WHAT HE WANTED.
SHUT UP...
*FX: CLANG
YOU SHOULD HAVE BEEN ABLE TO HEAR IT.
WHAT HE DEFINITELY SAID LAST...
SHUT UP...

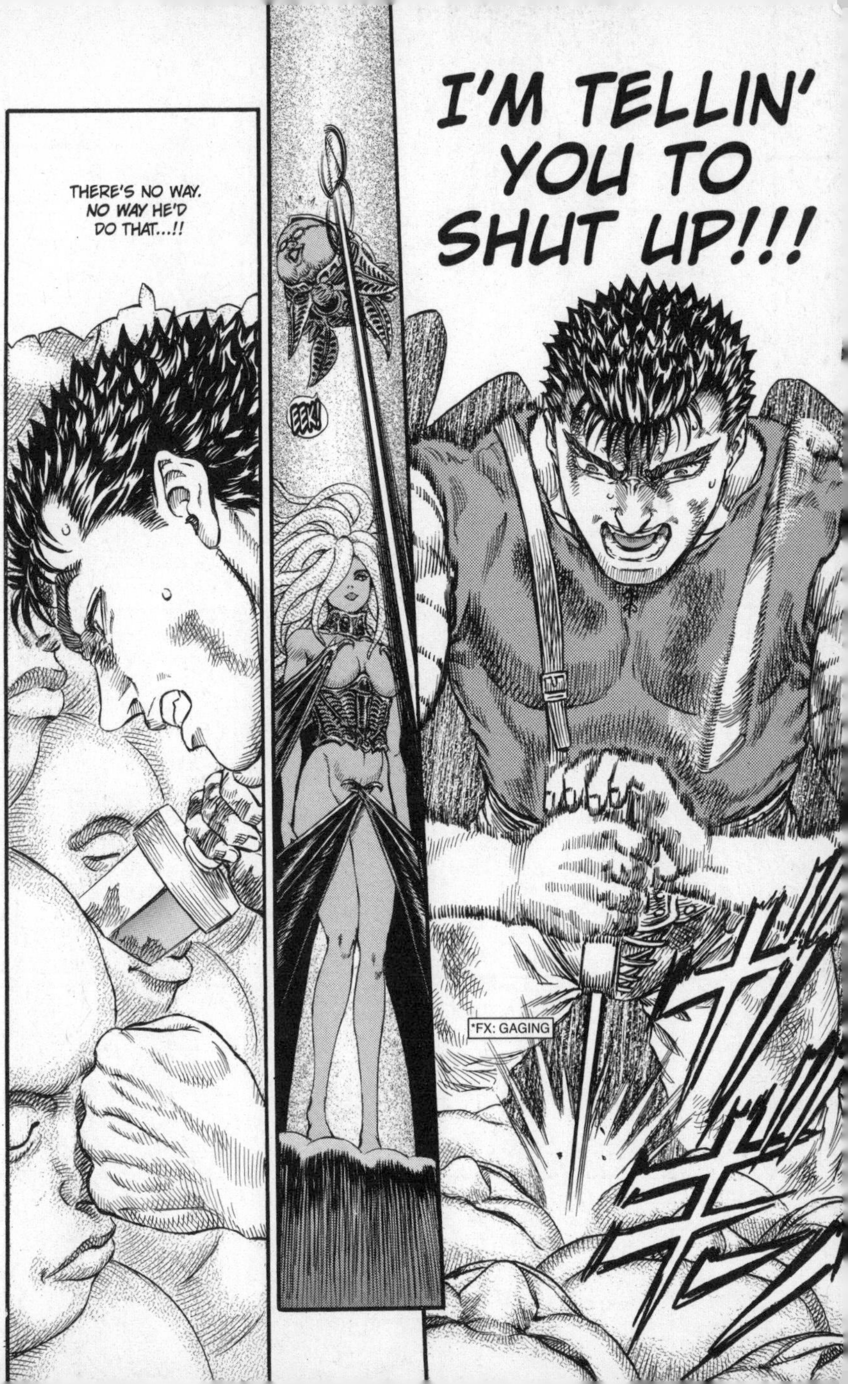
I'M TELLIN' YOU TO SHUT UP!!!
*FX: GAGING
EEK!
THERE'S NO WAY. NO WAY HE'D DO THAT...!!

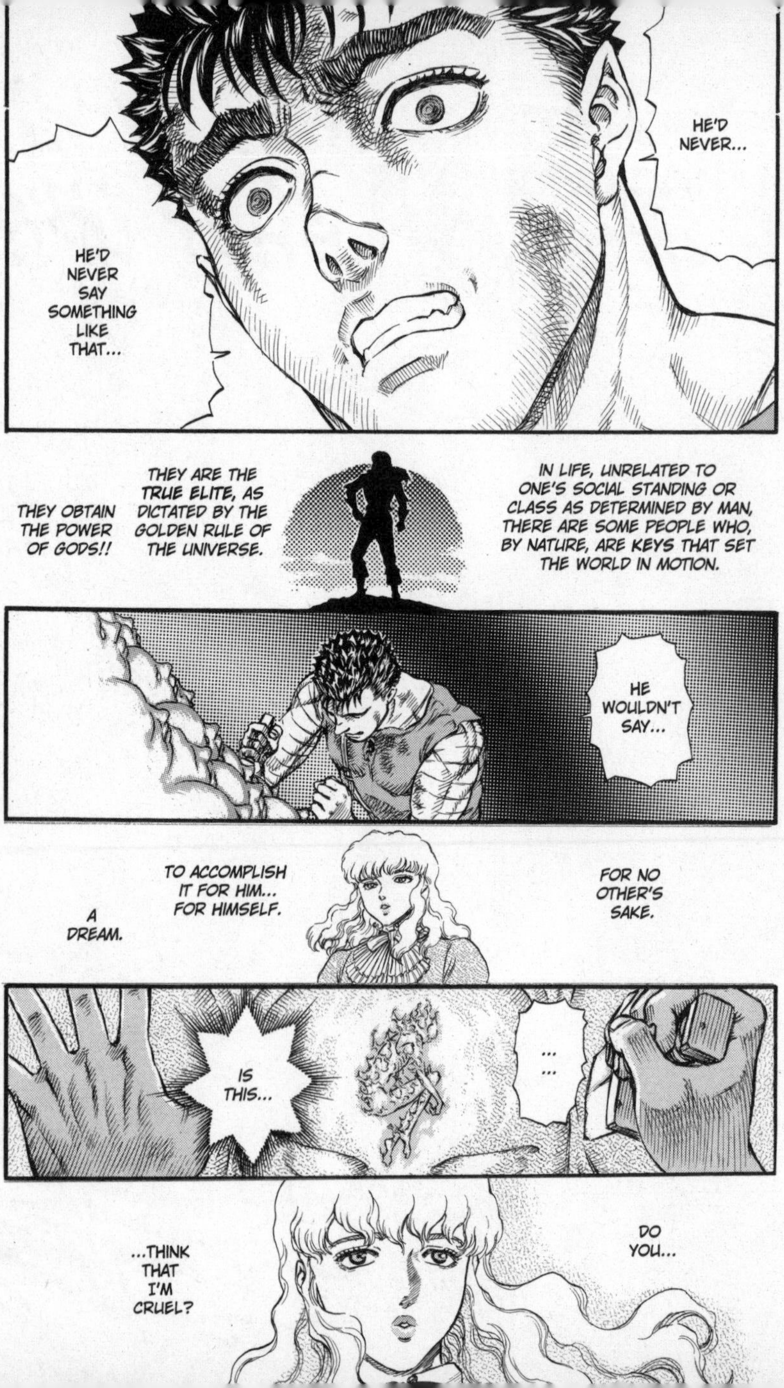
HE'D NEVER...
HE'D NEVER SAY SOMETHING LIKE THAT...
IN LIFE, UNRELATED TO ONE'S SOCIAL STANDING OR CLASS AS DETERMINED BY MAN, THERE ARE SOME PEOPLE WHO, BY NATURE, ARE KEYS THAT SET THE WORLD IN MOTION.
THEY ARE THE TRUE ELITE, AS DICTATED BY THE GOLDEN RULE OF THE UNIVERSE.
THEY OBTAIN THE POWER OF GODS!!
HE WOULDN'T SAY...
FOR NO OTHER'S SAKE.
TO ACCOMPLISH IT FOR HIM... FOR HIMSELF.
A DREAM.
... ...
IS THIS...
DO YOU...
...THINK THAT I'M CRUEL?

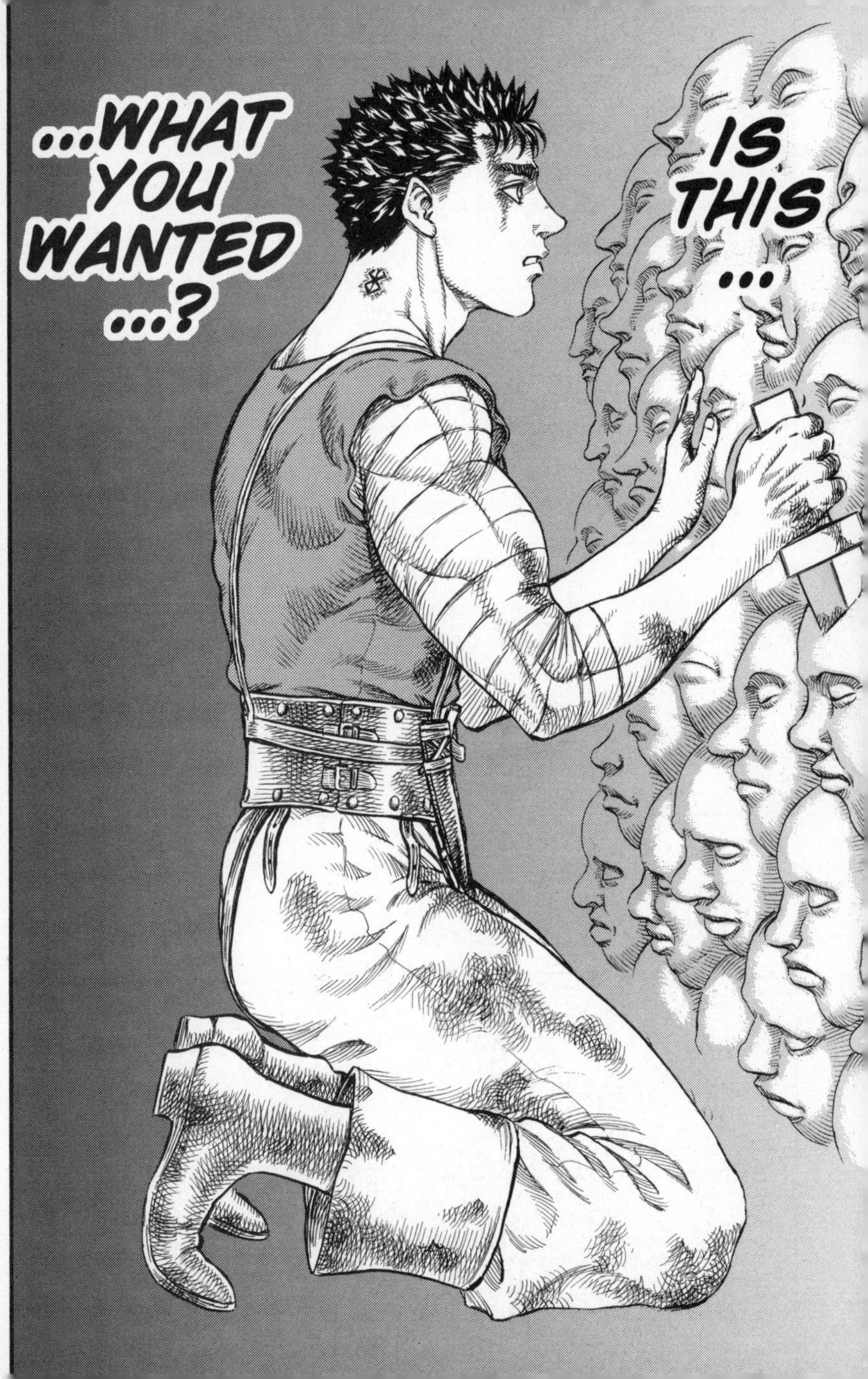
IS THIS ...
...WHAT YOU WANTED ...?

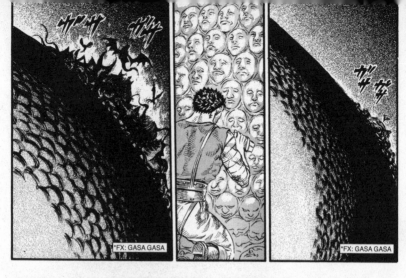

*FX: GASA GASA

*FX: GASA GASA

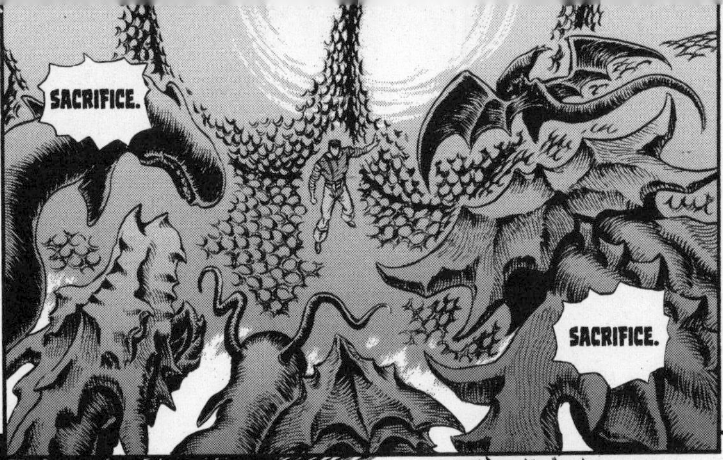
SACRIFICE.
SACRIFICE.

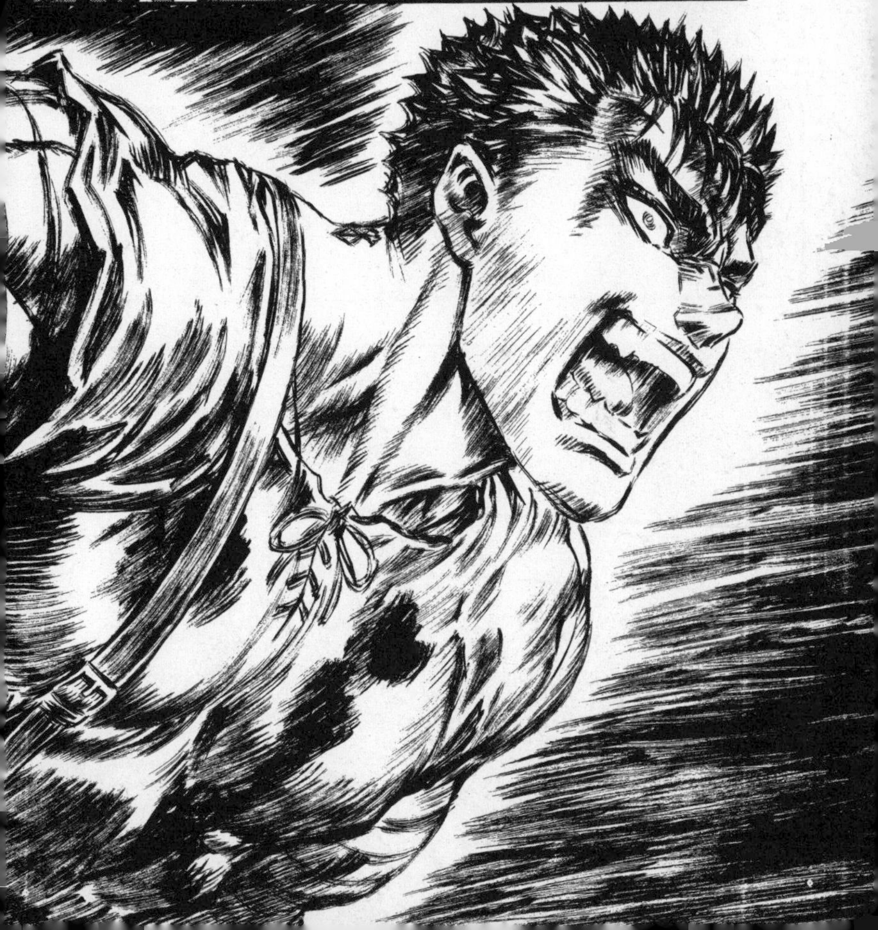

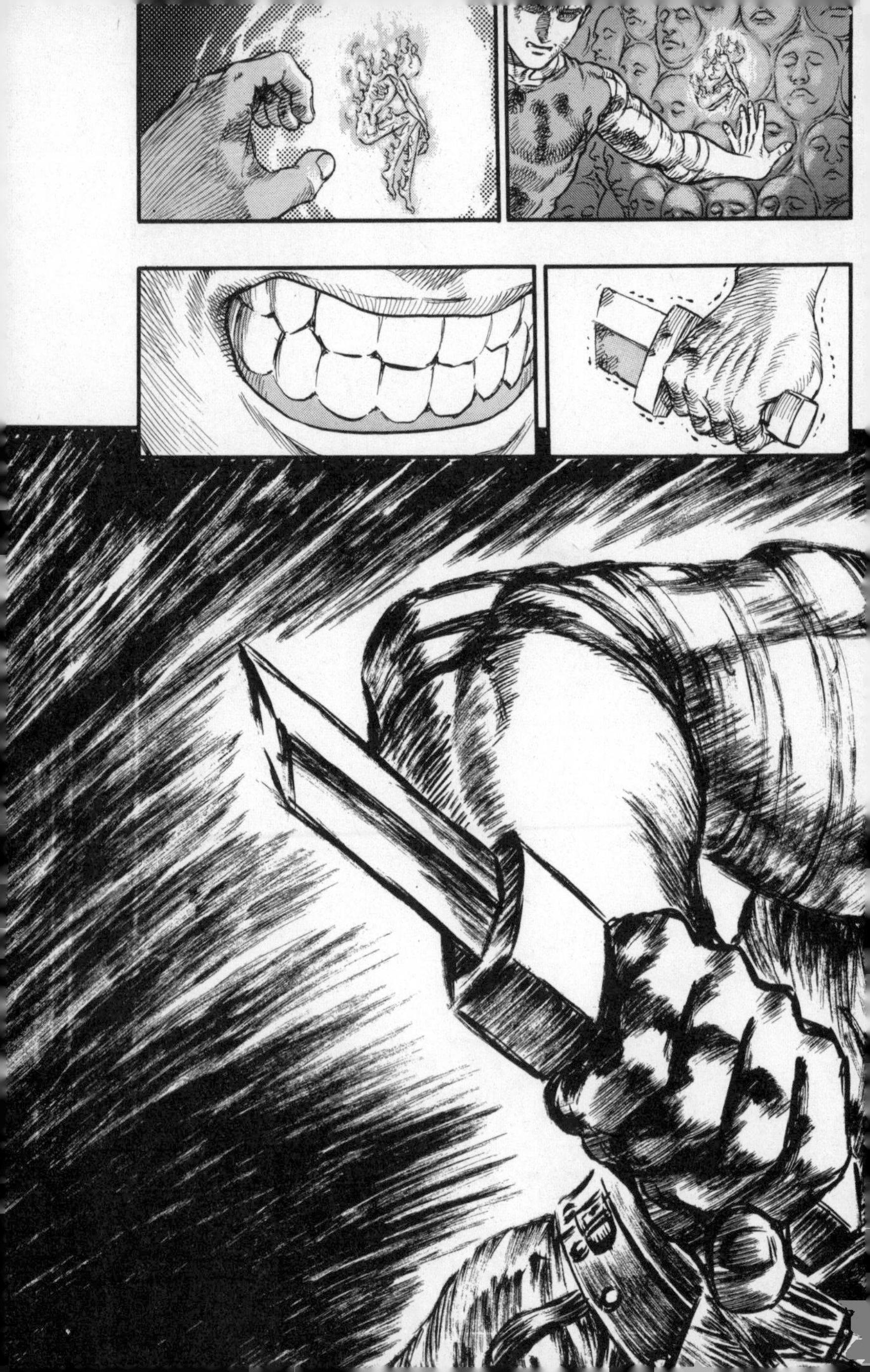

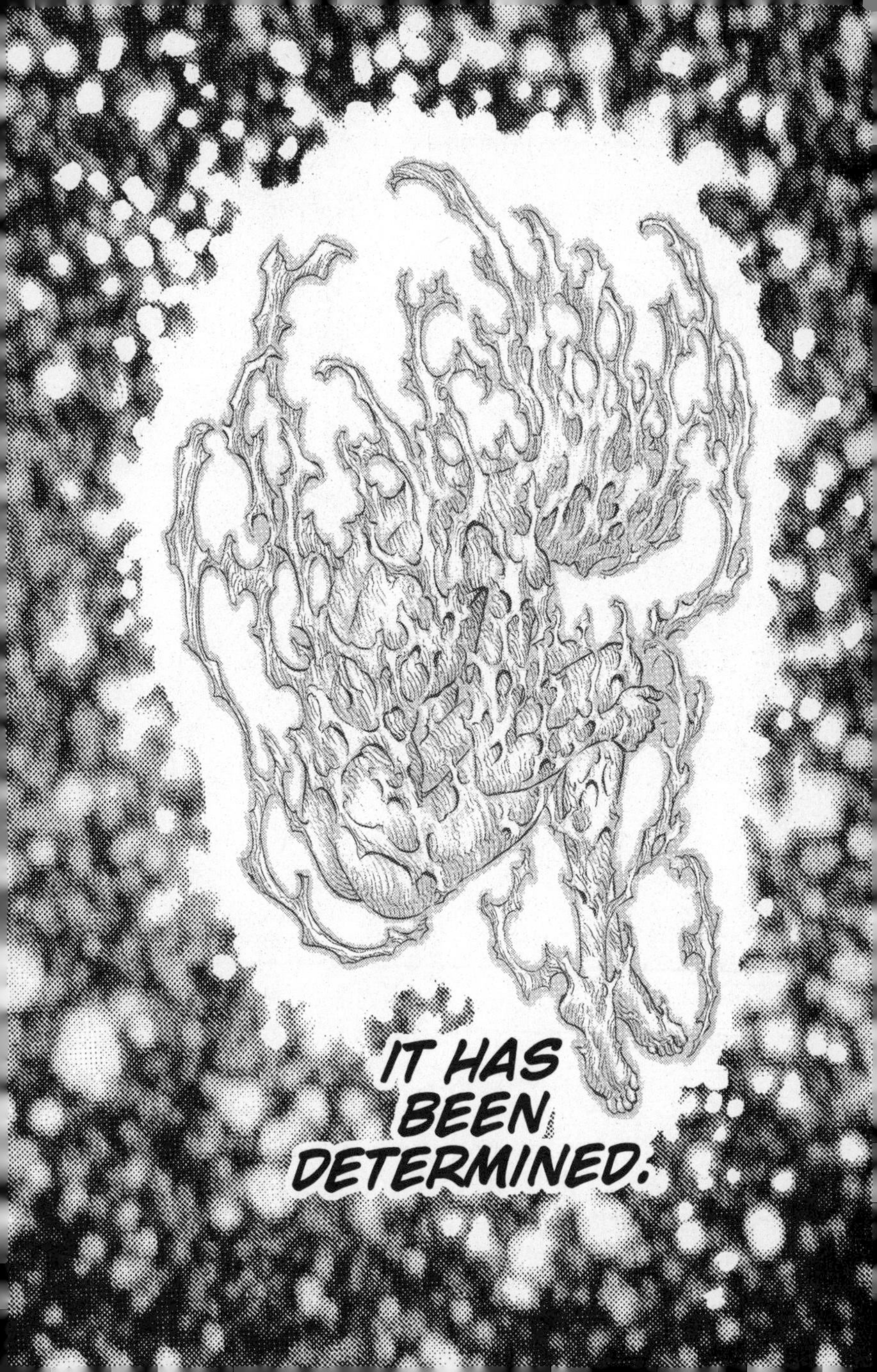
IT HAS BEEN DETERMINED.

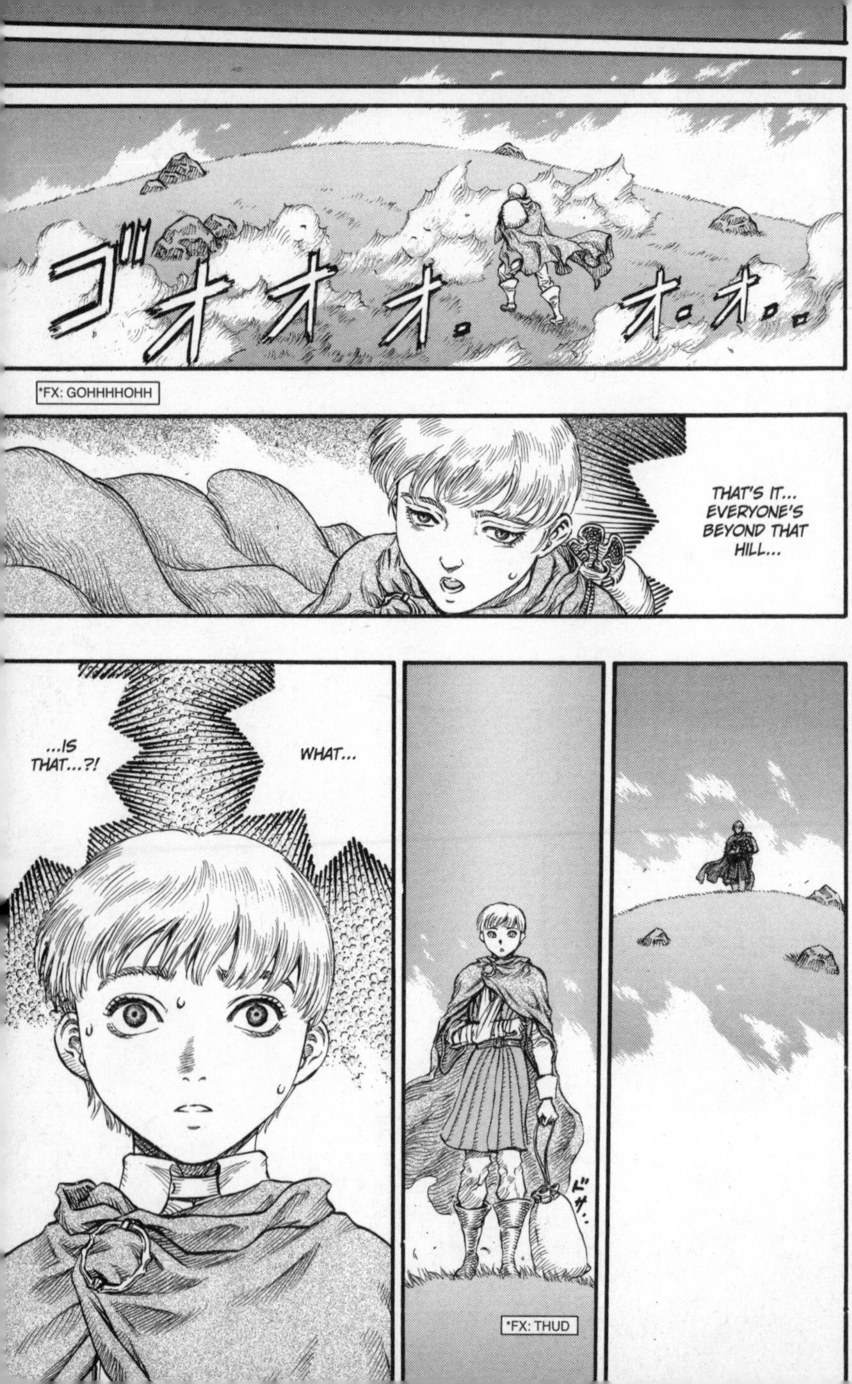
ゴオオオ。オ。オ。。
*FX: GOHHHHOHH
THAT'S IT... EVERYONE'S BEYOND THAT HILL...
ドサ‥
*FX: THUD
WHAT...
...IS THAT...?!

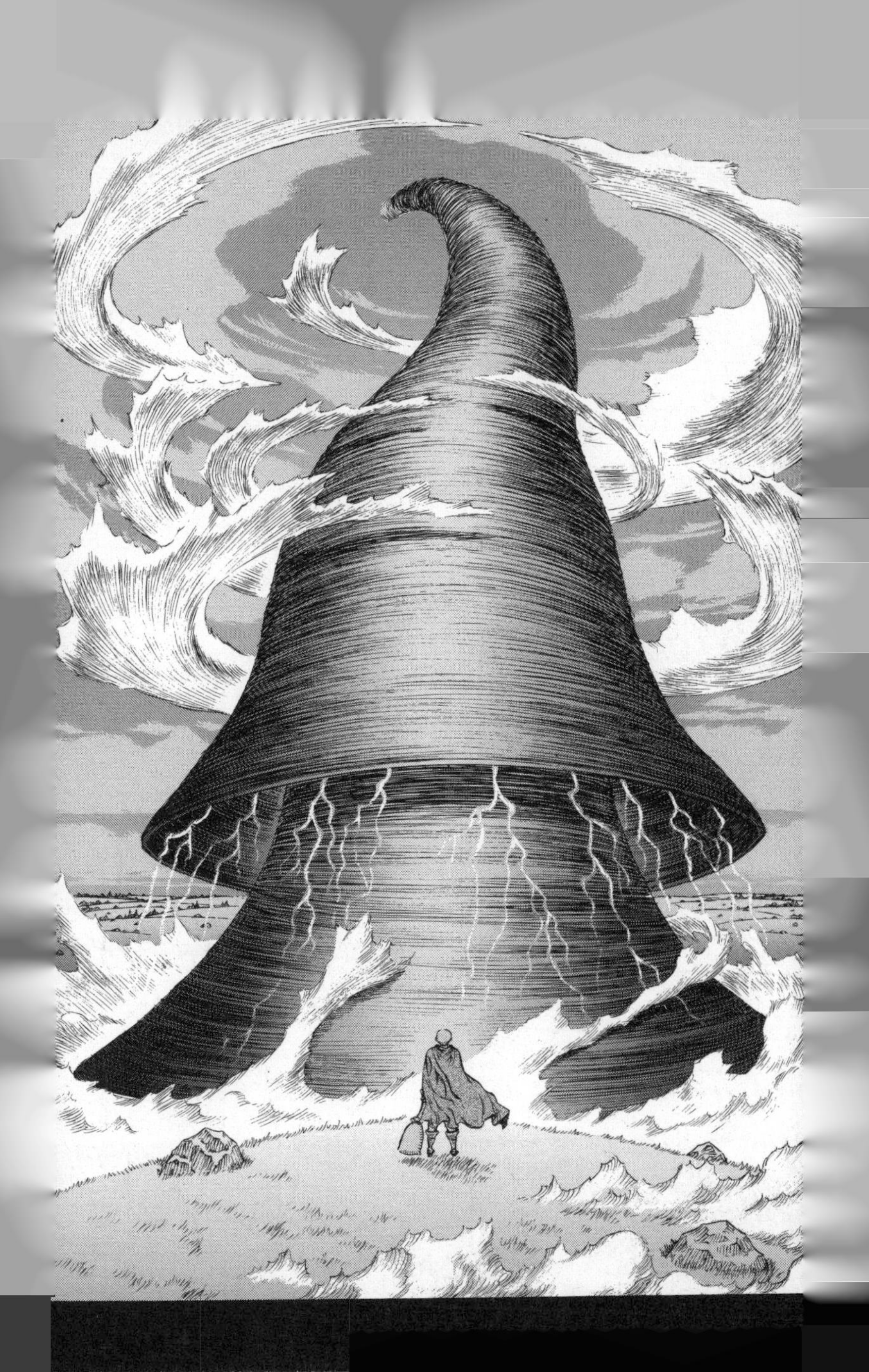

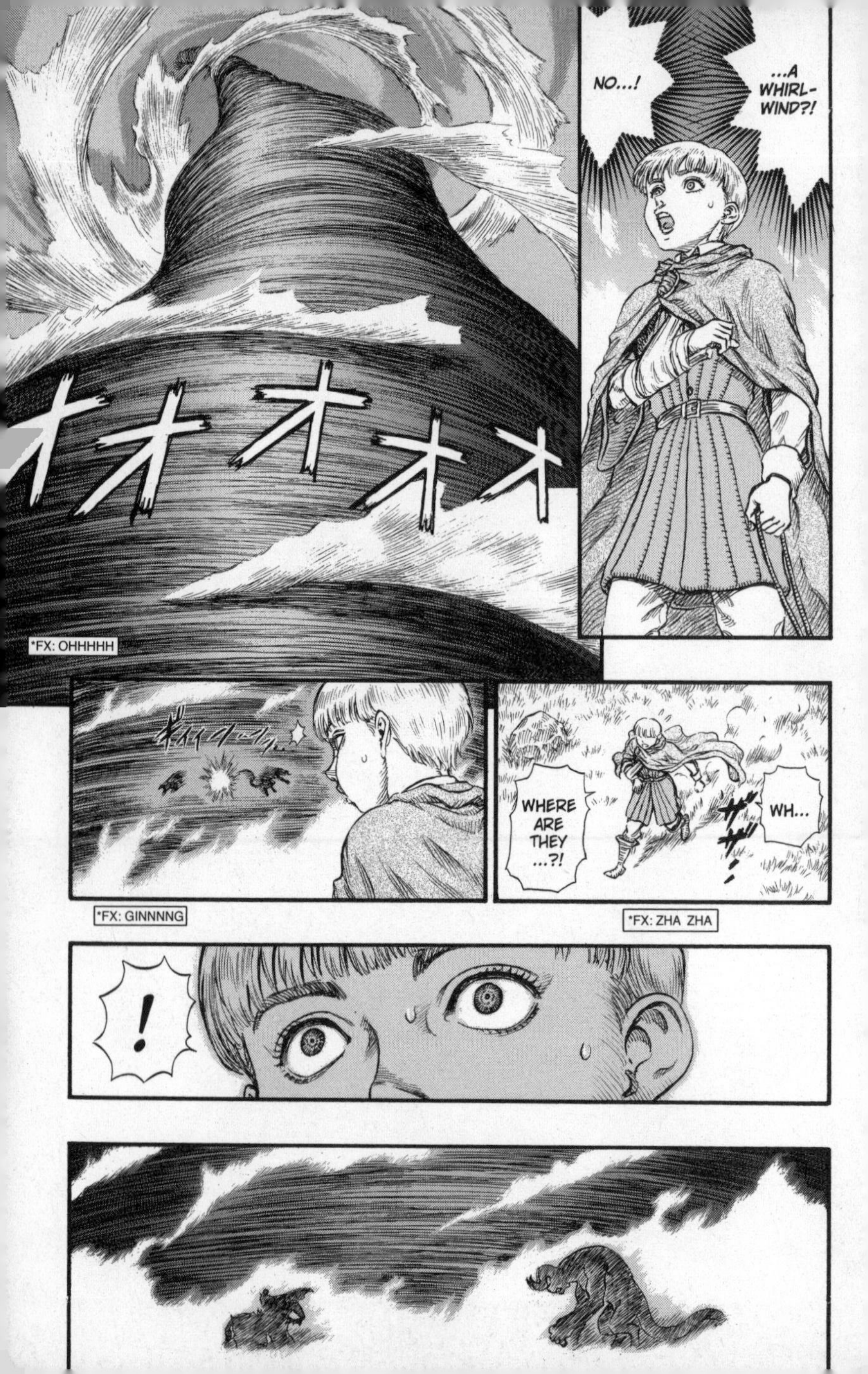

...A WHIRL-WIND?!
NO...!
オオオオオ
*FX: OHHHHH
WH...
WHERE ARE THEY ...?!
*FX: ZHA ZHA
*FX: GINNNNG
!

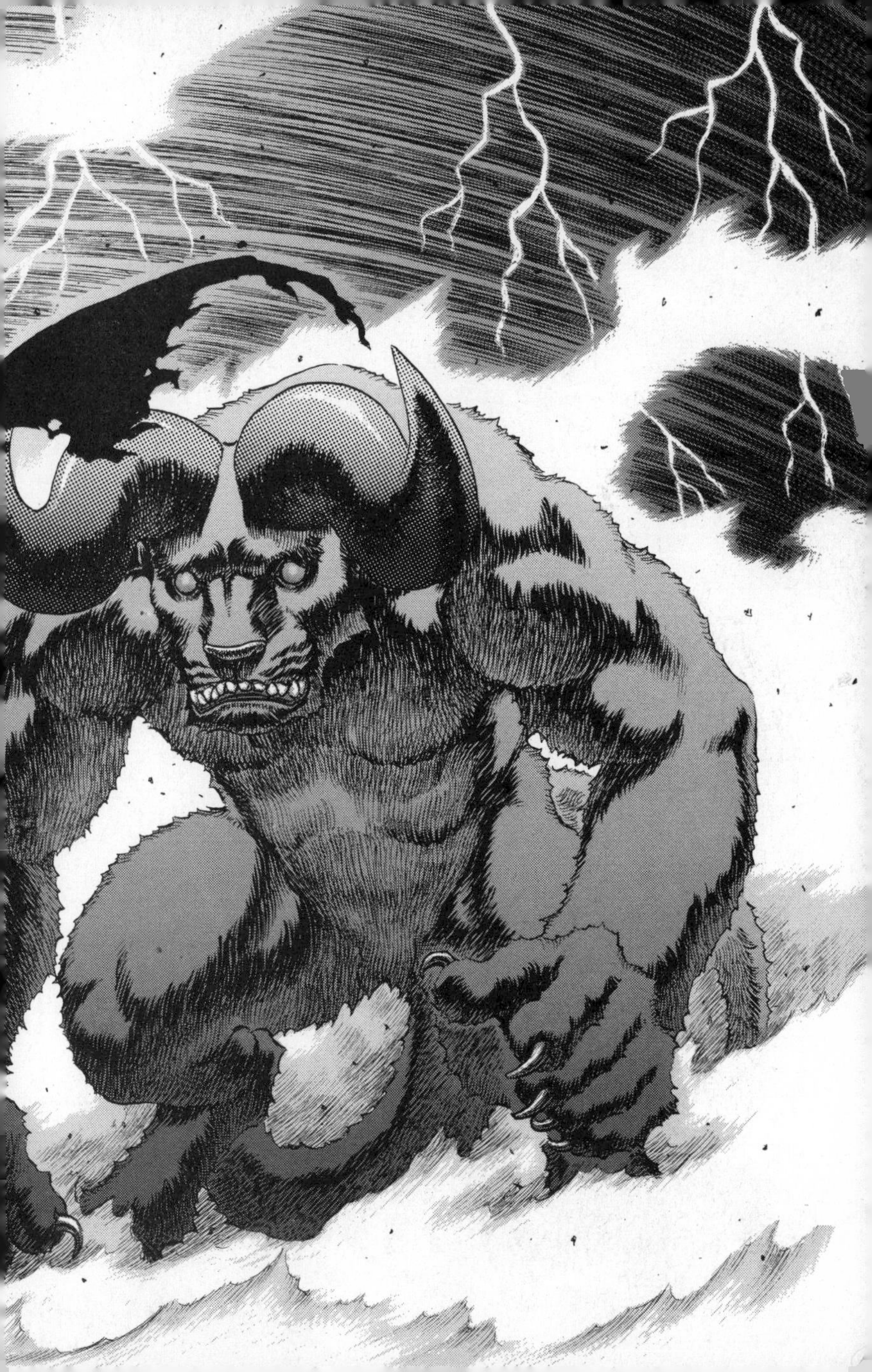

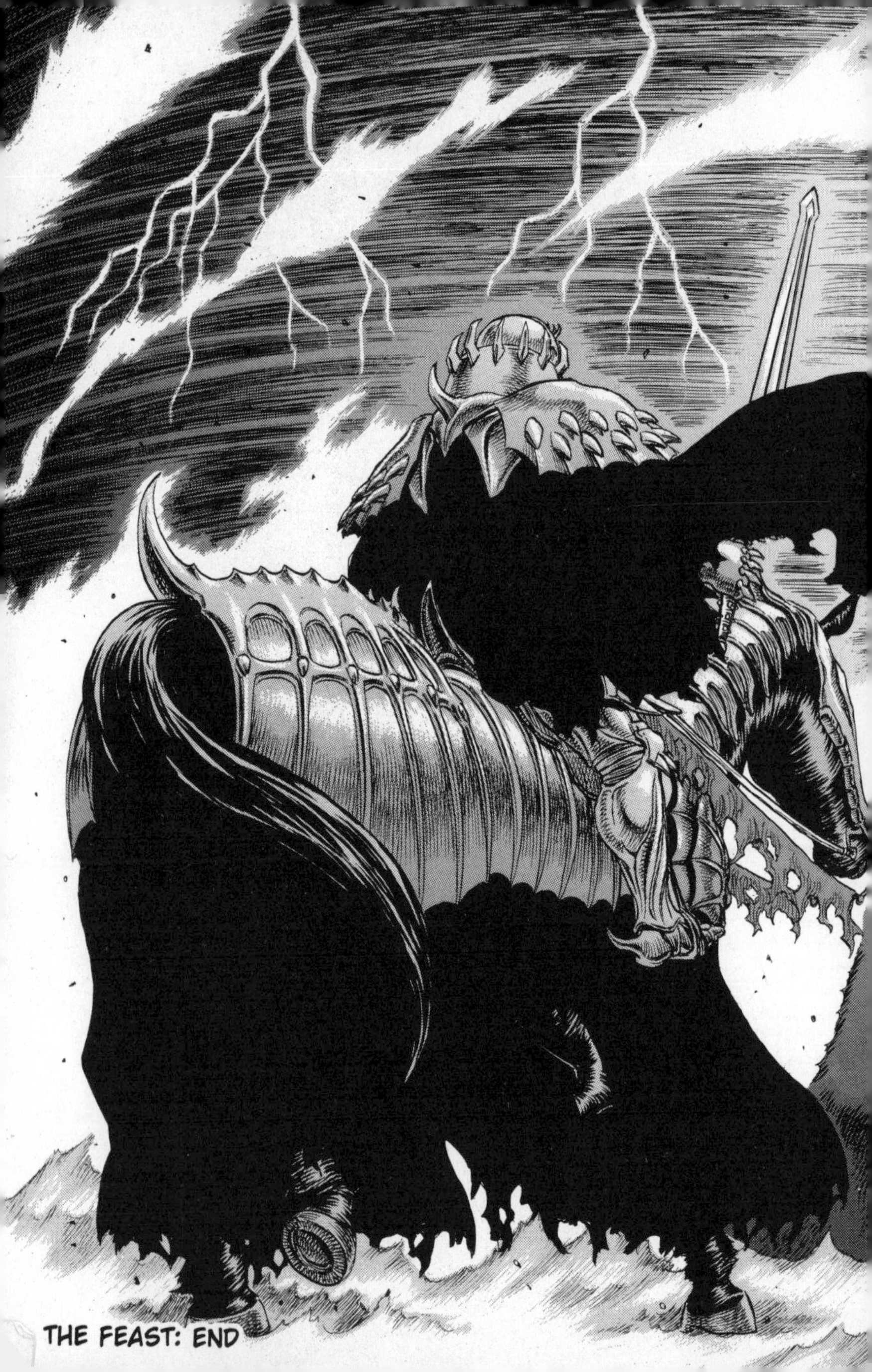
THE FEAST: END

BERSERK

Created by Kentaro Miura, *Berserk* is manga mayhem to the extreme—violent, horrifying, and mercilessly funny—and the wellspring for the internationally popular anime series. Not for the squeamish or the easily offended, *Berserk* asks for no quarter—and offers none!

Presented uncensored in the original Japanese format!

VOLUME 1
ISBN 978-1-59307-020-5

VOLUME 2
ISBN 978-1-59307-021-2

VOLUME 3
ISBN 978-1-59307-022-9

VOLUME 4
ISBN 978-1-59307-203-2

VOLUME 5
ISBN 978-1-59307-251-3

VOLUME 6
ISBN 978-1-59307-252-0

VOLUME 7
ISBN 978-1-59307-328-2

VOLUME 8
ISBN 978-1-59307-329-9

VOLUME 9
ISBN 978-1-59307-330-5

VOLUME 10
ISBN 978-1-59307-331-2

VOLUME 11
ISBN 978-1-59307-470-8

VOLUME 12
ISBN 978-1-59307-484-5

VOLUME 13
ISBN 978-1-59307-500-2

VOLUME 14
ISBN 978-1-59307-501-9

VOLUME 15
ISBN 978-1-59307-577-4

VOLUME 16
ISBN 978-1-59307-706-8

VOLUME 17
ISBN 978-1-59307-742-6

VOLUME 18
ISBN 978-1-59307-743-3

VOLUME 19
ISBN 978-1-59307-744-0

VOLUME 20
ISBN 978-1-59307-745-7

VOLUME 21
ISBN 978-1-59307-746-4

VOLUME 22
ISBN 978-1-59307-863-8

VOLUME 23
ISBN 978-1-59307-864-5

VOLUME 24
ISBN 978-1-59307-865-2

VOLUME 25
ISBN 978-1-59307-921-5

VOLUME 26
ISBN 978-1-59307-922-2

VOLUME 27
ISBN 978-1-59307-923-9

VOLUME 28
ISBN 978-1-59582-209-3

VOLUME 29
ISBN 978-1-59582-210-9

VOLUME 30
ISBN 978-1-59582-211-6

VOLUME 31
ISBN 978-1-59582-366-3

VOLUME 32
ISBN 978-1-59582-367-0

VOLUME 33
ISBN 978-1-59582-372-4

VOLUME 34
ISBN 978-1-59582-532-2

VOLUME 35
ISBN 978-1-59582-695-4

VOLUME 36
ISBN 978-1-59582-942-9

VOLUME 37
ISBN 978-1-61655-205-3

$14.99 each!

DMP Digital Manga Publishing™
DMPBooks.com

DARK HORSE MANGA
DarkHorse.com

AVAILABLE AT YOUR LOCAL COMICS SHOP OR BOOKSTORE
To find a comics shop near your area, call 1-888-266-4226. For more information or to order direct: •On the web: darkhorse.com •E-mail: mailorder@darkhorse.com •Phone: 1-800-862-0052 Mon.–Fri. 9 AM to 5 PM Pacific Time.

HELLSING

STOP

This is the back of the book!

This manga collection is translated into English but oriented in right-to-left reading format at the creator's request, maintaining the artwork's visual orientation as originally published in Japan. If you've never read manga in this way before, take a look at the diagram below to give yourself an idea of how to go about it. Basically, you'll be starting in the upper right corner and will read each balloon and panel moving right to left. It may take some getting used to, but you should get the hang of it very quickly. Have fun!

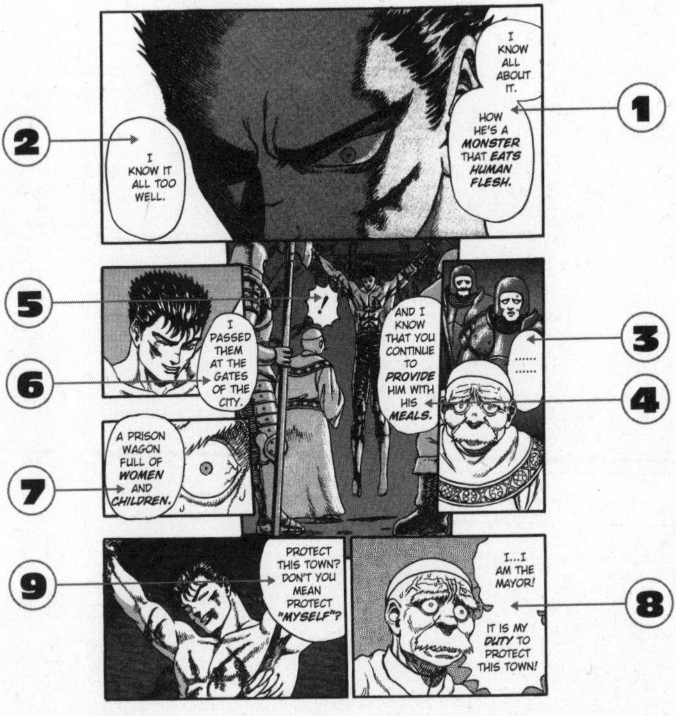
1
I KNOW ALL ABOUT IT.
HOW HE'S A MONSTER THAT EATS HUMAN FLESH.
2
I KNOW IT ALL TOO WELL.
3
......
......
4
AND I KNOW THAT YOU CONTINUE TO PROVIDE HIM WITH HIS MEALS.
5
!
6
I PASSED THEM AT THE GATES OF THE CITY.
7
A PRISON WAGON FULL OF WOMEN AND CHILDREN.
8
I...I AM THE MAYOR!
IT IS MY DUTY TO PROTECT THIS TOWN!
9
PROTECT THIS TOWN? DON'T YOU MEAN PROTECT "MYSELF"?